T0224746

Real-Time C++

Christopher Kormanyos

Real-Time C++

Efficient Object-Oriented and Template Microcontroller Programming

Fourth Edition

Christopher Kormanyos
Reutlingen
Germany

ISBN 978-3-662-62998-7 ISBN 978-3-662-62996-3 (eBook)
https://doi.org/10.1007/978-3-662-62996-3

This Springer imprint is published by the registered company Springer-Verlag GmbH, DE, part of Springer Nature.
The registered company address is: Heidelberger Platz 3, 14197 Berlin, Germany

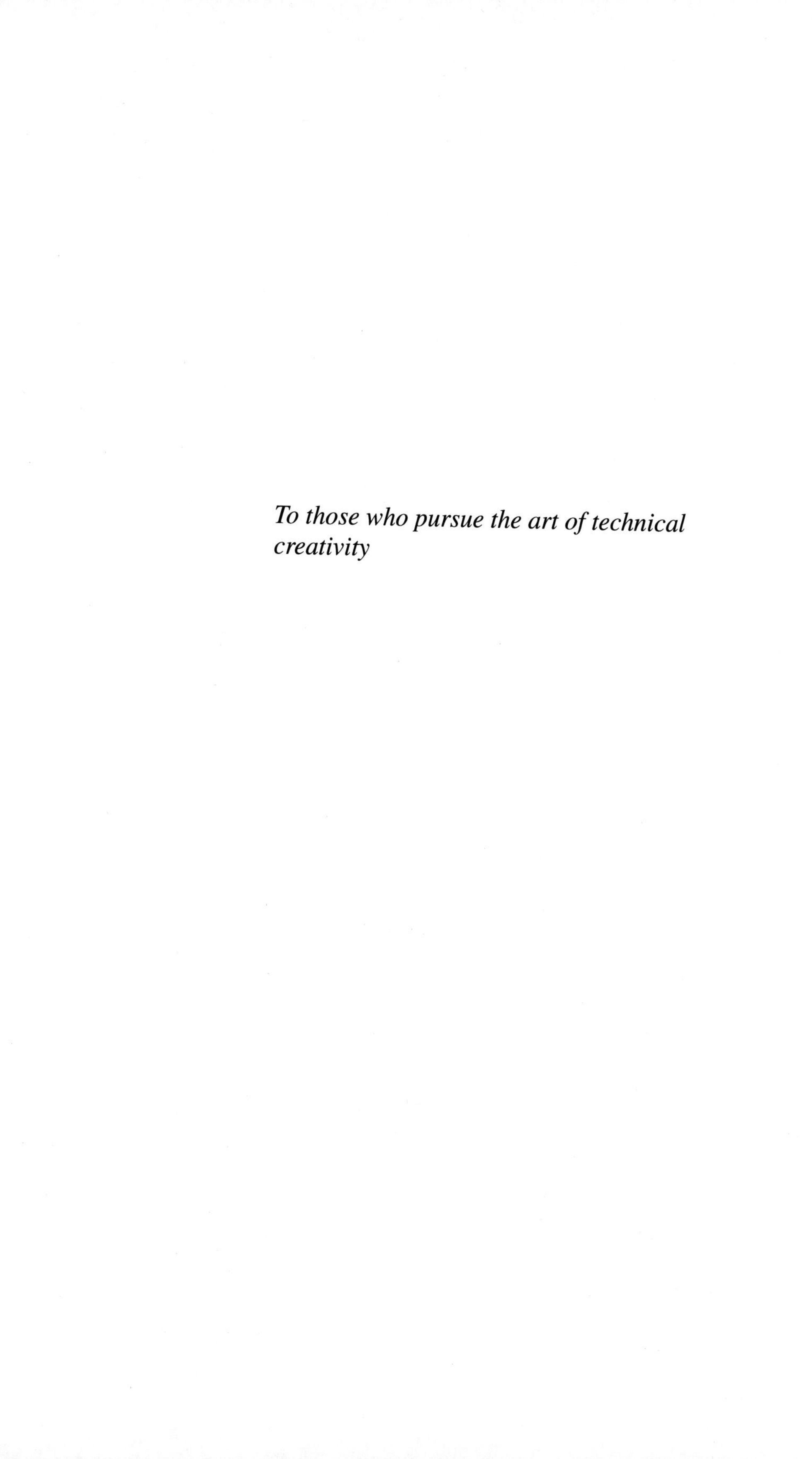

To those who pursue the art of technical creativity

Preface to the Fourth Edition

C++20, the newest evolution of C++, adds various major new language features that can significantly simplify and clarify program expression. At the same time, using C++ in microcontroller programming is steadily gaining popularity and the methods of its use are maturing in the embedded systems community. These steps are matched by the widespread support of modern post-C++11,14,17 adherence delivered by many high-quality microcontroller compiler vendors.

The fourth edition of this book keeps up with these progressions in C++. In addition to covering new C++ language elements, particular emphasis is placed on improving and extending the depth of the examples. Several interesting sample projects requiring additional chips and exercising advanced software and laboratory techniques have been added. Furthermore, one of the new computationally intensive examples has also been adapted to both our target with the 8-bit microcontroller as well as to a modern single-board computer with a powerful 32-bit processor.

These efforts are intended to widen the scope of applicability of this book for students, practitioners, and hobbyists alike by exemplifying practical, hands-on methods to leverage the power of portable C++ with lean, efficient real-time code.

New or Significantly Modified Sections

The fourth edition of this book contains several new or significantly modified parts. These include:

- Section 1.10 adapted to add detailed comments regarding using **`reinterpret_cast`** sparingly,
- Section 3.2 extended to include example `chapter03_02` that calculates prime numbers and provides an insightful preview of numerous C++ techniques,
- Section 3.21 (new) on `std::span` from C++20's `<span>` library that can be used for delimiting pointer ranges,

- Section 3.22 (new) briefly showing how to use the `<random>` library for generating sequences of pseudo-random integers,
- Section 4.4 which has been significantly expanded to include two full detailed examples exercising dynamic polymorphism with an intuitive LED class hierarchy,
- Chapters 4, 7, and 8 which have been reworked in order to improve code sequences and clarity of text passages,
- Section 5.13 (new) describing how to make effective and powerful use of template integer sequences at compile time with `std::integer_sequence`,
- Section 6.14 with the addition of example `chapter06_14` extending the original CRC32 calculation of example `chapter06_01` to make use of custom ROM-based iterators and containers specifically designed for accessing read-only program code,
- Section 6.21 (new) quantifying potential resource consumption resulting from using runtime type information (RTTI),
- Section 9.5 has been reworked to implement a portable, all-software SPI™ driver subsequently used in examples `chapter04_04`, `chapter04_04a`, `chapter10_08`, `chapter10_08a`, `chapter10_09`, and `chapter16_08`,
- Section 10.8 (new) providing a detailed example that uses external SRAM ICs to calculate up to $100,001$ decimal digits of π with an application architecture that uses custom SRAM pointers, iterators and containers, and numerical algorithms,
- Section 10.9 (new) which adapts the π calculations of Sect. 10.8 to the powerful 32-bit Arm®-based Raspberry Pi®Zero WH single-board computer system,
- Section 11.7 has been modified to include a sample that exemplifies preemptive multitasking scheduling,
- Section 12.2 has been slightly expanded to include common standardized mathematical constants such as $\sqrt{2}$, π, $\log 2$, e, etc. in the `<numbers>` header,
- Section 16.7 (new) describing a portable implementation of big integer types such as `uint128_t`, `uint256_t`, `uint512_t`, etc.,
- Section 16.8 (new) which develops a basic hardware-based custom random engine that can serve as an efficient and practical, hobby-quality drop-in replacement for `std::default_random_engine` and also presents example `chapter16_08` which performs primality testing of random 128-bit big integers,
- Section 16.9 (new) on the *freestanding* implementation,
- Section A.9 enlarged to treat C++20 enhancements of lambda expression syntax including template parameter lists and new capture style for **`this`**,
- Section A.16 broadened to include `std::variant` from C++20 in the new `<variant>` addition to the STL,
- Section A.18 (new) covering a three-way comparison with the co-called *spaceship* operator within the context of generalized equality and inequality,

Improved or New Examples and Code Snippets

Several new examples have been added. All of the example projects have been modernized and checked for compatibility with GCC version 10.1.0 built for `avr-g++`. The portability and range of use of each example project have been improved. In particular, test and verification of the examples have been carried out with various GCC versions ranging from 5 through 9 using the language standards flags `-std=c++11`, `-std=c++14`, `-std=c++17`, and `-std=c++20` (as available).

☞ The `chapter03_02` sample project (new) in Sect. 3.2 uses fixed-size integer types and various other C++ techniques to compute the first 100 prime numbers.
☞ The `chapter04_04` and `chapter04_04a` sample projects (new) in Sect. 4.4 exercise various forms of polymorphism and class relationships through the example of an LED class hierarchy.
☞ The `chapter06_14` sample project (new) in Sect. 6.14 shows how to create custom ROM-based iterators and containers used to calculate a CRC32 checksum.
☞ The sample projects `chapter10_08` and `chapter10_08a` (new, advanced) found in Sect. 10.8 use external memory ICs to extend available SRAM to up to 2 Mbyte for calculations of as many as 100, 001 decimal digits of the mathematical constant π.
☞ The `chapter10_09` sample project (new, advanced) in Sect. 10.9 adapts the π calculations of example `chapter10_08a` to the well-known 32-bit Arm®-based Raspberry Pi®Zero WH single-board computer system, running OS-less in bare metal mode. Seamlessly porting this application's C++ algorithms from an 8-bit platform to a high-performance 32-bit Arm®–based system provides keen insight into effective cross development on multiple systems.
☞ The `chapter11_07` sample project (new, advanced) exemplifies intuitive use of a preemptive multitasking scheduler constrained by small RAM/ROM resource footprint.
☞ The `chapter16_08` sample project (new, advanced) in Sect. 16.8 computes 128-bit prime numbers using a Miller–Rabin primality test.

With the fourth edition of this book, the detailed code snippets available in the public domain now cover approximately two-thirds of code samples in the text. Each code snippet comprises a complete and portable, single-file C++ program. Every program can be compiled and run on a PC or easily adapted to a microcontroller environment.

To obtain run-ability on a PC, code snippets have usually been embellished with a `main()` subroutine. Some code snippets have been augmented with `<thread>` support, simulated hardware registers or other C++ mechanisms in order to elucidate the topic of the program. Outputs of the code snippets are typically printed to the console with `<iostream>` and potentially formatted with the help of `<iomanip>`. File names of the code snippets correspond to chapter and section numbers in the book.

Companion Code

Based on new and reworked material in the fourth edition, the companion code has been significantly improved and extended.

The entire companion code can be found here:

http://github.com/ckormanyos/real-time-cpp

The complete reference application is at:

http://github.com/ckormanyos/real-time-cpp/tree/master/ref_app

Example projects are stored here:

http://github.com/ckormanyos/real-time-cpp/tree/master/examples

Code snippets are located at:

http://github.com/ckormanyos/real-time-cpp/tree/master/code_snippets

Further Notes on Coding Style

The coding style in the fourth edition of this book stays consistent with that used in the first through third editions. The code is intended to be easy to read and straightforward to comprehend while simultaneously utilizing the full spectrum of C++'s traditional and modern features.

Christopher Kormanyos

Reutlingen, Germany
November 2020

Updated Trademarks and Acknowledgments

In the prefaces to first and third editions, several trademarks and acknowledgments are listed. Meanwhile, the authors/holders of certain trademarks/copyrights and the scope of some of the acknowledgments have changed.

- Microchip® and AVR® are registered trademarks of Microchip Technology Incorporated or its subsidiaries in the USA and other countries.
- ARDUINO® is a registered trademark of the Arduino Group.
- Arm®, Arm11™ and Arm1176JZF-S™ are trademarks or registered trademarks of Arm Limited (or its subsidiaries) in the USA and/or elsewhere.
- The word AUTOSAR is a registered trademark of the AUTOSAR Development Partnership.
- Cypress® and MoBL® are registered trademarks of Cypress Semiconductor Corporation. At the time of writing the fourth edition, Cypress is an Infineon Technologies Company.
- Broadcom® is a registered trademark of Broadcom Corporation and/or its affiliates in the USA, certain other countries, and/or the EU.
- Raspberry Pi® is a registered trademark of the Raspberry Pi Foundation.
- SPI™ is a trademark of Motorola, Inc.
- LCD character displays used in various examples including `chapter10_08a`, `chapter10_09`, and `chapter16_08` and pictured in the associated Figs. 10.2, 10.4 and 16.4 are products of Newhaven Display International that are bound by the terms and conditions provided at Newhaven Display International's Internet website.
- Several other trademarks are associated with electronic components that appear prominently in some of the figures. These components and trademarks include 74xx logic ICs in Figs. 10.4 and 16.4 from Harris® Corp. Semiconductor Sector, an LM2903 dual voltage comparator in Fig. 16.4 from Fairchild™ Semiconductor International, Inc., electrolytic capacitors in various figures from Vishay® Roederstein, potentiometers in various figures from Piher Sensing Systems (an Amphenol® company), an SMD-to-DIP adapter of type PA0208 with text PROTO-ADVANTAGE.COM in Fig. 10.2, and a micro SD card inserted in a

tray in Fig. 10.4 from Transcend® Information, Inc. All these and any other trademarks mentioned or shown in the figures are the property of their respective companies.

- Nonetheless this is neither an official publication of nor has it been authorized, sponsored, or approved by any of the aforementioned copyright authors, copyright holders, or their subsidiaries.
- The circuits of all target hardware described and depicted in various chapters and appendices have been designed and assembled on solderless prototyping breadboards by myself.
- All photographs of target hardware shown in various chapters and appendices were taken by myself.

Preface to the Third Edition

C++ is a modern, expressive object-oriented programming language that continues to evolve. In keeping up with the exciting development of C++, the third edition of this book has been updated for C++17.[1]

With this iteration of the language, the purpose of this book remains the same—to show through example and text how to leverage C++'s powerful object-oriented and template features in the realm of microcontroller programming with the goal of improving software quality and robustness while simultaneously fulfilling efficiency requirements.

Several new sections have been added and others have been modified or adapted. These changes cover new language elements and library features in C++17. They also reflect the trend of improved compiler support for C++11 and C++14.

More errors have been identified, predominantly reported by careful and patient readers. All errors that have been found have been corrected.

New or Significantly Modified Sections

The third edition of this book contains several new or significantly modified sections. These include:

- Section 2.2 updated for a newer GCC toolchain with a more simple decorated name (i.e., GCC version 7.2.0 built for the target `avr-g++`).
- Section 3.4 adding information on C++17 nested namespace definitions,
- Section 3.17 now including descriptions of the (in the second edition of this book missing) standardized suffixes `if`, `i`, and `il` from the `<complex>` library,
- Section 3.18 (new) detailing the specifiers **`alignof`** and **`alignas`**,

[1] At the time of writing the third edition of this book, state-of-the-art compilers support C++17. The specification process is ongoing, and some language experts predict that C++20 will be the next revision of the C++ standard, potentially available in 2020.

- Section 3.19 (new) for the specifier `final`,
- Section 3.20 (new) on defining types with C++11 alias,
- Section 9.8 (new) portraying a full example that animates an RGB LED to produce a colorful light display,
- Section 12.4 covering inclusion of additional mathematical special functions in `<cmath>` specified in the C++17 standard,
- several sections in Chap. 13 reflecting improvements of the `fixed_point` class in the companion code,
- Section 16.6 (new) presenting an extended-complex template class that promotes the functionality of the `<complex>` library to user-defined types other than **`float`**, **`double`**, and **`long double`**,
- Chapter 17 (new) showing how to use C code in a C++ project (hereby "Additional Reading" has been moved from Chaps. 17 to 18),
- the tutorial of Appendix A, in particular Sect. A.4 updating **`static_assert`** for C++17, Sect. A.15 (new) about the `<type_traits>` library, Sect. A.16 (new) on using `std::any` from the C++17 `<any>` library, and Sect. A.17 (new) introducing structured binding declarations (also from C++17).

Improved or New Examples and Code Snippets

All sample projects have been modernized for GCC version 7.2.0 built for `avr-g++`, and five new examples have been added.

☞ The `chapter06_01` sample project (new) shows step-by-step how to perform the benchmark of the CRC calculation described in Sects. 6.1 and 6.2.

☞ The `chapter09_07` example in Sect. 9.7 has been adapted to architectural improvements found in the new `chapter09_08` sample of Sect. 9.8,

☞ The `chapter09_08` sample project (new) animates an industry-standard off-the-shelf RGB LED. This example incorporates several real-time C++ features including object-oriented design, peripheral driver development, and multitasking. They are merged together within the context of a coherent, intuitive, and visible project. By means of simulation on a PC, the `chapter09_08` sample also exemplifies cross-development and methods for creating portable code.

☞ The `chapter12_04` example (new) performs highly detailed calculations of several mathematical special functions. These are used to provide a benchmark of floating-point operations.

☞ The `chapter17_03` sample project (new) takes an existing C library used for CRC calculations and wraps the procedural functions in classes that can be employed in object-oriented C++. This practical exercise shows how to leverage the power of valuable existing C code within a modern C++ project.

☞ The `chapter17_03a` sample project (new) uses the CRC classes of the `chapter17_03` example and distributes the work of the calculations among successive time slices in a multitasking environment.

With the third edition of this book, code snippets have been made available in the public domain. The code snippets correspond to certain code samples that appear in the text. Each code snippet comprises a complete and portable, single-file C++ program. Every program can be compiled and run on a PC or easily adapted to a microcontroller environment.

To obtain run-ability on a PC, code snippets have been embellished with a `main()` subroutine. Some code snippets have been augmented with `<thread>` support or other higher-level mechanisms in order to elucidate the topic of the program. Outputs are printed to the console with `<iostream>`. The file names of the code snippets correspond to chapter and section numbers in the book.

Companion Code

The companion code has been improved and extended based on new and reworked sections of the third edition. Contemporary compiler toolchains are used. Legacy directories that previously provided for certain aspects of C++11 compatibility have been removed, as modern compilers now support these.

The entire companion code can be found here:

http://github.com/ckormanyos/real-time-cpp

The reference application is at:

http://github.com/ckormanyos/real-time-cpp/tree/master/ref_app

Example projects can be found here:

http://github.com/ckormanyos/real-time-cpp/tree/master/examples

Code snippets are located at:

http://github.com/ckormanyos/real-time-cpp/tree/master/code_snippets

Further Notes on Coding Style

The coding style in the third edition of this book stays consistent with that used in the first and second editions. The code is intended to be easy to read and straightforward to comprehend while simultaneously utilizing the full spectrum of C++'s traditional and modern features.

Updated Trademarks and Acknowledgments

In the preface to first edition of this book, we listed several trademarks and acknowledgments. Meanwhile the authors/holders of certain trademarks/copyrights and the scope of some of the acknowledgments have changed.

- MICROCHIP®, ATMEL®, and AVR® are registered trademarks of Microchip Technology Incorporated or its subsidiaries in the USA and other countries.
- *Real-Time C++: Efficient Object-Oriented and Template Microcontroller Programming, Third Edition* is a book authored by Christopher Kormanyos and published by Springer Verlag and has not been authorized, sponsored, or otherwise approved of by Microchip Technology Incorporated.
- ARDUINO® is a registered trademark of the Arduino Group.
- The word AUTOSAR is a registered trademark of the AUTOSAR Development Partnership.
- The circuits of all target hardware described in this book and depicted in various chapters such as Chaps. 2, 9, and Appendix D, were designed and assembled on solderless prototyping breadboards by Christopher Kormanyos.
- All photographs of target hardware in this book shown in chapters including Chaps. 2, 9, Appendix D and any others were taken by Christopher Kormanyos.

Reutlingen, Germany
February 2018

Christopher Kormanyos

Preface to the Second Edition

C++ seamlessly blends object-oriented techniques with generic template methods, creating a modern powerful programming language useful for problem-solving in countless domains. The most recent evolution of C++ from C++11 to C++14 has brought yet further improvements to this rich language.[1] As C++ becomes even more expressive, growing numbers of embedded systems developers are discovering new and fascinating ways to utilize its multifaceted capabilities for creating efficient and effective microcontroller software.

The second edition of this book retains its original purpose to serve as a practical guide to programming real-time embedded microcontroller systems in C++. New material has been incorporated predominantly reflecting changes introduced in the C++14 standard. Various sections have been reworked according to reader suggestions. Selected passages have been reformulated in a continued effort to improve clarity. In addition, all known errors throughout the text have been corrected.

New sections have been added (in particular for C++14) covering:

- digit separators (Sect. 3.15),
- binary literals (Sect. 3.16),
- user-defined literals (Sect. 3.17),
- variable templates (Sect. 5.12),
- and the `chapter09_07` sample project (Sect. 9.7) controlling an industry-standard seven-segment display.

Two new sample projects, `chapter02_03a` and `chapter09_07`, have been added to the companion code.

[1] At the time of writing the second edition of this book, C++14 is brand new. World-class compilers are shipped with support for C++14. Work is in progress on C++1z, the next specification of C++ (sometimes known as C++17). Experts anticipate that the specification of C++1z could be finished in 2017.

☞ The `chapter02_03a` sample project implements LED toggling at 1/2 Hz with timing provided by a simple multitasking scheduler in combination with a timer utility.
☞ The `chapter09_07` sample project in the newly added Sect. 9.7 uses many of the advanced programming methods in this book to animate an industry-standard seven-segment display.

Significantly reworked or corrected parts of this book include:

✓ corrections and clarifications in Chap. 1 on getting started with C++,
✓ the description of the `chapter02_02` project in Sect. 2.2,
✓ parts of Chap. 3 on the jump-start in real-time C++,
✓ corrections and clarifications in Chap. 5 on templates,
✓ Sects. 6.1 and 6.2 on optimization and performance,
✓ parts of Chap. 10 on custom memory management,
✓ parts of Chaps. 12 and 13 on mathematics,
✓ the literature list in Sect. 18.1,
✓ parts of Appendix A in the C++ tutorial,
✓ and repairs and extensions of the citations in some chapter references.

Companion Code

The companion code continues to be supported and numerous developers have successfully worked with it on various cross-development platforms. The scope of the companion code has been expanded to include a much wider range of target microcontrollers. In addition, the `chapter02_03a` and `chapter09_07` sample projects that are mentioned above have been added to the companion code.

The companion code is available at:

http://github.com/ckormanyos/real-time-cpp

More Notes on Coding Style

The second edition of this book features slight changes in coding style. These can be encountered in the code samples throughout the text.

Compiler support for standard C99 and C++11 macros of the form `UINT8_C()`, `UINT16_C()`, `UINT32_C()`, etc. and corresponding macros for signed types in the `<stdint.h>` and `<cstdint>` headers has become more prevalent (see also Sect. 3.2). Consequently, these macros are used more frequently throughout the code samples.

These macros are useful for creating integer numeric literal values having specified widths. The code below, for example, utilizes `UINT8_C()` to initialize an 8-bit integer variable with a numeric literal value.

```
#include <cstdint>

std::uint8_t byte_value = UINT8_C(0x55);
```

Digit separators have become available with C++14 (Sect. 3.15). These are used in selected code samples to improve clarity of long numeric literals. Digit separators are shown in the code sample below.

```
#include <cstdint>

constexpr std::uint32_t prime_number =
  UINT32_C(10'006'721);

constexpr float pi = 3.1415926535'8979323846F;
```

Other than these minor changes, however, the coding style in the second edition of this book remains consistent with that of the first edition and is intended to be clean and clear.

Reutlingen, Germany
Seattle, Washington
May 2015

Christopher Kormanyos

Preface to the First Edition

This book is a practical guide to programming real-time embedded microcontroller systems in C++. The C++ language has powerful object-oriented and template features that can improve software design and portability while simultaneously reducing code complexity and the risk of error. At the same time, C++ compiles highly efficient native code. This unique and effective combination makes C++ well-suited for programming microcontroller systems that require compact size, high performance, and safety-critical reliability.

The target audience of this book includes hobbyists, students, and professionals interested in real-time C++. The reader should be familiar with C or another programming language and should ideally have had some exposure to microcontroller electronics and the performance and size issues prevalent in embedded systems programming.

About This Book

This is an interdisciplinary book that includes a broad range of topics. Real-world examples have been combined with brief descriptions in an effort to provide an intuitive and straightforward methodology for microcontroller programming in C++. Efficiency is always in focus, and numerous examples are backed up with real-time performance measurements and size analyses that quantify the true costs of the code down to the very last byte and microsecond.

Throughout the chapters, C++ is used in a bare-bones, no-frills fashion without relying on any libraries other than those specified in the language standard itself. This approach facilitates portability.

This book has three parts and several appendices. The three parts generally build on each other with the combined goal of providing a coherent and effective set of C++ methods that can be used with a wide range of embedded microcontrollers.

- Part I provides a foundation for real-time C++ by covering language technologies. Topics include getting started in real-time C++, object-oriented methods, template programming, and optimization. The first 3 chapters have a particularly hands-on nature and are intended to boost competence in real-time C++. Chapter 6 has a unique and important role in that it is wholly dedicated to optimization techniques appropriate for microcontroller programming in C++.
- Part II presents detailed descriptions of a variety of C++ components that are widely used in microcontroller programming. These components can be either used as presented, or adapted for other projects. This part of the book uses some of C++'s most powerful language elements, such as class types, templates, and the STL, to develop components for microcontroller register access, low-level drivers, custom memory management, embedded containers, multitasking, etc.
- Part III describes mathematical methods and generic utilities that can be employed to solve recurring problems in real-time C++.
- The appendices include a C++ language tutorial, information on the real-time C++ development environment, and instructions for building GNU GCC cross-compilers and a microcontroller circuit.

C++ is a rich language with many features and details, the description of which can fill entire bookshelves. This book, however, primarily concentrates on how to use C++ in a real-time microcontroller environment. Along those lines, C++ language tutorials have been held terse, and information on microcontroller hardware and compilers is included only insofar as it is needed for the examples. A suggested list of additional reading material is given in Chap. 18 for those seeking supplementary information on C++, the C++ standard library and STL, software design, C++ coding guidelines, the embedded systems toolchain, and microcontroller hardware.

When units are needed to express physical quantities, the MKS (meter, kilogram, second) system of units is used.

Companion Code, Targets, and Tools

The companion code includes three introductory projects and one reference project. The introductory projects treat various aspects of the material presented in Chaps. 1 and 2. The reference project is larger in scope and exercises many of the methods from all the chapters.

The companion code is available at:

http://github.com/ckormanyos/real-time-cpp

The C++ techniques in this book specifically target microcontrollers in the *small-to-medium* size range. Here, small-to-medium spans the following approximate size and performance ranges.

- 4 kbyte ... 1 Mbyte program code
- 256 byte ... 128 kbyte RAM

- 8-bit ... 32-bit CPU
- 8 MHz ... 200 MHz CPU frequency

Most of the methods described in this book are, however, scalable. As such, they can be used equally well on larger or smaller devices, even on PCs and workstations. In particular, they can be employed if the application has strict performance and size constraints.

A popular 8-bit microcontroller clocked with a frequency of 16 MHz has been used as the primary target for benchmarking and testing the code samples in this book. Certain benchmarks have also been performed with a well-known 32-bit microcontroller clocked at 24 MHz. An 8-bit microcontroller and a 32-bit microcontroller have been selected in order to exercise the C++ methods over a wide range of microcontroller performance.

All the C++ examples and benchmarks in the book and the companion code have been compiled with GNU GCC versions 4.6.2 and 4.7.0. Certain examples and benchmarks have also been compiled with other PC-based compilers.

The most recent specification of C++11 in ISO/IEC 14882:2011 is used throughout the text. At the time this book is written, the specification of C++11 is brand new. The advent of C++11 has made C++ significantly more effective and easy-to-use. This will profoundly influence C++ programming. The well-informed reader will, therefore, want to keep in touch with C++11 best practice as it evolves in the development community.

Notes on Coding Style

A consistent coding style is used throughout the examples in this book and in the companion code.

Code samples are written with a `fixed-width font`. C++ language keywords and built-in types use the same font, but they are in boldface. For instance,

```
constexpr int version = 7;
```

In general, the names of all symbols such as variables, class types, members, and subroutines are written in lower case. A single underscore (_) is used to separate words and abbreviations in names. For instance, a system-tick variable expressed with this style is shown in the code sample below.

```
unsigned long system_tick;
```

Using prefixes, suffixes, or abbreviations to incorporate type information in a name, sometimes known as *Hungarian notation*, is not done. Superfluous prefixes, suffixes, and abbreviations in Hungarian notation may obscure the name of a symbol, and symbol names can be more intuitive and clear without them. For example,

```
std::uint16_t name_of_a_symbol;
```

Names that are intended for use in public domains are preferentially long and descriptive rather than short and abbreviated. Here, clarity of expression is preferred over terseness. Symbols used for local subroutine parameters or private implementation details with obvious meanings, however, often have terse or abbreviated names.

The global subroutine below, for example, uses this naming style. It returns the **float** value of the squared Euclidean distance from the origin of a point in two-dimensional Cartesian space $\mathbb{R}^2$.

```
float squared_euclidean_distance(const float& x,
                                 const float& y)
{
  return (x * x) + (y * y);
}
```

C++ references are heavily used because this can be advantageous for small microcontrollers. Consider an 8-bit microcontroller. The work of copying subroutine parameters or the work of pushing them onto the stack for anything wider than 8-bits can be significant. This workload can potentially be reduced by using references. In the previous code sample, for instance, the floating-point subroutine parameters `x` and `y`, each four bytes wide, have been passed to the subroutine by reference (i.e., **const float&**).

Fixed-size integer types defined in the `std` namespace of the C++ standard library such as `std::uint8_t`, `std::uint16_t`, `std::uint32_t`, and the like are preferentially used instead of plain built-in types such as **char**, **short**, **int**, etc. This improves clarity and portability. An unsigned login response with exactly 8 bits, for instance, is shown below.

```
std::uint8_t login_response;
```

Code samples often rely on one or more of the C++ standard library headers such as `<algorithm>`, `<array>`, `<cstdint>`, `<limits>`, `<tuple>`, `<vector>`, etc. In general, code samples requiring library headers do not explicitly include their necessary library headers.

The declaration of login_response above, for example, actually requires <cstdint> for the definition of std::uint8_t. The library file is, however, not included. In general, the code samples focus on the core of the code, not on the inclusion of library headers.

It is easy to guess or remember, for example, that std::array can be found in <array> and that std::vector is located <vector>. It can, however, be more difficult to guess or remember that std::size_t is in <cstddef> or that std::accumulate() is in <numeric>. With assistance from online help and other resources and with a little practice, though, it becomes routine to identify what standard library parts can be found in which headers.

In cases for which particular emphasis is placed on the inclusion of a header file, the relevant **#include** line(s) may be explicitly written. For instance,

```
#include <cstdint>

std::uint8_t login_response;
```

Namespaces are used frequently. In general, though, the **using** directive is not used to inject symbols in namespaces into the global namespace. This means that the entire namespace must be typed with the name of a symbol in it. This, again, favors non-ambiguity over brevity.

The unsigned 16-bit counter below, for example, uses a type from the std namespace. Since the "**using namespace** std" directive is not used, the name of the namespace (std) is explicitly included in the type.

```
std::uint16_t counter;
```

Suffixes are generally appended to literal constant values. When a suffix is appended to a literal constant value, its optional case is uppercase. For example,

```
constexpr float pi = 3.14159265358979323846F;

constexpr std::uint8_t login_key = 0x55U;
```

Certain established C++ coding guidelines have strongly influenced the coding style. For the sake of terseness and clarity, however, not every guideline has been followed all the time.

One clearly recognizable influence of the coding guidelines is the diligent use of C++-style casts when converting built-in types. The following code, for instance, explicitly casts from **float** to an unsigned integer type.

```
float f = 3.1415926535897932384 6F;

std::uint8_t u = static_cast<std::uint8_t>(f);
```

Even though explicit casts like these are not always mandatory, they can resolve ambiguity and eliminate potential misinterpretation caused by integer promotion.

Another influence of the coding guidelines on the code is the ordering of class members according to their access level in the class. The `communication` class below, for example, represents the base class in a hierarchy of communication objects. The members in the class definition are ordered according to access level. In particular,

```
class communication
{
public:
  virtual ~communication();

  virtual bool send(const std::uint8_t) const;
  virtual bool recv(std::uint8_t&);

protected:
  communication();

private:
  bool recv_ready;
  std::uint8_t recv_buffer;
};
```

C-style preprocessor macros are used occasionally. Preprocessor macros are written entirely in uppercase letters. Underscores separate the words in the names of preprocessor macros. The `MAKE_WORD()` preprocessor macro below, for example, creates an unsigned 16-bit word from two unsigned 8-bit constituents.

```
#define MAKE_WORD(lo, hi) \
  (uint16_t) (((uint16_t) (hi) << 8) | (lo))
```

Acknowledgments

First and foremost, I would like to thank my wife and my daughter for encouraging me to write this book and also for creating a peaceful, caring atmosphere in which I could work productively. Thank you for your support and your time. You have my gratitude.

I would also like to express appreciation to family, friends, and associates, too numerous to list, who contributed to this project with their innovative ideas, support, friendship, and companionship.

Thanks go to the members of the C++ standards committee, Boost, the volunteers at GCC and all the developers in the vibrant C++, and embedded systems communities. Through your efforts, often times for no pay whatsoever, C++ has evolved to an unprecedented level of expressiveness, making object-oriented and generic programming more effective and easier than ever.

Working with Springer Verlag was a delightful experience. I thank my editor, who first identified the merit of this work and supported me throughout the writing process. I also thank the copy editing team and all the staff at Springer Verlag for their professionalism and capable assistance.

- ATMEL® and AVR® are registered trademarks of Atmel Corporation or its subsidiaries, in the USA and other countries.
- *Real-Time C++: Efficient Object-Oriented and Template Microcontroller Programming* is a book authored by Christopher Kormanyos and published by Springer Verlag and has not been authorized, sponsored, or otherwise approved of by Atmel Corporation.
- ARDUINO® is a registered trademark of the Arduino Group.
- SPI™ is a trademark of Motorola Corporation.
- The circuit of the target hardware described in this book and depicted in Chap. 2 and Appendix D was designed and assembled on a solderless prototyping breadboard by Christopher Kormanyos.
- The photographs of the target hardware described in this book and depicted in Chap. 2 and Appendix D were taken by Christopher Kormanyos.

Reutlingen, Germany
Seattle, Washington
September 2012

Christopher Kormanyos

Contents

Acronyms

$\mathbb{C}$	$\mathbb{C}$ represents the set of complex numbers in mathematics.
$\mathbb{R}$	$\mathbb{R}$ represents the set of real numbers on the real axis in mathematics.
$\mathbb{R}^2$	$\mathbb{R}^2$ represents two-dimensional Cartesian space in mathematics and geometry.
$\mathbb{R}^3$	$\mathbb{R}^3$ represents three-dimensional Cartesian space in mathematics and geometry.
$\mathbb{Z}$	$\mathbb{Z}$ represents the set of integer numbers in mathematics.
ADC	Analog-Digital Converter.
ASCII	American Standard Code for Information Interchange [25] is a numerical representation of characters, often used in areas such as computer programming and telecommunication.
AUTOSAR	AUTomotive Open System ARchitecture [2] is a worldwide cooperation of automotive manufacturers and companies supplying electronics, semiconductors and software that concentrates on, among other things, a standardized architecture for automotive microcontroller software.
AWG	American Wire Gauge.
binutils	Binary Utilities [6] are the GNU binary utilities such as archiver, assembler, linker, object file parsers, etc. for GCC.
C	C is the C programming language, which is often referred to as ANSI–C [1] or C89 [2]. Later versions of C include C99 [13] and C11 [17].
C99	C99 refers to the C programming language, as specified in ISO/IEC 9899:1999 [13].
C11	C11 refers to the C programming language, as specified in ISO/IEC 9899:2011 [17].
C++	C++ refers to the C++ programming language.
C++98	C++98 refers to the C++ programming language, as specified in ISO/IEC 14882:1998 [12].
C++03	C++03 refers to the C++ programming language, as specified in ISO/IEC 14882:2003 [15].

C++11	C++11 refers to the C++ programming language, as specified in ISO/IEC 14882:2011 [18].
C++14	C++14 refers to the C++ programming language, as specified in ISO/IEC 14882:2014 [19].
C++17	C++17 refers to the C++ programming language, as specified in ISO/IEC 14882:2017 [20].
C++20	C++20 [26] is predicted by some C++ language experts to be the next revision of the C++ standard, possibly to become available in the year 2020.
CLooG	Chunky Loop Generator [4] is a software library used for geometric polyhedron analysis.
CRC	Cyclic Redundancy Check [27].
CPU	Central-Processing Unit.
ctor	constructor of a class object in object-oriented programming is a special subroutine that is called when an object is created.
DIL	Dual In-Line electronic component packaging.
DSP	Digital Signal Processor.
dtor	destructor of a class object in object-oriented programming is a special subroutine that is called when an object is destroyed or deleted.
FIR	Finite-Impulse Response is a kind of digital filter.
FLASH	Flash Memory is a nonvolatile computer memory that can be electrically written and erased. Flash is commonly used as an alternative to ROM.
FPU	Floating-Point Unit implements floating-point arithmetic in hardware. Many modern high-performance microcontrollers use an FPU to accelerate floating-point calculations.
GAS	is the GNU ASsembler.
GCC	GNU Compiler Collection [7] is a collection of free compilers for several popular programming languages including, among others, C and C++. GCC is supported for a wide range of targets.
GMP	GMP is the GNU Multiple-Precision library [9]. It implements highly efficient multiple-precision representations of integer and floating-point data types.
GNU	Is a ∗nix-like computer operating system consisting entirely of free software [8].
GUI	Graphical User Interface.
HEX	Hexadecimal representation is a base-16 numerical representation commonly used to store program data in computer engineering.
ICE	In-Circuit Emulator is a highly sophisticated hardware device used to debug embedded microcontroller software with an emulated bond-out processor.
ISL	Integer Set Library [11] is a software library used for manipulating sets of integers.

ISP In-System-Programming is the act of programming the program code of a microcontroller using a communication interface while the microcontroller is fitted in the application, rather than as a standalone non-soldered component.

ISR Interrupt Service Routine.

JTAG Joint Test Action Group, later standardized as IEEE 1149.1 [10], is a protocol and hardware interface used for printed circuit board testing, boundary scan and recently more and more for debugging embedded systems.

LED Light-Emitting Diode is a semiconductor-based light source used in diverse applications such as lighting, consumer electronics, and toys.

MCAL Microcontroller Abstraction Layer is a low-level layer in a layered software architecture (such as AUTOSAR). The interface of the MCAL is typically written in a portable fashion. The MCAL implementation itself, however, contains partially non-portable components that access microcontroller peripherals and their registers, such as PWM signal generators, timers, serial UARTs, and other communication interfaces.

MinGW Minimalist GNU [21] is an open-source programming toolset that emulates ∗nix-like environments.

MKS Meter, Kilogram, Second is a system of units used to express physical quantities.

MPC Multiple-Precision Complex [22] is a GNU C library that implements multiple-precision arithmetic of complex numbers.

MPFR Multiple-Precision Floating-Point with correct Rounding [5, 23] is the GNU multiple-precision floating-point library. It is built on top of GMP and places special emphasis on efficiency and correct rounding.

MSYS Minimal SYStem [21] is a collection of GNU utilities that enhance and extend the MinGW shell.

newlib newlib [24] is a free implementation of the C standard library. It is well-suited for use with embedded systems and has been ported to a variety of CPU architectures.

nop No OPeration is a common assembly instruction that simply does *no operation*. One or more nops are often chained sequentially in order to be used for ultra low-level functions such as creating very short delays or flushing an instruction pipeline.

opcode OPeration CODE is a machine language instruction containing the operation to be done.

PC Personal Computer.

POSIX Portable Operating System Interface is an open standardized operating system specified in ISO/IEC 9945:2003 [14].

PPL Parma Polyhedra Library [3] is a software library for abstract geometrical polyhedron representations.

PWM Pulse-Width Modulated signal is a square wave that usually has a fixed period and a variable duty cycle.

RAM	Random Access Memory is computer memory with nearly constant access time regardless of address or memory size. RAM is volatile in the sense that data are typically lost when the power is switched off.
ROM	Read-Only Memory is a class of computer memory that, once written, can only be modified with external programming tools—or not be modified at all. ROM has permanent character in the sense that data are retained throughout power on/off cycles.
SPI™	Serial Peripheral Interface bus is a four-wire serial communication interface commonly used for communication between a microcontroller and one or more off-chip devices on the printed circuit board.
STL	Standard Template Library is part of the C++ standard library. The standard template library contains a vast collection of generic containers, iterators and algorithms.
TO–220	Transistor Outline electronic component packaging, number 220.
TR1	C++ Technical Report 1 includes the standard library extensions that are specified in ISO/IEC TR 19768:2007 [16]. TR1 has been predominantly integrated in C++11 (ISO/IEC 14882:2011 [18]).
UART	Universal Asynchronous Receiver/Transmitter is an asynchronous receiver and transmitter commonly used for serial communication between a PC and a microcontroller.

References

1. ANSI, *ANSI X3.159-1989 American National Standard for Information Systems – Programming Language C* (American National Standard for Information, New York, 1989)
2. AUTOSAR, *Automotive Open System Architecture* (2017), http://www.autosar.org
3. BUGSENG, *Parma Polyhedra Library (PPL)* (2012), http://www.bugseng.com/products/ppl
4. CLooG, *Chunky Loop Generator* (2015), http://www.cloog.org
5. L. Fousse, G. Hanrot, V. Lefèvre, P. Pélissier, P. Zimmermann, MPFR: a multiple-precision binary floating-point library with correct rounding. ACM Trans. Math. Soft. **33**(2) (2007). Article 13
6. Free Software Foundation, *GNU Binutils* (2011), http://www.gnu.org/software/binutils
7. Free Software Foundation, *GNU Compiler Collection* (2015), http://gcc.gnu.org
8. Free Software Foundation, *GNU Operating System* (2015), http://gnu.org
9. GMP, *GNU Multiple Precision Arithmetic Library* (2012), http://gmplib.org
10. IEEE Computer Society, *IEEE Std 1149.1 – 1990: IEEE Standard Test Access Port and Boundary-Scan Architecture* (1990). Available at http://standards.ieee.org/findstds/standard/1149.1-1990.html
11. ISL, *Integer Set Library* (2015), http://isl.gforge.inria.fr
12. ISO/IEC, *ISO/IEC 14882:1998 : Programming languages – C++* (International Organization for Standardization, Geneva, 1998)
13. ISO/IEC, *ISO/IEC 9899:1999 : Programming languages – C* (International Organization for Standardization, Geneva, 1999)
14. ISO/IEC, *ISO/IEC 9945:2003 : Information Technology – Portable Operating System Interface (POSIX)* (International Organization for Standardization, Geneva, 2003)
15. ISO/IEC, *ISO/IEC 14882:2003 : Programming languages – C++* (International Organization for Standardization, Geneva, 2003)

16. ISO/IEC, *ISO/IEC TR 19768:2007 : Information technology – Programming languages – Technical Report on C++ Library Extensions* (International Organization for Standardization, Geneva, 2007)
17. ISO/IEC, *ISO/IEC 9899:2011 : Programming languages – C* (International Organization for Standardization, Geneva, 2011)
18. ISO/IEC, *ISO/IEC 14882:2011 : Information technology – Programming languages – C++* (International Organization for Standardization, Geneva, 2011)
19. ISO/IEC, *ISO/IEC 14882:2014 : Information technology – Programming languages – C++* (International Organization for Standardization, Geneva, 2014)
20. ISO/IEC, *ISO/IEC 14882:2017 : Programming languages – C++* (International Organization for Standardization, Geneva, 2017)
21. MinGW, *Home of the MinGW and MSYS Projects* (2012), http://www.mingw.org
22. MPC, *GNU MPC* (2012), http://www.multiprecision.org
23. MPFR, *GNU MPFR Library* (2013), http://www.mpfr.org
24. Red Hat, *newlib* (2013), http://sourceware.org/newlib
25. Wikipedia, *ASCII* (2017), http://en.wikipedia.org/wiki/ASCII
26. Wikipedia, *C++20* (2017), http://en.wikipedia.org/wiki/C%2B%2B20
27. Wikipedia, *Cyclic Redundancy Check* (2017), http://en.wikipedia.org/wiki/Cyclic_redundancy_check

Part I
Language Technologies for Real-Time C++

Chapter 1
Getting Started with Real-Time C++

C++ programs combine class types that encapsulate objects with procedural subroutines in order to embody the functionality of the application. This chapter presents these main language elements of C++ using a short, intuitive program that toggles an LED on a microcontroller output port pin. In addition, other language features are introduced including the syntax of C++, namespaces, the C++ standard library and optimization with compile time constants. This chapter uses our target system with the 8-bit microcontroller.

1.1 The LED Program

A simple microcontroller application is shown in Fig. 1.1 on the following page. The circuit in this figure has one LED connected to a digital output port pin on the microcontroller over a resistor to ground. Switching the port pin to high drives current through the resistor and the LED, and thereby switches the LED on. Setting the port pin to low stops current flow through the resistor and the LED, subsequently turning the LED off.

The LED circuit shown in Fig. 1.1 is part of the circuit belonging to our target system with the 8-bit microcontroller. Further details on the entire circuit in this application and its electrical components can be found in the figure here and also in Sect. 2.1 and Appendix D.

An object-oriented C++ program designed to control the LED circuit in Fig. 1.1 is shown below. It is called the *LED program*. In the LED program, an `led` object called `led_b5` is created on `portb.5`. The LED object `led_b5` is subsequently toggled from low to high and vice versa indefinitely without pause, break or return in an iterative loop in the `main()` subroutine.

C. Kormanyos, *Real-Time C++*, https://doi.org/10.1007/978-3-662-62996-3_1

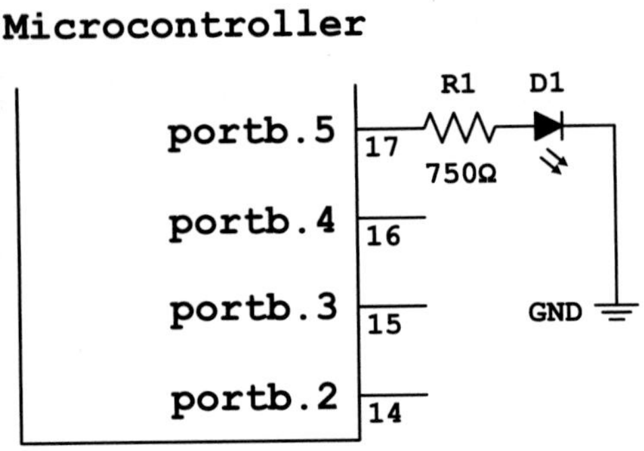

Fig. 1.1 The circuit of the LED `D1` on our target with the 8-bit microcontroller is shown. `D1` is connected to `portb.5` on microcontroller pin 17 over a 750 Ω resistor `R1` to ground


```
// chapter01_01-001_led_program.cpp

// The LED program.

#include <cstdint>
#include "mcal_reg.h"

class led
{
public:
  // Use convenient class-specific typedefs.
  typedef std::uint8_t port_type;
  typedef std::uint8_t bval_type;

  // The led class constructor.
  led(const port_type p,
      const bval_type b)  : port(p),
                            bval(b)
  {
    // Set the port pin value to low.
    *reinterpret_cast<volatile bval_type*>(port)
      &= static_cast<bval_type>(~bval);

    // Set the port pin direction to output.

    // Note that the address of the port direction
    // register is one less than the address
    // of the port value register.
    const port_type pdir = port - 1U;

    *reinterpret_cast<volatile bval_type*>(pdir)
      |= bval;
  }
```

```
  void toggle() const
  {
    // Toggle the LED via direct memory access.
    *reinterpret_cast<volatile bval_type*>(port)
      ^= bval;
  }

private:
  // Private member variables of the class.
  const port_type port;
  const bval_type bval;
};

namespace
{
  // Create led_b5 on portb.5.
  const led led_b5
  {
    mcal::reg::portb,
    mcal::reg::bval5
  };
}

int main()
{
  // Toggle led_b5 in a loop forever.
  for(;;)
  {
    led_b5.toggle();
  }
}
```

The LED program uses various C++ language elements. These include classes, namespaces, type definitions, C++ cast operators, register access via direct memory access and even a little bit of the C++ standard library.

In particular, the predominant parts of the LED program are:

- the inclusion of header files with **`#include`**,
- the `led` class,
- the `led` class constructor and class members that encapsulate the initialization and toggling of the LED via direct memory access,
- the anonymous **`namespace`** containing the `led_b5` object,
- and the `main()` subroutine that toggles the `led_b5` object indefinitely in a never-ending **`for`**`(;;)`-loop.

In the following sections of this chapter, we will investigate in detail how each one of these parts of the LED program is written and how each one works. Along the way, we will briefly discuss many aspects of the syntax of C++ and efficient ways to use the C++ language with real-time embedded systems.

1.2 The Syntax of C++

The syntax of C++ is similar to that of C. In fact, C++ is based on C. With a few minor exceptions, nearly all valid C language constructs can also be used in a C++ program.

As with C, the C++ language uses curly braces `{ ... }` to delimit scope. Parenthesizing and operator priorities are the same in C++ and C. The C++ language has familiar built-in types such as **`char`**, **`short`**, **`int`**, **`long`**, **`float`**, **`double`**, etc. C++ also supports C's well-known **`#include`** syntax for inclusion of user-defined header files and standard library files.

C++ uses C's iteration statements **`for`**, **`while`** and **`do-while`**. Source-level comments in C++ can be written in either slash-slash form (`// ...`) or block form (`/* ... */`). Most C++ developers, however, preferentially use slash-slash comments instead of C-style block comments. See also Item 4 in Meyers [4].

1.3 Class Types

Classes, structures (structs) and unions are *class types* in C++. The LED program has a class called `led`. In particular,

```
class led
{
  // ...
};
```

Class types enable object-oriented programming in C++ because they group data together with functions operating on them in a self-contained entity. The `led` class, for example, encapsulates the real LED hardware by grouping the LED's port pin together with its toggle function.

Classes, structures and unions typically have a mixture of data, functions and overloaded operators called *members*. The public interface of the `led` class, for instance, has a *constructor* (also known as a *ctor*) and a member function called `toggle()`.

A class constructor has the same name as its containing class. Constructors can have any number of input parameters. The constructor of `led` has two input parameters. They characterize the address of the port data register and the bit-position of the output port pin of the LED hardware.

Class initialization code can be placed in the body of the constructor. In particular, the port hardware of the LED is initialized in the body of the `led` constructor.

```
class led
{
public:
  // The led class constructor.
  led(const port_type p,
      const bval_type b) : port(p),
                           bval(b)
  {
    // Set the port pin value to low.
    *reinterpret_cast<volatile bval_type*>(port)
      &= static_cast<bval_type>(~bval);

    // Set the port pin direction to output.

    // Note that the address of the port direction
    // register is one less than the address
    // of the port value register.
    const port_type pdir = port - 1U;

    *reinterpret_cast<volatile bval_type*>(pdir)
      |= bval;
  }
  // ...
};
```

Here, the address of the LED's port direction register is calculated from the address of its port data register. In addition, the port pin value is set to low *before* the port pin direction is set to output. This strategy eliminates potential spikes on I/O pins. These kinds of electrical characteristics of I/O ports are specific to the underlying microcontroller hardware and need to be modified when porting the `led` class to another system.

The so-called *constructor initialization list* is placed after the constructor function parameters and a colon, but before the opening brace of the constructor body. In particular,

```
led(const port_type p,
    const bval_type b)  : port(p),
                          bval(b)
{
  // ...
}
```

In the constructor initialization list of the `led` class here, for example, we initialize the member variables `port` and `bval` with the corresponding values supplied by the input parameters `p` and `b`.

Constant member variables *must* be initialized in the constructor initialization list. Non-constant member variables *should* be initialized in the constructor initialization list. The order of all member variables present in the constructor initialization list should be identical to their order of appearance in the class definition because the compiler initializes them in the order they are declared. See also Item 13 in Meyers [4].

The implementation of the `led` class shown above is entirely contained within its definition. Alternatively, part or all of the implementation of a class type can be placed in a separate source file.

The definition of the `led` class, for instance, could be placed in a header file called `led.h`. In other words,

```
// In the file led.h
class led
{
public:
  led(const port_type p,
      const bval_type b);

  void toggle() const;
  // ...
};
```

The corresponding implementation details of the `led` class could be put in the `led.cpp` source file. For example,

```
// In the file led.cpp
#include "led.h"

led::led(const port_type p,
         const bval_type b) : port(p),
                              bval(b)
{
    // Set the port pin value to low.
    *reinterpret_cast<volatile bval_type*>(port)
      &= static_cast<bval_type>(~bval);

    // Set the port pin direction to output.

    // Note that the address of the port direction
    // register is one less than the address
    // of the port value register.
    const port_type pdir = port - 1U;

    *reinterpret_cast<volatile bval_type*>(pdir)
      |= bval;
}

void led::toggle() const
{
  // Toggle the LED.
  *reinterpret_cast<volatile bval_type*>(port)
    ^= bval;
}

// ...
```

When members are defined outside of a class definition, the *scope resolution operator* (`::`) is used to resolve the class name from the names of members in the implementation file. For example,

```
// The scope resolution operator (::).
void led::toggle() const
{
  // ...
}
```

Including implementation details directly in the class definition can improve optimization via *inlining*. There is no need to explicitly *recommend* inlining to the compiler with the **inline** keyword because a function implemented directly in the class declaration is per default inline. Short, non-virtual subroutines that require the utmost performance may be implemented in the class definition, allowing for potential compiler inlining. Long calculations and polymorphic functions that may be less time critical or rely on the runtime virtual mechanism (Sect. 4.4) should generally be localized in the source file corresponding to the class definition.

1.4 Members

The `led` class has a member function called `toggle()`. In particular,

```
void toggle() const
{
  // Toggle the LED.
  *reinterpret_cast<volatile bval_type*>(port)
    ^= bval;
}
```

The `toggle()` function is responsible for toggling the LED from off to on or, respectively, from on to off depending on the state of the LED. The toggling of the port pin is carried out with bit manipulation through direct memory access. This, as well as C++'s template **reinterpret_cast** operator, will be described in greater detail in Sects. 1.10 and A.1.

The trailing **const** qualifier means that `toggle()` is a *constant* member function. A constant member function is not usually intended to alter the state of any class member variables. A constant function can, however, modify class member variables that are qualified with the keyword **mutable**.[1] Here, *mutable* means capable of being changed. Class member functions that *do* modify member variables should, in general, be non-constant (see also Sect. 4.9).

The `led` class also has two private constant member variables (data members). These are `port` and `bval`. In particular,

```
private:
  const port_type port;
  const bval_type bval;
```

Once set, the value of a constant class data member can not be modified. So after `port` and `bval` are set, they retain their values for the lifetime of the class instance.

[1]The **mutable** keyword—although quite useful at times—is not frequently used in this book.

The variable port represents the LED's port address and the variable bval stores the numerical value corresponding to the pin position of the LED on the port.

Both member variables, port as well as bval, have the underlying type of std::uint8_t, which is itself type defined from the built-in type **unsigned char**. For the sake of convenience and intuitive legibility, the types of port and bval have been declared as class-local types using **typedef** statements.[2] The suggestive names port_type and bval_type (as in *bit-value* type) are used.

In C++, members of a class type have one of three *access controls*. These are public, private or protected, whereby protected access has not been used yet. For example,

```
class led
{
public:
  // ...

protected:
  // ...

private:
  // ...
};
```

The public members of a class constitute its user interface because they can be accessed by any part of the program. Private members can only be accessed by the class itself and its *friends*. Class friends are described in Sect. 4.11. Private members make it possible to hide selected data and implementation details when desired. Protected members are useful for code re-use via *inheritance* in class hierarchies (Sect. 4.3). Class inheritance is also subject to access control.

Some C++ programming guidelines recommend ordering the appearance of class members according to access control. Public members should appear first because users of a class type are most interested in the public interface. Protected members should come second because authors of derived classes are also interested in the protected interface. Private members should come last because they are only of interest to the class author.

If left unspecified, the default levels of member access and inheritance are private for classes and public for structures. This is the only non-stylistic difference between classes and structures in C++. Some C++ guidelines do, however, recommend exclusively using classes for objects having member functions and restricting the use of structures to more simple *data* structures that only have data members and possibly a trivial constructor.

[2]See also Sect. 3.20 for an intuitive alternative to type definitions provided by the C++11 alias.

1.5 Objects and Instances

A class type is an *object* that represents an actual thing, concept, or group or collection thereof that can be manipulated as a cohesive entity. An *instance* is an occurrence of a class type. A class defines how instances of it behave. In object-oriented programming, *object* is often used interchangeably with *instance of a class*.

In the LED program, `led_b5` is an instance of the `led` class. In other words,

```
const led led_b5
{
  mcal::reg::portb,
  mcal::reg::bval5
};
```

The parameters in the constructor of `led_b5` use C++'s *uniform initialization syntax* (Sect. A.2). This convenient braced initialization syntax allows for uniform initialization of, well, *anything* including built-in types, class types, STL containers and C-style arrays alike. Uniform initialization was introduced with C++11.

Here, `led_b5` is a constant object that will not be modified for the entire lifetime of the program. As such, it is declared using the **`const`** keyword. Furthermore, `led_b5` is created using constant register values contained in a user-defined namespace called `mcal::reg`. When the register addresses are resolved, the code of `led_b5`'s constructor is equivalent to the following.

```
const led led_b5
{
  0x25, // The address of portb.
  0x20  // The bit-value of portb.5 (1 << 5).
};
```

The LED `D1` on our target with the 8-bit microcontroller is connected to `port-b.5` on the microcontroller. When the constructor code of `led_b5` is executed, the physical address of `portb` (`0x25`) is stored in the `port` member and the pin's bit value (`0x20`) is stored in the `bval` member.

Since `led_b5` is a static instance, its constructor requires initialization code that needs to execute before the object is used in `main()`. The compiler takes care of this by automatically generating an internal subroutine for `led_b5`'s constructor that is called from a static initialization mechanism in the so-called *startup code*. The startup code executes before the jump to `main()`, ensuring that `led_b5` will be properly initialized before it is used. See Chap. 8 for more information on startup code and static initialization.

The `led_b5` instance is toggled by calling its `toggle()` member function in the **`for`**`(;;)`-loop in `main()`. In particular,

```
led_b5.toggle();
```

Notice, in the way `toggle()` is called, how `led_b5` really does behave like an encapsulated object in the sense of object-oriented programming, see Chap. 4. The toggling is also carried out in real-time on our target with the 8-bit microcontroller, as we will see when we build, flash and run the LED program in Chap. 2.

1.6 #include

Files such as library files or user-defined header files can be included in another file with the **`#include`** syntax. For example,

```
#include <cstdint>
#include "mcal_reg.h"
```

With these two lines, the standard library header file `<cstdint>` and a project-specific header file called `"mcal_reg.h"` are included in the LED program. Here, the acronym MCAL stands for *MicroController Abstraction Layer*, inspired by the AUTOSAR [1] software architecture from the automotive industry. The MCAL directly interfaces with the microcontroller peripherals, and we will be using it in various parts of this book.

Path information uses dots and forward slashes in the ∗nix-way. In addition to forward slash, C++ compilers also understand backward slash. It is even possible mix forward and backward slashes in the same **`#include`** line. The forward slash, however, is considered standard in C++ and should be used consistently throughout the project.

The C++ compiler has its own specific collection of default include paths including, among others, the location of the standard library headers. It is also possible to add other directories to the compiler's search path using command line options in order to improve coding ease and portability. Angled brackets (`< ... >`) should be used for files that are in the compiler's default include paths. Quotation marks (`" ... "`) should delimit the names of user-defined include files that are not in the compiler's default include paths.

1.7 Namespaces

A *namespace* is a collection of related symbol names. For example, the symbols in the C++ standard library are contained in the namespace `std`. In particular,

```
#include <stdint.h>

namespace std
{
  // Inject global ::uint8_t into namespace std.
  using ::uint8_t;

  // Lots of other standard library stuff
  // in lots of files.
  // ...
}
```

Namespaces can be used to create unique names for symbols by adding additional naming information. For instance,

```
// chapter01_07-001_namespace.cpp

namespace this_space
{
  constexpr int version = 1;
}

namespace another_space
{
  constexpr int version = 3;
}
```

In this case, there are two versions of `version` in individual namespaces occurring in the same file-level scope. However, since the two versions of `version` are in different namespaces, they are unique. In particular, `this_space::version` and `another_space::version` are distinct. If namespaces were not used, there would be a naming conflict due to ambiguity. The scope resolution operator (`::`) is used to resolve symbols in namespaces.

The LED program presents another example of a namespace, this time using an unnamed namespace.

```
namespace
{
  const led led_b5
  {
    // ...
  };
}
```

A unnamed namespace is called an *anonymous* namespace. An anonymous namespace limits the scope of anything within itself to file-level. A file-local anonymous namespace guarantees unique names for otherwise same-named symbols occurring in different files. The anonymous namespace may be considered superior to C-style **static**. In fact, some developers consider the anonymous namespace to be the preferred mechanism for file-level scope localization and reduction of naming ambiguity in C++ projects.

An optional **using** directive may be used to eliminate the necessity to type the namespace prefix. For example,

```
using namespace std;
```

When the "**using namespace** `std`" directive is present, the code beneath it can use all the symbols in the namespace `std` without explicitly typing the `std` prefix and scope resolution operator. In particular,

```
// chapter01_07-002_namespace.cpp

#include <cstdint>

using namespace std;

uint8_t my_u8; // No need for (std::) with uint8_t
```

It is also possible to inject individual symbols from a named namespace into the global namespace by using a **using** directive for only that symbol. For example,

```
#include <cstdint>

using std::uint8_t;

uint8_t my_u8; // No need for std:: with uint8_t
```

In this book, however, we generally do not use the **using** directive in non-library code. We thereby prefer clarity over terseness in style.

1.8 C++ Standard Library

The namespace std contains all the symbols in the C++ *standard library*. The standard library is a vast collection of types, functions and classes that is an essential part of the C++ language. The standard library also contains an extensive set of generic containers and algorithms called the *standard template library* (STL). In this book, we will make considerable use of the C++ standard library and the STL part of it. See also Sects. 5.8 and A.6–A.8.

The LED program uses the C++ standard library for std::uint8_t, one of several available fixed-size integer types. Readers familiar with the C99 specification of the C language [2] might have experience with <stdint.h>. This C library file defines identical fixed-size integer types, but in the global namespace. Using C++'s fixed-size integer types can improve portability because potentially non-portable user-defined types such as, say, my_uint8, my_uint16, etc. no longer need to be defined manually and managed with potentially hard-to-read preprocessor switches. See Sects. 3.2 and 6.10 for additional details on fixed-size integer types.

1.9 The main() Subroutine

The work of the LED program takes place in the main() subroutine. In particular,

```
int main()
{
  for(;;)
  {
    led_b5.toggle();
  }
}
```

Every C++ program is required to have one and only one implementation of main(). In C++, the return type of main() is plain integer, in other words **signed int**. When we just write **int** in C++, we mean **signed int**. This is because the default for integral types (if left blank) is **signed**, unless explicitly declared as **unsigned**.

The main() subroutine in the LED program lacks an explicit return code. The C++ compiler can, however, automatically generate the return code for main() if needed. If the compiler *does* generate return code for main(), its type is **signed**

int and its value is zero. The implicit generation of code to return a value is specific to the main() subroutine only. All subroutines other than main() returning any type other than **void** must supply explicit return code.

The main() subroutine is called from the startup code after the *static initialization* mechanisms for RAM and static constructors have been carried out. See Chap. 8 and Sect. 3.6.2 in [3] for additional information on startup code and static initialization.

Two portable definitions of main() are allowed according to the C++ standard (Sect. 3.6.1 in [3]):

```
int main()
{
  // ...
}
```

and

```
int main(int argc, char* argv[])
{
  // ...
}
```

The second form is used when program arguments are passed to main(). For our embedded microcontroller programs, no arguments are passed to main() and the first form is used.

1.10 Low-Level Register Access

Microcontroller programming in C++ requires low-level register access. For example, both the constructor as well as the toggle() function of the led class manipulate registers via direct memory access to control the LED hardware. See Chap. 7 for further discussions of register manipulation.

In particular, led's member function toggle() is responsible for toggling the LED.

```
void toggle() const
{
  // Toggle the LED.
  *reinterpret_cast<volatile bval_type*>(port)
    ^= bval;
}
```

The template cast operator **reinterpret_cast** is one of four specialized cast operators available in C++. See Sect. A.1 for a description of C++ cast operators. The **reinterpret_cast** operator is the one that is designed for casting integral types to pointers and back. Readers familiar with low-level register access in C might find the following equivalence example helpful.

```
// C++ register access.
*reinterpret_cast<volatile bval_type*>(port)
  ^= bval;

// Equivalent C-style.
*((volatile bval_type*) port) ^= bval;
```

The powerful **reinterpret_cast** operator should be used sparingly because it is rather uncommon in C++ to actually *need* manual conversion of pointer types without another more program-technically gentle option being available. Low-level microcontroller register manipulation via direct memory access is one of the rare cases when integral-to-pointer conversion is, in fact, mandatory.

As mentioned above, this topic is treated with greater detail in Sect. A.1. Furthermore, all of Chap. 7, deals with handling microcontroller registers including, in particular, Sects. 7.2 and 7.3 which introduce self-written dedicated abstractions specifically designed for generic microcontroller register read/write manipulation.

1.11 Compile-Time Constant

In the LED program, registers are defined with C++'s generalized constant expression syntax using the **constexpr** keyword. In particular,

```
namespace mcal
{
  // Compile-time constant register addresses.
  namespace reg
  {
    // The address of portb.
    constexpr std::uint8_t portb = 0x25U;

    // The values of bit0 through bit7.
    constexpr std::uint8_t bval0 = 1U;
    constexpr std::uint8_t bval1 = 1U << 1U;
    constexpr std::uint8_t bval2 = 1U << 2U;
    constexpr std::uint8_t bval3 = 1U << 3U;
```

```
    constexpr std::uint8_t bval4 = 1U << 4U;
    constexpr std::uint8_t bval5 = 1U << 5U;
    constexpr std::uint8_t bval6 = 1U << 6U;
    constexpr std::uint8_t bval7 = 1U << 7U;
  }
}
```

A generalized constant expression, denoted with the keyword **constexpr**, is guaranteed to be a compile-time constant. In general, using **constexpr** is considered superior to the preprocessor **#define** because generalized constant expressions have clearly defined type information. See Sect. 3.8 for more information on **constexpr** and generalized constant expressions, and also Sect. 7.1 for additional details on register addresses.

An alternative for ensuring that an integral value is a compile-time constant is with a static constant member of a class type. See also Item 1 in Meyers [4]. There will be more on static constant integral class members in Sect. 4.10.

Using compile-time constants almost always facilitates optimization in C++. As mentioned previously in Sect. 1.5, for example, `led_b5`'s constructor code is equivalent the following.

```
const led led_b5
{
  0x25, // Address of portb.
  0x20  // Bit-value of portb.5.
};
```

Since the constructor's parameters are compile-time constants, the compiler can directly initialize `led_b5`'s member variables without using the stack or intermediate CPU registers. This efficient kind of optimization is called *constant folding*, and is often useful in real-time C++ programming. Section 2.6 describes methods for improving performance even further by combining constant folding with C++ templates.

References

1. AUTOSAR, *Automotive Open System Architecture* (2017). http://www.autosar.org
2. ISO/IEC, *ISO/IEC 9899:1999 : Programming Languages – C* (International Organization for Standardization, Geneva, 1999)
3. ISO/IEC, *ISO/IEC 14882:2011 : Information Technology – Programming Languages – C++* (International Organization for Standardization, Geneva, 2011)
4. S. Meyers, *Effective C++: 55 Specific Ways to Improve Your Programs and Designs, Third Edition* (Addison-Wesley, Boston, 2005)

Chapter 2
Working with a Real-Time C++ Program on a Board

This chapter presents a complete example of building, flashing and executing a microcontroller C++ program using the LED program. The LED program will be built with GCC cross tools in the MinGW/MSYS [10] environment. Our target microcontroller is an 8–bit Microchip® AVR® microcontroller. This popular microcontroller has state-of-the-art quality and widespread availability. In addition, there is a well-maintained GCC port for this microcontroller making it well-suited for our example. In the second half of this chapter, we will investigate efficiency aspects and compiler warnings and errors based on the example of the LED program.

2.1 The Target Hardware

Our target hardware is shown in Fig. 2.1. It is a single-chip microcontroller circuit that has been hand-built on a solderless prototyping breadboard. This board uses an 8-bit Microchip® AVR® microcontroller [2], featuring 32 kB of program code, 2 kB of RAM and 1 kB of EEPROM. The microcontroller is clocked with an external quartz at 16 MHz. The schematic for the circuit of our target hardware and details about building it with discrete components on a board are given in Appendix D.

Our target hardware uses the same microcontroller and LED port pin as the well-known and versatile ARDUINO® open source project [1, 8, 13]. In addition, an ARDUINO® or an ARDUINO®–compatible board can optionally be used for the exercises in this chapter. Note, though, that our target hardware is not fully ARDUINO®–compatible because it lacks the circuitry for the serial UART interface that the ARDUINO® uses for communication with its bootloader.

C. Kormanyos, *Real-Time C++*, https://doi.org/10.1007/978-3-662-62996-3_2

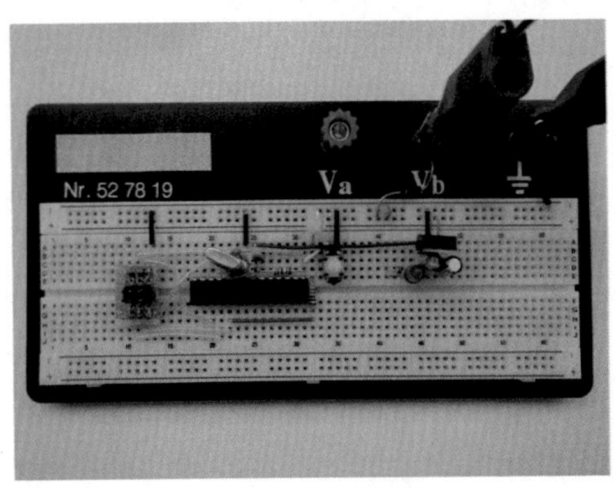

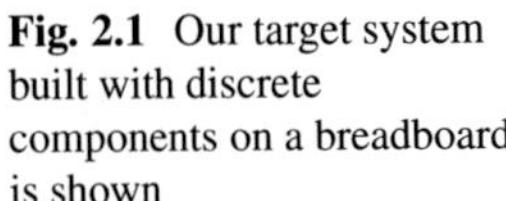
Fig. 2.1 Our target system built with discrete components on a breadboard is shown

2.2 Build and Flash the LED Program

The workflow for building and flashing a C++ program is shown in Fig. 2.2. The main steps include compiling the sources, linking the object files, extracting the HEX-file and flashing it in the microcontroller. We will build the LED program according to the workflow in Fig. 2.2. We will use traditional ∗nix-style commands within the MinGW/MSYS [11] environment.[1]

Here, we assume that the GNU GCC cross compiler [5] has been built and installed and that its path is known and can be used in a command shell.[2] See Appendix C for details on building and installing a GNU GCC cross compiler.

We will now build the example in the `chapter02_02` project of the companion code. In the MinGW/MSYS command shell, navigate to the directory `chapter-02_02` and locate the batch file `build.bat`. The batch file accepts two command-line parameters, the path of the GCC executable programs and the *prefix* of GCC.[3]

An example of the syntax for calling `build.bat` in the MinGW/MSYS command shell for the `chapter02_02` project is shown below.

```
build.bat "C:\gcc-9.2.0-avr\bin" avr
```

`build.bat` is intended to compile and link the LED program and subsequently extract the executable HEX-file according to the workflow in Fig. 2.2. Additional files containing C++ symbol information, an assembly listing, a report on code

[1]There are numerous tools and methods available for building microcontroller C++ projects. In addition to traditional command boxes and ∗nix-style shells, other popular build facilities include GNUmake [4], CMake [3] or even the Python programming language [12]. Furthermore, a variety of both cost-free as well as commercial GUIs are available for project management and build.

[2]Here, for instance, we are using GCC 9.2.0.

[3]Here, the prefix of GCC is the target-specific decoration in the name of the toolchain (such as `avr`, or the somewhat decorated prefix `avr-unknown-elf`, or other well-known GCC prefixes), as described in Appendix C. In this case, GCC has been built for `avr`.

Fig. 2.2 The workflow for building, flashing and running a C++ program is shown

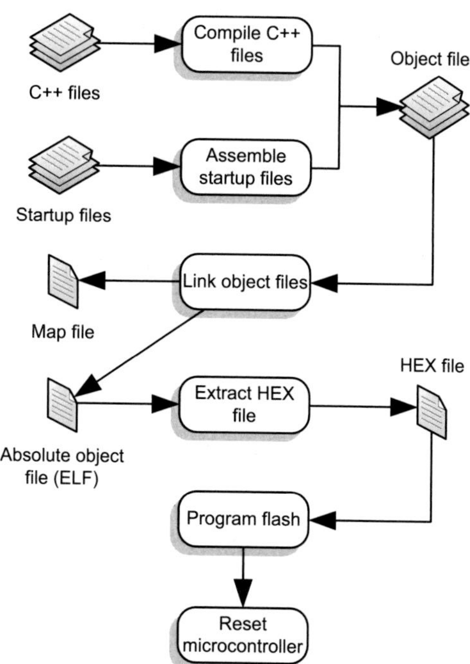

size, etc. are also created by `build.bat`. The results of the build are stored in the `bin`-directory. In the following paragraphs, we will investigate the most important commands in `build.bat`.

The startup code `crt0.s` (see Sect. 8.1) is assembled with the following command.

```
avr-g++ -mmcu=atmega328p \
  -x assembler crt0.s -c -o bin/crt0.o
```

This command means:

- Invoke the cross compiler `avr-g++` as an assembler. Here and subsequently, we use the decorated name of `g++` specially built for our target with the 8-bit microcontroller (Appendix C).
- Select the microcontroller architecture with the target-specific flag `-mmcu=atmega328p`.
- Assemble `crt0.s` with `avr-g++` using the assembler flags `-x assembler crt0.s -c -o bin/crt0.o`. This produces the object file `bin/crt0.o`.

The source file `led.cpp` is compiled with the following command.

```
avr-g++ -mmcu=atmega328p \
  -O2 -std=c++11 -I. -c led.cpp -o bin/led.o
```

This command means:

- Invoke the cross compiler `avr-g++` as a C++ compiler.
- Select the microcontroller architecture with the target-specific flag `-mmcu=atmega328p`.
- Use level 2 optimization (a medium-high level) with the `-O2` flag, see also Sect. 6.1.
- Use the C++11 language standard with the `-std=c++11` flag.[4]
- Include the current directory in the compiler's default include path. This is accomplished by using the `-I.` flag. This is needed for finding the header file `<cstdint>` present in the `chapter02_02` directory itself. The header file `<cstdint>` is self-written for this particular example. Normally, it would be present in the compiler's default include path for the standard library.
- Compile `led.cpp` using `-c led.cpp -o bin/led.o`. This produces the object file `bin/led.o`.

The following command links the LED program to create an absolute object file. Here, the compiled startup code in `bin/crt0.o` will be linked with `bin/led.o` to create the absolute object file `led.elf`.

```
avr-g++ -mmcu=atmega328p \
  -nostartfiles -nostdlib \
  -Wl,-Tavr.ld,-Map,bin/led.map \
  bin/led.o bin/crt0.o -o bin/led.elf
```

This command means:

- Invoke the cross compiler `avr-g++` as a linker.
- Select the microcontroller architecture with the `-mmcu=atmega328p` flag.
- Use the `-nostartfiles` flag to prevent the linker from linking with the compiler's own startup files. We have provided our own startup code in `crt0.s`.
- Use the `-nostdlib` flag to eliminate any standard library object code since we do not use any standard library functions.
- Use the memory definitions in the linker input file `avr.ld` and create an output memory map file `led.map` with the flags `-Wl,-Tavr.ld,-Map,-led.map`.
- Link the object files `bin/led.o` and `bin/crt0.o`. This command creates the absolute object file `bin/led.elf` using `bin/led.o bin/crt0.o -o bin/led.elf`. The absolute object file is in ELF binary format, the Executable and Linkable Format [14].

---

[4]With more modern GCC versions, the newer flags `-std=c++14`, `-std=c++17` can be used to select the C++14, or C++17, etc. language standard. With even more recent compilers, `-std=-c++20` can be used to activate C++20 compilation.

The following command extracts the HEX-file from the absolute object ELF-file using the program objcopy, which is part of GCC's binary utilities (binutils). This command creates the executable HEX-file bin/led.hex.

```
avr-objcopy -O ihex bin/led.elf bin/led.hex
```

This command means:

- Invoke object copy avr-objcopy.
- Create an output HEX-file in a well-known 16–bit text-based hexadecimal file format with the -O ihex flags.
- Extract bin/led.hex from bin/led.elf supplying the input filename and output filename as bin/led.elf bin/led.hex.

We should now have the HEX-file bin/led.hex that contains the executable code of the LED program. It is a short, text-based file that should be similar to the one shown in the listing below.

```
:040000000E94020058
:1000040011241FBEC0E0D8E0DEBFCDBF0E941100A6
:100014000E941D000E9426000E943700FFCF11E0BD
:10002400A0E0B1E0ECE9F0E002C005900D92A03050
:10003400B107D9F7089511E0A2E0B1E001C01D9223
:10004400A230B107E1F7089510E0C6E6D0E004C09D
:100054002297FE010E943300C436D107C9F70895E0
:100064004000059OF491E02D0994E0910001F0E046
:100074009091010180818927808 3FCCFE0E0F1E049
:1000840085E2808380E281832D98E081E150F0E075
:080094008081806280830895E1
:0400000300000064 95
:00000001FF
```

This executable HEX-file file can be flashed into the microcontroller's program FLASH memory using any of several available cost-free or commercial tools such as a JTAG [7] debugger, an ICE, etc. The instructions in the chapter02_02 directory show how to flash the HEX-file using a commercially available JTAG SPI™ ISP flash tool.

Users of the ARDUINO® should, however, note that the bootloader that comes pre-programmed in the ARDUINO® will be erased when we flash the LED program. If needed for development in the ARDUINO® environment, the ARDUINO® bootloader can be re-flashed [1].

When the LED program is executed, the LED D1 should light up because it will be toggling. The toggling will, however, be extremely rapid, with a frequency of approximately 1.1 MHz. This is far too fast for the human eye to resolve. Toggling can be viewed with a digital oscilloscope if available. Alternatively, the toggling frequency can be reduced using a delay loop or a timer, as shown in the following section.

2.3 Adding Timing for Visible LED Toggling

As mentioned above, the LED program toggles the LED too quickly to observe. Therefore, we will slow down the toggling in another version of the LED program that uses timing. This version of the program is included in the `chapter02_03` project of the companion code and it is partially listed below.

```
// The LED program with timing.

#include <cstdint>
#include <util/utility/util_time.h>
#include <mcal/mcal.h>

class led
{
  // ...
};

namespace
{
  // Define a convenient local 16-bit timer type.
  typedef util::timer<std::uint16_t> timer_type;

  // Create led_b5 at port B, bit-position 5.
  const led led_b5
  {
    mcal::reg::portb,
    mcal::reg::bval5
  };
}

int main()
{
  // Enable all global interrupts.
  mcal::irq::enable_all();

  // Initialize the mcal.
  mcal::init();

  // Toggle led_b5 forever with a 1s delay (0.5Hz).
```

```
  for(;;)
  {
    led_b5.toggle();

    // Wait 1s in a blocking delay.
    timer_type::blocking_delay(timer_type::seconds(1));
  }
}
```

The major change here is the inclusion of a 1 s blocking delay following the LED `toggle()`. This is can easily be identified in the `main()` subroutine, as emphasized below.

```
// Toggle led_b5 forever with a 1s delay (0.5Hz).
for(;;)
{
  led_b5.toggle();

  // Wait 1s in a blocking delay.
  timer_type::blocking_delay(timer_type::seconds(1U));
}
```

This reduces the LED toggling frequency to 1/2 Hz, allowing the toggling to be observed with the human eye. In order to implement timing, we have included more software components. In particular, we have included a timer utility header file `util_time.h` and simplified the code with a convenient **`typedef`** for a `timer_type`. See Sects. 6.9 and 15.3. We have also initialized a small MCAL in order to create a system tick, as described in Sect. 9.3.

Try to build, flash and run the LED program with timing in the way previously described for the original LED program. This should result in a program that has visually pleasing LED toggling with a frequency of 1/2 Hz.

As mentioned above, the LED toggling frequency in the `chapter02_03` project comes from a 1 s blocking delay. Using a blocking delay may, however, be considered poor style. Multitasking methods (Chap. 11) could result in a superior implementation. To exemplify this, an additional project called `chapter02_03a` has been created for Sect. 2.3 and included in the companion code. Example `chapter02_03a` also uses material from later in the book to implement a tiny multitasking scheduler which manages an LED application task. The LED application task uses a 1 s timer to generate the LED toggling frequency.

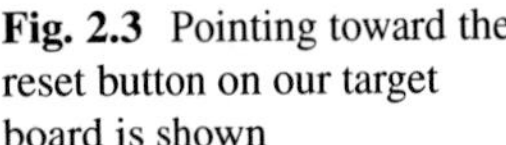

Fig. 2.3 Pointing toward the reset button on our target board is shown

2.4 Run and Reset the LED Program

After the program has been flashed, it stays in flash memory even when the board is powered off and disconnected from the PC or any other electrical supply. When the board is supplied with power, the microcontroller boots and program execution begins. It should not be necessary to push the reset button or do anything else other than simply plug in the power jack.

It may seem remarkable how quickly the microcontroller boots. It only requires a few milliseconds for the target system to boot and work through the startup code (Sect. 8.1). As a result, the LED will seem to start toggling essentially immediately after power-up.

The program can also be manually reset anytime while it is running using the *reset* button on the board. A photograph depicting the microcontroller reset button on our target system is shown in Fig. 2.3. The reset button gives the microcontroller an electrical soft-boot signal. This results in immediate program reset and subsequent execution of the startup code, etc. just like normal power-up.

It may be helpful to become familiar with both power-on reset using the power jack as well as soft reset using the manual reset button on the board. Try each one out a few times and make sure everything is working as expected.

2.5 Recognizing and Handling Errors and Warnings

Properly handling errors and warnings is an essential part of learning the C++ language. If a mistake in typing or syntax is present in the code, the compiler will report an *error* upon the attempted compilation of it.

We will now provoke an error in order to experience how this works. Consider typing some nonsensical characters such as "asdf" in one of the blank lines of led.cpp in the LED program from Sect. 1.1. For example,

```
// The LED program.

#include <cstdint>
#include "mcal_reg.h"
asdf
class led
{
  // ...
};

// ...
```

The led.cpp file now contains an error. If we save the faulty file and try to compile it, GCC will report an error message similar to the one shown below.

```
led.cpp:5:1: error: 'asdf' does not name a type
```

It is easy to interpret the error message within the context of the offending code. The compiler reports an error in line 5 at column 1 of led.cpp.

In addition to errors, the compiler can issue *warnings*. A warning indicates that the compiler has encountered ambiguous code. Warnings should be taken seriously and corrected because the compiler is reporting a potentially false interpretation of the code.

We will now provoke a warning. Consider removing the "**int**" part of the code preceding main() in led.cpp. For instance,

```
// ...

main()
{
  // ...
}
```

When compiling this code with the -pedantic warning option (see below), GCC issues the following warning.

```
led.cpp(50) :6: warning: ISO C++ forbids declaration
  of 'main' with no type [-pedantic]
```

Here, GCC is warning that the subroutine main() has been declared with no type. The warning is in line 50 at the beginning of column 6, whereby the beginning of column 6 is in the middle of the parentheses of the declaration of main().

For GCC, the warning options shown below result in a depth of warning that can be appropriate for most C++ projects.[5]

```
-Wall -Wextra -pedantic
```

This means:

- report warnings for *all* normal issues,
- also report *extra* warnings,
- and issue warnings in a *pedantic* fashion regarding ISO C++ adherence.

Another useful warning option is `-Weffc++`, which warns about failure to conform with certain guidelines in Meyers' well-known books [9, 10].

When the compiler encounters one or more warnings, it nonetheless completes compilation. The warning option `-Werror` can be used to treat all warnings as errors, thereby stopping compilation upon warning (well, now an error).

The error and warning messages shown previously are easy to understand. Error and warning messages can, however, become quite verbose including long symbol names and recursive file references. This can complicate tracing the origin of the offending code. In particular, it can be difficult to properly decipher error and warning messages originating from C++ templates. With a little practice, though, properly interpreting error and warning messages becomes routine.

Error and warning messages in C++ can be of immense help when trying to diagnose coding problems. Using a high warning level will also improve the overall quality of the code.

2.6 Reaching the Right Efficiency

C++ is a rich language with powerful features, giving vast control over the implementation details. In order to effectively program microcontrollers in C++, then, developers need to make insightful and sensible design choices.

When considering the `led` class in the LED program of Chap. 1, for example, an experienced microcontroller programmer might be thinking, *That class has a lot of overhead for simply toggling an LED! It may be a poor design choice.*

This astute observation would, in fact, be correct in this particular case. Indeed, the storage requirement alone for `led`'s member variables is at least two bytes, possibly even four bytes or eight—depending on the CPU architecture and the memory alignment characteristics of the compiler. Add to this the overhead of a potentially non-inlined call to the `toggle()` function, and the `led` class may be excessively bulky for its modest functionality.

---

[5] See also [6], in both Chap. 1, Sect. *Exploring C Warning Messages* as well as Appendix A in the same source for comprehensive information on GCC warning options.

C++ *templates* can be used to remedy this situation. A C++ template is a function or class that can have parameters of different types. See Chap. 5 for more information on C++ templates.

We will now convert the `led` class to a template class. In particular,

```
template<typename port_type,
         typename bval_type,
         const port_type port,
         const bval_type bval>
class led_template
{
public:
  led_template()
  {
    // Set the port pin value to low.
    *reinterpret_cast<volatile bval_type*>(port)
      &= static_cast<bval_type>(~bval);

    // Set the port pin direction to output.
    *reinterpret_cast<volatile bval_type*>(pdir)
      |= bval;
  }

  static void toggle()
  {
    // Toggle the LED.
    *reinterpret_cast<volatile bval_type*>(port)
      ^= bval;
  }

private:
  static constexpr port_type pdir = port - 1U;
};
```

In the `led_template` class, the types and member variables present in the original `led` class have been replaced with *template parameters*. This remarkable method profoundly improves efficiency because template parameters and their corresponding code are entities known at compile time. Templates can improve efficiency and reduce potentially redundant code by providing *scalability*. In this sense, templates offer high performance and strong *generic* character. We will discuss template programming in greater depth in Chap. 5.

Using the `led_template` class in code is straightforward. For example,

```
namespace
{
  // Create led_b5 at port B, bit-position 5.
  const led_template<std::uint8_t,
                     std::uint8_t,
                     mcal::reg::portb,
                     mcal::reg::bval5> led_b5;
}

int main()
{
  // Toggle led_b5 forever.
  for(;;)
  {
    led_b5.toggle();
  }
}
```

In this version of `main()`, the template instance of `led_b5` is used in exactly the same fashion as the non-template instance has been used previously in Sect. 1.1. We see that template classes can also be used to encapsulate objects. It can take a bit of trial-and-error to get accustomed with the syntax of templates and find stylistically appealing ways to write them in code. These issues are matters of style and they can be readily resolved with a bit of practice.

This version of the LED program is available in the companion code for Chap. 2. We can build this template version of the program for our target with the 8–bit microcontroller and create an *assembly listing* for the `led.cpp` file (Sect. 6.4). The assembly listing reveals that the efficiency of the `led_template` class approaches that of hand-programmed assembler. Remarkably, though, we are programming with a C++ class that utilizes the benefits of object-oriented design and data encapsulation.

We will now investigate how the efficiency and resource consumption of the template version of the LED program compare with those of the non-template version. The storage requirement of the `led_template` class have been reduced because the member variables `port` and `bval` have been replaced by template parameters that are compile-time constants. These template parameters can be eliminated at compile-time via constant folding. In addition, the `toggle()` function has been made **`static`**. This potentially reduces the call overhead when servicing the `toggle()` member.

As shown in Table 2.1, the template version of the program is both smaller *and* faster than the non-template one. It is somewhat remarkable, but not uncommon,

Table 2.1 The resources required for `led.cpp` for both the template as well as the non-template versions of the LED program are shown

Class version	Code size `main()` [byte]	RAM size `led_b5` [byte]	Runtime **`for`**`(;;)`-loop [μs]
Non-template	36	2	0.44
Template	16	0	0.31

that template-based design decreases memory consumption while simultaneously improving performance.

Selecting a template or a non-template LED class is an example of a typical design choice in microcontroller C++ programming. Although this is just one small example from infinitely many potential design choices, it does show how decisions about design and implementation can crucially impact efficiency.

References

1. ARDUINO®, ARDUINO® (2015). http://www.arduino.cc
2. ATMEL®, 8-bit ATMEL® Microcontroller with 4/8/16/32K Bytes in-system programmable flash (ATmega48A, ATmega48PA, ATmega88A, ATmega88PA, ATmega168A, ATmega168PA, ATmega328, ATmega328P), Rev. 8271D–AVR–05/11 (ATMEL®, 2011)
3. CMake (from Kitware), CMake (2020). http://cmake.org
4. Free Software Foundation, GNUmake version 3.81 (2006). http://www.gnu.org/software/make
5. Free Software Foundation, The GNU compiler collection version 7.2.0 http://gcc.gnu.org (2017)
6. W. von Hagen, *The Definitive Guide to GCC* (Apress, Berkeley, 2006)
7. IEEE Computer Society, IEEE Std 1149.1 – 1990: IEEE standard test access port and boundary-scan architecture (1990). http://standards.ieee.org/findstds/standard/1149.1-1990.html
8. M. Margolis, *ARDUINO® Cookbook, Second Edition* (O'Reilly, Sebastopol, 2011)
9. S. Meyers, *More Effective C++: 35 New Ways to Improve Your Programs and Designs* (Addison-Wesley, Boston, 1996)
10. S. Meyers, *Effective C++: 55 Specific Ways to Improve Your Programs and Designs, Third Edition* (Addison-Wesley, Boston, 2005)
11. MinGW, Home of the MinGW and MSYS projects (2012). http://www.mingw.org
12. Python Software Foundation, Python programming language—official website (2012). http://www.python.org
13. M. Schmidt, *ARDUINO®: A Quick-Start Guide* (Pragmatic Programmers, Raleigh, 2011)
14. Wikipedia, Executable and linkable format (2012). http://en.wikipedia.org/wiki/Executable_and_Linkable_Format

Chapter 3
An Easy Jump Start in Real-Time C++

Developers new to real-time C++ may want to obtain some useful results quickly before taking the time to master all the intricate details of the C++ language. This chapter addresses this desire by presenting a simple, yet effective, subset of the C++ language specifically designed for those seeking a lightweight and reliable jump start in real-time C++. The C++ subset in this chapter represents a judicious selection of some of the most easy-to-do things in C++ that can potentially be used in the widest possible range of programming situations. The strategy of this C++ subset is shown in Fig. 3.1. In addition, a complete working moderately detailed project that calculates prime numbers with a sieving method is presented in Sect. 3.2.

3.1 Declare Locals When Used

In C++, local variables can be declared where they are first used. They do not necessarily need to be bound to the opening curly brace of a scope. This can improve code readability and facilitate compiler optimization.

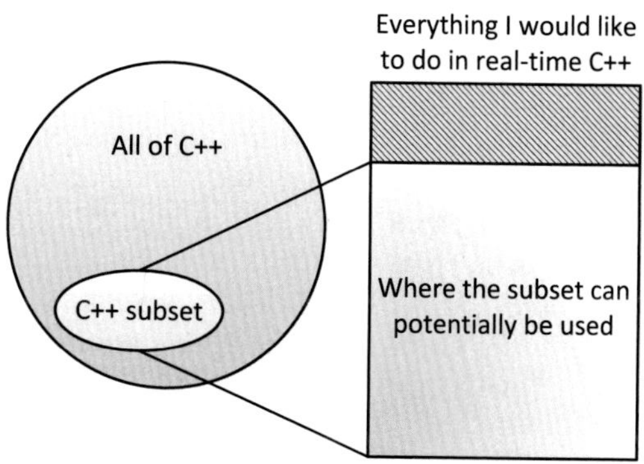

Fig. 3.1 The sketch suggests how a small subset of C++ can potentially be used for a wide variety of programming situations

C. Kormanyos, *Real-Time C++*, https://doi.org/10.1007/978-3-662-62996-3_3

The code below, for example, conveniently declares integral variables `i`, `j` and `k` near where they are first used in the subroutine.

```
// chapter03_01-001_declare_locals.cpp

void initialize();
void use_i(const int);
void use_j(const int);
void use_k(const int);

void do_something()
{
  // Initialize someting.
  initialize();

  // Declare i when using it in use_i().
  const int i = 3;
  use_i(i);

  // Declare j when using it in use_j().
  const int j = 7;
  use_j(j);

  // Declare k in the scope of the for-loop.
  for(int k = 0; k < 10; ++k)
  {
    use_k(k);
  }
}
```

3.2 Fixed-Size Integer Types and Prime Number Example

The C++ standard library has a complete set of portable fixed-size integer types in its `<cstdint>` header file. As mentioned in Sect. 1.8, user-defined types for built-in integral types such as `my_uint8`, `my_uint16`, and the like can potentially be clumsy, difficult to maintain and potentially error-prone, especially when used across multiple environments. Starting with C++11, however, non-standard user-defined types such as those can be replaced with standard fixed-size integer types such as `std::uint8_t`, `std::uint16_t`, `std::uint32_t`, etc.[1]

The code below, for instance, uses integer variables having specified widths such as *exactly* 16 bits and *at least* 32 bits.

```
// chapter03_02-001_fixed_size_integer.cpp

#include <cstdint>

// This has *exactly* 16-bits signed.
constexpr std::int16_t value16 = INT16_C(0x7FFF);

// This has *at least* 32-bits unsigned.
constexpr std::uint_least32_t value32 =
  UINT32_C(4'294'967'295);
```

Standard macros of the form `UINT8_C()`, `UINT16_C()`, `UINT32_C()`, etc. and corresponding macros for signed types are also defined in the `<cstdint>` header file.[2] As shown above, they can be convenient for creating numeric literal integral values having specified widths.

These macros also improve the integrity of code. In particular, they can be superior to commonly used suffixes such as `U`, `L`, `UL`, `LL`, `ULL`, etc.

Consider, for example, the initialization of 10, 006, 721, which is the 664, 999th prime number.

```
// chapter03_02-002_prime_number.cpp

#include <cstdint>

// The suffix U means unsigned int.
constexpr std::uint32_t prime_664999 = 10'006'721U;
```

This code could potentially be non-robust or suffer from portability problems. The integer literal constant `10'006'721U`, represents the 664, 999th prime number.[3] This literal representation, however, relies on the suffix `U`, meaning

[1]Fixed-size integer types have been available in the C header file `<stdint.h>` since C99 (in the global namespace) and in the C++ header file `<cstdint>` since C++11 (in both the global namespace as well as in namespace `std`).

[2]These macros have been available in the C header file `<stdint.h>` since C99 and in the C++ header file `<cstdint>` since C++11.

[3]A listing of all prime numbers up to and including 10, 006, 721 can be found in [8], which has been reconstructed in a more modern digital work [9].

unsigned int. When porting this code, especially to small 8-bit platforms, **unsigned int** might not be 32 bits wide. It might be only 16 bits wide or even merely 8 bits wide. In such cases, **unsigned int** is not large enough to contain the integer value 10, 006, 721 and the initialization could be potentially confusing (or even incorrect).

We will now slightly modify the initialization of `prime_664999` in order to improve coding integrity. In particular,

```
// chapter03_02-002_prime_number.cpp

#include <cstdint>

// Initialize the 664,999th prime number.
// Macros like UINT32_C() are portable.

constexpr std::uint32_t prime_664999 =
  UINT32_C(10'006'721);
```

In this case, the initialization is unequivocal, clearly formulated and portable. The macro `UINT32_C()` is guaranteed to handle all values within the full range of the unsigned 32-bit integer data type from 0 ... 4, 294, 967, 295.

In practice, consistent use of fixed-size integer types does not strongly contribute to functionality, but rather tends to blend into the prominent style of code. This usually results in improved portability by increasing the likelihood that the code will behave similarly and obtain identical results on different platforms.

Using fixed-size integer types within the context of a moderately large and diverse program is exhibited in the code of example `chapter03_02`. In this example, a sieve of Eratosthenes [14] is used to compute sequential prime numbers on our target with the 8-bit microcontroller.

Example `chapter03_02` uses several features of C++ that are described later in this book. These include, among others, template programming (Chap. 5), using the STL in a microcontroller environment (Sect. 5.8), hardware drivers (Chap. 9), custom memory management such as with a ring allocator (Sect. 10.5), multitasking (Chap. 11), floating-point calculations (Chap. 12), etc. This example is presented at this early point in this book in order to provide a complete working and moderately detailed project.

The theoretical background of example `chapter03_02` begins with mathematical special functions, in particular the logarithmic integral function [11], i.e.,

$$\begin{aligned} \mathrm{Li}\,(x) &= \mathrm{li}\,(x) - \mathrm{li}\,(2) \\ &= \int_2^x \frac{dt}{\log t}\,. \end{aligned} \tag{3.1}$$

Here li (x) is known as the logarithmic integral function and Li (x) is the *offset* logarithmic integral function.

An estimate of the number of primes below a given upper limit can be obtained from the prime counting function $\pi(x)$ in the prime number theorem [3, 4, 13, 15]. This remarkable and well-known theorem relates the offset logarithmic integral function Li (x) to the prime counting function in the asymptotic limit via

$$\pi(x) \sim \mathrm{Li}(x)\,. \tag{3.2}$$

Consider again for instance, as mentioned above, the 664, 999th prime which is 10, 006, 721. For this prime number, Eqs. 3.1 and 3.2 result in

$$\begin{aligned} \frac{\mathrm{Li}\,(10,006,721)}{664,999} &\approx \frac{665,335.4\ldots - 1.045\ldots}{664,999} \\ &\approx 1.000504\ldots \\ &\overset{?}{\sim} 1\,, \end{aligned} \tag{3.3}$$

where li $(2) \approx 1.045\ldots$. At this particular numerical point of $x = 10,006,721$, the ratio in Eq. 3.2 is 1.000504..., which slightly larger than 1. This ratio gets even closer to 1 for increasing x and is conjectured to reach unity for infinite x.

In example `chapter03_02`, the intent is to calculate at least 100 prime numbers. In order to identify and verify the proper limits of the sieve calculation, we consider an elementary divergent asymptotic series expansion of the logarithmic integral function for large x

$$\mathrm{li}\,(x) \sim \frac{x}{\log x} \sum_{k=0}^{\infty} \frac{k!}{(\log x)^k}\,. \tag{3.4}$$

This produces the asymptotic numerical approximation

$$\pi(x) \sim \left(\frac{x}{\log x} \sum_{k=0}^{\infty} \frac{k!}{(\log x)^k} \right) - \mathrm{li}\,(2)\,, \tag{3.5}$$

where x is sufficiently large. When implementing this calculation in software, the loop in the expansion should be terminated just after the terms in the summation reach their minimum and subsequently after this point begin increasing because the series is divergent.

Knowing beforehand that the 100th prime is 541, we plug the number 542 into Eq. 3.5. This results in

$$\pi\,(542) \sim \left(\frac{542}{\log 542} \sum_{k=0}^{7} \frac{k!}{(\log 542)^k} \right) - 1.045\ldots$$
$$\approx 108\,, \tag{3.6}$$

where the loop of the divergent series expansion runs from 0 … 7. This confirms that the first hundred primes can be comfortably calculated by setting the upper limit of the sieving loop to the value of the integral floor of the square root of 542,

$$\left\lfloor \sqrt{542} \right\rfloor = 23\,. \tag{3.7}$$

A specialized container composed of bit-packed unsigned integral values is used to hold the sieve. This container is implemented as a template class called `dynamic_bitset`. Memory storage in the container uses the specialized `ring_allocator` of Sect. 10.5.

The code sequence below shows a partial listing of the template subroutine `compute_primes_via_sieve`. It is taken directly from example `chapter03_02`.

```
template<const std::size_t maximum_value,
         typename forward_iterator_type,
         typename alloc>
void compute_primes_via_sieve
  (forward_iterator_type first)
{
  // Use a sieve algorithm to generate
  // a table of primes.

  // ...
  // ...

  // Create the sieve of primes.

  // ...
  // ...

  for(local_value_type i = 2U;
      i < local_value_type(imax);
      ++i)
```

```
  {
    if(sieve.test(i) == false)
    {
      const local_value_type i2 = i * i;

      for(local_value_type j = i2;
          j < maximum_value;
          j += i)
      {
        sieve.set(j);
      }
    }
  }

  // ...
  // ...

  // Fill the prime numbers into the data table
  // by extracting them from the sieve of primes.

  // ...
  // ...
}
```

This listing shows the inner loops of the sieve calculation. When calculating prime numbers in a sieve to upper limit n, the so-called *order* of the computational complexity of the nested loops is roughly given by $O\,(n \log \log n)$ [14]. For further discussion on the order of an algorithm's computational complexity, see also Sect. 6.3.

The sieve calculation is initialized and runs completely from start to finish. This is done cyclically in the `app::prime` task with a frequency of approximately 20 Hz (i.e., about once every 50 ms). Numerical verification is performed by ensuring that the value of the calculated 100th prime is agrees with the expected value of 541. Timing measurements use a digital oscilloscope with the method of Sect. 9.6. In this particular example, `portd.3` is toggled at the start and end of the sieve calculation. The measured runtime of each individual execution of the sieve calculation is approximately 4.3 ms on out target with the 8-bit microcontroller.

The study of prime numbers can lead to fascinating topics in numerous and diverse areas of pure and applied mathematics, number theory, high-performance computing and more. For further information on the prime counting function, see [12] and the references therein. Comprehensive coverage of computing prime numbers can be found in works including [1] and Vol. 2 of [7].

Later in this book, example `chapter16_08` in Sect. 16.8 uses randomly selected 128-bit integers to explore the prime number theorem.

3.3 The `bool` Type

C++ includes a built-in Boolean type **`bool`** that has two and only two possible values, **`true`** and **`false`**. In C++, the result of a Boolean test has the type **`bool`** and its value is either **`true`** or **`false`**. Using C++'s built-in Boolean type can improve the clarity of logic and simplify coding.

The code below, for instance, uses C++'s built-in Boolean type **`bool`** in logical statements.

```
// chapter03_03-001_bool_type.cpp

bool valid();
bool login();

void start_session();

void do_something()
{
  // This Boolean test yields true or false.
  const bool session_is_ok = (valid() && login());

  // This tests if (session_is_ok == true).
  if(session_is_ok)
  {
    start_session();
  }
}
```

3.4 Organization with Namespaces

C++ supports namespaces. Namespaces can be used to improve program organization and code readability. Namespaces can optionally be employed to correspond to different parts or functional groups of the software. Namespaces were first introduced in Sect. 1.7.

The code below, for example, uses C++ namespaces to organize several parts of the microcontroller abstraction layer (MCAL) in the software architecture.[4]

[4]See Sect. 1.6 for the first mention of the MCAL in this book and also Sect. B.2 for additional details on software architecture.

```
// chapter03_04-001_namespaces.cpp

// Namespace for the microcontroller abstraction layer.
namespace mcal
{
  // The mcal initialization.
  void init();

  // The general purpose timer stuff in the mcal.
  namespace gpt
  {
    void init();
    std::uint32_t get_time_elapsed();
  }

  // The ADC stuff in the mcal.
  namespace adc
  {
    void init();
    std::uint16_t read_value(const unsigned);
  }
}

// Initialize the mcal.
// Note the clean organization with namespaces.
void mcal::init()
{
  mcal::gpt::init();
  mcal::adc::init();
}
```

An unnamed namespace (i.e., an anonymous namespace) can be used for file-level localization. For example,

```
// chapter03_04-002_anonymous_namespace.cpp

// A file-local anonymous namespace.
namespace
{
  unsigned local_counter;
}
```

As mentioned previously in Sect. 1.7, using unnamed (anonymous) namespaces can provide an effective mechanism for defining file-level scope localization of variables, functions, class types, objects, etc.

C++17 introduced support for nested namespace definitions. These can be used to reduce typing effort when defining multiple layers of nested namespaces.

Consider, for instance, the traditional definition of a nested namespace in a made-up example. It is called `namespace X::Y::Z`.

```
// A traditional namespace definition.
namespace X
{
  namespace Y
  {
    namespace Z
    {
      int value;
    }
  }
}
```

As of C++17, the definition of a nested namespace such as `X::Y::Z` can be written equivalently as

```
// chapter03_04-003_nested_namespace.cpp

// A C++17 nested namespace definition.
namespace X::Y::Z
{
  int value;
}
```

In this example, the namespace `X::Y::Z` contains one integer `value` that can be accessed in the usual fashion. In particular,

```
void do_something()
{
  X::Y::Z::value = 1;
}
```

3.5 Basic Classes

It is not difficult to start working with class types in C++. As a first step, simple C-style structures can be replaced with C++ classes or structures having just a constructor, a few data members and possibly some simple functions. To keep things easy at first, it may be preferable to avoid using inheritance and runtime polymorphism. One can, and really should, use these powerful object-oriented features when confident enough to do so in order to make full use of C++. Additional information on classes and object-oriented programming can be found in Chap. 4.

The class below, for instance, encapsulates an unsigned integer coordinate `point` located in the first quadrant of two-dimensional Cartesian space $\mathbb{R}^2$.

```
// chapter03_05-001_basic_classes.cpp

#include <cstdint>

// An unsigned xy-coordinate point with some geometry.
class point
{
public:
  std::uint8_t my_x;
  std::uint8_t my_y;

  point(const std::uint8_t x = UINT8_C(0),
        const std::uint8_t y = UINT8_C(0)) : my_x(x),
                                              my_y(y)
  { }

  std::uint16_t squared_euclidean_distance() const
  {
    // Squared Euclidean distance from the origin.
    const std::uint16_t x2(std::uint16_t(my_x) * my_x);
    const std::uint16_t y2(std::uint16_t(my_y) * my_y);

    return x2 + y2;
  }
};
```

```
point p1;

point p2
{
  UINT8_C(31),
  UINT8_C(47)
};

// The squared Euclidean distance d1 is 0.
std::uint16_t d1 = p1.squared_euclidean_distance();

// The squared Euclidean distance d2 is 3,170.
std::uint16_t d2 = p2.squared_euclidean_distance();
```

3.6 Basic Templates

C++ templates use the same code for different types. Templates can reduce the effort of code upkeep and eliminate redundant sources of error. C++ templates also allow for *scalability*. When beginning with templates, it may be preferable to keep template depth and subroutine complexity low. C++ templates are described in detail in Chap. 5.

The code below, for instance, implements a template subroutine for computing the sum of two objects.

```
template<typename T>
T add(const T& a, const T& b)
{
  return a + b;
}
```

This template can be used to add different kinds of objects, as long as these support the addition operator. In particular,

```
// chapter03_06-001_basic_templates_add.cpp

template<typename T>
T add(const T& a, const T& b)
{
  return a + b;
}

const int   n = add(1, 2);
// n is 3.
```

```
const float f = add(1.2F, 3.4F);
// f is 4.6.

const std::string str = add(std::string("abc"),
                            std::string("xyz"));

// str is "abcxyz".
```

An example of a *class* template is shown below. It implements a **signed** or **unsigned** xy-coordinate point, potentially residing in any of the four quadrants of two-dimensional Cartesian space $\mathbb{R}^2$. This class is similar to the one shown in the previous section. But it is implemented as a template class intended to accept either signed or unsigned integral xy-components.

```
// chapter03_06-002_basic_templates_xy_point.cpp

#include <cstdint>
#include <type_traits>

// Template version of the xy-coordinate class.

template<typename short_type,
         typename long_type>
class point
{
public:
  static_assert(
       std::is_integral<short_type>::value
    && std::is_integral<long_type>::value,
       "the short and long types must be integral");

  short_type my_x;
  short_type my_y;

  point(const short_type& x = short_type(),
        const short_type& y = short_type()) : my_x(x),
                                              my_y(y)
  { }

  long_type squared_euclidean_distance() const
  {
    // Squared Euclidean distance from the origin.
    const long_type x2(long_type(my_x) * my_x);
    const long_type y2(long_type(my_y) * my_y);
```

```
    return x2 + y2;
  }
};

point<std::int16_t, std::int32_t> p
{
  INT16_C(-2129),
  INT16_C(+5471)
};

const std::int32_t d = p.squared_euclidean_distance();
// d is 34,464,482
```

This code snip introduces additional useful C++ language features that are described later. Note, for instance, the use of compile-time assert (via `static_assert`, Sects. 3.9 and A.4) in combination with the `<type_traits>` library (Sect. A.15). This ensures that the template parameters are integral types.

3.7 `nullptr` Replaces `NULL`

C++ offers the **`nullptr`** keyword (since C++11). The **`nullptr`** keyword eliminates the need for redundant and potentially conflicting definitions of `NULL` or testing with possibly awkward hand-written zero-pointers.

The code below, for example, uses the **`nullptr`** keyword to test if a pointer to some object, a `something*`, is non-zero.

```
// chapter03_07-001_nullptr.cpp

class something
{
public:
  something() { }
};

namespace
{
  // Default initialized to nullptr (i.e., 0).
  something* ps;
}
```

```
void do_something()
{
  // Any kind of zero pointer equals nullptr.
  if(ps == nullptr)
  {
    // Initialize ps.
    // ...
  }

  // Do something with ps.
  // ...
}
```

3.8 Generalized Constant Expressions with `constexpr`

Compile-time constants can be defined with **constexpr** or by using integral class members of type **static constexpr** or (the older) **static const**.[5] As briefly mentioned in Sect. 1.11, constants defined this way are known at compile time and have clearly defined type information.

The code below depicts various ways to use the **constexpr** keyword to make compile-time constants.

```
// chapter03_08-001_constexpr.cpp

// A compile-time constant version number.
constexpr unsigned int version = 3U;

// A compile-time floating-point value.
constexpr float pi = 3.1415926535'8979323846F;
```

The **constexpr** keyword can make compile-time constants from a wider variety of things than the original **const** keyword.[6] In particular, **constexpr** can also be used to define subroutines adhering to low-complexity constraints, certain constant-valued aggregates such as `std::arrays` (Sect. 3.11), and member variables of class types.

[5]The **constexpr** keyword has been available since C++11.

[6]Both the **const** keyword as well as the **constexpr** keyword are available for declaring constant symbols for various use cases in C++11 and beyond.

```
// chapter03_08-002_constexpr_more.cpp

#include <array>

// A compile-time constant function of low complexity.
constexpr int three() { return 3; }

// A constant array of integers.
constexpr std::array<int, 3U> my_array
{
  { 1, 2, 3 }
};

struct version_information
{
  // A compile-time constant member variable.
  static constexpr unsigned version = 3U;
};
```

Generalized constant expressions with **constexpr** can also be used to carry out significant computational work in the compile stage, in this way potentially reducing the costly runtime of an embedded project. This can be done for compile-time constants, tables and algorithms.

The ubiquitous integer power function x^n, for instance, might be used to calculate a result such as $10^3 = 1,000$. We will consider x^n for $(x, n) \in \mathbb{Z}^+$, where x and n are positive integers or zero. A compile-time implementation of x^n is shown below with the pown constant expression.

```
// chapter03_08-003_constexpr_pown.cpp

constexpr std::uintmax_t pown(std::uintmax_t x,
                              std::uintmax_t n)
{
  return ((n == UINTMAX_C(0))
           ? UINTMAX_C(1) : pown(x, n - 1U) * x);
}

// 1000 is computed at compile time.
constexpr std::uintmax_t t3 = pown(10U, 3U);

// OK because t3 is compile-time constant.
static_assert(t3 == 1000U,
              "Error: Unexpected constexpr");
```

These kinds of compile-time calculations can be similar to the methods of template metaprogramming, in particular when combined with template arguments, as briefly shown in Sect. 5.10. Also floating-point functions with sufficiently low computational complexity can be evaluated at compile time with **constexpr**, as described in Sect. 12.6.

3.9 static_assert

The C++ compiler can perform checks on Boolean expressions that are known at compile time using the **static_assert** facility. There are additional details on **static_assert** in Sect. A.4.

The code below, for instance, uses **static_assert** to ensure that the program version is high enough. The test with **static_assert** is performed at compile time.

```
// chapter03_09-001_static_assert.cpp

constexpr unsigned int version = 3U;

// Print an error if version is less than 2.
static_assert(version >= 2U, "Version is too low!");
```

3.10 Using <limits>

The C++ standard library includes portable and convenient numeric limits in its `<limits>` header. These can be used for obtaining and querying the limits of built-in types or also be extended (specialized) for user-defined types. The classes in `<limits>` are templates and, as mentioned above, it is common to implement template specializations of `std::numeric_limits` for custom user-defined types. The `<limits>` library is described in greater detail in Sect. A.5

The code below uses some members of `std::numeric_limits` to obtain and check information on limits for built-in integral and floating-point types.

```
// chapter03_10-001_limits.cpp

#include <limits>

// This is 31 on a system with 4 byte int.
```

```
// The sign bit is not included in digits.
constexpr int n_dig = std::numeric_limits<int>::digits;

// This is 2,147,483,647 if int is 4 bytes.
constexpr int n_max = std::numeric_limits<int>::max();

// Compile-time check if float conforms to IEEE-754.
static_assert(std::numeric_limits<float>::is_iec559,
              "float is not IEEE754 conforming!");

constexpr bool is_ieee754_conform =
  std::numeric_limits<float>::is_iec559;
```

3.11 `std::array`

Perhaps the simplest STL container is `std::array`. In C++, `std::array` can be used as a drop-in replacement for C-style arrays. Since `std::array` is a sequential STL container, it offers the additional benefits of iterators, container size, compatibility with STL algorithms, etc.

Using the `std::array` container is key for microcontroller programming because `std::array` has a fixed size known at compile-time. The compiler can, therefore, allocate a known amount of storage for an `std::array` where needed—on the stack, in static memory, even on-the-fly for an `std::array` declared as a **`constexpr`**, etc. Using `std::array` provides the comfort of a sequential container while simultaneously reducing concerns about potential memory fragmentation from dynamic memory allocation and the complexity of allocators (see also Sect. 10.3).

The code below creates a login key consisting of three 8-bit unsigned integers.

```
// chapter03_11-001_array.cpp

#include <array>
#include <cstdint>

// A login key stored in an std::array.
constexpr std::array<std::uint8_t, 3U> login_key
{
  {
    UINT8_C(0x01),
    UINT8_C(0x02),
```

```
    UINT8_C(0x03)
  }
};
```

3.12 Basic STL Algorithms

Using STL algorithms in C++ can significantly reduce coding effort and eliminate potential sources of error from hand-written code sequences. It is easy to get started with a few intuitive and easy-to-use STL algorithms such as simple min/-max operations `std::min()` and `std::max()`, mutating (i.e. change-causing) sequence operations like `std::fill()` and `std::copy()`, or non-modifying sequence operations including `std::all_of()`, `std::for_each()`, etc. See also Sects. 5.8, 6.17, and A.6–A.8 in the C++ tutorial for more information on STL algorithms.

The code below, for example, initializes (and re-initializes) four unsigned integer counters in an array using the `std::fill()` algorithm.

```
// chapter03_12-001_basic_stl.cpp

#include <algorithm>
#include <array>
#include <cstdint>

namespace
{
  // Four counters.
  std::array<std::uint8_t, 4U> counters;
}

void do_something()
{
  // (Re-)Initialize the counters with std::fill().
  std::fill(counters.begin(),
            counters.end(),
            static_cast<std::uint8_t>(0U));

  // Do something with the counters.
  // ...
}
```

3.13 <numeric>

The STL's `<numeric>` library has some particularly useful algorithms for micro-controller programming including, among others, `std::accumulate()` and `std::inner_product()` which can be used for computations such as check-sums, vector-matrix mathematics, etc. The functions in `<numeric>` can reduce code complexity and bring the heart of the algorithm at hand into clear focus. See Sect. A.8 for further information on `<numeric>`.

The example below computes the inner product of two arrays.

```
// chapter03_13-001_basic_stl_numeric.cpp

#include <array>
#include <numeric>

const std::array<int, 3U> u
{
  { 1, 2, 3 }
};

const std::array<int, 3U> v
{
  { 4, 5, 6 }
};

const int uv = std::inner_product(u.begin(),
                                  u.end(),
                                  v.begin(),
                                  0);

// The result is 32.
```

The result is $(4 + 10 + 18) = 32$. Readers familiar with physics or vector mathematics might recognize this as the dot-product

$$\vec{u} \cdot \vec{v} = uv \tag{3.8}$$

in three-dimensional Cartesian space $\mathbb{R}^3$, the result of which is a scalar.

3.14 `atomic_load()` and `atomic_store()`

The C++ standard library includes a collection of safe and portable atomic operations in its `<atomic>` library. The `<atomic>` library is large with many functions. It is, however, possible to get an easy start in the `<atomic>` library with two simple functions, `std::atomic_load()` and `std::atomic_store()`.

The code below, for example, uses `std::atomic_load()` to perform a consistent read of the 32-bit system tick on an 8-bit CPU. Here, it is assumed that `system_tick` is modified in a timer interrupt service routine, thereby making a consistent read via means such as `std::atomic_load()` mandatory.

```
// chapter03_14-001_atomic_operations.cpp

#include <atomic>
#include <cstdint>

namespace
{
  // The one (and only one) 32-bit system tick.
  volatile std::atomic<std::uint32_t> system_tick;
}

std::uint32_t get_time_elapsed()
{
  // Ensure 32-bit consistency on an 8-bit CPU.
  return std::atomic_load(&system_tick);
}
```

3.15 Digit Separators

The single quote character is used for separating groups of digits in numeric literals. Digit separators were introduced with C++14.

Consider initializing an integer number with many digits such as 1 trillion, in other words 10^{12}. In particular,

```
// chapter03_15-001_digit_separators.cpp

constexpr std::uint64_t one_trillion =
  UINT64_C(1'000'000'000'000);
```

Digit separators make the initialization of `one_trillion` easy-to-read because groups of three zeros can be readily identified.

Digit separators can also be used with floating-point numeric literals. The code below, for example, initializes a floating-point representation of Archimedes' constant π.[7]

```
// chapter03_15-002_digit_separators.cpp

constexpr long double pi =
  3.1415926535'8979323846'2643383279'5028841972L;
```

Here, we use the built-in floating-point type **`long double`**. The floating-point initialization is carried out with 40 decimal digits of precision after the decimal point. Digit separators are used between groups of ten digits. This makes the initialization more legible and appear in a well-organized fashion.

The granularity of digit separators is not restricted to clusters of three digits or ten digits or any other grouping. Digit separators can be used with arbitrary numbers of digits between the separations. As such, digit separators can improve the readability of numeric literals according to the standardizations of different locales.

3.16 Binary Literals

Binary literals are numeric literals written in binary form using any of the prefixes `0b`, `0B`, `b` or `B`. Binary literals were introduced with C++14.

The following code, for example, initializes easy-to-recognize constant unsigned integer values using binary literals.

```
// chapter03_16-001_binary_literals.cpp

constexpr std::uint8_t one   = UINT8_C(0b1);

constexpr std::uint8_t seven = UINT8_C(0b0000'0111);
```

In microcontroller programming, binary literals are particularly useful because hardware registers often have detailed bit-level descriptions. Manipulating hardware registers via binary literals can make it easier to understand which register bits will be set and cleared. The following example uses a binary literal numeric constant to switch the value of `portb.5` from low to high.

[7] See also Sect. 12.2 and [2] for more information on mathematical constants.

```
// chapter03_16-002_binary_literals.cpp

void do_something()
{
  // The address of the portb register.
  constexpr std::uint8_t portb = UINT8_C(0x25);

  // Switch portb.5 from low to high.
  *reinterpret_cast<volatile std::uint8_t*>(portb)
    |= UINT8_C(0b0010'0000);
}
```

3.17 User-Defined Literals

User-defined literals provide a syntax for applying custom suffixes to literal values. The following code, for instance, uses the specialized user-defined suffixes `_inch`, `_foot` and `_yard` for conversions from traditional length units to units of meters in the MKS system.[8]

```
// chapter03_17-001_user_defined_literals.cpp

inline constexpr float
operator"" _inch(long double inches)
{
  return static_cast<float>(inches * 0.0254L);
}

inline constexpr float
operator"" _foot(long double feet)
{
  return static_cast<float>(feet * 0.294L);
}

inline constexpr float
operator"" _yard(long double yards)
```

[8]The conversions are approximate, based on 3–4 decimal digits of precision resulting from common conversion factors. As such, the conversions here are not carried out with full scientific precision of **`long double`**.

```
{
  return static_cast<float>(yards * 0.9144L);
}
```

With these suffixes, lengths expressed as literal values in inches, feet and yards are converted to meters at compile time. For example,

```
constexpr float
one_foot          =  12.0_inch; // 0.3048m

constexpr float
basketball_player =   7.0_foot; // 2.058m

constexpr float
football_field    = 100.0_yard; // 91.44m
```

Here, we convert `one_foot` to 0.3048 m, `basketball_player` to 2.058 m and `football_field` to 91.44 m.

Several user-defined literals were standardized with C++14. In particular, the standard library supports a string suffix `s` for character string literals, such as those used with `std::string`.[9] For example,

```
// chapter03_17-002_user_defined_literals.cpp

#include <string>

using namespace std::string_literals;

std::string str = "creativity"s;
```

There are also several standardized chronological suffixes `h`, `min`, `s`, `ms`, `us` and `ns`. These are used for expressing time spans in common units. The standardized chronological suffixes are available in `<chrono>`.[10] The code sequence below, for instance, portrays a 10 ms time span.

[9]Standardized suffixes are defined in various namespaces. In particular, the string suffix `s` can be found in any of `std::literals`, `std::string_literals` and `std::literals::string_literals`.

[10]Along the same lines, the standardized chronological suffixes are available in the namespaces `std::literals`, `std::chrono_literals` and `std::literals::chrono_literals`.

```
// chapter03_17-003_user_defined_literals.cpp

#include <chrono>

using namespace std::chrono_literals;

// time_span is 10.
std::chrono::milliseconds time_span = 10ms;
```

When considering the suffix `s`, it could stand for character string or time in seconds. The compiler can, however, properly identify the theme of the use-case. This renders the suffix `s` non-ambiguous and contextually meaningful for use with both literal strings as well as literal chronological values.

In addition, standardized suffixes are available in `<complex>` for signifying the imaginary part of a complex number.[11]

Consider a potential floating-point expression of the complex number

$$z = 1.2 + 3.4i \ . \tag{3.9}$$

This complex number could be represented in C++ as shown below.

```
// chapter03_17-004_user_defined_literals.cpp

#include <complex>

using namespace std::complex_literals;

std::complex<float> z = 1.2f + 3.4if;
```

In this example, z approximates a complex number from the standard library's `std::complex` template class made from real and imaginary parts composed of the built-in floating-point type **`float`**. The suffix `if` appended to the floating-point literal value 3.4 is used to initialize the imaginary part of z.

The complex suffixes `if`, `i` and `il` are defined in the `<complex>` library. The complex suffixes are intended to be used with literal values of the built-in floating-point types **`float`**, **`double`**, and **`long double`** respectively. See also Sect. 12.5 for additional information on the `<complex>` library and complex-valued math in C++.

In the following practical example, we will compute and print the approximate value of

$$\sin(1.2 + 3.4i) \approx 13.979408806018 + 5.4228154724634\,, \tag{3.10}$$

[11]Similarly, the standardized complex suffixes are present in the namespaces `std::literals`, `std::complex_literals` and `std::literals:: complex_literals`.

where the result is expressed as std::complex<**double**>.

```
// chapter03_17-005_user_defined_literals.cpp

#include <complex>

using namespace std::complex_literals;

const std::complex<double> z = 1.2f + 3.4i;

// (13.979408806018, 5.4228154724634)
const std::complex<double> s = std::sin(z);
```

The standardized complex suffixes can also be used with integral literal values. The sequence below defines the **double** representation of $z = 1 + i$, where the complex part of z is actually written as a *binary* literal constant. See also Sect. 3.16 for more information on binary literals.

```
// chapter03_17-006_user_defined_literals.cpp

#include <complex>

using namespace std::complex_literals;

// (1,1)
std::complex<double> z = 1.0 + 0b0000'0001i;
```

3.18 Using alignof and alignas

In embedded microcontroller programming, it can often be useful to investigate the memory alignment of an entity. This can be accomplished with the **alignof** operator. For instance,

```
// chapter03_18-001_alignment.cpp

auto as  = alignof(short);      // Could be 2, 4,...
auto ai  = alignof(int);        // Could be 2, 4,...
auto al  = alignof(long);       // Could be 4, 8,...
auto all = alignof(long long);  // Could be 8,...
```

The result of **alignof** is specified as an unsigned integral value having type std::size_t. Values returned from **alignof** are typically unique for a given microcontroller-compiler system and may vary from one system to another depending on the underlying microcontroller and compiler characteristics.

The related specifier alignas can be used to ensure that an entity is actually stored with a particular memory alignment. The alignas specifier can be especially useful in embedded microcontroller programming, for instance, when creating memory-mapped structures and objects that are intended to be exactly aligned with the corresponding addresses of a piece of underlying hardware such as a microcontroller peripheral unit. Consider, for example, the registers of a made-up timer shown below.

```
// chapter03_18-002_alignment.cpp

struct alignas(16) timer_register_type
{
  std::uint32_t tmr_ctrl1;
  std::uint32_t tmr_ctrl2;
  std::uint32_t tmr_cntr1;
  std::uint32_t tmr_cntr2;
};
```

In this code sample, we have defined a structure that maps a fictive timer register set aligned on a 16-byte boundary.

3.19 The Specifier final

Another very useful specifier is known as final. The specifier final can be used to restrict the ability to derive a from another class previously occurring in its hierarchy. Consider the code sample below.

```
// chapter03_19-001_final.cpp

class base
{
public:
  virtual ~base() { }

  base& operator=(const base&) = default;

protected:
  base() { }
```

```
};

class derived final : public base
{
public:
  derived() { }

  virtual ~derived() { }

  derived& operator=(const derived&) = default;
};
```

This sample presents a simple class hierarchy with one base class and one derived class. The derived class is specified as `final`. It is not intended to subsequently derive additional classes from `derived`. Attempting to do so results in an error.

Embedded systems with microcontrollers often feature very specific electronic sub-circuits that exist only within the application.[12] When this kind of system element is embodied in a class, it might be a good design choice to exclude class inheritance via `final`. This can make sense if the class already represents the highest level of abstraction expected to be necessary for the underlying object.[13]

The following code sequence shows an attempt to derive *another* class from the `derived` class. But since `derived` is already specified as `final`, there is an error.

```
// chapter03_19-002_final.cpp

class derived_another : public derived
{
  // This class should result in an error.
};
```

3.20 Alias as an Alternative to typedef

In C++11 and beyond, a so-called *alias* can be used as an alternative to a classical **`typedef`** (see also Sect. 6.9). Consider the traditional type definition of an unsigned integral type below.

[12] An example of this is the simple LED circuit shown in the first chapter of this book in Sect. 1.1.

[13] It might also be desirable to make this sort of class *non-copyable* (Sect. 15.2). In particular, this can be done if the class uniquely maps a given electronic sub-circuit or peripheral device in the application that is not intended to be copied.

```
// chapter03_20-001_alias.cpp

// Traditional typedef.
typedef unsigned int uint_type;
```

With a C++11 alias, this can be written similarly as follows.

```
// C++11 alias.
using uint_type = unsigned int;
```

Some developers find the syntax of C++11 alias to be more legible and intuitive than that of the original C-style **typedef**. This can be particularly noticeable when dealing with long names of types. For instance,

```
// chapter03_20-002_alias.cpp

#include <algorithm>
#include <array>
#include <cstdint>

void do_something()
{
  // Alias for unsigned int.
  using uint_type     = unsigned int;

  // Alias for array of uint_type.
  using array_type    = std::array<uint_type, 3U>;

  // Alias for reverse iterator of array of uint_type.
  using reverse_iterator_type =
    array_type::const_reverse_iterator;

  constexpr array_type my_array( {{ 1U, 2U, 3U }} );

  // Find result is 2.
  const reverse_iterator_type ri =
    std::find(my_array.crbegin(),
              my_array.crend(),
              2U);
}
```

3.21 Delimiting Pointer Ranges with `<span>`

Starting with C++20, the standard library includes support for the `std::span` template in the `<span>` library. An `std::span` represents an efficient abstraction of a continuous span of values, such as those in a buffer or in a table in constants in program code. Using a span can be convenient when handling ranges of values or memory buffers, in particular if these are stored as traditional C-style arrays or similar memory constructs that are ubiquitous in real-time programming.

Consider, for instance, the code below. This code sequence uses `std::span` to clear a traditional legacy buffer that has a length known at compile time.

```
// chapter03_21-001_span.cpp

#include <span>

void clear_buffer(std::span<std::uint8_t> pb)
{
  for(auto u : pb)
  {
    u = UINT8_C(0);
  }
}

#define LEGACY_BUFFER_LENGTH 64U

uint8_t legacy_buffer[LEGACY_BUFFER_LENGTH];

void do_something()
{
  clear_buffer(legacy_buffer);
}
```

3.22 Generating Random Numbers with `<random>`

Starting with C++11, the standard library supports easy-to-use pseudo-random number generators (PRNG). C++11's `<random>` library is intended to be used for these, and `<random>` offers numerous convenient functions for calculating and retrieving pseudo-random numbers and their distributions. See also [6] as well as [7], Vol. 2, Chap. 3 "*Random Numbers*" for further detailed information on algorithmically generating and computing random numbers.

Consider the code below.

```
// chapter03_22-001_mersenne_twister_19937.cpp

#include <cstdint>
#include <random>

void do_something()
{
  using res_type =
    typename std::random_device::result_type;

  std::random_device  device;
  const res_type seed(device());
  std::mt19937          gtor(seed);
  const std::uniform_int_distribution<res_type>
   distribution(1U, 1023U);

  const unsigned random_numbers[3U] =
  {
    distribution(gtor),
    distribution(gtor),
    distribution(gtor)
  };
}
```

This code uses a Mersenne Twister 19937 [10] engine to generate a uniform integer `distribution` with range 1 ... 1023. This distribution is subsequently used to generate three pseudo-random numbers.

One of the interesting details in this code sequence is the so-called *seed* of the pseudo-random number generator taken from an unsigned integer value obtained from `std::random_device`. In microcontroller programming, it can be challenging and important to select a seed that is as random as possible. For this purpose, it can be useful to implement a custom random device or use a specialized on-chip hardware peripheral such as a *true random number generator* (TRNG).

There is a special `entropy()` function intended to represent the library author's determination of the *entropy* (i.e., the randomness) of `std::random_device`. The `entropy()` method of `std::random_device` returns a **`double`** value ranging from 0.0 ... 32.0, where a higher result indicates higher confidence regarding the randomness of the device.

Mersenne Twister 19937 (`std::mt19937`) can generate pseudo-random numbers with up to 32 unsigned bits. A 64-bit unsigned version is also available in the `<random>` library. It is called `std::mt19937_64`. Both `std::mt19937` as well as `std::mt19937_64` are specializations of the underlying template class std::mersenne_twister_engine<>. The corresponding type definitions for these useful twisters are standardized as

```
// chapter03_22-001_mersenne_twister_19937.cpp

#include <random>

// For std::mt19937.
using std::mt19937 =
  std::mersenne_twister_engine<
    std::uint_fast32_t,
    32,
    624,
    397,
    31,
    UINT32_C(0x9908B0DF),
    11,
    UINT32_C(0xFFFFFFFF),
    7,
    UINT32_C(0x9D2C5680),
    15,
    UINT32_C(0xEFC60000),
    18,
    UINT32_C(1812433253)>;
```

and

```
// For std::mt19937_64.
using std::mt19937_64 =
  std::mersenne_twister_engine<
    std::uint_fast64_t,
    64,
    312,
    156,
    31,
    UINT64_C(0xB5026F5AA96619E9),
    29,
    UINT64_C(0x5555555555555555),
    17,
    UINT64_C(0x71D67FFFEDA60000),
    37,
    UINT64_C(0xFFF7EEE000000000),
    43,
    UINT64_C(6364136223846793005)>;
```

Table 3.1 The random engines and adapters specified in Sect. 26.5.5 of [5] are listed

Engine or adapter	Specialization of template	10,000th consecutive random (with default seed)
`minstd_rand0`	`linear_congruential_engine`	1043618065
`minstd_rand`	`linear_congruential_engine`	399268537
`mt19937`	`mersenne_twister_engine`	4123659995
`mt19937_64`	`mersenne_twister_engine`	9981545732273789042
`ranlux24_base`	`subtract_with_carry_engine`	7937952
`ranlux48_base`	`subtract_with_carry_engine`	61839128582725
`ranlux24`	`discard_block_engine`	9901578
`ranlux48`	`discard_block_engine`	249142670248501
`knuth_b`	`shuffle_order_engine`	1112339016

There are various random engines or engine adapters provided in `<random>` including, in addition to `std::mersenne_twister_engine<>`, others such as `std::linear_congruential_engine<>` and more. These are specified in Sect. 26.5.5 of [5] and also listed here in Table 3.1. Especially `std::linear_-congruential_engine<>` can be efficient yet strong enough for numerous lightweight embedded applications of random numbers.

It is straightforward to perform a cursory check of the compiler's (or your own) implementation of a standard random engine or adapter. Consider, for instance, the code below which tests the $10,000$th consecutive random value produced by a default-seeded instance of `std::minstd_rand0`, the expected value of which is 1043618065.

```
// chapter03_22-002_test_random_engines.cpp

bool do_something()
{
  std::minstd_rand0 engine;

  engine.discard(9999U);

  return (engine() == UINT32_C(1043618065));
}
```

Further information on customizing `std::random_device` and specializing random engines within an embedded environment can be found in Sect. 16.8. That section also includes example `chapter16_08`, a fascinating program that generates 128-bit random prime numbers.

References

1. R. Crandall, C. Pomerance, *Prime Numbers: A Computational Perspective, Second Edition* (Springer, New York, 2005)
2. S.R. Finch, *Mathematical Constants* (Cambridge University Press, Cambridge, 2003)
3. L.J. Goldstein, A history of the prime number theorem. Am. Math Month. (80), 599–615 (1973)
4. L. Goodman, E.W. Weisstein, *Riemann Hypothesis*. From MathWorld–A Wolfram Web Resource (2020). http://mathworld.wolfram.com/RiemannHypothesis.html
5. ISO/IEC, *ISO/IEC 14882:2017 : Information Technology – Programming Languages – C++* (International Organization for Standardization, Geneva, 2017)
6. R.T. Kneusel, *Random Numbers and Computers* (Springer International Publishing, Cham Switzerland, 2018)
7. D.E. Knuth, *The Art of Computer Programming Volumes 1–3, Third Edition* (Addison-Wesley, Boston, 1998)
8. D.N. Lehmer, *List of Prime Numbers from 1 to 10,006,721* (Carnegie Institution of Washington, Washington D.C., 1914)
9. LORIA, D. Roegel, *The LORIA COLLECTION of MATHEMATICAL TABLES, DTL (Digital Tables Library)—Reconstructed Tables—A Reconstruction of Lehmer's Table of Primes (1914), HAL Id: hal-00654443* (2017). http://locomat.loria.fr/locomat/reconstructed.html and http://locomat.loria.fr/lehmer1914/lehmer1914doc.pdf
10. M. Matsumoto, T Nishimura, Mersenne twister: A 623-dimensionally equidistributed uniform pseudo-random number generator. ACM Trans. Model. Comput. Simul. Special Issue on Uniform Random Number Generation **8**(1), 3–30 (January 1998)
11. Wikipedia, *Logarithmic integral function* (2019). http://en.wikipedia.org/wiki/Logarithmic_integral_function
12. Wikipedia, *Prime-counting function* (2017). http://en.wikipedia.org/wiki/Prime-counting_function
13. Wikipedia, *Prime number theorem* (2019). http://en.wikipedia.org/wiki/Prime_number_theorem
14. Wikipedia, *Sieve of Eratosthenes* (2019). http://en.wikipedia.org/wiki/Sieve_of_Eratosthenes
15. E.W. Weisstein, *Prime Counting Function*. From MathWorld–A Wolfram Web Resource (2020). http://mathworld.wolfram.com/PrimeCountingFunction.html

Chapter 4
Object-Oriented Techniques for Microcontrollers

Object-oriented programs are built from various class objects that intuitively embody the application through their actions and interrelations among each other. This chapter introduces object-oriented C++ methods in the domain of embedded systems programming using classes for LEDs, PWM signal generators and communication interfaces.

4.1 Object Oriented Programming

Consider the application shown in Fig. 4.1.

This application has four LEDs and two peripheral timers used as pulse-width modulated (PWM) signal generators. The LEDs `L0` and `L1` are connected to port pins `P2.0` and `P2.1`, respectively. These LEDs have the same circuit as the one shown previously in Chap. 1, Fig. 1.1. They are controlled with bit manipulation of the microcontroller's port `P2`, as introduced in the LED program of Sect. 1.1.

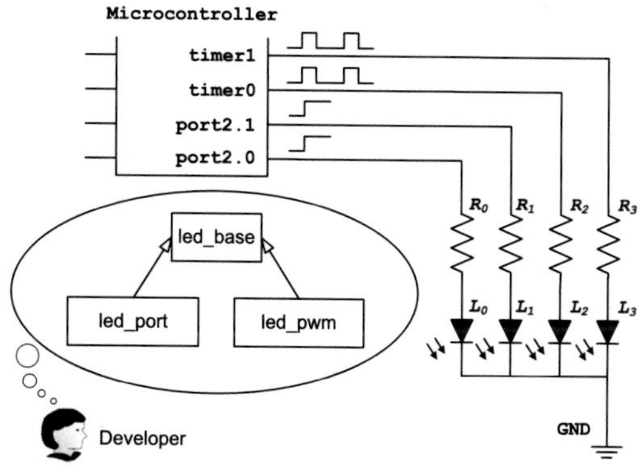

Fig. 4.1 An application with four LEDs is shown

C. Kormanyos, *Real-Time C++*, https://doi.org/10.1007/978-3-662-62996-3_4

The LEDs L2 and L3 are connected to PWM signals generated from peripheral timers in the microcontroller. L2 is connected to timer0 and L3 is connected to timer1. Setting the duty cycle of the PWM signal to 0% or 100% switches the corresponding LED off or on, respectively. Intermediate duty cycles with values greater than 0% but less than 100% can be used for dimming the corresponding LED. Dimming is an additional feature that an LED on a simple digital I/O pin does not have.

We will now design a *class hierarchy* for the LED objects in Fig. 4.1. This is the class hierarchy that the developer in Fig. 4.1 is considering. The two types of LEDs can be represented with a *base class* and two *derived classes*. The base class is called led_base. The two derived classes are called led_port and led_pwm.

One potential implementation of the led_base class is shown below.

```
// chapter04_01-001_led_hierarchy.cpp

class led_base
{
public:
  virtual void toggle() = 0; // Pure abstract.
  virtual ~led_base() { }    // Virtual destructor.

  // Interface for querying the LED state.
  bool state_is_on() const { return is_on; }

protected:
  bool is_on;

  // A protected default constructor.
  led_base() : is_on(false) { }

private:
  // Private non-implemented copy constructor.
  led_base(const led_base&) = delete;

  // Private non-implemented copy assignment operator.
  const led_base& operator=(const led_base&) = delete;
};
```

The public interface of the led_base class has two *virtual functions*, the virtual toggle() function and a virtual destructor called ~led_base().

In object-oriented programming, a derived class provides its own specific version of a virtual function in its base class. This is called a function *override*. When calling a member function on a base class pointer or reference to an object, the virtual function in the derived class will be used.

This is the virtual function mechanism in C++, and it is an essential part of *dynamic polymorphism* in object-oriented programming.

In dynamic polymorphism, derived classes in a class hierarchy can be manipulated with a common interface yet still exhibit specialized behavior. In our case here, it means that any kind of LED derived from `led_base` can `toggle()` in its own way.

In general, the destructor of a derived class should be virtual. This ensures that the proper derived class destructor is called when destroying an object via a base class pointer.

For more information on virtual function overrides and virtual destructors, consult Eckel [4], Chap. 15, Sect. "*virtual functions*" and also Sect. "*Destructors and virtual destructors*".

Another interesting feature of the `led_base` class is its protected constructor. The protected constructor can not be called from any other parts of the program except classes derived from `led_base`. This makes sense because `led_base` is intended to be just that, a base class. No one is actually supposed to create instances of `led_base`. Furthermore, if one were to try, the compiler would forbid it.

Now that we have the `led_base` class, we can derive another class from it called `led_port`.

```
// chapter04_01-001_led_hierarchy.cpp

class led_port : public led_base
{
public:
  typedef std::uint8_t port_type;
  typedef std::uint8_t bval_type;

  led_port(const port_type p,
           const bval_type b) : port(p),
                                bval(b)
  {
    // ...
  }

  virtual ~led_port() { }

  virtual void toggle()
  {
    // Toggle the LED.
    *reinterpret_cast<volatile bval_type*>(port)
      ^= bval;

    // Toggle the is_on indication flag.
    is_on = (!is_on);
  }
```

```
private:
  const port_type port;
  const bval_type bval;
};
```

The `led_port` class is specifically designed to toggle LEDs connected to a port pin. In our case here, this means `L0` and `L1` in Fig. 4.1. The `led_port` class is similar to the `led` class from the LED program in Sect. 1.1. There is nonetheless an important distinction between the two. The `led_port` class is derived from `led_base`.

Take a moment to notice how both `led_base` as well as `led_port` have the virtual `toggle()` function. This is a common interface that is shared by `led_port` and `led_base`.

A virtual override in a derived class does not need to explicitly use the **`virtual`** keyword, unless this is required for further derived classes. Some developers feel that supplying the optional **`virtual`** keyword in a derived class is redundant and should be avoided. Others consider it to be a helpful reminder that the function is virtual and is, in fact, overriding a function with the same signature in its base class.

For the LEDs on PWM signal generators in Fig. 4.1, we need an LED class that encapsulates a second kind of LED driver. Instead of manually switching an LED on and off by toggling a port pin, this class controls the brightness of its LED with a PWM signal generator. In particular,

```
// chapter04_01-001_led_hierarchy.cpp

class led_pwm : public led_base
{
public:
  explicit led_pwm(pwm* p) : my_pwm(p) { }

  virtual ~led_pwm() { }

  virtual void toggle()
  {
    // Toggle the duty cycle.
    const std::uint8_t duty =
      (my_pwm->get_duty() > 0U) ? 0U : 100U;

    my_pwm->set_duty(duty);

    // Toggle the LED with the PWM signal.
    is_on = (my_pwm->get_duty() > 0U);
  }
```

```
  // This LED class also supports dimming.
  void dimming(const std::uint8_t duty)
  {
    my_pwm->set_duty(duty);
    is_on = (duty != 0U);
  }

private:
  pwm* my_pwm;
};
```

Just like the `led_port` class, `led_pwm` has its own override of the `toggle()` function. This is `led_pwm`'s specialized way to `toggle()`. Notice in the implementation of the `toggle()` member how the `led_pwm` class uses its private variable `my_pwm` for manipulating the PWM signal generator connected to its corresponding LED.

In addition to the `toggle()` function, `led_pwm` also has a `dimming()` function. As mentioned above, dimming can be used to set intermediate values of LED brightness that lie between 0% and 100%. There is additional logic in the `toggle()` algorithm that synchronizes dimming with toggling. If the PWM signal has any non-zero duty cycle upon entering the `toggle()` function, then the LED is assumed to be on and it will be switched off by setting the duty cycle to 0%. If the PWM signal has a duty cycle of 0%, then `toggle()` switches the LED on by setting the duty cycle to 100%.

The constructor of the `led_pwm` class is declared with the **`explicit`** keyword. This ensures that the constructor can only be used if the input parameters are supplied and prevents potential unintended automatic compiler conversion of the class to another type. See also Eckel [4], Chap. 12, Sect. "*Preventing constructor conversion*".

The PWM signal generators can be encapsulated with a `pwm` class. In particular,

```
// chapter04_01-001_led_hierarchy.cpp

class pwm final
{
public:
  explicit pwm(const std::uint8_t c)
    : channel   (c),
      duty_cycle(0U) { }

  ~pwm() { }
```

```
  void set_duty(const std::uint8_t duty)
  {
    // Limit the duty cycle to 0...100.
    duty_cycle = (std::min)(std::uint8_t(duty),
                            std::uint8_t(100U));

    // Set the duty cycle in the PWM hardware.
    // ...
  }

  std::uint8_t get_duty() const
  {
    return duty_cycle;
  }

  std::uint8_t get_channel() const
  {
    return channel;
  }

private:
  std::uint8_t channel;
  std::uint8_t duty_cycle;
};
```

The pwm class has a simple public interface consisting of its constructor and two functions, `set_duty()` and `get_duty()`. These two functions are designed for setting and retrieving the value of the pwm's duty cycle. In our example here, we assume that the duty cycle can be set from 0 ... 100% in 101 discrete steps. The microcontroller-specific code sequences required for initializing the PWM hardware and setting the duty cycle are not shown. These are treated in greater detail in Sect. 9.4.

4.2 Objects and Encapsulation

Objects, through their actions and relations among each other (both concrete as well as abstract), compose the functionality of an object-oriented application. Objects for microcontrollers usually encapsulate electronic sub-circuits or control functions such as digital filters, regulation loops, communication devices, measurement equipment, graphical instruments, etc.

The LED class hierarchy and the pwm class, for example, encapsulate the electronic sub-circuits shown in Fig. 4.1 by uniting their respective functionalities with their internal data. In particular, the code sample below shows some possible instances of the `led_port`, `led_pwm` and `pwm` objects.

```
// chapter04_01-001_led_hierarchy.cpp

namespace
{
  // Two LEDs on port2.0 and port2.1
  led_port led0
  {
    mcal::reg::port2,
    mcal::reg::bval0
  };

  led_port led1
  {
    mcal::reg::port2,
    mcal::reg::bval1
  };

  // Two PWMs on channels timer0 and timer1.
  pwm pwm0 { 0U };
  pwm pwm1 { 1U };

  // Two LEDs connected to pwm0 and pwm1.
  led_pwm led2 { &pwm0 };
  led_pwm led3 { &pwm1 };
}
```

This code has instances of all four LEDs (`led0–led3`) and the two PWM signals from Fig. 4.1. The `pwm` instances, objects themselves, are used to initialize the `led_pwm` objects.

Now that we have our LEDs, it is straightforward to toggle them. For example,

```
// chapter04_01-001_led_hierarchy.cpp

void do_something()
{
  // Toggle led0-led3.
  led0.toggle();
  led1.toggle();
  led2.toggle();
  led3.toggle();
}
```

This code toggles `led0–led3`. Notice how the uniform `toggle()` interface makes it convenient to toggle both kinds of LEDs using the same function call. This is an example of object-oriented microcontroller programming in C++.[1]

4.3 Inheritance

Consider class inheritance in object-oriented C++ programming. For example,

```
// chapter04_01-001_led_hierarchy.cpp

class led_port : public led_base
{
  // ...
};
```

A derived class inherits data members and methods from its base(s) and can use them subject to access control. For example, `led_port` can use `led_base`'s public and protected members. In particular, `led_port` can directly manipulate `led_base`'s protected member `is_on`.

```
// chapter04_01-001_led_hierarchy.cpp

class led_port : public led_base
{
public:
  virtual void toggle()
  {
    // Toggle the LED.
    *reinterpret_cast<volatile bval_type*>(port)
      ^= bval;

    // Toggle the is_on indication flag.
    is_on = (!is_on);
  }

  // ...
};
```

[1]This code does not yet make use of the runtime virtual function mechanism. We will re-examine this example in association with dynamic polymorphism and the runtime virtual function mechanism in Sect. 4.4.

The `toggle()` function also toggles the state of `is_on` from **`false`** to **`true`** and vice versa after toggling the LED. Since `led_port` is publicly derived from `led_base`, it is allowed to manipulate the protected member variable of its base class. Clients of classes derived from `led_base` can query the state of `is_on` by calling the `state_is_on()` method.

Each successively more derived class adds to the inheritance chain. For example, `led_port` and `led_pwm` add their individualized `toggle()` capabilities. In addition, `led_pwm` adds its dimming function. We could potentially derive another kind of PWM-based LED class, say `led_pwm2`, from `led_pwm`. This new class would inherit both the `toggle()` function as well as the `dimming()` function—and could even add other functions of its own.

As mentioned earlier in Sect. 1.4, inheritance has three access controls: public, protected and private. When not explicitly specified, the default inheritance level of a class is private. The default inheritance level of a struct is public. Private inheritance is less common, but can be useful. The `noncopyable` class of Sect. 15.2 shows an interesting example of private inheritance used to control the access level of class copying. The access level of inheritance allows for fine-tuning copy semantics and hiding private data in class hierarchies.

Inheritance runs through the class hierarchy, providing for distribution of program complexity. Armed with the right object granularity and prudent design of class hierarchies, it is possible to build powerful and expressive object-oriented microcontroller programs in C++.

4.4 Dynamic Polymorphism and a Detailed LED Example

Dynamic polymorphism, or runtime polymorphism, is one of the most powerful tools in object-oriented C++ programming. Dynamic polymorphism in C++ uses a runtime virtual function mechanism to call methods of a derived class by accessing them from a base class pointer or reference. For example,

```
// chapter04_04-001_dynamic_polymorphism.cpp

void led_toggler(led_base* led)
{
  // Use dynamic polymorphism to toggle
  // a base class pointer.
  led->toggle();
}
```

```
void do_something()
{
  led_toggler(&led0); // Toggle an led_port.
  led_toggler(&led1); // Toggle an led_port.
  led_toggler(&led2); // Toggle an led_pwm.
  led_toggler(&led3); // Toggle an led_pwm.
}
```

In this code, `led_toggler()` uses dynamic polymorphism on a base class pointer (`led_base*`) to call the `toggle()` function for two different kinds of LED objects (*i.e.*, `led_port` and `led_pwm`). The virtual function mechanism selects the right `toggle()` function at runtime. The compiler has automatically generated a small amount of object code for this.

In the calls to `led_toggler()` above, the compiler will automatically downcast the `led_port` and `led_pwm` pointers to base class pointers. Explicit downcast with **`static_cast`** is possible, and exemplified below.

```
// chapter04_04-002_dynamic_polymorphism_cast.cpp

void do_something()
{
  led_toggler(static_cast<led_base*>(&led0));
  led_toggler(static_cast<led_base*>(&led1));
  led_toggler(static_cast<led_base*>(&led2));
  led_toggler(static_cast<led_base*>(&led3));
}
```

According to stylistic preferences and coding guidelines, some developers prefer to supply the explicit downcast. Others consider a non-necessary downcast redundant. They believe that it makes code "over-casted" and reduces legibility.

Dynamic polymorphism also works with a base class reference. For example,

```
// chapter04_04-003_dynamic_polymorphism_ref.cpp

void led_toggler(led_base& led)
{
  // Use dynamic polymorphism to toggle
  // a base class reference.
  led.toggle();
}
```

```
void do_something()
{
  // Toggle led0-led3.
  led_toggler(led0); // Toggle an led_port.
  led_toggler(led1); // Toggle an led_port.
  led_toggler(led2); // Toggle an led_pwm.
  led_toggler(led3); // Toggle an led_pwm.
}
```

The microcontroller programmer needs to be aware that dynamic polymorphism has slight runtime and size costs. When designing classes and class hierarchies, one should be sure that the benefits of dynamic polymorphism are worth its overhead. The following section provides more detail on this.

Dynamic polymorphism and the runtime virtual function mechanism are powerful object-oriented methods. They allow specialized objects that share a common inheritance to be treated identically while still retaining their own specific characteristics. This allows for enormous design flexibility because a uniform interface can be used throughout the entire class hierarchy.

We will now discuss examples `chapter04_04` and `chapter04_04a`. These sample projects use an intuitive LED class hierarchy similar to the one shown in Fig. 4.1 in order to exercise dynamic (and a little bit of static) polymorphism. See also Sect. 5.7 for further and more complete information on static polymorphism.

In this application, five individual discrete LEDs blink nearly simultaneously with a toggle frequency of approximately 1/2 Hz. This is the same familiar toggle frequency that has been used in example `chapter02_03` from Sect. 2.3. In addition, a parallel independent PC-based project configuration with its own MCAL layer has been implemented in order to simulate this application on a PC using console output as toggle indication.

The hardware setup used in example `chapter04_04` on our target system with the 8-bit microcontroller is shown in Fig. 4.2. This hardware setup utilizes commonplace discrete components fitted on a solderless prototyping breadboard.

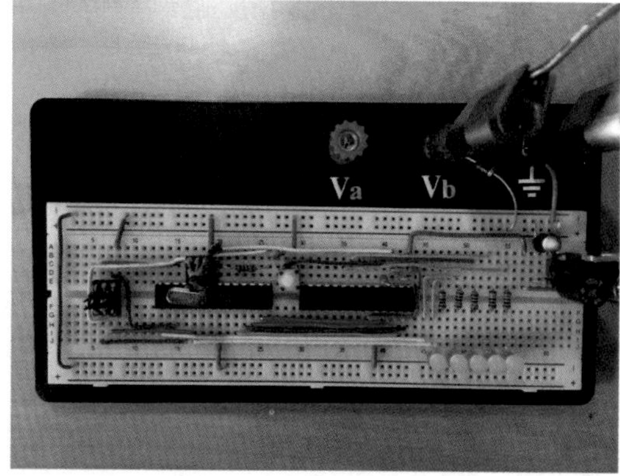

Fig. 4.2 The target hardware used in example `chapter04_04` is shown. There are five port-controlled LEDs on the board exhibiting three different toggle mechanisms and having three corresponding class types

Table 4.1 The pin connections of the port expander chip in examples `chapter04_04` and `chapter04_04a` are listed

Pin on port expander	Port expander function	Electrical connection
9	V_{DD}	+5 V
10	V_{SS}	GND
11	$\overline{CS}$	`portc.4`
12	SCK	`portc.3`
13	SI	`portc.1`
14	SO	`portc.2`
15	A0	+5 V
16	A1	+5 V
17	A2	+5 V
18	$\overline{RESET}$	15 kΩ to +5 V pullup, switch to GND
21	GPA0	750 Ω to LED_2
22	GPA1	750 Ω to LED_3
23	GPA2	750 Ω to LED_4

The LEDs are rated at approximately 10 mA. LED current is limited through 750 Ω, 1/ 10 W leading resistors. Similar resistor-LED combinations can be used according to availability and electrical design of the circuit. Hereby, it is essential to remain within the specified electrical current ratings of the port pins on the microcontroller and port expander.

The five LEDs are animated with three individual kinds of port control. The port pins include one regular microcontroller port pin on `portb.5`, a PWM microcontroller peripheral port pin on `portb.1` and three additional LEDs hooked up to GPA0, GPA1 and GPA2 on an external port expander chip of type Microchip® MCP23S17 [8]. The pinning of the port expander chip is listed in Table 4.1.

The all-software SPI™ driver from Sect. 9.5 controls the external port expander chip. The instruction set of the port expander chip is realized within a header-only MCAL-specific class called `port_expander_microchip_mcp23s17`.

In the example `chapter04_04` sample project, the `led_base` class provides the interface for two derived LED classes. The two LED classes, `led_port` and `led_pwm`, are very similar to the ones described previously in Sect. 4.1 of this chapter (see Fig. 4.1).

The particular implementation of the `led_port` class here, however, uses a template parameter that describes the "`port_type`" being used to control the LED. The template parameter is used as a placeholder that describes exactly how the port is being toggled. Basically the LED control is handled with the static public interface of the `port_type`, which follows that of the I/O port pin driver template class presented in Sect. 9.1. Templates and template parameters will be covered fully in Chap. 5.

The public interface of the LED base class `led_base` is summarized in the code below.

```
class led_base : private util::noncopyable
{
public:
  virtual void toggle() = 0;
  virtual bool state_is_on() const = 0;

  virtual ~led_base() = default;

  // ...
};
```

The public interface and some of the implementation details of the `led_port` class are depicted in the code sample below.

```
template<typename port_type>
class led_port : public mcal::led::led_base
{
public:
  led_port() : is_on(false)
  {
    port_type::set_pin_low();
    port_type::set_direction_output();
  }

  virtual ~led_port() = default;

  virtual void toggle()
  {
    // Toggle the LED state.
    is_on = (!is_on);

    port_type::toggle_pin();
  }

  // ...
};
```

Each of the derived LED classes in example `chapter04_04` implements its own version of the `toggle()` method. As mentioned above, the `led_port` class uses common port toggle functionality as described in Sect. 9.1 to toggle its corresponding LED. The `led_pwm` class, on the other hand, uses a `dimming()` method to toggle its LED by switching the duty cycle completely on or off. Although not used in this example, an intermediate duty cycle can also be adjusted with `led_pwm`'s `dimming()` function.

The application layer can be found in the file `app_led.cpp`. The application declares a static container of type `std::array` (Sect. 3.11) containing five `led_base` class pointers. In particular,

```
std::array<mcal::led::led_base*, 5U>
app_led_base_class_pointers =
{{
  mcal::led::led0(),
  mcal::led::led1(),
  mcal::led::led2(),
  mcal::led::led3(),
  mcal::led::led4()
}};
```

Each `led_base` class pointer object is retrieved from a unique singleton function (Sect. 8.6) that wraps a corresponding static derived class instance. The singleton objects and the implementation details of their LED classes are hidden within the MCAL layer.

In order to exemplify one of these singleton functions, the `led2()` object pointer which embodies the LED on port expander pin GPA0 is shown below.

```
mcal::led::led_base* mcal::led::led2()
{
  using led2_port_type =
    mcal::port::port_pin_expander<0U>;

  using led2_led_type =
    mcal::led::led_port<led2_port_type>;

  static led2_led_type l2;

  return &l2;
}
```

The five LEDs are toggled nearly in unison with a frequency of approximately 1/2 Hz in the application task. This is shown in the code below.

```
void app::led::task_func()
{
  if(app_led_timer.timeout())
  {
    app_led_timer.start_interval(app_led_one_sec);

    for(auto& p_led : app_led_base_class_pointers)
    {
      p_led->toggle();
    }

    // ...
  }
}
```

The task function `app::led::task_func()` is cyclically polled by the multitasking scheduler and called every $\sim\ 2\,ms$. In this cycle task, `app_led_timer` times out approximately each second. Upon each timeout occurrence, the range-based **for**`(:)` loop (Sect. A.12) iterates over the base class pointers in the array to toggle each LED.

We will now briefly turn our attention to example `chapter04_04a`. Consider the array of LED base class pointers `app_led_base_class_pointers` shown above. This array stores LED base class pointers of type `led_base*`. Some C++ designs could use LED base class references having type `led_base&` instead of LED base class pointers.

One harmless hitch encountered when doing so is that references can not be stored directly in STL containers. This makes it difficult to directly replace the LED base class pointers with LED base class references in our example. References can, however, be stored in containers when wrapped by the standard library's `std::reference_wrapper` template.[2]

In particular, when we redesign the singleton instances such as `mcal::led::led0()`, etc. to return LED base class references instead of LED base class pointers, the array of LEDs becomes

[2]The `std::reference_wrapper` template can be found in the `<functional>` header and is available as of C++11.

```
using app_led_ref_type =
  std::reference_wrapper<mcal::led::led_base>;

std::array<app_led_ref_type, 5U>
app_led_base_class_refs =
{{
  mcal::led::led0(),
  mcal::led::led1(),
  mcal::led::led2(),
  mcal::led::led3(),
  mcal::led::led4()
}};
```

Example `chapter04_04a` composes this array of LED base class references in the form of wrapped in instances of `std::reference_wrapper`. These are used in order to accomplish the same LED toggle functionality using dynamic polymorphism in essentially the same way as in example `chapter04_04`.

Examples `chapter04_04` and `chapter04_04a` exemplify how dynamic polymorphism can provide a powerful means to unify object interfaces for underlying classes having differing implementation details. These examples exhibit the use of this object oriented technology by seamlessly accessing each different LED's specialized `toggle()` method. This effectively shields the application layer from the implementation details of the LED classes, thereby radically reducing the core application's complexity to essentially nothing more than container management and the polymorphic calling of a single virtual method.

4.5 The Real Overhead of Dynamic Polymorphism

One may wonder how much overhead is associated with dynamic polymorphism and the runtime virtual function mechanism in C++. Since the implementation details of the virtual function mechanism depend on the compiler's internals, there is no exact answer to this question. In general, though, the best compilers in the market have remarkably low overhead for dynamic polymorphism.

We will now examine a scheme commonly used to implement the runtime virtual mechanism in C++. Many compilers store the addresses of virtual functions in a compiler-generated table at a location that could be either in static RAM or program code. A general rule-of-thumb, then, is that each virtual function of a class costs one chunk of memory large enough to hold a function pointer. Consider an 8-bit platform. If a function pointer requires two bytes on this platform and a derived class has three virtual functions, then the implementation of the derived class might require six bytes of storage for its virtual function table.

Calling a virtual function can be efficient because all the compiler needs to do is select the proper entry from the virtual function table and call it. This might be only slightly slower than a normal function call. In addition, the call overhead of a virtual function remains the same regardless of how many levels of inheritance there are. It is always the same effort for accessing the virtual function table. Readers interested in additional details on the overhead associated with the runtime virtual function mechanism can consult FAQ 20.4 of Parashift [1] or Eckel [4], Chap. 15, Sect. "*Under the hood*".

Even though modern C++ compilers have little overhead associated with dynamic polymorphism, low-level drivers that are called very often (*e.g.* in high-frequency interrupts) may be unsuited for dynamic polymorphism. Procedural methods or static polymorphism (Sect. 5.7) could be better options for extremely time critical code. Functions in the application layer that are less time critical can greatly benefit from well-designed class hierarchies because the advantages of dynamic polymorphism usually far outweigh its modest costs.

4.6 Pure Virtual and Abstract

Examination of the `led_base` class implementation reveals that its `toggle()` function does not have a body. Rather, the `toggle()` function of `led_base` is a so-called *pure virtual* function, implemented with the unmistakably recognizable syntax "`= 0`". In other words,

```
// chapter04_01-001_led_hierarchy.cpp

class led_base
{
public:
  virtual void toggle() = 0; // Pure abstract.

  // ...
};
```

A class that has one or more pure virtual methods is called an *abstract* class. An abstract class is the generalized notion of something, as opposed to a concrete example of a specific thing. As such, the pure virtual functions of an abstract class are not intended to be called. Instead, pure virtual functions define a mandatory interface for derived classes. In other words, pure virtual functions define a sort of *blueprint* for derived classes.

Consider an abstract base class. Any to-be-instantiated class derived from it *must* implement overrides for each pure virtual method of its base(s). Otherwise, no objects of the derived class can be instantiated.

For example, both `led_port` as well as `led_pwm` are derived from the abstract `led_base` class. Therefore, both of them must provide a member override for `toggle()`. In this way, C++ provides clear language semantics for data abstraction.

Say we derive a class called `led_no_toggle` from `led_base` but fail to include the required virtual `toggle()` function. If anyone attempted to instantiate an instance of `led_no_toggle`, there would be a compilation error. In particular,

```
// chapter04_06-001_abstract_compile_error.cpp

class led_no_toggle : public led_base
{
public:
  led_no_toggle() { }
  virtual ~led_no_toggle() { }

  // Does not have a toggle function.
  // ...
};

namespace
{
  led_no_toggle led_no; // Compilation error!
}
```

As mentioned above, an abstract object is an idealization—not intended to be created. It is usually a good idea to protect the constructor of an abstract class type. This is why the constructor of `led_base` is protected. The protected constructor ensures that no one is able to create `led_base` objects. Yet the constructor is *only* protected, and not private. Publicly derived classes are, therefore, granted access to the base class constructor.

A derived class can, itself, contribute methods to the abstract interface by adding pure virtual functions of its own. However, it is always important to remember that class types with pure virtual functions are not intended to be instantiated and hence will lead to a compilation error.

4.7 Class Relationships

There is a variety of well-known class relationships in object-oriented design. In fact, we have already worked with some of them without even explicitly mentioning them. Possibly the most important class relationship is the *is-a* relationship for which a derived class *is-a* subclass of a base class. In other words, `led_port` *is-a* subclass of `led_base`, and `led_pwm` also *is-a* subclass of `led_base`.

Another special relationship is that of *has-a*, in the sense of *having* something. The led_pwm class exhibits the *has-a* relationship with its member variable pwm. In other words, the led_pwm class *has* its own PWM signal generator. Since it has its own pwm object, it can use this for the internal workings of the toggle() function.

There is also the *uses-a* relationship. The relationship of *using* usually requires some way to pass the thing-being-used to its user. This can be done, for example, via function parameter or by accessing an existing instance through pointer or reference.

The difference between *has-a* and *uses-a* can be subtle, but important. In particular, if led_pwm were to *use* a pwm and not *have* one, then its toggle() function would need an input pwm pointer or reference parameter. Note, though, that this would break the uniformity of the toggle() interface within the class hierarchy.

We will now visualize these important class relationships with a few simple code snippets.

The led_pwm class *is-a* specialized kind of led_base.

```
// chapter04_01-001_led_hierarchy.cpp

class led_pwm : public led_base
{
  // led_pwm is-a led_base.
  // ...
};
```

The led_pwm class *has-a* class-owned pwm.

```
// chapter04_01-001_led_hierarchy.cpp

class led_pwm : public led_base
{
  // ...

private:
  // led_pwm has-a pwm.
  pwm* my_pwm;
};
```

Perhaps in a different implementation, the led_pwm class might *use-a* PWM signal. In this case, a pointer to a PWM signal, in other words a pwm*, could be used as a subroutine input parameter to the toggle() function instead of being a class member. Even though this would wreck the uniformity of the toggle() interface in our example, the *use-a* relationship can be a useful class relationship in many other cases.

```
// chapter04_07-001_led_hierarchy_uses_pwm.cpp

class led_pwm : public led_base
{
  // ...

  // This led_pwm uses the use-a relationship
  // to toggle.
  virtual void toggle(pwm* p)
  {
    // ...
  }
};
```

Careful consideration of class relationships is necessary for successful object-oriented design because class relationships strongly influence the efficiency and cleanliness of the interfaces in a software project. A thorough description of class relationships can be found in Sect. 6.4 in Coplien [2]. Additional information on the *is-a* relationship is available in Eckel [4], Chap. 1, Sect. "*Is-a vs. is-like-a relationships*".

4.8 Non-copyable Classes

The `led_base` class has private yet non-implemented declarations of a copy constructor and a copy assignment operator. In particular,

```
// chapter04_01-001_led_hierarchy.cpp

class led_base
{
public:
  // ...

private:
  // Private non-implemented copy constructor.
  led_base(const led_base&) = delete;

  // Private non-implemented copy assignment operator.
  const led_base& operator=(const led_base&) = delete;
};
```

This means that the led_base class and its derived classes are non-copyable. Declaring a private copy constructor and a private copy assignment operator and qualifying them with the **delete** keyword tells the compiler that a given class and its derived classes should be treated as strictly non-copyable without exception.

When using non-copyable classes, the compiler will issue an error for any code, including compiler-generated code, that tries to copy the class. This technique is often done on purpose in order to eliminate the risk of both intentional as well as unintentional attempts to copy a class instance.

Explicitly making certain classes non-copyable can be particularly useful in real-time C++ because some classes or class instantiations may be intimately linked to a particular hardware unit or peripheral device. For instance, an LED on a port pin, a PWM signal on a timer output or a communication interface such as a serial UART may be bound to a unique microcontroller peripheral resource.

If only one instance of a class should be allowed to use a single resource, then non-copyable semantics can reduce the risk of unintentionally using the resource with multiple class instances. Non-copyable semantics can also improve intuitive clarity in the code by unmistakably indicating if a class is intended to be copied or not.

In fact, the non-copyable mechanism is so widely established that some high-reliability guidelines [9] recommend using it when appropriate. In addition, a standard C++ utility called noncopyable in Boost [3] has been invented to simplify the semantics of making a class object non-copyable. See Sect. 15.2 for our own version of the noncopyable utility.

Class copying is a rich topic involving issues such as eliminating reliance on compiler generated default copy, deep-copy mechanisms for pointer members, checking for self-assign, etc. For additional information on class copying, see Eckel [4], all of Chap. 11 "*References & the Copy-Constructor*" and also Chap. 12, Sect. "*Overloading assignment*". Meyers [7] describes deep-copy mechanisms in Item 11 and copy assignment in Items 15, 16 and 17.

4.9 Constant Methods

We have already encountered several examples of constant member functions previously. For example, the toggle() function in the LED program of Sect. 1.1 and the squared_euclidean_distance() member of the point structure in Sect. 3.5 are both constant methods.

Constant member functions have read-only character regarding the member variables of a class. As such, they can not modify the value of any class member variable. If there are good reasons to do so, however, a constant member function can modify a non-constant variable if that variable is qualified with the **mutable** keyword.

We will now examine an example of a richer class that has both constant as well as non-constant member functions. Consider a communication class designed to send and receive single-byte data frames.

```
// chapter04_08-001_const_com_class.cpp

extern "C"
void com_recv_isr() __attribute__((interrupt));

class communication
{
public:
  communication() : recv_buf(0U),
                    has_recv(false) { }

  ~communication() = default;

  bool send_byte(const std::uint8_t by) const
  {
    *tbuf = by;

    return true;
  }

  bool recv_ready() const { return has_recv; }

  std::uint8_t recv_byte()
  {
    if(has_recv)
    {
      has_recv = false;

      recv_buf = *rbuf;

      return recv_buf;
    }

    return 0U;
  }

private:
  static constexpr std::uint8_t* tbuf =
    reinterpret_cast<std::uint8_t*>(0xAAU);

  static constexpr std::uint8_t* rbuf =
    reinterpret_cast<std::uint8_t*>(0xABU);
```

```
  std::uint8_t recv_buf;
  bool has_recv;

  communication(const communication&) = delete;

  const communication& operator=
    (const communication&) = delete;

  friend void com_recv_isr();
};
```

The `communication` class is simple and versatile. It is designed for low-level asynchronous communication with a microcontroller peripheral interface. With slight modification, the `communication` class can be used with physical layers such as SPI™, CAN [6], etc. The serial SPI™ driver class in Sect. 9.5, for example, is based on the `communication` class shown above.

For now, we need not be concerned about the *friend* function `com_recv_isr()` nor about its interrupt `__attributes__()`. Class friends are described in greater detail in Sect. 4.11, and additional information on interrupts and GCC's language extensions for them is provided in Sect. 9.2.[3]

Byte transmission is carried out with the `send_byte()` member using direct memory access to write a to-be-transmitted byte to `communication`'s transmit buffer `tbuf`. As such, `send_byte()` does not modify any class-internal data and can be declared as **`const`**. In particular,

```
// chapter04_08-001_const_com_class.cpp

class communication
{
public:
  // ...

  bool send_byte(const std::uint8_t by) const
  {
    *tbuf = by;

    return true;
  }
};
```

[3]In the example here, however, simplified interrupt attributes have been used for the sake of clarity.

A client using a constant instance of class can only call constant members of the class. For instance,

```
// chapter04_08-001_const_com_class.cpp

// Emphasize: com is a const reference.
bool wakeup(const communication& com)
{
  // Call the const send_byte() function
  // on a const reference.
  return com.send_byte(0x12U);
}
```

In this code, `wakeup()` uses a constant communication reference, in other words **`const`** `communication&`, to send the wake-up pattern. The wake-up is sent with a call to the constant `send_byte()` member. This is expected to compile without error.

Consider the implementation of a communication login that sends the wake-up pattern `0x12` and expects to receive the login response `0x34`. In particular,

```
// chapter04_08-002_nonconst_com_class.cpp

// Emphasize: com is a const reference.
bool login(const communication& com)
{
  // OK. Call the const send_byte() function
  // on a const reference.
  const bool wakeup_is_ok = wakeup();

  if(wakeup_is_ok)
  {
    // Receive the byte.
    // Since com is a const reference,
    // there should be a compilation error
    // when calling com.recv_byte().

    return (com.recv_byte() == 0x34U);
  }
  else
  {
    return false;
  }
}
```

In login(), the call of the constant send_byte() member on the constant communication class reference compiles without error. The attempted call of the non-constant recv_byte() member, however, does not. The compilation should result in an error because calling a non-constant member on a constant object is not allowed.

In order to call recv_byte(), the reference to communication must be made non-constant in the input parameter to the login() function. In other words,

```
// chapter04_08-002_nonconst_com_class.cpp

// Emphasize: com is a non-const reference.
bool login(communication& com)
{
  // OK.
  const bool wakeup_is_ok = wakeup(com);

  if(wakeup_is_ok)
  {
    // OK.
    return (com.recv_byte() == 0x34U);
  }
  else
  {
    return false;
  }
}
```

Many development guidelines recommend making member functions constant whenever it makes sense to do so. This provides additional intuitive insight into how a class and its interface are intended to be used. This is a part of what is generally known as *const-correctness* in the literature.

There are no added runtime or storage costs associated with qualifying member functions as **const**. So the microcontroller programmer can freely use constant methods to improve program clarity without introducing undue resource consumption.

4.10 Static Constant Integral Members

The communication class has two static constant integral data members, tbuf and rbuf. These represent made-up register addresses of a fictive 8-bit microcontroller communication peripheral. The registers are declared as compile-time constants with the **constexpr** keyword.[4] In particular,

```
// chapter04_08-001_const_com_class.cpp

class communication
{
public:
  // ...

private:
  static constexpr std::uint8_t* tbuf =
    reinterpret_cast<std::uint8_t*>(0xAAU);

  static constexpr std::uint8_t* rbuf =
    reinterpret_cast<std::uint8_t*>(0xABU);

  // ...
};
```

We first encountered static constant integral members of a class in Sect. 3.8. Similar to symbols defined with a preprocessor **#define**, static constant integral members of class types are compile-time constants. As described earlier, however, use of **constexpr** can offer significant advantages over the preprocessor **#define**.

For effective C++ design, it is essential to understand that static constant integral members have distinct advantages over preprocessor **#define**s. For example, static constant integral members have a clearly defined type and name. They may, thus, potentially have compiler symbol information. Symbols that have been defined with a preprocessor **#define**, on the other hand, are used exclusively by the preprocessor and lack these. Type and symbol information can be useful with a debugger or when examining program contents in a linker *map file* (see also Sect. 6.5).

At the same time, static constant integral class members are guaranteed to be known at compile time. Using them often eliminates the code overhead associated with runtime address load or move operations by taking advantage of constant folding (Sect. 2.6). For further discussions of static constant integral members versus preprocessor **#define**s, see Item 1 in Meyers [7].

[4]See also Sect. 3.8 for details on **constexpr**. In addition, the relevant code snippets for the PC simulate these registers using the constant addresses of static variables.

4.11 Class Friends

Byte reception in the `communication` class of the previous section uses the member function `recv_byte()`. This receive function does not directly retrieve the byte by reading the UART's hardware buffer register. Instead, `recv_byte()` reads the *software* receive buffer, `recv_buf`. It thereby also checks and clears the `has_recv`-flag. In this way, `communication` is designed for asynchronous byte reception.

To provide a mechanism for asynchronous receive, `communication` uses a *friend* subroutine called `com_recv_isr()`. As perhaps expected, the "`isr`"-part of the friend subroutine's name is, in fact, intended to indicate that this an interrupt service routine.

```
// chapter04_08-002_const_com_class.cpp

extern "C"
void com_recv_isr() __attribute__((interrupt));

class communication
{
  // ...

  friend void com_recv_isr();
};
```

A friend of a class is allowed to access any class member variable or method regardless of its access level, public, protected or private. Class friends can be either global or local functions, member functions or even other class types. Note that friend functions do not necessarily need to have C-linkage (qualified with **extern** `"C"`). This is a characteristic of the particular example at hand which uses a friend function that just so happens to be an interrupt service routine.

A possible implementation of `com_recv_isr()` is shown below.

```
// chapter04_08-002_const_com_class.cpp

extern "C"
void com_recv_isr() __attribute__((interrupt));

communication com;

// Communication's friend and also an ISR.
```

```
void com_recv_isr()
{
  // Asynchronous byte reception can use the
  // private members of com.

  // Simulate receiving a byte
  // in the hardware register.
  *com.rbuf = 0x34U;

  com.has_recv = true;
}
```

The communication object `com` is a static instance of the `communication` class with global scope. When an asynchronous hardware receive interrupt occurs, the microcontroller calls `com_recv_isr()`. This interrupt service routine subsequently reads the hardware receive buffer (`communication::rbuf`) and fills `com`'s receive buffer with the received byte. The `com_recv_isr()` interrupt also activates the `has_recv`-flag. This announces the new reception to a polling listener. In this way, `com_recv_isr()` executes asynchronous byte-reception. Notice in all this how the interrupt service routine—a friend of the `communication` class—can access `communication`'s private members.

Another part of the program such as a cyclical task could potentially poll `com`, thereby querying its Boolean member function `recv_ready()` to find out if a new byte has been received. Upon reception of a new byte, `recv_ready()` returns **`true`**. The new byte in the receive queue can be retrieved with the `recv_byte()` subroutine. For example,

```
// chapter04_08-003_poll_communication.cpp

extern communication com;

void task_poll_communication()
{
  if(com.recv_ready())
  {
    const std::uint8_t the_byte = com.recv_byte();

    // Do something with the_byte.
    // ...
  }
}
```

Some developers avoid using class friends, arguing they break data hiding and fragment encapsulation.[5] This is not necessarily the case. Using class friends in certain cases can actually improve data encapsulation by eliminating thin `set()`-and-`get()` interfaces that might weaken class boundaries by exposing internal class details. For such reasons, using class friends tends to ensure that private members remain *private*. See also FAQ 14.2 at Parashift [1] for a further discussion of this.

It can be wise to use class friends, but sparingly, and only if the use of friendship is justified by tangible design improvement beyond mere convenience. For example, interrupt service routines require static C-linkage, making them difficult to be encapsulated in a class while simultaneously included in the interrupt vector table (Sect. 9.2). When accessing a global object such as `com` within an interrupt service routine, class friendship can provide just the right mechanism to retain encapsulation while adhering to the constraints of interrupt programming.

4.12 Virtual Is Unavailable in the Base Class Constructor

The virtual function mechanism for a given class is neither available in its own class constructor nor in any base class constructor because the object is not fully formed yet. Any attempt to use the virtual function mechanism within a base class constructor will result in undefined behavior. In the code below, `communication_base` is a base class for communication and `communication_serial` is a specialized class derived from it. In particular,

```
class communication_serial : public communication_base
{
public:
  communication_serial(const std::uint16_t c,
                       const std::uint8_t  b)
    : channel(c),
      baud(b) { }

  virtual ~communication_serial() { }
```

[5]The high-integrity coding guidelines in [9], for example, recommend avoiding the use of class friends (with certain justified exceptions), indicating that class friends may potentially degrade the strength of encapsulation.

```
  virtual void init()
  {
    // Initialize this communication_serial class.
    // ...
  }

private:
  const std::uint8_t channel;
  const std::uint16_t baud;
};
```

The candidate base class `communication_base` is shown below. It makes erroneous, undefined use of the virtual function mechanism in the base class constructor.

```
class communication_base
{
public:
  virtual ~communication_base() { }

  // A virtual initialization function.
  virtual void init() { }

protected:
  communication_base()
  {
    // Undefined use of the virtual mechanism!
    init();
  }
};
```

Here, the constructor of `communication_base` attempts to use the virtual function mechanism to call `init()`. Unfortunately, this code might not do what its author intended. The code is meant to use the virtual function mechanism to call the `init()` function of the derived class in the base class constructor. The virtual function mechanism is, however, unavailable in the base class constructor. Therefore, the `communication_serial` object might be created using the empty `init()` function of `communication_base`.

The compiler might not even issue a warning for attempting to use the virtual mechanism in a base class constructor. This is because the compiler cannot differentiate between an inadvertent virtual function call that might not work and an intended call of a base class member function.

In order to properly initialize `communication_serial`, its `init()` function could be called explicitly *after* the constructors are finished. In particular, we will redesign `communication_base` such that its constructor no longer calls `init()`.

```
class communication_base
{
public:
  // ...

protected:
  // Remove initialization from
  // the base class constructor.
  communication_base() { }
};

class communication_serial : public communication_base
{
  // ...
};
```

Now the constructor of the `communication_base` class no longer attempts to call the virtual `init()` function. Clients of the `communication_serial` class need to explicitly call the `init()` method *after* the object has been created. For example,

```
void do_something()
{
  // Create com_serial on channel 1 with 9600bps.
  communication_serial com_serial(1U, 9600U);

  // Explicitly initialize com_serial.
  // It is fully formed.
  com_serial.init();

  // Use com_serial.
  // ...
}
```

Understandably, it can be all too easy to forget to explicitly call the `init()`-like functions of a class needing explicit initialization after creation. One possible remedy for this problem uses an abstract interface (often called a *factory*) to dynamically create objects and simultaneously ensure that they are explicitly initialized when fully formed, but before being used.[6]

Through empirical investigations or trial-and-error, one may find compilers for which, by chance, the virtual function mechanism seems to be available in the base class constructor. Relying on this behavior, however, is unreliable and can be confusing because the code might work with one compiler yet be broken by another.

Always remember that the C++ language specification is clear on this matter. The virtual function mechanism is not available in the base class constructor. Potential confusion can be spared by remembering and adhering to this rule. See Item 23.5 at Parashift [1] for more information on the unavailability of the virtual function mechanism in the base class constructor.

References

1. M. Cline, *Parashift C++ FAQ* (2012). http://www.parashift.com/c++-faq
2. J.O. Coplien, *Advanced C++ Programming Styles and Idioms* (Addison-Wesley, Boston, 1992)
3. B. Dawes, D. Abrahams, *Boost C++ Libraries* (2012). http://www.boost.org
4. B. Eckel, *Thinking in C++ Volume 1: Introduction to Standard C++*, 2nd edn. (Pearson Prentice Hall, Upper Saddle River, 2000)
5. E. Gamma, R. Helm, R. Johnson, J. Vlissides, *Design Patterns: Elements of Reusable Object-Oriented Software* (Addison-Wesley, Boston, 1994)
6. ISO, *ISO 11898–1:2003 : Road vehicles – Controller area network (CAN) – Part 1: Data Link Layer and Physical Signaling* (International Organization for Standardization, Geneva, 2003)
7. S. Meyers, *Effective C++: 55 Specific Ways to Improve Your Programs and Designs*, 3rd edn. (Addison-Wesley, Boston, 2005)
8. Microchip, *MCP23S17 16-Bit SPI I/O Expander with Serial Interface* (2020). www.microchip.com/wwwproducts/en/MCP23S17
9. Programming Research Ltd., *High Integrity C++ Coding Standard Version 4.0* (2015). http://www.codingstandard.com/HICPPCM/index.html

[6]Factories are described in good design books such as [5]. In addition, Sect. 5.9 in this book uses a simple factory to introduce variadic templates.

Chapter 5
C++ Templates for Microcontrollers

C++ templates use the same source code for different types. This can improve code flexibility and make programs easier to maintain because code can be written and tested once, yet used with different types. Templates can also be used in generic programming that treats different types with the same semantics. This chapter introduces templates and static polymorphism, the STL, template metaprogramming and some generic programming methods, and shows how these can be used effectively for microcontrollers.

5.1 Template Functions

Consider the simple template function below.

```
// chapter05_01-001_template_add.cpp

template<typename T>
T add(const T& a, const T& b)
{
  return a + b;
}
```

The template function `add()` returns the sum of (`a` + `b`), where `a`, `b` and the return value of `add()` all have the same type as the *template parameter* `T`. A template parameter can be considered a placeholder for a not-yet-specified type. Template parameters can be class types, built-in types, constant integral or pointer values, but not floating-point values. See Sect. 4.3 in Vandevoorde and Josuttis [4].

C. Kormanyos, *Real-Time C++*, https://doi.org/10.1007/978-3-662-62996-3_5

When a template is used in code, the compiler *instantiates* it for a known type by filling in the template code corresponding to its template parameters at compiler time. This is the same vocabulary that is used for instances of a class types in object-oriented programming. The context should be considered when discerning the two.

The code below, for example, uses `add()` twice, one time to add two integer variables and a second time to add two variables of type `std::string`, the standard library's string class.

```
// chapter05_01-001_template_add.cpp

const int n = add(1, 2); // 3

const std::string s =
  add(std::string("abc"),
      std::string("xyz")); // "abcxyz".
```

In the calls to `add()` above, the template parameter is not explicitly given. The compiler can automatically *deduce* the types of template parameters if it has sufficient information to do so from the context of usage. Even if the template parameters could be deduced, though, they can still be optionally provided. For example,

```
const int c = add<int>(a, b);
```

The template parameters must be compatible with the functionality of the template code. In order to be used with `add()`, for example, a given template parameter must support the binary addition operator (in other words **`operator`**`+`).

The compiler does not automatically perform type conversion for templates. So if the function's parameters do not exactly match those of the template, then the template parameters must be explicitly provided. For example,

```
double d1 = add(1.1, 2.2);         // OK, 3.3, double
double d2 = add(1.1, 2);           // Not OK, ambiguous
double d3 = add<double>(1.1, 2); // OK, 3.1, double
```

If multiple types are needed, template functions can have more than one template parameter.[1]

[1] Multiple template parameters are provided in a comma-separated template parameter list in angled brackets.

For instance,

```
// chapter05_01-002_template_add2.cpp

template<typename T1,
         typename T2>
T1 add(const T1& a, const T2& b)
{
  return a + T1(b);
}

const double d =
  add(1.1, 2); // OK, 3.1, double
```

5.2 Template Scalability, Code Re-Use and Efficiency

Templates are scalable. For instance, we will now consider a scalable template function that may be useful in microcontroller programming. It is based on the ubiquitous "`MAKE_WORD()`" preprocessor macro. The `MAKE_WORD()` macro is normally used to *make* a 16-bit unsigned integer from two constituent 8-bit unsigned bytes. One possible implementation of `MAKE_WORD()` using a C-style preprocessor macro with **`#define`** is shown below.

```
// chapter05_02-001_make_word.cpp

#define MAKE_WORD(lo, hi) \
          (uint16_t) (((uint16_t) (hi) << 8) | (lo))
```

We will now replace the C-style `MAKE_WORD()` preprocessor macro with a more generic template function called `make_large()`. In particular,

```
// chapter05_02-002_make_large.cpp

template<typename ularge_type,
         typename ushort_type>
ularge_type make_large(const ushort_type& lo,
                       const ushort_type& hi)
```

```
{
  constexpr int ushort_digits
    = std::numeric_limits<ushort_type>::digits;

  constexpr int ularge_digits
    = std::numeric_limits<ularge_type>::digits;

  // Ensure proper width of the large type.
  static_assert(ularge_digits == (2 * ushort_digits),
                "error: ularge_type size mismatch");

  // Shift the high part to the left.
  const ularge_type uh
    = static_cast<ularge_type>(hi) << ushort_digits;

  // Return the composite result.
  return static_cast<ularge_type>(uh | lo);
}
```

The `make_large()` template function returns the composite value of a larger unsigned type `ularge_type` made from two constituents of a smaller unsigned type `ushort_type`. Here, `ularge_type` is twice as wide as `ushort_type`. The high-part of the composite value is first shifted left by an amount corresponding to the width of the smaller unsigned type `ushort_type`. Afterward, the low-part is OR-ed with the shifted high-part to generate the result.

The standard library's `std::numeric_limits` template is used to obtain the number of binary digits in the large and short types (Sect. A.5). This template function also uses **`static_assert`** to ensure that the `ularge_type` has exactly twice as many binary digits as `ushort_type`. It can be wise to build these types of checks into template utilities to prevent error caused by instantiation with non-compatible types. Further security could be included by adding compile-time assertions that verify that `ularge_type` and `ushort_type` are both unsigned integer types.

Using `make_large()` in code is simple. For example,

```
// chapter05_02-002_make_large.cpp

std::uint8_t  lo8  = UINT8_C(0x34);
std::uint8_t  hi8  = UINT8_C(0x12);
std::uint16_t u16
  = make_large<std::uint16_t>(lo8, hi8);
```

```
std::uint16_t lo16 = UINT16_C(0x5678);
std::uint16_t hi16 = UINT16_C(0x1234);
std::uint32_t u32
  = make_large<std::uint32_t>(lo16, hi16);

std::uint32_t lo32 = UINT32_C(0x9ABC'DEF0);
std::uint32_t hi32 = UINT32_C(0x1234'5678);
std::uint64_t u64
  = make_large<std::uint64_t>(lo32, hi32);
```

This code uses `make_large()` to make three results of widths 16, 32 and 64-bit, respectively. The results are made from their corresponding half-width constituents. This shows how templates are *scalable*. Notice how `make_large()` automatically scales its width at compile time to accommodate different integer types.

One of the great features of templates is code re-use. To provide the same scalability with preprocessor macros, three individual ones would be needed. In particular, we would need equivalent preprocessor macros such as `MAKE_WORD()` for 16-bit results, `MAKE_DWORD()` for 32-bit results and `MAKE_QWORD()` for 64-bit results. The `make_large()` template is superior to multiple preprocessor macros because it only needs to be implemented once and maintained in one place.

A generic template, tested and written in a type-safe fashion, is a tool that can be used, re-used and readily ported to other platforms without needing redesign. Furthermore, preprocessor macros can be plagued by non-safe side-effects such as unwanted parameter modification, etc. C++ Templates are freed from the problems of C-style macros and generally improve code portability and robustness.

Templates are not necessarily expanded inline by default because template inlining is relegated to the compiler's internal optimization characteristics. The **`inline`** keyword can be used in order to *recommend* to the compiler to treat a template function as inline. The compiler can, however, still optionally choose to disregard the **`inline`** keyword based on its optimization settings, and the length and complexity of a given template. See Sect. 6.1 for further information on optimization.

Templates facilitate efficiency because they make all of their code and template parameters known to the compiler at compile time. Templates can, however, also incur additional code costs. Each time the compiler encounters a template subroutine or object, it must create new code for each individual instance. This phenomenon can potentially lead to excessive *code bloat* if left unchecked. For additional discussion on code bloat and how to avoid it, see Eckel [1], Chap. 5, Sect. "*Preventing template code bloat*". The microcontroller C++ programmer must be aware of this trade-off and wisely find the right mixture of templates and non-templates when designing code. When used properly, templates can be highly effective for optimized programming. The benefits of improved performance and scalability often far outweigh any potential costs.

5.3 Template Member Functions

Member functions of class types can be templates. For example, consider a simplified version of the `communication` class from Sect. 4.9.

```
// chapter05_03-001_communication_nontemplate.cpp

class communication
{
public:
  communication() { }

  virtual ~communication() { }

  virtual bool send_byte(const std::uint8_t b) const
  {
    // ...
  }

  std::uint8_t recv_byte() const
  {
    return recv_buffer;
  }

private:
  std::uint8_t recv_buffer;
};
```

Say we would like to add the capability of sending larger chunks of data with the `communication` class. For example, in addition to 8-bit unsigned bytes (`std::uint8_t`), we would also like to send 16-bit or 32-bit unsigned integers over the `communication` interface. In order to do this, we could add a new template `send_uint()` member function. For example,

```
// chapter05_03-002_communication_template.cpp

class communication
{
public:
  // ...

  // Add a template send_uint function.
  template<typename unsigned_type>
```

```
  bool send_uint(const unsigned_type& u) const
  {
    constexpr bool type_is_signed
      = std::numeric_limits<unsigned_type>::is_signed;

    // Ensure that unsigned_type is unsigned.
    static_assert(type_is_signed == false,
                  "error: type must be unsigned");

    constexpr std::size_t count =
      std::numeric_limits<unsigned_type>::digits / 8;

    std::size_t i;

    for(i = 0U; i < count; i++)
    {
      const std::uint8_t by(u >> (i * 8U));

      if(send_byte(by) == false)
      {
        break;
      }
    }

    return (i == count);
  }
};
```

In this listing, the template Boolean member function `send_uint()` has been added to the `communication` class. The type of `unsigned_type` is intended to be a right-shift-capable unsigned integral type. Similar to the `send_byte()` function, `send_uint()` performs data transmission. However, instead of transmitting a single byte, `send_uint()` transmits the number of bytes contained in its template parameter type `unsigned_type`. For example, `send_uint()` sends one byte if `unsigned_type` is `std::uint8_t`, two bytes for `std::uint16_t`, four bytes for `std::uint32_t` and eight bytes for `std::uint64_t`.

Calling template class member functions is straightforward. In fact, template class methods can be called just like non-template ones using the usual member selection operators (`.`) and (`->`). For example, we will now use the modified `communication` class to simulate communication with an external target system.

```
// chapter05_03-003_communication_session.cpp

class communication
{
  // ...
};

bool start_session(const communication& com)
{
  constexpr std::uint32_t login_key =
    UINT32_C(0x12345678);

  // Send the 32-bit login key.
  const bool start_session_is_ok =
    com.send_uint(login_key);

  return start_session_is_ok;
}
```

The `start_session()` subroutine above depicts a made-up command for starting a communication session with an off-chip target system. The new template `send_uint()` member function added to the `communication` class is used to send the 32-bit `login_key`. The subroutine returns **`true`** if the login send is successful.

Notice, as an aside, how a constant reference (*i.e.*, a **`const`** `communication&`) is used as the input parameter to the `start_session()` subroutine. Remember from Sect. 4.3 how this technique could also use dynamic polymorphism if `communication` were to be a base class.

Just as with non-class template subroutines, the compiler is capable of deducing the template parameters of template class methods. Of course, sufficient information still needs to be available to the compiler for automatic template deduction via the type(s) of the input argument(s).

Template member functions can improve coding quality and clarity of design when used sensibly. For example, the template `send_uint()` member function adds flexibility and scalability to `communication`'s send mechanisms. In addition, the template `send_uint()` function only needs to be implemented and debugged once. Furthermore, it works for various types. This eliminates potential sources of error and reduces coding complexity when using `communication` to send multiple bytes of data.

5.4 Template Class Types

A class types can also be a template. This can be convenient for making re-usable or scalable objects. For example, a coordinate `point` in two-dimensional Cartesian space $\mathbb{R}^2$ can be implemented as a scalable template. In particular,

```
// chapter05_04-001_template_point.cpp

template<typename x_type,
         typename y_type>
class point
{
public:
  x_type my_x;
  y_type my_y;

  point(const x_type& x = x_type(),
        const y_type& y = y_type()) : my_x(x),
                                      my_y(y) { }
};

// An (x16, y16) point.
point<std::uint16_t,
      std::uint16_t>
pt16_16
{
  UINT16_C(1234),
  UINT16_C(5678)
};

// An (x8, y8) point.
point<std::uint8_t,
      std::uint8_t>
pt08_08
{
  UINT8_C(12),
  UINT8_C(34)
};

// An (x8, y16) point.
point<std::uint8_t,
      std::uint16_t>
pt08_16
{
```

```
  UINT8_C(34),
  UINT16_C(5678)
};
```

5.5 Template Default Parameters

Template functions and class types support default template parameters. For example,

```
// chapter05_05-001_template_point.cpp

template<typename x_type = std::uint16_t,
         typename y_type = x_type>
class point
{
  // ...
};

// An (x16, y16) point.
point<> pt16_16
{
  UINT16_C(1234),
  UINT16_C(5678)
};

// An (x8, y8) point.
point<std::uint8_t>
pt08_08
{
  UINT8_C(12),
  UINT8_C(34)
};

// An (x8, y16) point.
point<std::uint8_t,
      std::uint16_t>
pt08_16
{
  UINT8_C(34),
  UINT16_C(5678)
};
```

A default template parameter type can be set to the symbolic typename of one of the previously supplied template parameters. For example, the default type of the template parameter `y_type` above is `x_type`.

When writing templates with default template parameters, it is not necessary to supply defaults for each template parameter. Template default parameters begin with the last template parameter and work sequentially toward the beginning of the template parameter list.

```
// chapter05_05-002_template_point.cpp

// Both template parameters have default types.
template<typename x_type = std::uint8_t,   // OK.
         typename y_type = std::uint16_t> // OK
class point
{
  // ...
};

// chapter05_05-003_template_point.cpp

// Only the second template parameter
// has a default types.
template<typename x_type,
         typename y_type = std::uint16_t> // OK
class point
{
  // ...
};

template<typename x_type = std::uint16_t, // Not OK
         typename y_type>
class point
{
  // ...
};
```

5.6 Template Specialization

Templates can be specialized for a particular type. This creates a unique *template specialization* for this type. When writing a template specialization, the to-be-specialized parameter is removed from original template parameter list and added to a second comma-separated template parameter list following the symbol name.

In particular, suppose that the project design rules discourage the use of floating-point types. In order to enforce this design rule, we might explicitly cause errors when using built-in floating-point types with the add template by making specialized versions with errors for **float**, **double** and **long double**. For example,

```
// chapter05_06-001_template_specialization.cpp

// The original add template function.
template<typename T>
T add(const T& a, const T& b)
{
  return a + b;
}

// Make template specializations of add() with
// easy-to-detect errors for float, double
// and long double.

template<>
float add<float>(const float&, const float&)
{
  // Explicitly create an erroneous result!
  return 0.0F;
}

template<>
double add<double>(const double&, const double&)
{
  // Explicitly create an erroneous result!
  return 0.0;
}

template<>
long double add<long double>(const long double&,
                             const long double&)
{
  // Explicitly create an erroneous result!
  return 0.0L;
}
```

Template specialization can be applied to templates with multiple parameters and also to specialize different parameters. When a subset of template parameters is specialized, it is called a *partial* template specialization. For example, we will now make a partial template specialization of the `point` class whose x-coordinate members are of type `std::uint8_t`. In particular,

```
// chapter05_06-002_template_point.cpp

// The original point template class.
template<typename x_type,
         typename y_type>
class point { ... };

// A partial specialization of the point
// class with x-axis having type std::uint8_t.

template<typename y_type>
class point<std::uint8_t, y_type>
{
public:
  std::uint8_t my_x;
  y_type       my_y;

  point(const std::uint8_t& x = x_type(),
        const y_type&       y = y_type()) : my_x(x),
                                            my_y(y)
  {
  }
};
```

5.7 Static Polymorphism

Templates provide a mechanism for static polymorphism, or in other words, for polymorphic behavior determined at compile time. This is distinctly different from the dynamic (runtime) polymorphism described in Sect. 4.4.

Consider once again the two LED classes in the class hierarchy of Sect. 4.1, `led_port` and `led_pwm`. We will now take a look at static polymorphism using these two LED classes. We will first slightly modify these classes to be better suited for static polymorphism instead of dynamic polymorphism. In particular, we will remove the classes from a class hierarchy and eliminate the virtual functions.

```
// chapter05_07-001_led_static_polymorphism.cpp

class led_port // No base class.
{
public:
  led_port(const port_type p,
           const bval_type b);

  void toggle() const // Not virtual.
  {
    // ...
  }

  // ...
};

class led_pwm // No base class.
{
public:
  led_pwm(pwm* p);

  void toggle() const // Not virtual.
  {
    // ...
  }

  // ...
};
```

These new LED classes are no longer related to each other through a class hierarchy. Both of these new LED classes do, however, now have a non-virtual `toggle()` function. Therefore, static polymorphism can be used to create a generic toggle mechanism for them. For example,

```
// chapter05_07-001_led_static_polymorphism.cpp

template<typename led_type>
void led_toggler(led_type& led)
{
  // Toggle with static polymorphism.
  led.toggle();
}
```

The `led_toggler()` subroutine accepts a reference to an `led_type`. Thus, any `led_type` object that has a `toggle()` member can be successfully toggled with `led_toggler()`. Instead of using the virtual function mechanism to select the right toggle function at runtime, the compiler generates the appropriate call of each object's `toggle()` member at compile time. This is static polymorphism.

As a final example of static polymorphism, we will redo the toggle code of the LEDs `L0`...`L3` from Sect. 4.2. This time we will use static polymorphism in place of dynamic polymorphism.

```
// chapter05_07-001_led_static_polymorphism.cpp

namespace
{
  // Two LEDs connected P2.0-P2.1
  led_port led0 { mcal::reg::port2, 1U };
  led_port led1 { mcal::reg::port2, 2U };

  // Two PWMs on channels T0 and T1.
  pwm pwm0 { 0U };
  pwm pwm1 { 1U };

  // Two LEDs connected to pwm0 and pwm1.
  led_pwm led2 { &pwm0 };
  led_pwm led3 { &pwm1 };
}

void toggle_all_leds()
{
  led_toggler(led0); // Uses led_port::toggle().
  led_toggler(led1); // Uses led_port::toggle().

  led_toggler(led2); // Uses led_pwm::toggle().
  led_toggler(led3); // Uses led_pwm::toggle().
}
```

Static polymorphism removes the runtime overhead caused by the virtual function mechanism. As such, static polymorphism *can* improve runtime performance. At the same time, though, a given implementation based on static polymorphism *might* have significantly more code than a comparable implementation based on dynamic polymorphism because of multiple instantiation. On the other hand, static polymorphism could just as well result in improved performance *and* reduced code due the potentially improved optimization made possible by templates. This can also be observed in Table 2.1 of Sect. 2.6.

The microcontroller programmer should be cognizant of the existence of static polymorphism and dynamic polymorphism and be aware of potential advantages or costs resulting from their use. When designing code, one should try to identify situations in which each one (or a mixture of the two) can produce the most effective and reliable results.

5.8 Using the STL with Microcontrollers

The Standard Template Library (STL) is an innovative collection of containers, iterators, algorithms, etc. The STL provides a remarkably complete and powerful set of generic tools and is highly regarded as an example of generic programming in C++. See Sect. 14.5, "Generic Programming" in [4].

The STL is part of the C++ standard library. This section provides only a brief introduction to the richness of the STL. Consult [3] and also Appendix A for further details on the STL.

The code below uses the STL's template `std::vector` container in combination with the `std::for_each()` algorithm.

```
// chapter05_08-001_using_the_stl.cpp

#include <algorithm>
#include <vector>

void do_something_with_the_stl()
{
  // Create v with the decimal values (1, 2, 3).
  // Initialize with a convenient initializer_list.

  std::vector<char> v { 1, 2, 3 };

  // Use an algorithm with a lambda function.
  // Convert from decimal char to ASCII char.

  std::for_each(v.begin(),
                v.end(),
                [](char& c)
                {
                  c += 0x30;
                });
}
```

In this example, the three characters in the vector `v` with decimal values `(1, 2, 3)` are converted to ASCII characters [6] having values `('1', '2', '3')`. The conversion from decimal to ASCII is carried out with a so-called *lambda expression* as the third input parameter to `std::for_each()`. The vector `v` is constructed and initialized at the same time using a convenient `std::initializer_list` in combination with uniform initialization syntax. The initializer list is also an STL container. See Sect. A.2 for more information on uniform initialization syntax, Sect. A.9 for lambda expressions and Sect. A.10 for initializer lists.

Sometimes more than one algorithm is available for a particular programming task. The conversion of the characters in `v` from decimal to ASCII could, for example, just as well be accomplished with `std::transform()`.

```
// chapter05_08-002_using_the_stl_algo.cpp

#include <algorithm>
#include <vector>

void do_something_with_the_stl()
{
  // Create v with the decimal values (1, 2, 3).
  // Initialize with a convenient initializer_list.

  std::vector<char> v { 1, 2, 3 };

  // Use std::transform.
  // Convert from decimal char to ASCII char.

  std::transform(v.cbegin(),
                 v.cend(),
                 v.begin(),
                 [](char& c) -> char
                 {
                   return c + 0x30;
                 });
}
```

These kinds of conversion operations—and many others like them—often arise in real-time C++ software. Although the conversion from decimal to ASCII is somewhat trivial, these examples do provide a glimpse into the power and flexibility of the STL.

The code of the STL can be found in the include path where the compiler's STL headers are stored.[2] Those curious about the implementation details of the compiler's STL can simply investigate the source code.

[2]It might be difficult to read the code, but it is expected to be available.

The `std::for_each()` algorithm, for example, could be implemented in the STL in a way similar to the code shown below.

```
// chapter05_08-003_std_for_each.cpp

namespace std
{
  template<typename iterator_type,
           typename function_type>
  function_type for_each(iterator_type first,
                         iterator_type last,
                         function_type function)
  {
    while(first != last)
    {
      function(*first);

      ++first;
    }

    return function;
  }
}
```

Using the STL can simplify programming, reduce error and improve efficiency and portability in microcontroller programming. Instead of arduously developing and testing hand-written containers and loops, the standardized components of the STL can be used *out-of-the-box*. With the consistent use of the standardized containers, iterators, algorithms, etc. of the STL, code will adopt a recognizable *look and feel* with easy-to-understand style.

One might also want to glance ahead to Sects. 10.3 and 10.5 which describe methods for outfitting STL containers with custom dynamic memory management mechanisms appropriate for microcontrollers. These techniques allow us to fit surprisingly many parts of the STL into the strictly limited memories of even the most tiny embedded controllers.

5.9 Variadic Templates

Variadic templates are template functions or class types that have a variable number of template parameters. Variadic templates were introduced in C++11.

Consider a simple software factory.

```
// chapter05_09-001_factory_simple.cpp

template<typename type_to_make>
type_to_make* factory(void* mem)
{
  // Construct a new pointer of kind type_to_make
  // with the placement-new operator.

  type_to_make* p = new(mem) type_to_make;

  return p;
}
```

This `factory()` makes products of kind `type_to_make`. The placement-**new**`()` operator, described in Sect. 10.2, is used to create the product in a caller-supplied memory pool.

We will now make *something* with this `factory()`. For example,

```
// chapter05_09-001_factory_simple.cpp

class something
{
  something() = default;

  ~something() = default;

  void do_something() const
  {
    // ...
  }
};

extern void* pool;

something* ps = factory<something>(pool);
```

Here, `ps` is created in the memory `pool`. The newly created `ps` is just like any other pointer. It can be used accordingly and deleted when no longer needed.

Consider, next, another class called something_else.

```
// chapter05_09-002_factory_variadic_template.cpp

class something_else
{
public:
  something_else(const int M,
                 const int N) : m(M),
                                n(N) { }

  virtual ~something_else() = default;

private:
  const int m;
  const int n;
};
```

Imagine that we would like to create a pointer to something_else. Unlike the constructor of the something class, the constructor of something_else supports has two input parameters. In this case, our factory() is not flexible enough to create something_else because it can only create things with parameter-less constructors.

In order to make a flexible factory(), then, we can use a variadic template. For example,

```
// chapter05_09-002_factory_variadic_template.cpp

template<typename type_to_make,
         typename ...parameters>
type_to_make* factory(void* mem,
                      parameters... params)
{
  // Construct a new pointer of kind type_to_make
  // with the placement-new operator
  // and a parameter pack argument.

  type_to_make* p = new(mem) type_to_make(params...);

  return p;
}
```

Here, the variadic template parameter `parameters` can contain any number of all kinds of things, including built-in types, class types, etc. Notice that **`operator...`** is used in two different ways. The **`operator...`** is used on the left side to declare a parameter pack in the template parameter list and on the right side to unpack the parameter pack into separate arguments in the function call. The parameter pack will be unpacked at compile time. In this case, C++ trades compilation effort for improved runtime efficiency, which is usually the right trade-off for real-time C++.

With this new, more flexible version of our `factory()`, we can successfully create objects of any class types having any kinds and numbers of constructor parameters. An instance of `something_else`, for example, can readily be made with the new `factory()`. In particular,

```
// chapter05_09-002_factory_variadic_template.cpp

class something_else
{
  // ...
};

extern void* pool;

something_else* p_else
  = factory<something_else>(pool, 12, 34);
```

Variadic templates add a new dimension of flexibility to template programming. They can be used to elegantly solve a class of problems that arise when multiple varying types need to be handled by a generic mechanism.

5.10 Template Metaprogramming

Template metaprogramming uses templates at compile time to do work that may otherwise need to be done during runtime. Template metaprogramming can be useful for sophisticated optimizations such as compile-time generation of constant values and loop unrolling.

The archetypal introductory template metaprogram computes the value of the unsigned integer factorial function at compile time. The factorial function $N!$ is defined by

$$N! \equiv N\,(N-1)\cdots 2\cdot 1\,. \tag{5.1}$$

A possible implementation of a template metaprogram for computing $N!$ is shown below.

```
// chapter05_10-001_metaprogram_factorial.cpp

template<const std::uint32_t N>
struct factorial
{
  // Multiply N * (N - 1U) with template recursion.
  static constexpr std::uint32_t value
    = N * factorial<N - 1U>::value;
};

template<>
struct factorial<0U>
{
  // Zero'th specialization terminates the recursion.
  static constexpr std::uint32_t value = 1U;
};
```

When the compiler instantiates `factorial<N>::value` for a given value of `N`, it recursively multiplies `N` with `factorial<N - 1>::value`. Template recursion terminates with the template specialization of `factorial<0U>::value`. The compiler produces no intermediate code and the result of the factorial is generated as a compile-time constant.

Consider, for example, the computation of 5! below.

```
// chapter05_10-001_metaprogram_factorial.cpp

constexpr std::uint32_t fact5 = factorial<5U>::value;
```

Here, the `factorial` template is used to calculate 5!, the result of which is $5 \times 4 \times 3 \times 2 \times 1 = 120$. This value is generated by the compiler and directly injected into the code as a compile-time constant. The factorial example, although somewhat trivial, shows how template metaprogramming uses recursive templates for radical compile-time optimization.

Template metaprogramming can also be used to compute powers of integral values at compile time. For instance,

```
// chapter05_10-002_metaprogram_pow10.cpp

template<const std::uint32_t n>
constexpr std::uint32_t pow10()
{
  static_assert(
    n <= 9U,
    "Error: n is limited to 9 or less.");
```

```
  return pow10<n - 1U>() * UINT32_C(10);
};

template<>
constexpr std::uint32_t pow10<UINT32_C(0)>()
{
  return UINT32_C(1);
};

// 1,000,000
constexpr std::uint32_t million = pow10<6U>();
```

Here, the `pow10` meta-function can compute 10^n at compile time, where $0 \leq n \leq 9$. The result is returned as a **constexpr** 32-bit unsigned integral value. The `pow10` template meta-function is, in fact, actually used later in this book to provide scaling with powers of ten in the π spigot program of example `chapter10_08` of Sect. 10.8.

A less trivial metaprogram computes the inner product of two equally sized ranges of adjacent iterator types. Consider the `inner_product` structure below.

```
// chapter05_10-003_metaprogram_inner_product.cpp

template<const std::size_t N,
         const std::size_t M = 0U>
struct inner_product
{
  template<typename iterator_left,
           typename iterator_right,
           typename result_type>
  static result_type sum(iterator_left u,
                         iterator_right v,
                         const result_type& init)
  {
    // Add (u[M] * v[M]) recursively.
    const result_type uvm
      = *(u + M) * result_type(*(v + M));

    return uvm
      + inner_product<N, M + 1U>::sum(u, v, init);
  }
};
```

```
template<const std::size_t N>
struct inner_product<N, N>
{
  template<typename iterator_left,
           typename iterator_right,
           typename result_type>
  static result_type sum(iterator_left,
                         iterator_right,
                         const result_type&)
  {
    // N'th specialization terminates the recursion.
    return result_type(0);
  }
};
```

The `inner_product` structure computes the inner product of the elements in the range [`M`, `N` − `1`). The template parameters `M` and `N` are used to represent the start index and total length of the inner product, respectively. The $\texttt{M}^{th}$ value of the sum is recursively passed to the $(\texttt{M} + 1)^{th}$ index in the inner product. Template recursion stops when the index parameter `M` reaches the upper bound of the inner product `N`. The `inner_product` template can be used with C-style arrays, `std::array`, `std::vector`, etc. (Sect. 5.8).

The template parameter `result_type` provides for optional scalability of the result. Notice that the start index `M` need not necessarily begin with zero. The inner product can start with an index higher than zero by appropriately setting `M` in the calling code.

The following code uses the `inner_product` metaprogram to compute the inner product of two `std::arrays`, `u` and `v`, where each array has three elements.

```
// chapter05_10-003_metaprogram_inner_product.cpp

constexpr std::array<unsigned, 3U> u
{
  { 1U, 2U, 3U }
};

constexpr std::array<unsigned, 3U> v
{
  { 4U, 5U, 6U }
};
```

```
// The result is 32.
const unsigned w =
  inner_product<3U>::sum(u.cbegin(),
                         v.cbegin(),
                         0U);
```

In this example, the values in both arrays u and v as well as the index parameters are known at compile time. Therefore, the compiler can fully compute the constant value of the inner product when setting w. This metaprogramming technique can be useful in areas involving coordinates such as linear algebra graphics, vehicle dynamic detection, navigation, etc.[3]

5.11 Tuples and Generic Metaprogramming

One very versatile template library added to the standard library with C++11 is `std::tuple`. The `std::tuple` template is a generalization of `std::pair` to triple, quadruple, quin-*tuple*, sex-*tuple*, etc. See Sect. A.13 for more information on tuples.

Unlike template STL containers such as `std::vector`, a tuple can contain different kinds of objects. For example,

```
// chapter05_11-001_tuple_things_simple.cpp

#include <tuple>

class apple
{
  // ...
};

class car
{
  // ...
};
```

[3]This example can be compared with the second example in Sect. 3.13, in which the same inner product was computed dynamically using `std::inner_product` from the standard library's `<numeric>` header.

```
class tiger
{
  // ...
};

std::tuple<apple, car, tiger> things;
```

Grouping objects of different types together can be useful if they need to be organized and manipulated as a cohesive collection. For example, the `things` tuple above can be passed by reference to a subroutine or included in a class as a member variable. In this way, tuples can improve program organization.

Another advantage of tuples is their ability to be manipulated with templates and metaprogramming. For example, imagine that all of the seemingly unrelated objects in the `things` tuple, the `apple`, `car` and `tiger`, have a same-named public member function called `setup()`. In other words, the `apple` class has `apple::setup()`, the `car` class has `car::setup()` and the `tiger` class has `tiger::setup()`. In this made-up example, the `setup()` member functions are responsible for setting up the internals of their respective class, such as the `apple`'s ripeness, the `car`'s fuel level or the `tiger`'s state of health. For instance,

```
// chapter05_11-001_tuple_things_simple.cpp

class apple
{
public:
  apple() = default;
  ~apple() = default;

  void setup() const
  {
    // ...
  }
};

class car
{
public:
  car() = default;
  ~car() = default;

  void setup() const
  {
    // ...
  }
};
```

```
class tiger
{
public:
  tiger() = default;
  ~tiger() = default;

  void setup() const
  {
    // ...
  }
};
```

We will now take our `things` tuple and explicitly `setup()` each element in it using the STL's template `std::get()` facility. In particular,

```
// chapter05_11-001_tuple_things_simple.cpp

void do_something()
{
  // Create the tuple of things.
  std::tuple<apple, car, tiger> things;

  // Setup the things.
  std::get<0>(things).setup();
  std::get<1>(things).setup();
  std::get<2>(things).setup();
}
```

Here, `std::get()` is used to *get* a reference to each object in the `things` tuple by index. Since each one of the objects in `things` has a `setup()` function, it can be called with the regular member selection operator (`.`) for references.

This situation lends itself well to generic metaprogramming. In particular, we could easily modify the inner product example from the last section to run through the indexes in a tuple and call each object's `setup()` function.

```
// chapter05_11-002_tuple_things_metaprogram.cpp

template<const unsigned N,
         const unsigned M = 0U>
struct tuple_setup_each
{
  template<typename tuple_type>
  static void setup(tuple_type& t)
```

```
  {
    // Setup the M'th object and the next higher one.
    std::get<M>(t).setup();
    tuple_setup_each<N, M + 1U>::setup(t);
  }
};

template<const unsigned N>
struct tuple_setup_each<N, N>
{
  template<typename tuple_type>
  static void setup(tuple_type&) { }
};
```

With the `tuple_setup_each` metaprogram, it's almost trivial to `setup()` the objects in the `things` tuple. In particular,

```
// chapter05_11-002_tuple_things_metaprogram.cpp

void do_something()
{
  // Create the tuple of things.
  std::tuple<apple, car, tiger> things;

  // Setup the things.
  tuple_setup_each<3U>::setup(things);
}
```

The `tuple_setup_each` metaprogram recursively generates setup code for each object in the `things` tuple via its `setup()` member.

This code can be made *even* more generic by strategically employing the standard `std::tuple_size` facility. The `std::tuple_size` facility returns the number of objects in a tuple-type as a compile-time constant. We will now slightly modify the code accordingly.

```
// chapter05_11-003_tuple_things_metaprogram.cpp

void do_something()
{
  // Use a convenient type definition
  // for the tuple_type.
  using tuple_type =
    std::tuple<apple, car, tiger>;
```

```
  tuple_type things;

  // Use tuple_size to get the size of the things.
  constexpr unsigned the_size
    = std::tuple_size<tuple_type>::value;

  // Setup the things.
  tuple_setup_each<the_size>::setup(things);
}
```

This metaprogramming technique can setup the things in any tuple with any number and all kinds of elements—as long as the type of each element in the tuple has a `setup()` function. Generic metaprogramming with tuples can be useful when objects with a partially or wholly common interface are to be treated with the same semantics.

5.12 Variable Templates

In addition to class types and functions, *variables* can also be templates. Variable templates were introduced with C++14. Variable templates can improve generic programming and reduce the complexity of template code.

The following code sets the value of the `prime_number` variable template equal to 541, the value of the 100th prime number. The variable template is instantiated as a 16-bit unsigned integer.

```
// chapter05_12-001_prime_number.cpp

template<typename T>
constexpr T prime_number = T(541);

constexpr std::uint16_t p =
  prime_number<std::uint16_t>;
```

Variable templates can be particularly useful in generic numeric programming (Sect. 12.7). The code sequences below, for example, define scalable representations of two well-known mathematical constants, Archimedes' constant ($\pi \approx 3.14159\ldots$),

```
// chapter05_12-002_constants.cpp

template<typename T>
constexpr T pi =
  T(3.1415926535'8979323846'2643383279'5028841972L);
```

and the natural logarithmic base ($e \approx 2.71828\ldots$).

```
// chapter05_12-002_constants.cpp

template<typename T>
constexpr T e =
  T(2.7182818284'5904523536'0287471352'6624977572L);
```

Consider a non-trivial mathematical computation such as Stirling's approximation of the Gamma function for large argument expanded to order 2. In particular,

$$\Gamma(x) \approx \left(\frac{x}{e}\right)^{x} \left\{\sqrt{\frac{2\pi}{x}} + \frac{1}{6}\sqrt{\frac{\pi}{2}}\left(\frac{1}{x}\right)^{3/2}\right\}, \quad \text{for } x \gg 1\,. \tag{5.2}$$

We can use the representations of π and e above to simplify typing in a template implementation of this approximation. A well-suited subroutine for this approximation, for instance, `tgamma_order_2`, could be written as shown below.

```
#include <cmath>

// chapter_05_12-003_stirlings_approx.cpp

template<typename T>
T tgamma_order_2(T x)
{
  using std::pow;
  using std::sqrt;

  const T      one_over_x = T(1.0L) / x;
  const T sqrt_one_over_x = sqrt(one_over_x);

  const T term0 =     sqrt(T(2.0L) * pi<T>)
                    * sqrt_one_over_x;
```

```
  const T term1 = (  sqrt(pi<T> / T(2.0L))
                   * (  sqrt_one_over_x
                      * one_over_x))
                  / T(6.0L);

  return pow(x / e<T>, x) * (term0 + term1);
}

// Test tgamma_order_2(20.0F).
// Result:       1.216442... e+17.
// Compare with: 1.216451... e+17.
```

In addition to the variable template representations of π and e, this order-2 implementation of Stirling's approximation also uses the elementary transcendental functions `std::pow()` and `std::sqrt()` from the `<cmath>` header file in the standard library (see also Sect. 12.3). These library functions have overloads (Sect. A.3) for the built-in data types **float**, **double** and **long double**.

The order-2 approximation of $\Gamma(20)$, as programmed above, obtains a result of $1.216442\ldots \times 10^{17}$. This agrees with the known value of $1.216451\ldots \times 10^{17}$ to within about 5–6 decimal digits of precision.

This template approximation of the Gamma function can be instantiated for **float**, **double** and **long double**. Via inclusion of the **using** directives for `std::pow` and `std::sqrt`, this template approximation can also be used with user-defined types that support elementary transcendental functions, such as the `fixed_point` class described in Chap. 13.

This example can also be programmed using, instead of self-written versions of constants π and e, C++20's standardized constants from the `<numbers>` library, described also in Sect. 12.2. A slightly modified implementation of `tgamma_order_2` using constants from `<numbers>` is shown below.

```
// chapter_05_12-004_stirlings_approx_cpp_numbers.cpp
#include <cmath>
#include <numbers>

template<typename T>
T tgamma_order_2(T x)
{
  using std::pow;
  using std::sqrt;

  const T       one_over_x = T(1.0L) / x;
  const T sqrt_one_over_x = sqrt(one_over_x);
```

```
  const T term0 =     sqrt(T(2.0L)
                    * std::numbers::pi_v<T>)
                    * sqrt_one_over_x;

  const T term1 =
        (  sqrt(std::numbers::pi_v<T> / T(2.0L))
      * (  sqrt_one_over_x
         * one_over_x))
         / T(6.0L);

  return    pow(x / std::numbers::e_v<T>, x)
          * (term0 + term1);
}

// Test tgamma_order_2(20.0F).
// Result:        1.216442... e+17.
// Compare with: 1.216451... e+17.
```

5.13 Template Integer Sequences

C++14 has introduced the `std::integer_sequence` utility. It can be found in the `<utility>` header of the STL. Integer sequences can be used to facilitate compile-time calculations such as summations, series expansions, etc.

A very straightforward integer sequence operation is the computation of the `sum` of a sequence of integers s_i from $i = 0 \ldots N$, for instance

$$\texttt{sum} = \sum_{i=0}^{N} s_i \,. \tag{5.3}$$

The code below shows a **constexpr** template function called `sequence_accumulate()` that computes this kind of sum at compile time.

```
template<typename integral_type,
         const integral_type... I>
constexpr integral_type sequence_accumulate(
  std::integer_sequence<integral_type, I...>)
{
  integral_type sum(0);
```

```
  for(const integral_type& i : { I... })
  {
    sum += i;
  }

  return sum;
}

constexpr
std::integer_sequence
  <unsigned, 1U, 3U, 5U, 7U> int_seq;

// 16
constexpr unsigned sum =
  sequence_accumulate(int_seq);

static_assert(sum == 16U);
```

In this code example, the sum of the integer sequence (1, 3, 5, 7), having result 16, is calculated and verified at compile time.

`std::integer_sequence` can also be used to unpack index-based template parameter packs at compile time. In Sect. "*Convert array to tuple*" in the original motivational paper for C++ compile-time integer sequences provided in [5], an example is presented that uses `std::integer_sequence` combined with `std::index_sequence` and `std::make_index_sequence` to convert an `std::array` to an `std::tuple`.

In the example below, a similar technique is used to convert a array of **`int`** to a tuple of **`float`**.

```
#include <array>
#include <tuple>
#include <utility>

template<typename array_type,
         unsigned... I>
decltype(auto)
  array_to_tuple_helper(
    const array_type& a,
    std::index_sequence<I...>)
{
  return std::make_tuple(1.0F * a[I]...);
}
```

```
template<typename T,
         const unsigned N,
         typename indices =
           std::make_index_sequence<N>>
decltype(auto)
  array_to_tuple(const std::array<T, N>& a)
{
  return array_to_tuple_helper(a, indices());
}

std::array<int, 4> a =
{{
  1, 2, 3, 4
}};

// Convert int array to float tuple.
// Here, the type of t is
// std::tuple<float, float, float, float>.
auto t = array_to_tuple(a);
```

In this example, the `array_to_tuple()` function together with its helper function convert an array with four integer elements (1, 2, 3, 4) to a tuple with four floating-point elements (1.0, 2.0, 3.0, 4.0).

We will now consider the well-known Taylor series approximation of the exponent function e^x for small argument x is given by

$$\begin{aligned} e^x &\approx \sum_{i=0}^{N} \frac{x^i}{i!} \\ &= 1 + x + \frac{x^2}{2} + \frac{x^3}{6} + \frac{x^4}{24} + \cdots . \end{aligned} \tag{5.4}$$

In the code below, the **constexpr** template function `exp_series()` computes this Taylor series approximation at compile time.

```
template<typename integral_type,
         const integral_type... I,
         typename floating_point_type>
constexpr floating_point_type exp_series(
  std::integer_sequence<integral_type, I...>,
  const floating_point_type x)
```

```
{
  static_assert(
    std::is_floating_point
      <floating_point_type>::value);

  floating_point_type term(1.0L);
  floating_point_type sum (0.0L);

  for(const integral_type& i : { I... })
  {
    sum += term;

    term *= x;
    term /= i;
  }

  return sum;
}

constexpr
std::integer_sequence
  <unsigned, 1U, 2U, 3U, 4U> int_seq;

// 1.10517...
constexpr float e =
  exp_series(
    std::integer_sequence
      <unsigned, 1U, 2U, 3U, 4U>(),
    0.1F);

static_assert((e > 1.10516F) && (e < 1.10518F));
```

The integer sequence is unpacked at compile time and used to calculate and accumulate the floating-point coefficients in the series expansion. This template is intended for the built-in floating-point data types **float**, **double** or **long double**.

We find that the compiler can properly calculate an order–4 approximation of $e^{0.1} \approx 1.10517$ at compile time with about 6 to 7 decimal digits of precision (known value is $e^{1/10} \approx 1.105170918\ldots$). This precision of this result is comparable to that of built-in **float**, assuming standard single-precision 32-bit representation according to IEEE–754:2008 [2] (see also Sect. 12.1).

Further descriptions of compile-time evaluation of floating-point functions are provided in Sect. 12.6, where several examples including computing the trigonometric sine function at compile time are presented.

References

1. B. Eckel, *Thinking in C++ Volume 2: Practical Programming* (Pearson Prentice Hall, Upper Saddle River, 2004)
2. IEEE Computer Society, *IEEE Std 1003.1 – 2008*, IEEE Standard 754–2008 (2008). http://ieeexplore.ieee.org/servlet/opac?punumber=4610933
3. N.M. Josuttis: *The C++ Standard Library: A Tutorial and Reference*, 2nd edn. (Addison-Wesley, Boston, 2011)
4. D. Vandevoorde, N.M. Josuttis, D. Gregor, *C++ Templates: The Complete Guide*, 2nd edn. (Addison-Wesley Professional, Boston, 2017)
5. J. Wakely, *Compile-time integer sequences: ISO/IEC JTC1 SC22 WG21 N3658 2013-04-18* (2019). http://www.open-std.org/JTC1/sc22/WG21/docs/papers/2013/n3658.html
6. Wikipedia, *ASCII* (2017). http://en.wikipedia.org/wiki/ASCII

Chapter 6
Optimized C++ Programming for Microcontrollers

Embedded systems software, possibly even more than other kinds of software, is time critical and often has cost-sensitive size constraints. Literally every *bit* of the microcontroller software costs precious code space and cycles. Even the most minute software weakness can lead to system-debilitating resource problems. Writing efficient C++ code for microcontrollers mandates command of the language and solid development practices. This chapter aids this endeavor by providing a selection of helpful tips for optimized C++ microcontroller programming.

6.1 Use Compiler Optimization Settings

Compiler optimization settings allow for flexible tuning of the compiler's code generation. It is possible to optimize with emphasis on space, speed or a combination thereof. GNU compilers have a particularly rich set of command-line optimization settings. See von Hagen [5] Chap. 5 and App. A for further information on optimization settings in GCC.

When researching microcontroller optimization techniques for this book, a computationally intensive code sequence rich in 32-bit operations implementing a CRC32 cyclic redundancy check [10] was benchmarked. There are numerous well-known types of CRC calculations with various bit widths ranging from 4 to 64-bits. In this benchmark, we use a CRC32 / MPEG-2 algorithm, also commonly used for data-integrity verification in MPEG-2 program streaming [6, 8]. For the investigation here, the code has been optimized and specially designed for reliable porting to 8, 16, and 32-bit microcontrollers.

After being prepared for efficient use with microcontrollers, the CRC32 code was compiled three times for our target with the 8-bit microcontroller, the first two times optimized for speed and the third time optimized for space.

C. Kormanyos, *Real-Time C++*, https://doi.org/10.1007/978-3-662-62996-3_6

Table 6.1 The code size and runtime for a CRC32 algorithm on our target with the 8-bit microcontroller with optimization tuned for space (with `-Os`) and speed (with `-O2` and `-O3`) are listed

Optimization goal	Code size CRC32 [byte]	Runtime CRC32(`0x31 ... 0x39`) [μs]
Space (with `-Os`)	280	320
Speed (with `-O2`)	320	300
Speed (with `-O3`)	1700	280

When benchmarking the CRC32 program for speed, two runs were made with optimization settings `-O2` and `-O3`. The space optimized run used the optimization setting `-Os`. For the GNU C++ compiler, optimization setting `-O2` performs most available optimizations that do not strongly increase code size. Optimization setting `-O3` performs all the optimizations of level `-O2` plus additional potentially expensive optimizations such as inline functions and loop distribution. See also [4, 5] for further details on GCC optimization settings.

Table 6.1 shows the benchmark results for the computation of the CRC32 of the 8-bit ASCII characters [9] representing the nine digits 1 to 9 (in other words: `0x31, 0x32, 0x33, 0x34, 0x35, 0x36, 0x37, 0x38, 0x39`).[1] Both the space-optimized version as well as each of the two speed-optimized versions obtain the correct result for the CRC32.[2] In particular,

$$\text{CRC32}\,(\texttt{0x31 ... 0x39}) = \texttt{0x0376'E6E7}. \tag{6.1}$$

The space-optimized version of the algorithm results in a code size about 20% smaller than the version optimized for speed with `-O2`, whereas, the version optimized for speed with `-O2` runs approximately 10% faster than the space-optimized one. In general, space and speed are opposing optimization goals. Improvements in speed are usually obtained at the cost of larger code size. The benchmark results shown above confirm this tendency.

Differences between speed and space optimization can be strongly pronounced if inline-depth control, loop unrolling and common subexpression elimination are available. In particular, the size and speed of template-intensive code can be significantly influenced by the compiler optimization settings.

[1]Calculating the CRC of the ASCII characters representing the nine digits 1 to 9 has evolved into a standard test for CRC checksum algorithms.

[2]This is another testament to the quality and language standards adherence capabilities of GCC. GCC correctly compiles this 32-bit computationally intensive CRC32 calculation with ease and absolute correctness—even for an 8-bit platform.

The impact of these factors can be observed in Table 6.1. Consider the code sizes and the runtime characteristics resulting from optimization settings `-O2` and `-O3`. The version fully optimized with `-O3` runs about 10% faster than the version optimized with `-O2`, as expected. The code size, however, significantly increases with optimization setting `-O3`. In fact, the resulting code size with optimization setting `-O3` is about a five times larger than the code size resulting from optimization setting `-O2`. Does a 10% improvement in runtime justify a five-fold increase in code size? This depends on the characteristics and design goals of the application.

It is usually best to carefully study the available compiler optimization settings. If possible, try to understand which optimization features get activated at each optimization level. Investigate the benefits of certain optimizations and determine if others are too expensive. Try to select the right overall compiler optimization settings for the project.

The CRC32 code used for the benchmark in this section is shown in its entirety below. It is also included in the companion code as a standalone header file in the reference project and also in the example project `chapter06_01`.

The CRC32 calculation is based on 4-bit nibbles. It uses a look-up table with sixteen unsigned 32-bit integer entries derived from the polynomial `0x04C1'1DB7`.

```
// chapter06_01-001_crc32_mpeg2.cpp

template<typename input_iterator>
std::uint32_t crc32_mpeg2(input_iterator first,
                          input_iterator last)
{
  // Name             : CRC-32/MPEG-2
  // Polynomial       : 0x04C11DB7
  // Initial value    : 0xFFFFFFFF
  // Test: '1'...'9'  : 0x0376E6E7

  // ISO/IEC 13818-1:2000
  // Recommendation H.222.0 Annex A

  // CRC-32/MPEG-2 Table based on nibbles.
  const std::array<std::uint32_t, 16U> table =
  {{
    UINT32_C(0x00000000), UINT32_C(0x04C11DB7),
    UINT32_C(0x09823B6E), UINT32_C(0x0D4326D9),
    UINT32_C(0x130476DC), UINT32_C(0x17C56B6B),
    UINT32_C(0x1A864DB2), UINT32_C(0x1E475005),
    UINT32_C(0x2608EDB8), UINT32_C(0x22C9F00F),
    UINT32_C(0x2F8AD6D6), UINT32_C(0x2B4BCB61),
    UINT32_C(0x350C9B64), UINT32_C(0x31CD86D3),
    UINT32_C(0x3C8EA00A), UINT32_C(0x384FBDBD)
  }};
```

```
  // Set the initial value.
  std::uint32_t crc = UINT32_C(0xFFFFFFFF);

  // Loop through the input data stream.
  while(first != last)
  {
    using std::iterator_traits;

    // Define a local value_type.
    using value_type =
      typename
      iterator_traits<input_iterator>::value_type;

    const value_type value = (*first) & UINT8_C(0xFF);

    const std::uint_fast8_t byte = uint_fast8_t(value);

    std::uint_fast8_t index;

    // Perform the CRC-32/MPEG-2 algorithm.
    index = (   (std::uint_fast8_t(crc   >> 28))
              ^ (std::uint_fast8_t(byte >>  4))
            ) & UINT8_C(0x0F);

    crc =    std::uint32_t(  std::uint32_t(crc << 4)
                           & UINT32_C(0xFFFFFFF0))
           ^ table[index];

    index = (   (std::uint_fast8_t(crc >> 28))
              ^ (std::uint_fast8_t(byte))
            ) & UINT8_C(0x0F);

    crc =    std::uint32_t(  std::uint32_t(crc << 4)
                           & UINT32_C(0xFFFFFFF0))
           ^ table[index];

    ++first;
  }

  return crc;
}
```

6.2 Know the Microcontroller's Performance

The same C++ code running on different microcontrollers can have vastly different performance on each of them. Consider the two microcontrollers used in this book, the 8-bit target running at 16 MHz and the 32-bit target clocked at 24 MHz. These are both excellent microcontrollers offering the industry's highest levels of product quality combined with world-class CPU architectures and peripherals. In addition, both microcontrollers can readily be programmed in C++ with the versatile GCC. The two microcontrollers are, however, in radically different performance classes, and this must be taken into account when assessing their ranges of application.

Table 6.2 compares the code size and runtime for the CRC32 algorithm from the previous section on these two microcontrollers. As mentioned above, this CRC32 code is computationally intensive and has numerous 32-bit integer operations. Consequently, the program runs significantly faster—about 30 times faster—on the 32-bit microcontroller than on the 8-bit machine. In addition, the code on the 32-bit target requires merely 1 / 3 of the program space taken up by the corresponding code on the 8-bit target.

The reasons for these performance and size differences are easy to understand. Basic operations on 32-bit integers such as shift and bitwise logic operations make up the core of the CRC32 algorithm. These operations require significant software support on the 8-bit microcontroller, whereas they are single opcodes on the 32-bit target. From the perspective of code size, on the other hand, 32-bit opcodes are wider than the 8-bit or 16-bit opcodes in the vocabulary of the 8-bit machine. So 32-bit code *could*, in general, be larger than corresponding 8-bit code.[3] In the case of the CRC32 algorithm, however, the improved efficiency of 32-bit operations is so overwhelmingly beneficial for the CRC32 that both the code size as well as the runtime are significantly better on the 32-bit machine.

Bigger and faster is not always better. If the application is cost-sensitive and only needs to perform a few functions, then a small 8-bit microcontroller can be the right choice. A big 32-bit microcontroller might be too expensive for the application. If,

Table 6.2 The code size and runtime for a CRC32 algorithm on our targets with 8-bit and 32-bit microcontrollers are listed. The compiler optimization has been tuned for speed

Target system	Code size CRC32 [byte]	Runtime CRC32(`0x31 ... 0x39`) [µs]
32-bit target at 24 MHz (`-O2`)	110	10
8-bit target at 16 MHz (`-O2`)	320	300

[3]In fact, it is not uncommon that code compiled for an 8-bit target is more compact than the corresponding code compiled for a 32-bit target. This usually only occurs if the code at hand can, without introducing error, be scaled to the architecture using, among other things, the so-called *native* integer width of the CPU (Sect. 6.10).

however, the microcontroller lacks sufficient resources for the requirements of the application, then the CPU may be overloaded and the system could be unreliable or might even fail. In this case, a larger 32-bit CPU may be necessary. In order to guarantee the right efficiency for the application, it is a good idea to select a microcontroller with the right performance and size.

A chunk of portable, computationally intensive microcontroller C++ code with a non-trivial result such as a CRC32 algorithm can be used as part of a benchmark to provide reliable data for proper microcontroller selection. There are additional notes on microcontroller selection in the checklist of Sect. B.1 and some details on establishing reliable runtime limits in Sect. B.3.

6.3 Know an Algorithm's Complexity

In computer science, the limiting behavior of algorithmic complexity can be characterized by the number of terms N in the algorithm's input size. The so-called *big-O* notation (pronounced *big-oh*) is often used to express the algorithmic complexity as a power of N. For example, counting loops, simple additive checksums such as CRCs and digital filters (Chap. 14) have linear complexity of order-N, in other words $O(N)$. Traditional grade-school multiplication of $a \times b$, where both a and b have N constituents, has quadratic complexity of $O\left(N^2\right)$.

The runtime of an algorithm may grow rapidly or—for all practical matters—become essentially unbounded as N increases. In such cases, it usually makes sense to find better algorithms for large N. For example, interpolation in an ordered set of points can use either a linear search or a binary search (Sect. 15.4). A linear search has complexity of $O(N)$ because it loops through the points until the interpolation pair is found. A binary search, on the other hand, uses interval-halving methods with logarithmic complexity of $O\left(\log_2 N\right)$. If N is 128, then a linear search has a maximum complexity of $\sim$128, while the corresponding binary search with the same N has a complexity of $\sim$7. Many searching and sorting algorithms in the STL use a binary search under-the-hood. These algorithms, therefore, benefit from the efficiency of logarithmic complexity, as opposed to linear complexity.

The speed of multiplication often determines the performance of mathematical calculations because many mathematical calculations spend the majority of their time doing multiplications. The efficiency of multiplication can have a particularly strong influence on common integer calculations such as graphics algorithms, sensor data analysis, hashing functions, fixed-point computations, etc. When designing code, then, writing multiplication operations in the optimum way can improve performance.

Consider the multiplication of two unsigned 16-bit integers with an unsigned 32-bit integer result. One potentially efficient way to express this multiplication in C++ on an 8-bit CPU architecture is shown below.

```
// chapter06_03-001_mul_16x16to32.cpp

std::uint16_t a = UINT16_C(55555);
std::uint16_t b = UINT16_C(61234);

void do_something()
{
  // Unsigned 16 x 16 --> 32-bit.
  // 55555 * 61234 = 3401854870

  // Cast and multiply.
  std::uint32_t result =
    a * static_cast<std::uint32_t>(b);
}
```

In this example, only one side of the multiplication of $a \times b$ has been casted to `std::uint32_t`. The compiler can, therefore, optionally choose between the better of $16 \times 16 \rightarrow$ 32-bit multiplication and $32 \times 32 \rightarrow$ 32-bit multiplication and still get the right answer. For an 8-bit CPU architecture, a good compiler will select $16 \times 16 \rightarrow$ 32-bit multiplication with algorithmic complexity $2^N = 2^2 = 4$. Casting both `a` and `b` to `std::uint32_t` would, however, force the compiler to use $32 \times 32 \rightarrow$ 32-bit multiplication with complexity $2^N = 2^4 = 16$. The code as written above is portable, yet still allows the compiler to take advantage of the optimization of half-sized multiplication when necessary.

In mathematics, graphics, signal processing, etc., a convolution such as a fast Fourier transform (FFT) is often used to reduce the computational complexity of an algorithm in the transform space. Transformation makes sense if the added runtime effort of the transformation is more than compensated by reduced work in the transform domain. There is often a cut-off point, in other words a particular value of N, above which the transformation reduces an algorithm's runtime and below which it does not.

Hardware accelerators and digital signal processors (DSP) can be integrated in microcontrollers to perform some functions faster than possible in software. They are commonly used for mathematical operations like multiplication and division, transformations such as FFT, checksums such as CRC, hashing algorithms, digital filters and other common signal processing tasks. If computationally intensive operations play a central role in the application, preferentially selecting a microcontroller with the appropriate accelerator or DSP can significantly reduce the CPU work load.

Knowing the algorithmic complexity of a computation is illustrated in examples `chapter10_08`, `chapter10_08a` and `chapter10_09` in Sects. 10.8 and 10.9 of this book. These examples involve high-precision computation of the mathematical constant π. Both the algorithmic complexity as well as the memory consumption of these particular calculations are, in fact, known in closed form. See

Eqs. 10.3 through 10.6 and their descriptions. This advanced knowledge allows us to make predictions in these examples regarding the expected runtime and memory consumption of these algorithms prior to coding and running them (or verify such predictions empirically, as shown in Table 10.2).

In general, it can be helpful to understand the algorithmic complexities and if possible to also predict the input sizes that are expected in the project. Is binary arithmetic coded with ideal operand sizes? Are linear algorithms adequate? Are optimized algorithms such as those in the STL consistently used? Does the application need hardware acceleration or even a dedicated DSP? These are the kinds of design questions that should be considered when selecting the chip and the software libraries or beginning with software design and implementation.

6.4 Use Assembly Listings

Assembly listings allow us to follow the original high-level C++ source code into the intricate depths of compiler-generated assembly language and machine-level opcodes. Analyses of assembly listings facilitate the process of designing and writing optimized code because assembly listings show the actual code which will run on the target processor in a very low-level form.

In general, the *way* in which C++ code is written strongly influences *how* the compiler generates assembly code and, ultimately, *which* machine-level opcodes are placed in the executable. A basic understanding of assembly file listings makes it possible to guide the implementations of time critical code sequences in a controlled and iterative fashion. In this way, highly optimized results can be achieved.

By studying assembly listings one will, over time, obtain an intuitive *feeling* for efficient coding. Developing this skill is a long-term process. Investigating assembly listings can teach us when and how to use templates and how to develop efficient class objects. Assembly listings can also reveal the benefits and costs of program artifacts such as runtime polymorphism, inline functions, templates, using the STL, etc.

With GNU compilers, an assembly listing can be generated with `objdump`. The object dump program is available in GCC's binary utilities (binutils) and also in the bash shell on most ∗nix-like environments. A sample command using `objdump` is shown below.

```
objdump -j .text -S my_file.o > my_file.lst
```

In this command, `my_file.o` is an object file that has been created with `g++`. The text-based results are piped into `my_file.lst`.

6.5 Use Map Files

Most linkers can generate a *map file*. Map files contain detailed information about the addresses, types and sizes of program components such as program code, static variables and objects, interrupt tables, debug sections, etc.

Map files can be used to verify that the program parts are properly located in memory and also to investigate their resource consumption. This facilitates guided size optimization. Together with assembly listings, it is possible to use map file information to iteratively find the best compromise between space and speed in the code.

With GNU compilers, a map file can be generated by the linker when creating the absolute object file. For example, `app.map` can be created with the following command.

```
g++ a.o b.o c.o -Wl,-Tldef.ld,-Map,app.map -o app.elf
```

In this command, the files `a.o`, `b.o` and `c.o` are object files compiled from the corresponding source codes `a.cpp`, `b.cpp` and `c.cpp`. The file `ldef.ld` is a linker definition file (Sect. 8.4). The absolute object file `app.elf` is the output of the linker in ELF binary format. In this particular example, the map file is a by-product of linking the program.

ELF files are in binary format and can be read with the utility program `readelf`. Again, `readelf` is a standard tool available in GCC's binary utilities (binutils) and on most ∗nix-like environments. A sample command using `readelf` is shown below.

```
readelf --syms app.elf > app.txt
```

Here, `app.elf` is the absolute object file mentioned above. The text-based results from `readelf` are piped into `app.txt`. The command program option `--syms` stands for *display the symbol table* and is equivalent to the short-hand option `-s`.

6.6 Understand Name Mangling and De-mangling

Symbol names created by the C++ compiler can be difficult to read in the map file. C++ supports namespaces, function overrides, etc. This means that symbols can potentially have the same name. For example, both integers in the two separate namespaces below are named `the_int`.

```
// chapter06_06-001_name_mangling.cpp

namespace this_space
{
  int my_integer;
}

namespace another_space
{
  int my_integer;
}
```

Same-named symbols such as `my_integer` shown above need to be uniquely identifiable. In order to guarantee non-conflicting symbol names in C++, the compiler needs to make *decorated* internal names for variables and subroutines using additional information based on the partial names of parameters, namespaces, classes, etc. These can be optionally combined with random numbers, letters and selected non-alphanumeric characters such as '&', '_', '?', '!', '@', etc. in order to create unique names.

In practice, the names that a C++ compiler makes can be so long and difficult to read that the name-decorating process has come to be known as *name mangling*. Name mangling is mandatory for establishing unequivocal symbol names in C++. As an aside, note that name mangling is dreadfully compiler-specific. Mangled names can not be found in the source code. Mangled names are constructed by the compiler for internal use and will only be encountered in map files, assembly listings, debuggers, etc.

Consider the rather uncomplicated subroutine declaration below.

```
// chapter06_06-002_name_mangling_get_event.cpp

os::event_type os::get_event(const os::task_id_type);
```

This is the name of a multitasking scheduler's `get_event()` function (such as the kind mentioned toward the end of Chap. 11). This function resides in the namespace `os`. Its sole input parameter is a **typedef**-ed enumeration for task-IDs, also located within the namespace `os`. GCC creates the mangled name shown below for the subroutine `os::get_event()`.[4]

```
// chapter06_06-002_name_mangling_get_event.cpp

_ZN2os9get_eventENS_12task_id_typeE
```

[4]Here we have used GCC 8.1.0 for the PC with `--target=x86_64-w64-mingw32`.

The essential elements of the original name are recognizable and it is possible to vaguely guess how the name mangling has augmented the original name with namespace and parameter information to create a unique name. Nonetheless, the mangled name is rather hard to read.

With the `c++filt` program, it is possible to *demangle* the mangled names created by `g++`. Yes, it really is called name demangling. The sample `bash` session below illustrates how `c++filt` can be used to demangle the mangled name of `os::get_event()`.

```
// chapter06_06-002_name_mangling_get_event.cpp

chris@chris-PC ~
$ c++filt _ZN2os9get_eventENS_12task_id_typeE
os::get_event(os::task_id_type)

chris@chris-PC ~
$ exit
```

It can also be convenient to initially produce a list of mangled names with `nm`, the *names* program, and subsequently demangle them with `c++filt`. For example, the following command extracts the mangled names from `app.elf` with `nm`, subsequently sorts them numerically (by address) and demangles them by piping the sorted list to `c++filt`.

```
// chapter06_06-002_name_mangling_get_event.cpp

nm --numeric-sort app.elf | c++filt
```

This simple command demangles even the most complicated names from `g++`, creating a clean, easy to read list of recognizable symbol names. A basic understanding of name mangling and how to de-mangle names with readily available tools can be helpful when interpreting map files.

6.7 Know When to Use Assembly and When Not to

Assembly programming, by its very nature, is non-portable and should be avoided in C++. Nonetheless, there are a few rare situations in microcontroller programming which require assembly. This can be the case either because assembly programming is the only way to accomplish the programming task at hand or because efficiency can be so radically improved for a frequently running, time critical sequence that programming it in assembly could be justified.

Assembly sequences should be buried within the microcontroller layer of the software architecture in order to shield the system and application layers from non-portability. See Sect. B.2 for information on layered software architecture. For short assembly sequences of just a few lines, it may be preferable to use so-called *inline assembly*, directly integrated into the C++ compiler via language extension. For larger assembly sequences with more than, say, ten or twenty lines (*e.g.*, for parts of an extended multitasking scheduler), a dedicated assembly file may be more appropriate.

GCC's inline assembly syntax uses microcontroller-specific assembly dialects expressed in the language of GAS, the GNU assembler. Other compilers have similar language extensions with varying forms of assembly syntax.

Inline assembly can be convenient for creating short inline functions for things such as global interrupt enable and disable, the *nop* operation, etc. For example,

```
// chapter06_07-001_assembly_sequences.cpp

namespace mcal
{
  namespace irq
  {
    // Interrupt enable/disable.
    inline void enable_all () { asm volatile("sei"); }
    inline void disable_all() { asm volatile("cli"); }
  }
}

namespace mcal
{
  namespace cpu
  {
    // The no-operation.
    inline void nop() { asm volatile("nop"); }
  }
}
```

Calling a C++ function, whether inline or non-inline, that is either partly or completely composed of assembly is done in the same way as calling a *normal* C++ function. For example, the code sample below enables global interrupts in `main()` via call of `mcal::irq::enable_all()`.

```
// chapter06_07-001_assembly_sequences.cpp

int main()
{
  // Initialize the mcal.
  // ...
```

```
  // Enable all global interrupts.
  // The enable_all() function uses assembly!
  mcal::irq::enable_all();

  // Start multitasking.
  // ...
}
```

6.8 Use Sensible Comments

A developer once wrote the following line of code:

```
// chapter06_08-001_comments.cpp

CalculateSpeed(); // Calculate speed.
```

Years after its origination, an amused code reviewer indicated that the comment does not foster understanding, but detracts from code legibility instead.

Long, redundant comments can obscure clarity and decrease readability. Comments can also be a potential source of error. Code evolves over time and comments, once written by a motivated programmer, often disagree with the code at a later stage in its evolution. In fact, a skeptical developer once said, *If the code and the comment disagree, then they are might be both wrong*. Trying to improve poorly written code by adding comments might simply sidestep an underlying quality problem because commenting clear code can be superfluous.

On the other hand, comments that explain non-obvious algorithm details or illuminate the obscure meaning of register bit assignments do *deserve* to be commented in the code. It is important to find the right compromise between legibility and understanding and, above all, it might be a good idea to write code that is clear, terse and has at least some level of being self-explanatory.

6.9 Simplify Code with `typedef` and Alias

Using **typedef** can reduce typing effort and simultaneously make code easier to read and understand. Equivalently a convenient C++11 alias (Sect. 3.20) can be used instead of a traditional **typedef**. In Sect. 7.3 ahead, we will define a template class used for generic access to microcontroller registers. In particular,

```
// chapter06_09-001_typedef_reg_access.cpp

template<typename addr_type,
         typename reg_type,
         const addr_type addr,
         const reg_type val>
struct reg_access_static
{
  static reg_type reg_get() { /* ... */ }
  static void     reg_set() { /* ... */ }
  static void     reg_and() { /* ... */ }
  static void     reg_or () { /* ... */ }
  static void     reg_not() { /* ... */ }
  static void     reg_msk() { /* ... */ }

  static void     bit_set() { /* ... */ }
  static void     bit_clr() { /* ... */ }
  static void     bit_not() { /* ... */ }
  static bool     bit_get() { /* ... */ }
};
```

The versatile `reg_access_static` template structure (see also Sects. 7.2 and 7.3) can be used for most common register manipulations. For example, we can use the `bit_not()` member to toggle `portb.5`. In other words,

```
// chapter06_09-001_typedef_reg_access.cpp

// Toggle portb.5.
reg_access_static<std::uint8_t,
                  std::uint8_t,
                  mcal::reg::portb,
                  5U>::bit_not();
```

That is quite a bit of typing for the modest task of toggling a port bit. It is, however, possible to reduce the typing effort of the toggle operation with a **typedef**. For instance,

```
// chapter06_09-001_typedef_reg_access.cpp

// Use a typedef to save tedious typing work.
typedef reg_access_static<std::uint8_t,
                          std::uint8_t,
```

```
                                            mcal::reg::portb,
                                            5U> port_b5_type;

// Toggle portb.5.
port_b5_type::bit_not();
```

It is also possible to define the type `port_b5_type` above using cppeleven alias. This is shown in Sect. 3.20.

Previously in Sect. 2.6, we defined the `led_template` class and used it to encapsulate an LED on `portb.5`. Combining the `reg_access_static` template from this example with **`typedef`**s can simplify the implementation of this class. In particular,

```
// chapter06_09-002_typedef_led_template.cpp

template<typename port_type,
         typename bval_type,
         const port_type port,
         const bval_type bval>
class led_template
{
public:
  led_template()
  {
    // Set the port pin value to low.
    port_pin_type::bit_clr();

    // Set the port pin direction to output.
    port_dir_type::bit_set();
  }

  static void toggle()
  {
    // Toggle the LED.
    port_pin_type::bit_not();
  }

private:
  static constexpr port_type pdir = port - 1U;

  // Type definition of the port data register.
  typedef reg_access_static<std::uint8_t,
                            std::uint8_t,
```

```
                                   mcal::reg::portb,
                                   port> port_pin_type;

  // Type definition of the port direction register.
  typedef reg_access_static<std::uint8_t,
                                   std::uint8_t,
                                   mcal::reg::portb,
                                   pdir> port_dir_type;
};
```

Here, the strategic use of templates and **typedef**s makes the functionality of the `led_template` class more intuitive and easier to understand. Throughout this book, **typedef** is used to simplify code and improve program clarity.

Optionally in this example, we could also use a C++11 alias to accomplish the same type definition of `port_b5_type` (see Sect. 3.20). In particular,

```
// chapter06_09-003_alias_reg_access.cpp

using port_b5_type =
  reg_access_static<std::uint8_t,
                    std::uint8_t,
                    mcal::reg::portb,
                    5U>;

// Toggle portb.5.
port_b5_type::bit_not();
```

6.10 Use Native Integer Types

Operations with integers have optimum performance if implemented with the so-called *native* integer type, in other words either the **signed** or **unsigned** version of plain **int**. These are the native integer types of the microcontroller. They are, in some sense, indigenous to the CPU architecture insofar as they typically have the same width as CPU registers. The C99 specification calls **signed** and **unsigned int** the *natural* integer types.

For example, 32-bit signed and unsigned integers are the native integer types on a 32-bit machine, whereas 8-bit integers are native to an 8-bit architecture.

Consider the loop operation shown in the subroutine `checksum()` below.

```
// chapter06_10-001_checksum_uint8_t.cpp

std::uint8_t checksum(const std::uint8_t* p,
                      const std::uint8_t len)
{
  std::uint8_t sum = UINT8_C(0);

  for(std::uint8_t i = UINT8_C(0); i < len; i++)
  {
    sum += *p;
    ++p;
  };

  return sum;
}
```

Here, the `checksum()` subroutine computes the byte-wise `std::uint8_t` sum as a simple additive summation. In other words,

$$\text{sum} = \sum_{i=0}^{i<\text{len}} p_i \,, \tag{6.2}$$

where p_i is the zero-based i^{th} element in an `std::uint8_t`-pointer sequence of length `len`, and

$$0 \le \text{len} < 256 \,. \tag{6.3}$$

We will now compile the `checksum()` subroutine for our target with the 32-bit microcontroller. The compiled subroutine requires 192 bytes of program code, which is excessively large for this simple checksum. Investigations of the assembly listing reveal that the compiler generates code for loading and manipulating 8-bit entities, struggling through numerous zero-clear actions on the three unused bytes in 32-bit registers after loading a value. These operations are inefficient for this 32-bit machine and not actually needed for the checksum algorithm.

Using native integer types improves efficiency. For example, we will now simply change the types of `sum`, `len` and the index `i` from `std::uint8_t` to the compiler's fastest 8-bit unsigned integer type `std::uint_fast8_t`. This is an integer type that is guaranteed to have at least 8-bits (but may optionally have more) and is intended to be the *fastest* one of its kind on its target architecture.[5] We have selected `std::uint_fast8_t` instead of, say, `std::uint_fast32_t` because the resulting code will also be fast on 8-bit and 16-bit architectures, yet still fulfill the requirements of the checksum operation.

The modified source code is shown below.

```
// chapter06_10-002_checksum_uint_fast8_t.cpp

std::uint8_t checksum(const std::uint8_t* p,
                      const std::uint_fast8_t len)
{
  std::uint_fast8_t sum = UINT8_C(0);

  for(std::uint_fast8_t i = UINT8_C(0); i < len; i++)
  {
    sum += *p;
    ++p;
  };

  return sum;
}
```

This minor code change switching from `std::uint8_t` with *exactly* 8 bits to `std::uint_fast8_t` with *at least* 8 bits vastly improves the algorithm's efficiency on the 32-bit target. In particular, the disassembled source code is markedly shorter.

The compiled subroutine using `std::uint_fast8_t` has a size of 24 bytes. Compare 24 bytes with the 192 bytes from the previous listing. Using the fastest 8-bit integer type for the inner loop of the algorithm has improved the space and performance by a factor of ∼8. Yes, that is right, an eightfold improvement. This striking betterment shows that using native integer types can really pay off.

6.11 Use Scaling with Powers of Two

Multiplication and division with powers of two can be replaced by efficient shift operations. For example, division by 4 can be replaced with a right-shift of 2. Multiplication with 32 can be replaced with a left-shift of 5. All good compilers do

[5]Here, the C++ specification leaves the interpretation of *fastest* open to the compiler implementation. In widespread practice, though, the *fast* integer types simply have the same width as CPU registers on the target architecture.

this automatically, assuming that the right-hand operator is a compile-time constant. One of the simplest and most effective ways to remove costly multiply and divide operations is to scale with powers of two.

Consider a software counter, in other words a prescaler, used to divide a timebase into slower secondary frequencies.

```
// chapter06_11-001_scale_with_powers_of_two.cpp

namespace { std::uint_fast8_t prescaler; }

void do_something()
{
  ++prescaler;

  do_something_at_01x_period();

  if((prescaler % 2U) == 0U)
  {
    do_something_at_02x_period();

    if((prescaler % 4U) == 0U)
    {
      do_something_at_04x_period();

      if((prescaler % 8U) == 0U)
      {
        do_something_at_08x_period();
      }
    }
  }
}
```

In this example, different software operations are carried out with frequencies of 1, 1/2, 1/4 and 1/8 of the base frequency. The conditional operations are performed with modulus 2^n so the compiler automatically uses shifts instead of costly division for them. If a base-10 prescaler were used instead, it would require division. This would be *much* less efficient. Here, we assume that the `do_something_at...()` functions are frequently-called inline functions, possibly in an interrupt service routine, quick enough in call and execution to warrant the use of optimization via `prescaler`. A further refinement is achieved by nesting the **`if`**-statements, reducing the average load of conditional-testing, making it non-constant though.

6.12 Potentially Replace Multiply with Shift-and-Add

For some microcontrollers, the compiler *might* replace potentially slow multiplication operations with fast shift-and-add sequences. This is particularly prevalent for small microcontrollers that lack fast hardware multiplication.[6] Good compilers should be capable of determining which is faster, a shift-and-add sequence or its corresponding multiplication operation. For example, a long sequence of shift-and-add algorithms might be slower than a single multiplication with a large integer or an integer having a non-simple prime factorization. Consider multiplication by 23, which needs three shifts and three adds (in other words, $23 = 16 + 4 + 2 + 1$). This is a lot of shift-and-add and it might be slower than the corresponding multiplication operation.

A typical multiplicative scaling operation is shown in the code sequence below. Here, we let the compiler decide whether to use shift-and-add or multiply.

```
// chapter06_12-001_mul_shift_and_add.cpp

std::uint32_t scale(const std::uint32_t x)
{
  // Let the compiler decide for
  // shift-and-add or multiply.
  return std::uint32_t(x * 23U);
}
```

Modern compilers are remarkably aware of these situations and preferentially select the faster of multiply or shift-and-add. Positive integers that are small-valued, even and non-prime lend themselves well to optimization with shift-and-add. Preferentially using them can lead to significant performance improvements. Check the assembly listings (Sect. 6.4) to ensure that the compiler is aware of optimization via shift-and-add, and preferentially use compile-time constants that lend themselves well to shift-and-add.

6.13 Consider Advantageous Hardware Dimensioning

Peripheral hardware can be dimensioned so that it simplifies microcontroller programming. In particular, carefully designed hardware can make it possible to write code for which the compiler can replace costly multiplication and/or division

[6] Even though most modern microcontrollers have fast hardware multiplication, replacing multiply with shift-and-add can still be useful for older microcontrollers or price-sensitive microcontrollers that emulate multiplication in software.

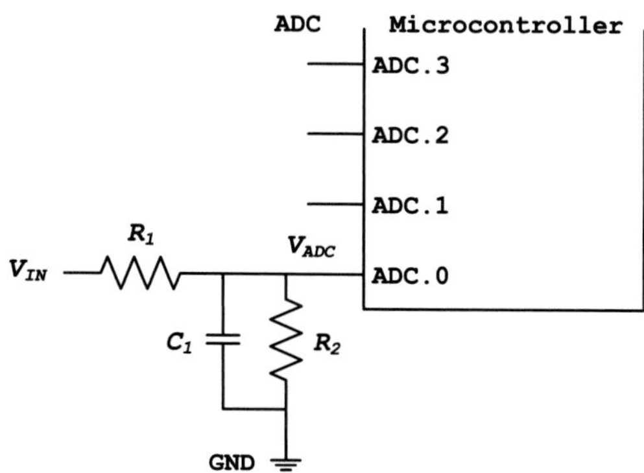

Fig. 6.1 An ADC circuit is shown

with shift operations. In this way, a few simple hardware design considerations can significantly improve software efficiency.

For example, scaling with 2^n can be directly designed into the microcontroller board. Consider the simple Analog-Digital Converter (ADC) circuit shown in Fig. 6.1. Suppose the ADC has 10-bit resolution and 5 V logic. Conversion results range from $0 \ldots 1023$ steps for ADC voltage after the voltage divider (V_{ADC}) ranging from $0 \ldots 5$ V.

We will now design the ADC circuit for input voltage $V_{IN} \lesssim 25$ V and simultaneously select the voltage divider parameters such that software conversion from ADC raw value to mV can be accomplished with multiplication by 32, which is a left shift by 5.

The maximum ADC result of 1023 steps should occur when the maximum readable input voltage of $32\,\text{V} \times 1023 = 32,736\,\text{mV}$ lies on V_{IN}. This corresponds to the maximum ADC voltage of 5 V (in other words 5000 mV) on V_{ADC}. So the voltage divider made from R_1 and R_2 should be dimensioned according to

$$\frac{V_{ADC}}{V_{IN}} = \frac{5000}{32,736} = \frac{R_2}{R_1 + R_2}, \tag{6.4}$$

which gives

$$R_2 = \left(\frac{5000}{27,736} \right) \times R_1 . \tag{6.5}$$

We will use resistors with 1% tolerance and limit the worst-case injection current on the ADC pin to $\lesssim 1/2\,\text{mA}$ for $V_{IN} = 25$ V by selecting the resistor $R_1 = 64.9\,\text{k}\Omega$. This results in $R_2 \approx 11.70\,\text{k}\Omega$, which is very close to the nearest standard 1% resistor value of $11.8\,\text{k}\Omega$. So, the final dimension of the voltage divider is $R_1 = 64.9\,\text{k}\Omega$ and $R_2 = 11.8\,\text{k}\Omega$. We can complete the circuit by selecting $C_1 = 22\,\text{nF}$ such that the low-pass filter has a rise time of $\tau \sim 1.4\,\text{ms}$.

We will now verify the dimension of the ADC circuit. For an input voltage V_{IN} of 16 V, the voltage on V_{ADC} is

$$16\,\text{V} \times \left(\frac{11.8}{64.9 + 11.8}\right) \approx 2.462\,\text{V}\,, \tag{6.6}$$

resulting in an integer conversion value of

$$1023 \times \left(\frac{2.462}{5.0}\right) = 503\,. \tag{6.7}$$

To check the result, multiply $503 \times 32\,\text{mV}$, giving $16,096\,\text{mV}$. This result is within 1% of the true value of $16,000\,\text{mV}$. The circuit dimension is quite acceptable. The accuracy of the software conversion is less than but comparable to the total hardware uncertainty, estimated by

$$\sqrt{2\,(0.01)^2 + \left(\frac{2}{1023}\right)^2} \lesssim 2\,\%\,, \tag{6.8}$$

originating from 2 resistors with 1% tolerance and 2 LSB tolerance (a typical value) for the ADC.

When the software designers write a conversion routine from ADC raw to mV for this circuit, it will be a simple multiplication with 32. For example,

```
// chapter06_13-001_adc_dimensioning.cpp

std::uint16_t raw2mv(const std::uint16_t& raw)
{
  return raw * UINT16_C(32);
}
```

6.14 Consider ROM-ability

In microcontroller programming, every resource is limited. In many projects, though, the most rare resource of all can be RAM. This makes it essential to preferentially use objects that can be entirely placed in read-only program memory, so-called *ROM-able* objects. A ROM-able object is entirely constant, in other words bitwise constant, and the compiler can save costly RAM by locating ROM-able objects in program code.

Consider the two version strings shown below.

```
// chapter06_14-001_romable_string.cpp

namespace
{
  // A version stored in a constant std::string.
  const std::string version_string1("1.23");

  // A version stored in a constant std::array.
  const std::array<char, 5U> version_string2
  {
    { '1', '.', '2', '3', '\0' }
  };
}
```

In this example, `version_string1` is stored in a constant `std::string` and `version_string2` is stored in a constant `std::array`. Both version strings have roughly equivalent values for the user. They both represent the ASCII character string "1.23" [9]. The storage requirements, however, can be quite different for the two version strings.

Benchmark examinations of various map files for a few different CPU architectures revealed that `version_string1` is generally stored in RAM, whereby `version_string2` can potentially be stored in read-only program code for some targets. Furthermore, `version_string1` typically requires the overhead of compiler-generated code for the pre-`main()` initialization of its static constructor (Sect. 8.3).

The instance of `version_string1` is not ROM-able because, among other reasons, it is a complex object involving runtime initialization with a constructor and memory allocation (*e.g.*, with a custom allocator, as described in Sect. 6.16 and Chap. 10). The instance of `version_string2`, on the other hand, is ROM-able because its contents are entirely known at compile time and can be directly placed in program code accordingly—or even used by the compiler *on-the-fly*.

In fact, instantiations of `std::array` composed of constant-valued built-in types usually fulfill the requirements for **`constexpr`** (see also Sect. 3.8). It is, therefore, possible to *force* the compiler to treat the version string as a compile-time entity by using **`constexpr`** instead of **`const`**. In particular,

```
// chapter06_14-002_romable_array.cpp

namespace
{
  // A version that is compile-time constant.
  constexpr std::array<char, 5U> version_string
  {
    { '1', '.', '2', '3', '\0' }
  };
}

static_assert(
  version_string[0U] == static_cast<char>('1'));
```

In addition, an `std::initializer_list` (Sect. A.10) whose elements are constant-valued data of built-in type is also compile-time constant. Consider, for example, the code sequence below.

```
// chapter06_14-003_romable_initializer_list.cpp

namespace
{
  constexpr std::initializer_list<char>
  version_string
  (
    { '1', '.', '2', '3', '\0' }
  );
}

static_assert(
  *version_string.begin() == char('1'));
```

In this code, **`static_assert`** (Sect. A.4) is used at compile time to verify that the value of the beginning of the sequence of version string characters is equal to one. In fact, both member functions `begin()` and `end()` of `std::initializer_list` are marked as **`constexpr`** and can be used accordingly in appropriate cases.

Initializer lists are also commonly used to initialize STL containers at compile time. For instance,

```
// chapter06_14-004_container_initializer_list.cpp

#include <initializer_list>
#include <iostream>
#include <vector>

std::vector<char>
  v( { '1', '.', '2', '3', '\0' } );
```

When programming with constant-valued objects, consider their ROM-ability and their potential to be treated as compile-time constant. Preferentially employing ROM-able constant objects can be used at discretion of the developer to save significant RAM in the project.

Example `chapter06_14`, introduces various dedicated ROM-based utilities intended to simplify potentially cumbersome program memory operations. These include

```
// See also example chapter06_14.

namespace mcal::memory::progmem
{
  template<>
  class forward_iterator;

  template<>
  class array;
}
```

The template classes above are intended to wrap low-level primitives such as `pgm_read_byte()`, `pgm_read_byte()`, etc. on out target with the 8-bit microcontroller or other similar architecture-specific instructions used for reading ROM. Abstracting such specific primitives can provide easy-to-use, intuitive support for standard iterator operations, containers and algorithms embedded in ROM.

We will now rework the CRC calculation from Sect. 6.1 using ROM-based iterators and containers. Consider, for instance, the ROM-based input data shown below. The array declaration and initialization are very similar to those of a standard array and are used accordingly in example `chapter06_14`.

```
// See also example chapter06_14.

static const
mcal::memory::progmem::array<std::uint8_t, 9U>
  app_benchmark_crc_data MY_PROGMEM =
  {{
    0x31U, 0x32U, 0x33U, 0x34U,
    0x35U, 0x36U, 0x37U, 0x38U,
    0x39U
  }};
```

Using our specialized ROM-based utilities, the resulting CRC32 calculation is essentially the same as the previous version shown in the beginning of this section. The ROM variables can, however, be iterated and read directly from constant program memory, thereby potentially saving significant amounts of precious RAM.

One trivial difference is the use of the word `MY_PROGMEM`, which is a user-invented abstraction of a memory attribute ensuring that storage is in constant program memory. `MY_PROGMEM` is implemented in a cross-development environment featuring our target with the 8-bit microcontroller in a semi-portable fashion as listed below.

```
// See also example chapter06_14.

#if defined(__GNUC__) && defined(__AVR__)
  #include <avr/pgmspace.h>

  #define MY_PROGMEM PROGMEM
#else
  #define MY_PROGMEM
#endif
```

A potential alternative for creating a custom ROM-iterator could be based on using `iterator_facade` from Boost [1]. Consider, for example, the pseudo-code below

```
// chapter06_14-005_iterator_facade.cpp

#include <boost/iterator/iterator_facade.hpp>

namespace mcal::cpu::progmem_boost
{
  template<class T>
  class iterator
    : public boost::iterator_facade<...>
```

```
  {
    // ...
    // Implement iterator.
  };
}
```

According to the *Iterator Façade* abstract in the Boost documentation [1], "...iterator_facade is a base class template that implements the interface of standard iterators in terms of a few core functions and associated types, to be supplied by a derived iterator class". Boost's *Iterator Façade* is based on the well-known and useful *curiously recurring template pattern* described in [2] and Chap. 5 of Eckel [3].

6.15 Minimize the Interrupt Frame

Interrupts can be called frequently, so it is essential they be programmed efficiently. We will now examine how the code in an interrupt service routine can influence the efficiency of its *interrupt frame*. The interrupt frame is the compiler-generated assembly code at the head and tail of the interrupt service routine that brackets the user-written code. The interrupt frame is responsible for context save and restore at interrupt entry and exit. See Sect. 9.2 for more information on interrupts.

The code below establishes a system timebase for the software project by incrementing the system_tick in timer interrupt __vector_timer Essentially the same code can be found in the general-purpose-timer part of the MCAL in the reference project of the companion code (in **namespace** mcal::gpt). It is the interrupt service routine for a timer register compare match event.

```
// chapter06_15-001_minimize_interrupt_frame.cpp

namespace
{
  volatile std::uint32_t system_tick;
}

// Attributes indicate interrupt service routine.
extern "C"
void __vector_timer() __attribute__((interrupt));

// This is the interrupt service routine.
// This interrupt occurs when the timer
// counter register reaches the value in the
// compare register.
```

```
void __vector_timer()
{
  // Increment the system tick.
  ++system_tick;
}
```

A summarized representation of the assembly code that the GNU compiler creates for the interrupt service routine `__vector_timer()` is shown below.

```
// chapter06_15-001_minimize_interrupt_frame.cpp

extern "C" void __vector_timer()
{
  ; Save the ISR context.
  ; 7 assembly lines to save the context.

  ; Increment the system tick.
  ; ++system_tick;
  ; 5 assembly lines to increment the system_tick.

  ; Restore the ISR context.
  ; 7 assembly lines to restore the context.
}
```

The interrupt frame is relatively brief. It uses 7 assembly lines to *push* a handful of registers in preparation for the interrupt. In the body of the interrupt service routine, the value of the 32-bit `system_tick` is incremented. This requires only two 8-bit CPU registers. Since just a few registers are used in the ISR, the compiler knows that it does not have to save and restore the entire register context information, just those registers that are actually used in the interrupt service routine itself. All good C and C++ compilers keep track of the registers used in an interrupt service routine. Consequently, the compiler generates a minimal interrupt frame.

If more complicated code is placed in an ISR, the interrupt frame grows accordingly. The worst situation results from calling a non-inline, external function in an ISR. Consider an alternative way to increment the system tick using a subroutine call in the interrupt service routine. For instance,

```
// chapter06_15-002_minimize_interrupt_frame.cpp

extern "C"
void __vector_timer() __attribute__((interrupt));

extern void increment_system_tick();
```

```
void __vector_timer()
{
  // Increment the system tick with a subroutine call.
  increment_system_tick();
}
```

This version of the interrupt service routine `__vector_timer()` also increments the system tick. The `system_tick` variable is, however, not directly incremented. Rather the increment operation takes place in a non-inline, external subroutine called `increment_system_tick()`.

The corresponding interrupt frame generated by the compiler for this version of the interrupt service routine is extensive. The synopsis is shown below.

```
// chapter06_15-002_minimize_interrupt_frame.cpp

extern "C" void __vector_timer()
{
  ; Save the ISR context.
  ; 17 assembly lines to save the context.

  ; Increment the system_tick in a function.
  ; increment_system_tick();

  ; Restore the ISR context.
  ; 17 assembly lines to restore the context.
}
```

This is certainly a drastic difference caused by changing just one line of code. The sizes of the head and tail in the interrupt frame have grown from 7 to 17 lines in the assembly listing. The increased size of the interrupt frame is, however, mandatory. As far as the compiler *knows*, there might be complicated operations or secondary subroutine calls in `increment_system_tick()`. In fact, the values of every register could potentially be changed or modified (*i.e.*, clobbered) by the subroutine call. Perhaps none or only some registers will really be clobbered. The compiler, however, has no clear way to determine what happens in the function call because compilers usually do not have full call-tree analysis capabilities.

Instead of saving and restoring the registers used before and after the call of `increment_system_tick()`, then, the compiler must perform a full context save and restore of *all* the user-registers in the interrupt frame of this version of `__vector_timer()` Each register is sequentially *push*-ed onto the stack in the head of the interrupt frame. Each register is subsequently restored via *pop* instruction in reverse order in the tail thereafter.

The difference in performance and size is striking. To do the same tick incrementing, the total work of the interrupt routine has grown significantly. This kind of hidden performance hit can be eliminated by avoiding complicated code in interrupts, especially calls to non-inline external functions. This minimizes the interrupt frame and can potentially save precious CPU cycles.

6.16 Use Custom Memory Management

In this section, we provide motivation to consider using specialized memory management with options such as placement-**new**. and custom allocators. Additional information on this topic can be found in Chap. 10.

Small and medium sized microcontrollers might have a tiny heap for dynamic memory allocation, or even no heap at all. When using **new** and **delete** during runtime, any heap memory that might be available could quickly run out of memory or become fragmented beyond repair, thereby taking on a non-usable, unpredictable form. In addition, the standard implementations of global operators **new** and **delete** might link in undesired object code from the C++ library or other code. For these reasons, it might be preferable to limit or avoid altogether use of operators **new** and **delete**.

Consider, for instance, the simple memory allocation and deallocation depicted in the code sample below.

```
// chapter06_16-001_operator_new.cpp

#include <algorithm>
#include <cstdint>
#include <memory>

std::uint8_t* local_buffer { nullptr };

void do_something()
{
  // Allocate 32 bytes for local_buffer
  // using global operator new.
  // This allocation might be problematic.

  local_buffer = new std::uint8_t[32U];

  // ...
}
```

```
void cleanup()
{
  // Cleanup the local_buffer memory
  // using global operator delete.
  delete [] local_buffer;

  local_buffer = nullptr;
}
```

Even straightforward memory operations like these could potentially be problematic for microcontroller programming, particularly if there are limitations caused by the lack of a heap or or other microcontroller-typical constraints.

Developers might inadvertently forget to `catch()` an `std::bad_alloc` exception thrown by a potentially failed allocation attempt, Sect. 10.7. This can result in a hard-to-find defect because a non-caught exception or a non-thrown one can be difficult to detect or reproduce during testing.

The problems outlined above can be avoided, and in most cases eliminated altogether, if careful, attentive use is made of user-defined memory management using placement-**new**. STL containers can also take advantage of user-defined memory allocation using custom allocators based on placement-**new**. User-defined allocation provides fine-grained control over dynamic memory resulting in efficient resource use and error reduction. Using placement-**new** and designing custom allocators for STL containers are described in Chap. 10.

6.17 Use the STL Consistently

Overall efficiency can potentially be improved by using the STL consistently throughout the entire microcontroller software project. In doing so, it is possible to significantly decrease coding complexity while simultaneously improving legibility, portability and performance. Manually programmed loops previously written with laborious attention to detail can become more simple, intuitive and eloquent, reducing the number of levels of scopes and their nesting. For all good compilers, the STL authors have meticulously optimized the STL implementation for the specific characteristics of the compiler at hand. One can be relatively certain that the library developers have used programming idioms that can be optimized particularly well by the compiler. When using anything from the STL, then, one can be relatively sure that these parts of the code will reach the highest level of efficiency that the compiler has to offer.

As a case in point, reconsider the checksum algorithm from Sect. 6.10. We will now investigate the efficiency of the summation if, instead of a manually-written algorithm, `std::accumulate()` from STL's `<numeric>` is used.

```
// chapter06_17-001_use_the_stl.cpp

#include <numeric>

std::uint8_t checksum(const std::uint8_t* p,
                      const std::uint_fast8_t len)
{
  // Use the STL's version of accumulate.
  return std::accumulate(p,
                         p + len,
                         std::uint_fast8_t(0U));
}
```

The implementation is a simple one-liner. In addition, it is equally or even more efficient than the second optimized implementation in Sect. 6.10. It is an interesting exercise to use reverse engineering in an effort to find out how the STL might program this particular algorithm with such high efficiency. After a few attempts via trial-and-error, the implementation shown below has been discovered. It has been found to have the same efficiency as the version in the STL that ships with the compiler for our target with the 32-bit microcontroller.

```
// chapter06_17-002_use_the_stl.cpp

std::uint8_t checksum(const std::uint8_t* p,
                      const std::uint_fast8_t len)
{
  // Compare with a manually written accumulate.
  std::uint_fast8_t   sum = UINT8_C(0);
  const std::uint8_t* end = p + len;

  while(p != end)
  {
    sum += *p;
    ++p;
  };

  return sum;
}
```

This, for example, may or may not be how one programs. It is, nonetheless, a quite efficient way to implement this particular algorithm in C++ for this compiler. When investigating this benchmark, for example, I did *not* innately program in such a way as to reach the compiler's highest efficiency. The STL implementation beat me by two lines of assembly.

A common algorithm rarely needs to be reinvented and programed from scratch because the algorithm is probably available in the STL. In addition, the STL authors have diligently optimized it and tested it. Using the STL throughout the project, therefore, results in a more legible, efficient and portable body of source code, automatically. In addition, other developers will find it easy to analyze and review source code that uses the STL because the standardized template interface encourages consistent style and reinforces coding clarity.

6.18 Use Lambda Expressions

The example below is based on part of the startup code as described in Sect. 8.3. The code initializes the static constructors before the jump to `main()`. The code calls the compiler-generated constructors in the range [`ctors_begin, ctors_end`) using the STL's `std::for_each()` algorithm.

We will now write this part of the startup code in two ways. The first uses the `std::for_each()` algorithm in combination with a lambda expression, whereas the second uses a function with static linkage.

The code below is written with a lambda expression.

```
// chapter06_18-001_use_lambdas.cpp

using function_type = void(*)();

function_type ctors_end[];
function_type ctors_begin[];

void init_ctors()
{
  std::for_each(ctors_begin,
                ctors_end,
                [](const function_type& pf)
                {
                  pf();
                });
}
```

The following code uses a static function.

```
// chapter06_18-001_use_lambdas.cpp

using function_type = void(*)();

function_type ctors_end[];
function_type ctors_begin[];

namespace
{
  void call_ctor(const function_type& pf) { pf(); }
}

void init_ctors()
{
  std::for_each(ctors_begin, ctors_end, call_ctor);
}
```

Analyses of the assembly listings of the two cases reveal that the version using the algorithm with the lambda expression has higher performance. In my benchmark, the version using the lambda expression had a savings of about 25% in runtime.

Lambda expressions offer the compiler more opportunities to optimize by making the function, its iterator range and its parameters *visible* to the compiler within a single block of code. In this way, the compiler has access to richer set of register combinations, merge possibilities, etc. and it can do a better optimization. Using lambda expressions consistently throughout an entire project can save significant code and generally improve the performance of the whole software.

6.19 Use Templates and Scalability

Templates expose all of their code, their template parameters, function calls, program loops, etc. to compiler optimization at compile time. This provides the compiler with a wealth of information allowing for many intricate optimizations such as constant folding and loop unrolling. Using templates can result in many (sometimes subtle) improvements in runtime performance.

Always remember, though, that additional template instantiation *could* result in the creation of additional code. Although this does not necessarily have to be the case because added code resulting from templates might be more than offset by size reductions gained from improved compilation efficiency. So, if performance and size really matter, consider template design. Write the code without templates.

Write it again with templates. If a mix is better, templates can be combined with non-templates. Analyze the assembly code listings along the way and strike the right balance between using templates and using non-template classes and subroutines.

As mentioned above in Sect. 6.17, one of the most effective ways in which templates can improve overall performance is simply by using the STL. In many senses, making consistent use of the STL is a kind of *global* project optimization.

Templates provide for *scalability*, allowing the scale and complexity of a particular calculation to be adjusted by changing the template parameters. For example, the timers of Sect. 15.3 are implemented as scalable templates. The best efficiency of these timers can be achieved if the template parameter uses the native unsigned integer type (Sect. 6.10). The digital filter classes of Chap. 14 are also scalable. Sect. 14.4 shows how to achieve maximum filter performance and functionality by properly scaling the template parameters.

6.20 Use Metaprogramming to Unroll Loops

Template metaprogramming can be used to improve code performance by forcing compile-time loop unrolling. An interesting analysis of this can be found by revisiting the inner product metaprogram in the code samples of Sect. 5.10.

In the original example, both sides of the dot-product ($\vec{u} \cdot \vec{v}$) including sizes of their vectors are compile-time constants, allowing for complete evaluation of the result at compile time. In other situations, however, the values of the container elements might not be known at compile time. For example, if dynamic containers with variable size unknown to the compiler are used or if a lower optimization level is applied, the inner product might *not* be unrolled by compiler optimization alone.

A template metaprogram could potentially force loop unrolling, regardless of the container type or optimization level. Care must be taken, though, to ensure that the range index stays in bounds when unrolling dynamic containers with metaprogramming. Loop unrolling with template metaprogramming is a versatile programming tool that can be employed to improve performance in many different situations.

6.21 Potential Costs of Runtime Type Information (RTTI)

Runtime type information (RTTI) can be used to obtain things such as type information. RTTI can, however, potentially incur unforeseen costs and should be used judiciously in real-time C++ programming.

Depending on the compiler, the RTTI implementation might rely on storing and manipulating data tables, performing string operations and possibly other activities, all of which may require memory and runtime for their execution. It can, therefore, be wise to analyze potential resource consumption when using RTTI.

We will now investigate the program space required by a simple use of the RTTI function `typeid()`. Consider the code sample below.

```
// chapter06_21-001_rtti_typeinfo.cpp

#include <cstring>
#include <typeinfo>

// Invent a simple, yet non-trivial
// structure for testing typeid().

struct test_typeid
{
  explicit test_typeid(const unsigned u)
    : my_u(u) { }

  ~test_typeid() = default;

private:
  unsigned my_u;
};

bool verify_typeid(const char* pn);

void do_something()
{
  // Create an instance of the struct.
  const test_typeid a(7U);

  // Obtain a const ref to the typeid of a.
  const std::type_info& tia = typeid(a);

  if(verify_typeid(tia.name()))
  {
    // tia.name() should be a constant
    // character string such as
    // "struct test_typeid" or similar,
    // depending on the compiler.

    // Do something that will not be
    // optimized away.
    ;
  }
}
```

```
// Put this subroutine in a file that
// differs from the file calling it.
bool verify_typeid(const char* pn)
{
  // Here, the actual text could be
  // "struct test_typeid" or similar,
  // depending on the compiler.

  const bool type_id_name_is_ok =
    (strcmp(pn, "struct test_typeid") == 0);

  return type_id_name_is_ok;
}
```

In this example, `typeid()` is used to obtain type information for the object `a`. The *type* of the type information is `std::type_info`. These facilities can be found in the library header file `<typeinfo>`.

The name of the type is expressed as a constant character string (*i.e.*, a **const char***). This name is verified in the subroutine `verify_typeid()`. It should be something similar to "*struct test_typeid*", with possible variations depending on the internal details of the compiler-specific implementation of `typeid()`.

This sample code has been compiled with GCC 7.3.1 for our target with the 32-bit microcontroller. A quick check of the resulting map files reveals that this simple use of the RTTI function `typeid()` requires approximately 500 bytes of program code for this system.

RTTI is enabled by default for GCC, however it can be intentionally *deactivated* with the command line option `-fno-rtti`. See also von Hagen [5] App. A, Sect. "Alphabetical GCC Option Reference" for descriptions of `-fno-rtti` and many more GCC command line options. In the companion code including all examples and the reference application, RTTI has been explicitly deactivated with this flag.

In this example, however, we are purposefully trying to measure the resource consumption caused by the use of RTTI and the `-fno-rtti` flag should not be used. In addition, the architecture of the code in this sample has been designed to prevent compile-time assessment of `typeid()`. In fact, a good modern compiler could potentially analyze type information at compile time. In order to increase the likelihood that the compiler avoids this and generates actual code to query type information during runtime instead of at compile time, the subroutine `verify_typeid()` should be placed in a source file that differs from the source file that calls it.

References

1. D. Abrahams, J. Siek, T. Witt, *Iterator Façade* (2020). http://www.boost.org/doc/libs/1_73_0/libs/iterator/doc/iterator_facade.html
2. J. Coplien, *Curiously Recurring Template Patterns*, C++ Report, February 1995, pp. 24–27
3. B. Eckel, *Thinking in C++ Volume 2: Practical Programming* (Pearson Prentice Hall, Upper Saddle River, 2004)
4. Free Software Foundation, *Invoking GCC: 3.10 Options That Control Optimization* (2018). http://gcc.gnu.org/onlinedocs/gcc/Optimize-Options.html
5. W. von Hagen, *The Definitive Guide to GCC* (Apress, Berkeley, 2006)
6. ISO/IEC, *ISO/IEC 13818–1:2000 : Information technology – Generic coding of moving pictures and associated audio information: Systems* (International Organization for Standardization, Geneva, 2010)
7. Microchip, *AVR Libc Reference Manual* (2019). http://www.microchip.com/webdoc/AVRLibcReferenceManual/index.html
8. Wikipedia, *MPEG program stream* (2015). http://en.wikipedia.org/wiki/MPEG_program_stream
9. Wikipedia, *ASCII* (2017). http://en.wikipedia.org/wiki/ASCII
10. Wikipedia, *Cyclic redundancy check* (2017). http://en.wikipedia.org/wiki/Cyclic_redundancy_check

Part II
Components for Real-Time C++

Chapter 7
Accessing Microcontroller Registers

Microcontroller programming requires efficient techniques for register access. Registers are used to configure the CPU and peripheral hardware devices such as flash access, clocks, I/O ports, timers, communication interfaces (UART, SPI™, CAN [1], etc. This chapter describes C++ methods that can be used to manipulate microcontroller registers. The focus of this chapter is placed on template methods that provide for efficient, scalable and nearly portable register access.

7.1 Defining Constant Register Addresses

When accessing microcontroller peripheral hardware such as flash access, clocks, I/O ports, timers, communication interfaces (UART, SPI™, CAN [1]), etc., C programmers often define register addresses with a preprocessor **#define**. For example,

```
// chapter07_01-001_register_address.c

// The 8-bit address of portb.
#define REG_PORTB ((uint8_t) 0x25U)
```

The preprocessor symbol REG_PORTB represents the 8-bit address of portb on our target with the 8-bit microcontroller. We first encountered this register in the LED program of Sect. 1.1. The value of portb's address is 0x25. The type of the address is uint8_t. In addition, the type information is tightly bound to the preprocessor definition with a C-style cast operator. All-in-all, this is a robust register definition in C.

As mentioned in association with the LED program in Sect. 1.10, portb can also be manipulated via direct memory access in the C language. For example, the following C code sets the value of portb to zero.

C. Kormanyos, *Real-Time C++*, https://doi.org/10.1007/978-3-662-62996-3_7

```
// chapter07_01-001_register_address.c

// Set portb to 0.
*((volatile uint8_t*) REG_PORTB) = UINT8_C(0);
```

In C++ it can be convenient to define register addresses with compile-time constant static integral members of a class type (such as a structure) or using the **constexpr** keyword. This technique has already been used a few times in this book and is described in greater detail in Sect. 4.10. In particular,

```
// chapter07_01-002_register_address.cpp

namespace mcal
{
  struct reg
  {
    static constexpr std::uint8_t portb =
      UINT8_C(0x25);

    // Additional registers
    // ...
  };
}
```

Register addresses can alternatively be defined as compile-time constants with **constexpr** possibly in a namespace for naming uniqueness. For example,

```
// chapter07_01-002_register_address.cpp

namespace mcal
{
  namespace reg
  {
    constexpr std::uint8_t portb = UINT8_C(0x25);

    // Additional registers
    // ...
  }
};
```

The `mcal::reg` structure (or the `mcal::reg` namespace) can be used to define a variety of microcontroller register addresses. Each register address needed in the program can be included as a compile-time constant. In the `mcal::reg` structure above, for example, the 8-bit address of `portb` on our target with the 8-bit microcontroller has a compile-time constant value equal to `0x25`.

Using the `mcal::reg` structure (or alternatively the namespace `mcal::reg`) it is straightforward to set `portb` via direct memory access in C++. For instance,

```
// chapter07_01-002_register_address.cpp

// Set portb to 0.
*reinterpret_cast<volatile std::uint8_t*>
  (mcal::reg::portb) = UINT8_C(0);
```

As mentioned in Sects. 1.10 and 4.10, compile-time constants are just as efficient as preprocessor **#define**s, but have superior type information. Compile-time constants are well-suited for defining register addresses because they require no storage and are available for constant folding. Register addresses defined as compile-time constants can also be used as parameters in C++ templates. This can be used to create highly optimized template class types that can be mapped to the peripherals of the microcontroller resulting in efficient hardware-access code that possesses a high degree of portability. This technique will be shown in the next section and also used for a serial SPI™ driver in Sect. 9.5.

7.2 Using Templates for Register Access

Consider the template structure below. It is a scalable template structure designed for setting the value of a microcontroller register.

```
// chapter07_02-001_register_access.cpp

template<typename addr_type,
         typename reg_type,
         const addr_type addr,
         const reg_type val>
struct reg_access_static
{
  static void reg_set()
  {
    *reinterpret_cast<volatile reg_type*>(addr) = val;
  }
};
```

The reg_access_static structure has four template parameters that specify the characteristics of the microcontroller register being accessed. The addr_type parameter defines the type of the register's address. When used with portb on our target with the 8-bit microcontroller, for example, the type of addr_type is std::uint8_t. The reg_type parameter defines the physical width of the register. This is also std::uint8_t for portb on our target with the 8-bit microcontroller.[1] The last two template parameters, addr and val, define the register's address and the value that should be written it. These two parameters must be integral compile-time constants.[2]

The reg_access_static template has one static method called reg_set(). This function is designed for setting a register at a fixed address with a constant value. For example,

```
// chapter07_02-001_register_access.cpp

// Set portb to 0.
reg_access_static<std::uint8_t,
                  std::uint8_t,
                  mcal::reg::portb,
                  UINT8_C(0x00)>::reg_set();
```

As in the examples in the previous section, this code also sets the value of the portb register to zero. This is accomplished by calling the reg_set() function. Notice how this code obtains the address of portb from the mcal::reg structure.

There are several advantages to implementing register access functions in a template class type such as reg_access_static. In particular, the reg_access_static structure offers scalability and a certain degree of portability because it can be used with different register types and microcontroller architectures.

In the code below, for example, a register with a 32-bit address and an 8-bit width is set with an 8-bit value.[3]

[1]Note, however, that the width of a register need not necessarily have the same type as its address. One often encounters registers with 8-bit width or 16-bit width on a 32-bit machine, etc.

[2]Sometimes the address and the value of a register to be set or modified are not known at compile time, but rather during program execution instead. When this happens, these parameters can not be used in templates but must be provided via other means such as through function arguments. For these cases, a second register access structure is provided in both the reference application as well as in the code snippets. It is called reg_access_dynamic.

[3]This example and the following one have been taken from code originally written to initialize timer0 for a well-known 32-bit microcontroller.

```
// chapter07_02-002_register_access.cpp

// Set timer0 mode register tm0ctl0 to zero.
reg_access_static<std::uint32_t,
                  std::uint8_t,
                  mcal::reg::tm0ctl0,
                  UINT8_C(0x00)>::reg_set();
```

In the following code, a register with a 32-bit address and 16-bit width is set with a 16-bit value.

```
// chapter07_02-002_register_access.cpp

// Set timer compare0 tm0cmp0 to 32,000 - 1.
reg_access_static<
  std::uint32_t,
  std::uint16_t,
  mcal::reg::tm0cmp0,
  std::uint16_t(32000UL - 1UL)>::reg_set();
```

In this particular example, the `timer0` compare register `tm0cmp0` had been set to a value of 32,000 − 1 with the underlying peripheral clock set to 32 MHz. The result was a compare event that subsequently triggered an interrupt at 1 kHz, thereby providing a software time base for a system tick having a frequency of approximately 1 MHz (using techniques similar to those described in Sect. 9.3).

The `reg_set()` function of the `reg_access_static` structure can be quite efficient because all the template parameters are compile-time entities. When compiling the sample above, for example, the compiler eliminates the `addr` and `val` template parameters via constant folding and is able to interpret the `reg_set()` statement as follows.[4]

```
// chapter07_02-003_register_access.cpp

*reinterpret_cast<volatile std::uint16_t*>
  (std::uint32_t(0xFFFFF694UL)) =
    std::uint16_t(32000UL - 1UL);
```

Since this code is entirely known at compile time, the compiler can optimize it to the best of its ability. In fact, the compiler could potentially substitute a single

[4]Here we are using the actual physical 32-bit address of the `timer0` compare register `tm0cmp0` (which is `0xFFFFF694`) for this particular microcontroller-specific peripheral timer.

opcode for the operation if one is available for the CPU architecture and if the compiler is capable of recognizing the opportunity to do so.

7.3 Generic Templates for Register Access

Based on the `reg_set()` subroutine in the previous section, we can add additional functions such as logic and bit operations to the `reg_access_static` For example, we will now add a function for the logical `or` operator to the `reg_access_static` structure.

```
// chapter07_03-001_register_access.cpp

template<typename addr_type,
         typename reg_type,
         const addr_type addr,
         const reg_type val>
struct reg_access_static
{
  static void reg_set()
  {
    *reinterpret_cast<volatile reg_type*>(addr) = val;
  }

  static void reg_or()
  {
    *reinterpret_cast<volatile reg_type*>(addr) |= val;
  }
};
```

The `reg_or()` function is similar to the `reg_set()` function. The only difference is that instead of setting the value with assignment via **`operator`**`=()`, the logical **`or`** operator is used. This subroutine can be used for **`or`**-ing the value of a register at a fixed address with a constant value. In particular,

```
// chapter07_03-001_register_access.cpp

// Set portb.5 to 1.
reg_access_static<std::uint8_t,
                  std::uint8_t,
                  mcal::reg::portb,
                  UINT8_C(0x20)>::reg_or();
```

This code is equivalent to

```
// chapter07_03-001_register_access.cpp

*reinterpret_cast<volatile std::uint8_t*>(0x25)
  |= UINT8_C(0x20);
```

and it performs a bitwise **or** of `portb` with the 8-bit value `0x20`. This sets `portb.5` on our target with the 8-bit microcontroller to high.

As a final example, we will add a dedicated bit operation to the `reg_access_static` structure. For example,

```
// chapter07_03-002_register_access.cpp

template<typename addr_type,
         typename reg_type,
         const addr_type addr,
         const reg_type val>
class reg_access_static
{
  // ...

  static void bit_not()
  {
    *reinterpret_cast<volatile reg_type*>(addr)
      ^= reg_type(reg_type(1U) << val);
  }
};
```

The `bit_not()` function performs a bitwise exclusive-or (`xor`) of a register with a bit mask containing a single bit. Notice that the `val` parameter here is used to create the bit mask from 1 shifted left `val` times.

The `bit_not()` function has the effect of toggling a bit from low to high and vice versa. For example,

```
// chapter07_03-002_register_access.cpp

// Toggle portb.5.
reg_access_static<std::uint8_t,
                  std::uint8_t,
                  mcal::reg::portb,
                  UINT8_C(5)>::bit_not();
```

This code is equivalent to

```
*reinterpret_cast<volatile std::uint8_t*>(0x25)
  ^= UINT8_C(0x20);
```

and it performs a bitwise `xor` of `portb` with `0x20`. This toggles `portb.5` on our target with the 8-bit microcontroller from low to high and vice versa. It is the same register manipulation that was introduced in the `toggle()` function of the `led` class in the LED program of Sect. 1.1.

The `reg_access_static` structure (or any similar template register access mechanism) could include useful functions for register set, logical `or` and bitwise `xor`. It is straightforward to add even more register functions. For example, the synopsis of a relatively complete extended `reg_access_static` structure is shown below.

```
// chapter07_03-003_register_access.cpp

template<typename addr_type,
         typename reg_type,
         const addr_type addr,
         const reg_type val>
struct reg_access_static
{
  static reg_type reg_get() { /* ... */ }
  static void     reg_set() { /* ... */ }
  static void     reg_and() { /* ... */ }
  static void     reg_or () { /* ... */ }
  static void     reg_not() { /* ... */ }
  static void     reg_msk() { /* ... */ }

  static void     bit_set() { /* ... */ }
  static void     bit_clr() { /* ... */ }
  static void     bit_not() { /* ... */ }
  static bool     bit_get() { /* ... */ }
};
```

This version of the `reg_access_static` structure is contained in the companion code of this book. It has functions for register set, get, various bit operations, etc. In this sense, the `reg_access_static` structure is a scalable, flexible and generic template that can be used for register manipulation on any microcontroller platform, regardless of the address widths and register types.

Register manipulation code is not usually considered to be truly portable because the addresses and purposes of registers are specific to a given microcontroller. The `reg_access_static` structure, however, makes no use of these kinds of microcontroller-specific details. So as long as the details such as numerical address values are localized somewhere else (for instance as in something like the `mcal::reg` structure), the `reg_access_static` structure remains relatively portable—perhaps nearly as portable as possible for microcontroller register access.

7.4 Bit-Mapped Structures

Microcontroller programmers often use C-style structures with bit-fields to represent bits or groups of bits in a register. This is useful for creating a bit-mapped structure that identically matches the bits in a hardware register. For example, an 8-bit port register can be represented with the C-style bit-mapped structure shown below.

```
// chapter07_04-001_register_access_bitmap.cpp

typedef struct bit8_type
{
  std::uint8_t b0 : 1;
  std::uint8_t b1 : 1;
  std::uint8_t b2 : 1;
  std::uint8_t b3 : 1;
  std::uint8_t b4 : 1;
  std::uint8_t b5 : 1;
  std::uint8_t b6 : 1;
  std::uint8_t b7 : 1;
}
bit8_type;
```

Using the `bit8_type` structure is straightforward. For example, the code below sets `portb.5` to high.

```
// chapter07_04-001_register_access_bitmap.cpp

reinterpret_cast<volatile bit8_type*>
  (mcal::reg::portb)->b5 = 1U;
```

It can also be convenient to combine a built-in integral type with a bit-mapped register structure in a C-style union. In particular,

```
// chapter07_04-002_register_access_union.cpp

typedef union reg_map_c
{
  std::uint8_t value;
  bit8_type    bits;
}
reg_map_c;
```

In this example, we have combined the eight bits in the `bit8_type` structure with an `std::uint8_t` in the `reg_map_c` union. This makes it possible to manipulate either the individual bits or the value of the entire register, depending on the coding situation. Consider, in particular,

```
// chapter07_04-002_register_access_union.cpp

// Set portb to 0.
reinterpret_cast<volatile reg_map_c*>
  (mcal::reg::portb)->value = UINT8_C(0);

// Set portb.5 to 1.
reinterpret_cast<volatile reg_map_c*>
  (mcal::reg::portb)->bits.b5 = 1U;
```

In C++, it is possible to take the concept of the `reg_map_c` union and create from it a generic template class type for register mapping. We will now exemplify this in the following code sample.

```
// chapter07_04-003_register_access_reg_map.cpp

template<typename addr_type,
         typename reg_type,
         typename bits_type,
         const addr_type addr>
struct reg_map
{
  static reg_type& value()
```

```
  {
    return *reinterpret_cast<reg_type*>(addr);
  }

  static bits_type& bits()
  {
    return *reinterpret_cast<bits_type*>(addr);
  }
};
```

The `reg_map` class has four template parameters similar to the ones in the `reg_access_static` structure from the previous sections of this chapter. In particular, the `addr_type` parameter specifies the type of the register's address. The `addr` parameter provides the constant value of the register's address. The `reg_type` gives the type of the register. The new `bits_type` template parameter is intended to be a bit-mapped structure representing the bit-mapping of the hardware register.

These template parameters are used by `reg_map`'s two static members functions to provide access the register as a value or a bit-map. The `value()` subroutine returns a non-constant (i.e., capable of being modified) reference to the value of the register. The `bits()` subroutine returns a non-constant reference to the bit-mapped value of the register.

Imagine we would like to use the `reg_map` class to access the `portb` register on our target with the 8-bit microcontroller. In particular,

```
// chapter07_04-003_register_access_reg_map.cpp

// Set portb to 0.
reg_map<std::uint8_t,
        std::uint8_t,
        bit8_type,
        mcal::reg::portb>::value() = UINT8_C(0);

// Set portb.5 to 1.
reg_map<std::uint8_t,
        std::uint8_t,
        bit8_type,
        mcal::reg::portb>::bits().b5 = 1U;
```

Bit-mapped structures can potentially provide an intuitive and effective way to identically *map* a software structure to a hardware register or set of registers. Using bit-mapped structures in this way can, however, result in potentially non-portable code. One of the reasons for this is because, according to specification, the types of bit-field members in a structure must be one of **`signed`** or **`unsigned int`**.

Bit-mapped structures, however, often use other integral types in order to obtain the right structure packing for the hardware.

If bit-mapped structures are to be used, one may want to check how the compiler handles them and ensure that the desired bit-mapping is actually carried out. The code of bit-mapped structures should also be clearly marked with a comment indicating potential non-portability.

Reference

1. ISO, *ISO 11898–1:2003 : Road vehicles – Controller Area Network (CAN) – Part 1: Data Link Layer and Physical Signaling* (International Organization for Standardization, Geneva, 2003)

Chapter 8
The Right Start

The *startup code* is called by the microcontroller hardware after reset and is the first code to execute before calling the `main()` subroutine. The startup code predominantly consists of initialization code and may include, among other things, CPU-initialization, zero-clear RAM initialization, ROM-to-RAM static initialization and static constructor call initialization. The compiler's default startup code is often tightly bound to the compiler's runtime libraries and may not be available as source code. In addition, even if the source of the startup code is available, it can be hard to understand because it may be written in assembly and cluttered with a multitude of options required for supporting a variety of chip derivatives. This chapter describes how to implement a custom startup code and its initializations written almost entirely in C++, from reset to `main()`.

8.1 The Startup Code

It can be preferable to write a custom version of the startup code. This makes it possible to include specialized initialization mechanisms for memory, I/O pins, oscillators, clocks, timers, watchdogs, etc. These might otherwise be postponed to an unduly late time, such as in the `main()` subroutine. The flowchart of a custom startup code is shown in Fig. 8.1.

We will now examine the main parts of a potential startup code going step-by-step through a real example. The code below shows the implementation of the startup code for our target with the 8-bit microcontroller in the reference project of the companion code.[1]

[1] An additional relatively complete description of a startup code in action on a completely different 32-bit single-board computer system is provided in the description of example `chapter10_09` in

C. Kormanyos, *Real-Time C++*, https://doi.org/10.1007/978-3-662-62996-3_8

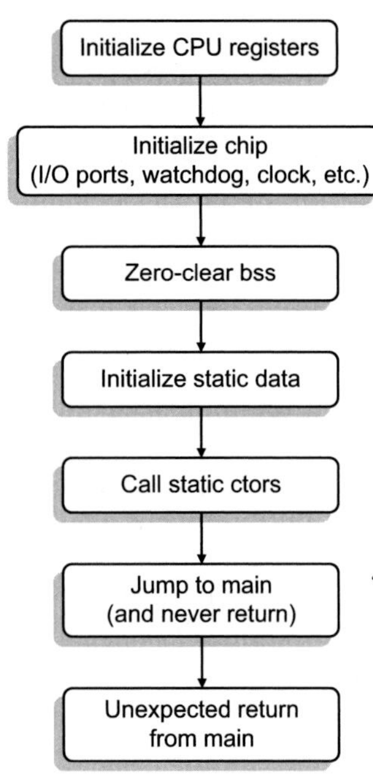

Fig. 8.1 The flowchart of a customized startup code is shown

```
// chapter08_01-001_my_startup.cpp

void __my_startup()
{
  // Load the sreg register.
  asm volatile("eor r1, r1");
  asm volatile("out 0x3f, r1");

  // Set the stack pointer.
  asm volatile
    ("ldi r28, lo8(__initial_stack_pointer)");
  asm volatile
    ("ldi r29, hi8(__initial_stack_pointer)");

  // Load the sph register (stack pointer high).
  asm volatile("out 0x3e, r29");

  // Load the spl register (stack pointer low).
  asm volatile("out 0x3d, r28");
```

Sect. 10.9. The general purpose and flow of the startup code is, nonetheless, the same even though these are two vastly different systems.

```
  // CPU Initialization, including watchdog,
  // port, oscillators (i.e. clocks).
  mcal::cpu::init();

  // Initialize statics from ROM to RAM.
  // Zero-clear default-initialized static RAM.
  crt::init_ram();
  mcal::wdg::secure::trigger();

  // Call all constructor initializations.
  crt::init_ctors();
  mcal::wdg::secure::trigger();

  // Call main (and never return).
  asm volatile("call main");

  // Catch an unexpected return from main.
  for(;;)
  {
    // Replace with a loud error if desired.
    mcal::wdg::secure::trigger();
  }
}
```

The first part of the startup code initializes the some CPU registers. For other architectures, it may also be necessary to initialize other kinds of CPU registers and data pointers needed for rudimentary operations such as bus access, subroutine calls, etc. These kinds of registers are target-specific and need to be carefully studied in the microcontroller handbook. This portion of the startup code usually needs to be written in assembly or, as is the case above, with one or more lines of inline assembly.

The remaining parts of the startup code can often be written in C++. These include low-level hardware initialization (Chap. 9), RAM initialization, static constructor initialization and the jump to `main()`.

This example of the startup code is primarily written in C++ with small hybrid assembly components. This makes it convenient to distribute the important parts of the initialization sequence in procedural subroutines with easy-to-recognize names. With this technique, it is possible to implement the startup codes for different microcontrollers in a similar fashion. This can potentially be a significant improvement over the all-assembly implementations predominantly found for many compilers and most target systems.

8.2 Initializing RAM

There are usually at least two kinds of RAM that need to be initialized in the startup code that runs prior to the `main()` subroutine. These include both non-initialized static variables as well as the initialized ones. Non-initialized, non-local static variables need to be zero-cleared. Non-local static variables that are initialized must be set with constant values extracted from a so-called ROM-to-RAM table. For example,

```
// chapter08_02-001_static_init_ram.cpp

namespace
{
  // Needs default initialization (zero-clear).
  std::uint16_t flag;

  // Needs ROM-to-RAM initialization.
  std::uint8_t  version = UINT8_C(3);
}
```

In this code, there are two static variables having file-level scope, `flag` and `version`. We note that the `flag` variable is not explicitly initialized. As such it needs to be initialized with its so-called *default value*, which is zero. The variable `version` is initialized with the value 3. Its initialization is carried out with a runtime mechanism that copies into it the initial value of 3.

All non-initialized static variables such as the `flag` variable shown above need to be zero-cleared. In order to facilitate this, the compiler and linker have located variables of this kind in special linker section. For GNU compilers, this is often called the `bss`-section.

In order to zero-clear the `bss`-section, the startup code loops through the `bss`-section from begin to end and sets its contents to zero. The code below shows a potential implementation of the zero-clear mechanism for the `bss`-section.

```
// chapter08_02-002_static_init_bss.cpp

// Linker-defined begin and end of the .bss section.
extern std::uint8_t* _bss_begin;
extern std::uint8_t* _bss_end;

void init_bss()
{
  // Clear the bss segment.
  std::fill(_bss_begin, _bss_end, 0U);
}
```

The `init_bss()` subroutine uses `std::fill()` to loop through the `bss`-section and zero-clear its contents. Notice how the external symbols `_bss_begin` and `_bss_end` have been made available to simplify the coding. These symbols are typically defined in the so-called *linker script*. We will discuss the linker script and some methods for defining these kinds of symbols in Sect. 8.4 below.

Initialized static variables such as `version` shown above should be initialized with constant values. The compiler and linker have, once again, created two special linker sections to facilitate these kinds of initializations. One linker section contains all the static variables needing initialization. This is often called the `data`-section. The other linker section contains a table of the actual values used to initialize them. This is sometimes referred to as the `rodata`-section, as in "read-only" data (or a similar tool-specific section name).

In order to initialize the static variables, then, all one needs to do is loop through the `data`-section and copy to it the contents of the `rodata`-section. For example,

```
// chapter08_02-003_static_init_data.cpp

// Linker-defined begin of rodata.
extern std::uint8_t* _rodata_begin;

// Linker-defined begin and end of data.
extern std::uint8_t* _data_begin;
extern std::uint8_t* _data_end;

void init_data()
{
  // Calculate the size of the data section.
  const std::size_t count = _data_end - _data_begin;

  // Copy the rodata section to the data section.
  std::copy(_rodata_begin,
            _rodata_begin + count,
            _data_begin);
}
```

The initialization sequence in `init_data()` uses `std::copy()` to loop through the `rodata`-section and copy the ROM-to-RAM initialization contents to the `data`-section. Again, this mechanism makes use of external symbols that have been defined in the linker script (Sect. 8.4).

8.3 Initializing the Static Constructors

As mentioned in Sect. 1.5, static constructors of class types have compiler-generated constructor code. The same is true for static variables initialized with the return value of a subroutine. For example, recall the constructor call of `led_b5`

```
// chapter08_03-001_static_constructor.cpp

// Create led_b5 on portb.5.
const led led_b5
{
  mcal::reg::portb,
  mcal::reg::bval5
};
```

This code was first introduced in the LED program of Sect. 1.1. It has a static instance of the `led` class called `led_b5`. Since `led_b5` must be fully formed before it can be used in `main()`, the compiler has automatically generated a subroutine for its constructor. For our target with the 8-bit microcontroller, for example, GCC creates a subroutine named `_GLOBAL__I_main()`. This compiler-generated subroutine carries out the initialization of `led_b5`.

The pseudo-code that the compiler generates for `_GLOBAL__I_main()` is shown below.

```
// chapter08_03-001_static_constructor.cpp

000000ba <_GLOBAL__I_main>:
;led(const port_type p, const bval_type b) : port(p),
;                                            bval(b)

; 4 assembly lines to initialize port, bval.

;{
;  // Set the port pin to low.
;  *reinterpret_cast<volatile bval_type*>(port)
;  &= static_cast<bval_type>(~bval);

   ; 1 assembly line to clear the port pin.

;  // Set the port pin to output.
;  *reinterpret_cast<volatile bval_type*>(port - 1U)
;  |= bval;

   ; 1 assembly line to set the port direction.
;}
```

The original C++ source code from the `led` class constructor has been included in this assembly listing in the form of comments. With the source code included, it is possible to recognize the assembly code sequences generated for both the constructor initialization list and also for setting the port pin direction to output and the port pin value to low.

Most C++ programs have numerous objects requiring construction. In general, the compiler generates a subroutine with construction code for each one of them. The addresses of these compiler-generated subroutines are stored in a special linker section. Different compilers use different names for the linker section containing the constructors. Section names such as `ctors`, `init_array` and the like are used by ports of GCC. Regardless of what the linker section is called, however, it is essentially just a table of function pointers.

In order to initialize the constructors, then, a mechanism is needed that loops through the `ctors`-section and sequentially calls each compiler-generated constructor function. For example,

```
using function_type = void(*)();

// Linker-defined begin and end of the ctors.
extern function_type _ctors_begin[];
extern function_type _ctors_end  [];

void init_ctors()
{
  std::for_each(_ctors_begin,
                _ctors_end,
                [](const function_type& pf)
                {
                  pf();
                });
}
```

This code was first introduced in Sect. 6.18 as an example intended to provide motivation to use lambda expressions. As mentioned in that section, the code calls the compiler-generated constructors in the range

$$\big[\texttt{ctors\_begin},\ \texttt{ctors\_end}\big), \tag{8.1}$$

where the STL's `std::for_each()` template from `<algorithm>` is used. Thereby, the code for each compiler generated static constructor is executed and every static class object is fully formed before the jump to `main()`. Actually, the real code runs through the range of constructors in reverse order using an iterator of type `std::reverse_iterator` because GCC stores its static constructors in reverse order. This detail is, however, irrelevant for the example.

8.4 The Connection Between the Linker and Startup

In the previous two sections, we have discussed three initializations that occur before the jump to `main()`. These include zero-clearing the `bss`-section, initializing statics in the `bss`-section and calling all of the static constructors in the `ctors`-section.

One might wonder how convenient symbols like `_bss_begin` and `_bss_end` for the `bss`-section or `_ctors_begin` and `_ctors_end` for the `ctors`-section come into existence and can be used like normal variables in C++ code. The answer lies in the so-called *linker definition file*, also known as a linker script. The linker definition file defines the addresses where all program components will be located. For example, all normal program code (also known as `text`) will be located in the `text`-section. Static variables that need to be zero-cleared will be located in the `bss`-section, and so on.

The linker definition file needs to be written with intimate knowledge of the microcontroller memory map in order to ensure that each program component gets located in the right place. Components such as program code, the list of static constructors and the ROM-to-RAM data table should be located in the read-only program memory of the microcontroller. The contents of the `bss`-section and the `data`-section need to be placed in static RAM.

GNU compilers use a specific language for the linker definition file. A simplified example of a linker definition file is shown below. For additional information on GNU linker definition files, turn to Barr's book [1].

```
ENTRY(start)

MEMORY
{
  ROM(rx)  : ORIGIN = 0x08000000, LENGTH = 128K
  RAM(rwx) : ORIGIN = 0x20000000, LENGTH = 8K
}

SECTIONS
{
  /* Program code, read-only data and static ctors */
  .text :
  {
    . = ALIGN(4);
    KEEP(*(.isr_vector))
    *(.text)
    *(.text.*)
    *(.rodata)
    *(.rodata*)
    _ctors_begin = .;
```

```
    KEEP (*(SORT(.init_array.*)))
    KEEP (*(.init_array))
    _ctors_end = .;
  } > ROM

  _rom_data_begin = .;

  /* The ROM-to-RAM initialized data section */
  .data :
  {
    . = ALIGN(4);
    _data_begin = . ;
    *(.data)
    *(.data.*)
    _data_end = . ;
  } > RAM AT > ROM

  /* The uninitialized (zero-cleared) data section */
  .bss :
  {
    . = ALIGN(4);
    _bss_begin = .;
    *(.bss)
    *(.bss*)
    _bss_end = . ;
  } > RAM
}
```

This sketch of a linker definition file shows how the most important linker sections and symbols can be defined in a linker script. It can be difficult to understand the language of the GNU linker. Even without understanding every part of it, though, it is possible to gain an intuitive feeling of how the linker definition file works. There are three main parts in this linker script. The first part uses the `ENTRY` directive to define the startup routine `startup()`. This is the routine that was first shown in Sect. 8.1. The second part of the linker definition file uses the `MEMORY` directive to define two important memory classes, `ROM` and `RAM`. The `MEMORY` directive also defines the addresses and sizes of the `ROM` and `RAM`. The third part of the linker definition file uses the `SEC-TIONS` directive to define how the various program sections should be located in `ROM` and `RAM`.

It is possible to define variables (in other words symbols) in the linker definition file. Symbols defined in this way become available for use in the source code as variables. For example, the `bss`-section begins at address `0x20000000` in `RAM` and includes all non-initialized statics. Bracketing the begin and end of the lines describing the `bss`-section are the symbols `_bss_begin` and `_bss_end`. These symbols can actually be used in C++ code, in particular for the C++ loop that initializes the bss-section in init_bss above. Similarly, other symbols such as _ctors_begin, _ctors_end, _data_begin, _data_end, etc. can be defined in the linker script used in their respective C++ initialization loops.

8.5 Understand Static Initialization Rules

Now that we have discussed RAM and static constructor initialization, we will consider some of the storage requirements pertaining to initialization. C++ has several rules governing the initialization of statics. It is essential to understand these rules in order to avoid redundant initialization code and avoid subtle pitfalls such as using an object before it has been initialized.

All statics with file-level or global scope, both built-in types and class types alike, are initialized by the startup code before the jump to main(). In particular, consider non-local statics with one of the built-in integer, character, floating-point or Boolean types. These are initialized by the startup code with the appropriate default values such as 0 for type **int**, '\0' for type **char**, 0.0F for type **float**, **false** for type **bool**, etc.

The statics in following code, for example, do not need explicit initialization because they are default initialized by the startup code.

```
// chapter08_05-001_static_initialization.cpp

namespace
{
  char         c;    // Default initialized.
  std::uint8_t key;  // Default initialized.
  float        f;    // Default initialized.
  bool         flag; // Default initialized.
}

struct protocol_frame
{
  static std::uint8_t count;
  protocol_frame() { }
};

// Default initialized.
std::uint8_t protocol_frame::count;
```

If the default value is the desired one, then explicit initialization is not necessary. For instance,

```
// chapter08_05-002_static_initialization.cpp

namespace
{
  char          c    = '\0';         // Not necessary.
  std::uint8_t key  = UINT8_C(0); // Not necessary.
  float         f    = 0.0F;         // Not necessary.
  bool          flag = false;        // Not necessary.
}

struct protocol_frame
{
  static std::uint8_t count;
  protocol_frame() { }
};

// Not necessary.
std::uint8_t protocol_frame::count = UINT8_C(0);
```

These static variables do no not need explicit initialization. In fact, extra initialization when the default suffices is redundant. It increases both the code size and the runtime of the pre-`main` by adding more entries to the initialization sequence.

A static with an initial value that differs from the default value must be explicitly initialized. For example,

```
// chapter08_05-003_static_initialization.cpp

namespace
{
  char          c    = 'A';          // Explicit init.
  std::uint8_t key  = UINT8_C(3); // Explicit init.
  float         f    = 4.56F;        // Explicit init.
  bool          flag = true;         // Explicit init.
}
```

```
struct protocol_frame
{
  static std::uint8_t count;
  protocol_frame() { }
};

// Explicit init.
std::uint8_t protocol_frame::count = UINT8_C(42);
```

8.6 Avoid Using Uninitialized Objects

The process of static initialization has runtime characteristics that should be kept in mind when designing stable software. For example, all non-subroutine-local statics *must* be initialized by the compiler before the call to `main()`. This is simply a necessity.

Furthermore, a non-subroutine-local static is *guaranteed* to be initialized before any function in its containing file uses it. This rule is simple enough to keep in mind for any given file. Because C++ supports the translation of separate files, though, no rule governs the *order* of initialization of different files. Even though this aspect of the C++ language is well-known, it understandably remains a big source of confusion that can lead to an unpredictable program crash.

We will now examine a case in point. Consider a simple structure called `alpha` and a static instance of it named `instance_of_alpha` residing in `alpha.cpp`. For example,

```
// chapter08_06-001_singleton_object.cpp

struct alpha
{
  alpha(const std::uint16_t a) : value(a) { }

  std::uint16_t value;
};

// In file alpha.cpp.
alpha instance_of_alpha { 3U };
```

Imagine, in addition, that the `value` member of `instance_of_alpha` is used to initialize an unrelated static unsigned integer called `beta` residing in `beta.cpp`. In particular,

```
// chapter08_06-001_singleton_object.cpp

// In file beta.cpp.
extern alpha instance_of_alpha; // From alpha.cpp.

// Oops, instance_of_alpha might be uninitialized!
// Meaning that beta's value might be unexpected.

std::uint16_t beta { instance_of_alpha.value };
```

Suppose that the static contents of `beta.cpp` just happen to be initialized *before* those of `alpha.cpp`. In this case, the `instance_of_alpha` object in `alpha.cpp` will be uninitialized when `beta` in `beta.cpp` tries to use it. This subtle, almost hidden, phenomenon can truly wreak havoc in the code of the unwary programmer. It afflicts simple built-in types and class types alike, regardless of an object's complexity. This makes it all too easy to use something *before* it has been initialized.

A well-known design pattern using a so-called *singleton instance* remedies this problem.

```
// chapter08_06-002_singleton_object.cpp

// In file alpha.cpp.
alpha& safe_reference_to_alpha()
{
  static alpha instance_of_alpha { 3U };

  return instance_of_alpha;
}

// In file beta.cpp.
// OK, but mind the overhead.
extern alpha& safe_reference_to_alpha();

// OK, safe_reference_to_alpha() returns
// an initialized, fully-formed object.
std::uint16_t beta
{
  safe_reference_to_alpha().value
};
```

The singleton instance solves this problem because a subroutine-local static will be initialized *one time only*, at the moment first encountered in the subroutine. The solution is simple enough, but it comes at the expense of overhead. In particular, the singleton instance has overhead for the call of the subroutine `safe_reference_to_alpha()`. This overhead includes both the first-time initialization of the local static object `instance_of_alpha` as well as the necessity to check its *guard-variables* every time `safe_reference_to_alpha()`. is called.[2] See Item 47 in Meyers [2] for additional details on the singleton instance.

8.7 Jump to `main()` and Never `return`

Near the end of the startup code listed in Sect. 8.1, there is a line which jumps to `main()`. In particular,

```
// chapter08_07-001_my_startup_and_main.cpp

extern "C" void __my_startup()
{
  // ...

  // Call main (and never return).
  asm volatile("call main");

  // ...
}
```

Since the C++ compiler forbids explicit call of the `main()` subroutine, the jump to `main()` must be programmed in assembly. This line, of course, must be written in the local assembly dialect of appropriate for the microcontroller being used.

In the startup code presented in this chapter, the program is never expected to return from `main()`. This is typical for a microcontroller application that starts at power-up and never stops execution, only stopping upon hard power-down (i.e., switching off the microcontroller power). If the application stops with a controlled shutdown, then the return from `main()` must be properly handled and a mechanism for calling each static destructor should be implemented.

[2]Guard-variables are compiler-generated flags used to mark the if a given file-local static has been initialized—a sort of "I am already set" marker preventing multiple initialization. Note also, as an aside, that guard-variables can have strongly distorted mangled names.

Most of the programs in this book are never expected to return from main(). An unexpected exit from main() is handled with an infinite loop that triggers the watchdog timer and never breaks. For example,

```
// chapter08_07-001_my_startup_and_main.cpp

extern "C" void startup()
{
  // ...

  // Catch an unexpected return from main.
  for(;;)
  {
    // Replace with a loud error if desired.
    mcal::wdg::secure::trigger();
  }
}
```

The strategy used here is to keep the hardware in its last known state and undertake no further actions as a sensible error reaction to an unexpected exit from main(). This may or may not be an appropriate reaction for a given microcontroller application. A reset or some other kind of error reaction may be better suited to another application.

8.8 When in main(), What Comes Next?

One might be tempted to implement large parts of the application in the main() subroutine. It can, however, be considered poor style to do so because this detracts from modularity and clarity of design.

The main() function in a typical real-time C++ project, therefore, might consist of just a few lines. For instance,

```
// chapter08_07-002_main_and_scheduler.cpp

namespace mcal
{
  void init();
}

void scheduler();
```

```
int main()
{
  // Initialize the microcontroller layer.
  mcal::init();

  // Call the multitasking scheduler
  // and never return.
  scheduler();
}
```

Here, `main()` is literally a two-liner. After initializing the MCAL (Sect. B.2), the program calls its multitasking scheduler. This scheme for `main()` is also used in Sect. 11.5.

Control never returns to the `main()` subroutine, and the application runs indefinitely in a multitasking environment. Ideally the application will be robust, designed with clear modularity, appropriate temporal efficiency and sensible architectural granularity, as described in Chap. B.

References

1. M. Barr, *Programming Embedded Systems with C and GNU Development Tools, Second Edition* (O'Reilly, Sebastopol, 2006)
2. S. Meyers, *Effective C++: 55 Specific Ways to Improve Your Programs and Designs, Third Edition* (Addison-Wesley, Boston, 2005)

Chapter 9
Low-Level Hardware Drivers in C++

Microcontroller applications usually require low-level drivers for peripheral devices such as I/O ports, interrupts, timers, communication interfaces like UART, CAN [6], SPI™, etc. This chapter presents several efficient methods for programming peripheral hardware drivers in C++. Low-level drivers are inherently dependent on the microcontroller and its peripherals. Even though the low-level hardware drivers in this chapter are primarily designed for our target with the 8-bit microcontroller, an effort has been made to keep them as portable as possible. In this way, they can be adapted to other microcontrollers. The final two sections in this chapter present complete, non-trivial examples. The first (`chapter09_07`) controls a seven-segment display [5]. The second (`chapter09_08`) produces colorful light by animating an RGB LED.

9.1 An I/O Port Pin Driver Template Class

General purpose I/O ports can be used for a variety of interfaces to on-board and off-board devices. A simple general purpose I/O port can be controlled via three registers, an output *data* register for setting the output value, a *direction* register for selecting input or output, and an *input* data register for reading the input value. Port pins often come grouped in registers that are 8, 16 or 32 bits wide. The general purpose I/O ports on our target with the 8-bit microcontroller, for example, can be controlled with three 8-bit registers, the data register, the direction register and the input register, as shown in Table 9.1.

C. Kormanyos, *Real-Time C++*, https://doi.org/10.1007/978-3-662-62996-3_9

Table 9.1 The registers of the general purpose I/O ports on our target with the 8-bit microcontroller are summarized

I/O port	Data register	Direction register	Input register
portb	0x25	0x24	0x23
portc	0x28	0x27	0x26
portd	0x2B	0x2A	0x29

We will now write a template port_pin class that encapsulates a port pin. It is intended to be used to control the general purpose I/O port pins, such as those found on portb, portc or portd, as summarized in Table 9.1. The public interface of port_pin is shown below.

```
// chapter09_01-001_port_pin_template.cpp

template<typename addr_type,
         typename reg_type,
         const addr_type port,
         const reg_type bpos>
class port_pin
{
public:
  static void set_direction_output();

  static void set_direction_input();

  static void set_pin_high();

  static void set_pin_low();

  static bool read_input_value();

  static void toggle();
};
```

The port_pin template is essentially a light-weight wrapper placed around target-specific register manipulation, i.e., such as might be accomplished via direct memory access. The reg_access_static template previously introduced in Chap. 7, for instance, could be used to provide implementation details of the port_pin template class. In order to manipulate the port pins, the fixed-bit subroutines of reg_access_static could easily be employed, as is done in the reference application of the companion code.

The member functions of the port_pin class are all qualified with the **static** keyword and there is no class constructor because port_pin is designed to be mapped to a specific, compile time constant port pin using a type definition or a similar alias. This means that objects of type port_pin are not intended to be instantiated.

Variations of the port_pin template class having the same public interface can be adapted to other microcontroller systems. The reference application in this book's companion code, for instance, has a handful of such variations. Using this kind of technique can provide for a nearly portable port pin class with a uniform interface that can be used in the same way with different targets. This method of port pin control can even be adapted for other port structures such as those on a port expander device, as is done in examples chapter04_04, chapter04_-04a, chapter10_08 and chapter10_08a.

Using the port_pin template is straightforward. The code below, for example, maps the port_pin template to portd.0 and subsequently sets the I/O pin to output with logic level high.

```
// chapter09_01-001_port_pin_template.cpp

void do_something()
{
  // Map portd.0 using a type definition.
  using port_d0_type = port_pin<std::uint8_t,
                                std::uint8_t,
                                mcal::reg::portd,
                                UINT8_C(0)>;

  // Set portd.0 to output with logic level high.
  // Set the value before direction to avoid spikes.

  port_d0_type::set_pin_high();
  port_d0_type::set_direction_output();
}
```

Additional security can be added to the port_pin class if desired. The functions that set the output value, for instance, could first ensure that the port pin direction is actually set to output before setting the logic level.

9.2 Programming Interrupts in C++

Developing low-level drivers in real-time C++ such as a timer counter or a serial UART interface may require the programming of one or more *interrupts*. An interrupt is an asynchronous signal caused by a hardware or software event that indicates that a special interrupt service routine should execute.

Interrupt service routines usually have higher CPU priority than the priority of the `main()` subroutine. Consider, for example, a microcontroller peripheral timer that is programmed to count in the upward direction. This up-counting timer can be configured to generate a hardware interrupt request when the value of the timer counter register reaches the value programmed in its compare register. In this way, a timer can be used to call an interrupt service routine with a fixed period. The resulting interrupt frequency is more precise than that which could be achieved with the CPU priority of the `main()` subroutine.

Programming an interrupt in C++ generally involves three main steps.

- Writing an interrupt service routine.
- Putting the interrupt service routine in the interrupt vector table.
- Activating the interrupt source and enabling global interrupts.

Among other timers, our target with the 8-bit microcontroller has an 8-bit peripheral timer called `timer0`. The `timer0` has a compare register `a`. The interrupt service routine shown below is designed to be called when the counter register of `timer0` register reaches the value set in its compare register `a`. This interrupt service routine has been discussed previously within the context of efficiency in Sect. 6.15.

```
// chapter09_02-001_programming_interrupts.cpp

// Attributes for an ISR and C-linkage.
extern "C"
void __vector_timer() __attribute__((interrupt));

// The timer0 compare-a interrupt service routine.
void __vector_timer()
{
  // This interrupt occurs when the counter
  // register reaches the compare-a register.

  // Do something...
}
```

The GNU C++ compiler [3] uses special *attributes* in the function prototype of an interrupt service routine. These are realized with the `__attribute__()` declaration syntax, for example in the prototype of `__vector_timer`. The `__attribute__()` declaration syntax is a language extension specific to GNU compilers.[1] The pairs of two leading and trailing underscores are intended to make the `__attribute__()` language extension uniquely visible.

GCC ports to other microcontrollers use different attribute keys and other compilers use different language extensions for declaring interrupt service routines, making interrupt syntax highly compiler-dependent. Declaring an interrupt service routine in C or C++ always relies on compiler-dependent syntax because it is not specified by ISO/IEC [7, 8], and is considered to be an implementation detail of the compiler.

Interrupt service routines abruptly interrupt normal program flow. The compiler may, therefore, need to create a special subroutine frame consisting of assembly sequences that save and restore the register context at interrupt entry and exit. The `__attribute__()` syntax shown above clearly indicates that this function is an interrupt service routine, allowing the compiler to generate the interrupt frame. Assuming that an interrupt service routine can be identified as such via language extensions, the compiler generates the interrupt frame automatically.

Depending on the characteristics of the underlying peripherals and the microcontroller architecture, it may be necessary to actively clear an interrupt request flag in software in the interrupt service routine. It is, on the other hand, just as common for the microcontroller hardware to automatically clear the interrupt request in the interrupt service routine. In `__vector_timer` above, for instance, it is not necessary to explicitly clear an interrupt request flag in software because the microcontroller hardware does it.

Interrupts can be generated for all sorts of hardware and software events, not only for timers. A communication device such as a serial UART, for instance, will usually have at least three unique interrupt sources, one for byte reception, a second for byte transmission and a third for framing error on a failed reception. Typically, these interrupts will be employed when developing a real-time asynchronous serial communication driver.

Small microcontrollers usually have a few tens of interrupt sources. Large microcontrollers may have hundreds of interrupt sources or even more. It is customary, then, to store the addresses of the interrupt service routines in what is known as an *interrupt vector table*.

In practice, the interrupt vector table is implemented as an array of function pointers, possibly with added fill bytes, containing the addresses of the interrupt service subroutines. For example, the interrupt vector table for the 8-bit microcontroller in the reference project is shown below.

---

[1]GNU compilers support numerous attributes for functions, variables, objects and types with its `__attribute__()` declaration syntax. See [2] and [4] for additional details.

```
// chapter09_02-001_programming_interrupts.cpp

// Declare the interrupt vector table.
extern "C"
const volatile isr_type isr_vectors[26U]
  __attribute__ ((section(".isr_vectors")));

// The interrupt vector table.
extern "C"
const volatile isr_type isr_vectors[26U] =
{
  {{0x0C, 0x94}, __my_startup },   //  1 reset
  {{0x0C, 0x94}, __unused_isr},    //  2 ext0
  {{0x0C, 0x94}, __unused_isr},    //  3 ext1
  {{0x0C, 0x94}, __unused_isr},    //  4 pin0
  {{0x0C, 0x94}, __unused_isr},    //  5 pin1
  {{0x0C, 0x94}, __unused_isr},    //  6 pin2
  {{0x0C, 0x94}, __unused_isr},    //  7 watchdog
  {{0x0C, 0x94}, __unused_isr},    //  8 timer2 cmp a
  {{0x0C, 0x94}, __unused_isr},    //  9 timer2 cmp b
  {{0x0C, 0x94}, __unused_isr},    // 10 timer2 ovf
  {{0x0C, 0x94}, __unused_isr},    // 11 timer1 cap
  {{0x0C, 0x94}, __unused_isr},    // 12 timer1 cmp a
  {{0x0C, 0x94}, __unused_isr},    // 13 timer1 cmp b
  {{0x0C, 0x94}, __unused_isr},    // 14 timer1 ovf
  {{0x0C, 0x94}, __vector_timer},  // 15 timer0 cmp a
  {{0x0C, 0x94}, __unused_isr},    // 16 timer0 cmp b
  {{0x0C, 0x94}, __unused_isr},    // 17 timer0 ovf
  {{0x0C, 0x94}, __unused_isr},    // 18 spi(TM)
  {{0x0C, 0x94}, __unused_isr},    // 19 usart rx
  {{0x0C, 0x94}, __unused_isr},    // 20 usart err
  {{0x0C, 0x94}, __unused_isr},    // 21 usart rx
  {{0x0C, 0x94}, __unused_isr},    // 22 adc
  {{0x0C, 0x94}, __unused_isr},    // 23 eep Ready
  {{0x0C, 0x94}, __unused_isr},    // 24 comparator
  {{0x0C, 0x94}, __unused_isr},    // 25 two-wire
  {{0x0C, 0x94}, __unused_isr}     // 26 spm
};
```

The first position in the interrupt vector table is often used by the microcontroller hardware as the entry point of the program. This is where program execution starts after microcontroller reset. In the sample above, for instance, `__my_startup()` is the program entry point. This is, for example, the same `__my_startup()`

routine that was described in Sect. 8.1. Notice how the `timer0` compare register a interrupt service routine `__vector_timer` is entered at the 15th position of the interrupt vector table, which is where it belongs for this particular microcontroller hardware.

The interrupt vector table must usually be mapped to a fixed physical address. The can be accomplished in software using a linker section. As shown above, placing objects in a linker section uses special section attributes, again a language extension particular to GCC. The interrupt vector table uses C-linkage in order to eliminate potential C++ name mangling. This produces a non-mangled name for the interrupt vector table and makes it easier to identify it in the map file, for example, when troubleshooting or verifying the proper location, alignment, contents and length. See Sects. 6.5, 6.6 and 8.4.

It can be good practice to fill unused entries in the interrupt vector table with a user-provided handler for unused interrupts. For example, unused interrupts in the `isr_vectors` table shown above use the subroutine `__unused_isr()`. The unused interrupt handler can generate a loud error such as waiting forever in en endless loop, optionally executing a nop-operation or, even louder, toggling a digital I/O port. A potential implementation of an unused interrupt service routine is shown below.

```
// chapter09_02-001_programming_interrupts.cpp

extern "C"
void __unused_isr() __attribute__((interrupt));

// The unused interrupt handler.
extern "C"
void __unused_isr()
{
  // Generate a loud error. It could be made
  // even louder by toggling an I/O port.
  for(;;)
  {
    mcal::irq::nop();
  }
}
```

For some microcontrollers, it may also be necessary to add fill bytes to the interrupt vector table. Fill bytes in the interrupt vector table generally have a special hardware purpose such as ensuring proper memory alignment or executing a low-level jump operation. The fill bytes `{0x0C, 0x94}` shown in the sample interrupt vector table above, for instance, constitute the opcode for a jump operation on our target with the 8-bit microcontroller. These aspects of interrupt programming in

C++ are notoriously non-portable. They are specific to a given microcontroller and compiler and usually can not be written in a generic form.

The final step involved in programming an interrupt is enabling the interrupt source. In practice, this is usually done by writing special enable bits in a special function register via direct memory access (Chap. 7). For example,

```
// chapter09_02-002_enable_timer_interrupt.cpp

// Enable the timer0 compare match a interrupt.
mcal::reg_access_static<
  std::uint8_t,
  std::uint8_t,
  mcal::reg::timsk0,
  UINT8_C(0x02)>::reg_set();
```

Here we enable bit-1 (value `0x02`) of the `timsk0` special function register for our target with the 8-bit microcontroller. This line of code can be found in the MCAL layer in the subroutine `mcal::gpt::init()` in the file "`mcal_-gpt.cpp`". This particular example enables a timer interrupt, as described in greater detail in the following section.

9.3 Implementing a System Tick

A system tick is typically an essential part of the low-level driver software because it provides the timebase for the entire software project. The multitasking scheduler described in Chap. 11, for instance, uses a timebase that originates from a system tick. In this section, we will use `timer0` on our target with the 8-bit microcontroller to create a system tick. The timer is configured to count in the upward direction in compare mode. Together with a small amount of software, this underlying timer is used to build a high-resolution 32-bit system tick with a frequency of 1 MHz.

Since `timer0` has counter and compare registers that are 8-bits in width, the 32-bit system tick needs to be synthesized from a combination of hardware and software. The lower byte of the system tick comes from the `timer0` counter register `tcnt0` and the upper three bytes are stored in the variable `system_tick`. This composite representation of the system tick is shown in Fig. 9.1.

One possible declaration of `system_tick` is shown below.

```
namespace
{
  // The one (and only one) 32-bit system tick.
  volatile std::uint32_t system_tick;
}
```

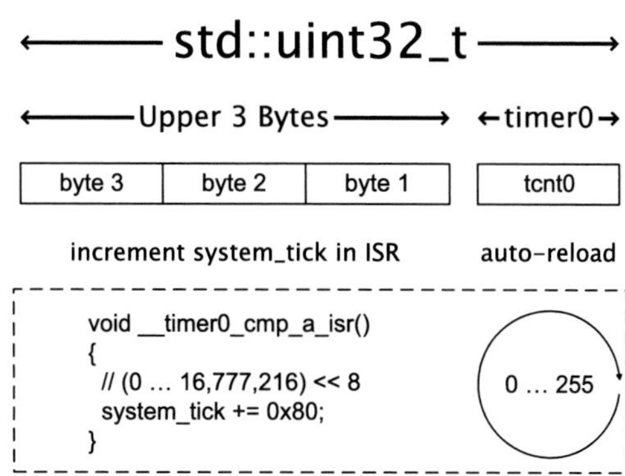

Fig. 9.1 The representation of the 32-bit system tick is shown. The three upper bytes of the software system tick are stored in the `system_tick` variable. The lower byte of the system tick originates from `timer0`'s counter register `tcnt0`

The `system_tick` variable is qualified as **`volatile`** This tells the compiler that it should avoid aggressive optimization involving `system_tick`. This can be helpful because the value of `system_tick` is changed via incrementation in the interrupt service routine, but used elsewhere.

We will now setup `timer0` to generate a periodic interrupt for incrementing the system tick. The code below initializes `timer0` to count in the upward direction. The frequency of the clock source is set to 2 MHz. The `timer0` compare register a is set to `0xFF` = 255 and the compare match interrupt is activated.

```
void mcal::gpt::init()
{
  // Clear the timer0 overflow flag.
  mcal::reg_access<std::uint8_t,
                   std::uint8_t,
                   mcal::reg::tifr0,
                   UINT8_C(0x02)>::reg_set();

  // Enable the compare match a interrupt.
  mcal::reg_access<std::uint8_t,
                   std::uint8_t,
                   mcal::reg::timsk0,
                   UINT8_C(0x02)>::reg_set();

  // Set ctc mode 2 for timer0 compare match a.
  mcal::reg_access<std::uint8_t,
                   std::uint8_t,
                   mcal::reg::tccr0a,
                   UINT8_C(0x02)>::reg_set();

  // Set the compare match a value to 255.
  mcal::reg_access<std::uint8_t,
                   std::uint8_t,
```

```
                         mcal::reg::ocr0a,
                         UINT8_C(0xFF)>::reg_set();

  // Set the timer0 source to 16MHz/8 = 2MHz and
  // start counting.
  mcal::reg_access<std::uint8_t,
                   std::uint8_t,
                   mcal::reg::tccr0b,
                   UINT8_C(0x03)>::reg_set();
}
```

The `mcal::gpt::init()` routine is designed to be called once, and only once, from the initialization mechanism of the MCAL. The result of the initialization code in `mcal::gpt::init()` is to set the `timer0` frequency to 2 MHz and activate an interrupt at every full cycle of its 8-bit timer period.

When the `timer0` counter register rolls over from 255 to 0, an interrupt for match on compare register `a` is generated. The corresponding interrupt service routine `__vector_timer` is called and it increments the upper three bytes of the system tick. One possible implementation of this mechanism is shown in the code sample below.

```
void __vector_timer()
{
  // This interrupt occurs every 128us.
  // Increment the 32-bit system tick by 128.
  system_tick += UINT8_C(0x80);
}
```

Here, the system tick is incremented with `0x80` which is 128. The 256 timer ticks required for the compare match interrupt have been divided by 2 because the underlying timer frequency is 2 MHz, which is double the system tick frequency. In this way, a 32-bit system tick with a frequency of 1 MHz and a resolution of 1 μs has been created with the 8-bit `timer0` hardware and a small amount of software.

To obtain the entire value of the 32-bit system tick, the timer counter register `tcnt0` is combined with the upper three bytes of the `system_tick` variable using logical `or`. Since the timer counter register is rapidly incremented by the timer hardware, a consistency check must be included in the routine that reads the `system_tick` variable.

The interface to the system tick can be found in the `gpt` namespace of the MCAL in the reference project of the companion code. Here, `gpt` stands for *general purpose timer*. The interface to the system tick uses a procedural subroutine called `get_time_elapsed()`. In other words,

```
mcal::gpt::value_type mcal::gpt::get_time_elapsed();
```

Complete details on the implementation of the system tick for both our targets with the 8-bit microcontroller and the 32-bit microcontroller can be found in the reference project of the companion code. For the 32-bit target, a 16-bit timer hardware counter register is combined with a quad-word in software to synthesize a 64-bit system tick with a frequency of 1 MHz and a resolution of 1 μs.

The standard library time facilities in `<chrono>` require the implementation of several clocks, one of them being a high-resolution clock. The system tick presented in this section is well-suited for providing the underlying timebase for the `high_resolution_clock` in `<chrono>`. A methodology for using the system tick as the timebase for `<chrono>`'s high-resolution clock is presented in Sect. 16.5.

9.4 A Software PWM Template Class

A pulse-width modulated signal (PWM) is a square wave that usually has a fixed period and a variable duty cycle. A PWM signal uses a cyclical counter that increments and is reset at the end of the PWM period. When the counter reaches the value matching the duty cycle of the PWM, the output switches from high to low, thereby creating a square wave. PWM signals with duty cycles of 20%, 50% and 80% are shown in Fig. 9.2. PWM signals can be generated with software or with a peripheral timer. The duty cycle, period and resolution of a PWM signal are determined by the configuration of the underlying software or timer.

Dedicated PWM units are often integrated in the microcontroller hardware peripherals. For example, a PWM signal can be created with a peripheral timer that has a counter, a compare register and a dedicated auto-toggle output pin associated with the compare event of the timer compare register. A hardware-based PWM signal can be set up and programmed to run independently without CPU supervision.

A typical user interface for a PWM signal generator provides public methods for setting and retrieving the duty cycle. This interface has been used with the pwm

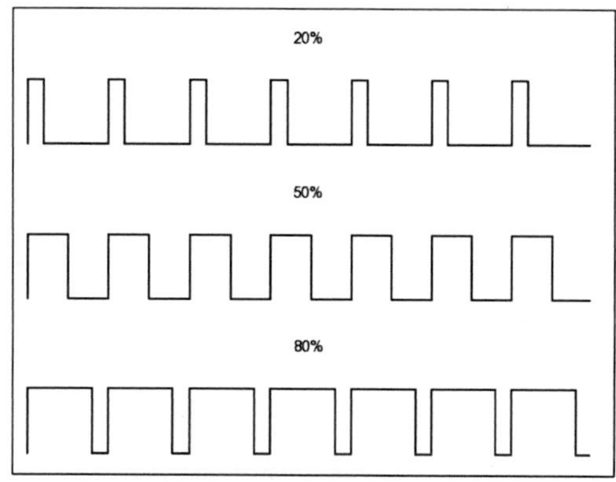

Fig. 9.2 PWM signals with duty cycles of 20%, 50% and 80% are shown

class in conjunction with the LED class hierarchy presented previously in Sect. 4.1. The example here makes a more detailed implementation of a dedicated PWM class called pwm_{type.

The synopsis of the pwm_type class is shown below.

```
class pwm_type
{
public:
  pwm_type(const std::uint8_t duty = UINT8_C(0));

  void set_duty(const uint8_t duty);

  std::uint8_t get_duty() const;
};
```

A PWM signal generated with software uses a timebase for the counter and manual manipulation of an I/O pin to toggle the signal. Generating a PWM signal with software may be more CPU-intensive than using a dedicated hardware peripheral. A software PWM signal generator does, however, have a slightly higher degree of flexibility than one in hardware and can also be used even if no dedicated PWM hardware is available.

We will now write a template class designed to encapsulate a software PWM signal generator on a digital I/O port.

```
template<typename addr_type,
         typename reg_type,
         const addr_type addr,
         const reg_type bpos,
         const std::uint8_t resol = UINT8_C(100)>
class pwm_type
{
public:
  pwm_type(const std::uint8_t duty = UINT8_C(0))
    : counter(0U),
      duty_cycle(duty),
      shadow(duty)
  {
    // Set the pin to output, low.
    port_pin_type::set_pin_low();
    port_pin_type::set_direction_output();
  }
```

```
  void set_duty(const uint8_t duty)
  {
    // Set new duty cycle in the shadow register.
    std::atomic_store(&shadow,
                      std::min(duty, resol));
  }

  std::uint8_t get_duty() const
  {
    // Retrieve the duty cycle.
    return std::atomic_load(&duty_cycle);
  }

  void service()
  {
    // Increment the counter.
    ++counter;

    // Set output according to duty cycle.
    if(counter <= duty_cycle)
    {
      port_pin_type::set_pin_high();
    }
    else
    {
      port_pin_type::set_pin_low();
    }

    if(counter >= resol)
    {
      // Latch in duty cycle from shadow register.
      duty_cycle = shadow;

      // Reset the counter for a new PWM period.
      counter = 0U;
    }
  }

private:
  std::uint8_t counter;
  volatile std::uint8_t duty_cycle;
  std::uint8_t shadow;
```

```
  // Define the type for the PWM port pin.
  typedef port_pin<addr_type,
                   reg_type,
                   addr,
                   bpos> port_pin_type;

  // Make the pwm_type class non-copyable.
  pwm_type(const pwm_type&) = delete;
  const pwm_type& operator=(const pwm_type&) = delete;
};
```

This software encapsulation of a PWM signal driver closely mimics a hardware PWM peripheral timer. When the internal counter is less than the duty cycle, the output pin is set to high. When the internal counter exceeds the duty cycle, the output pin is set to low. In this way, the requested signal is generated on the output pin. The `service()` member should be called with a fixed tick cycle, such as from a timer interrupt service routine with a period of 50 μs. If there are, say, 100 ticks specified with the `resol` template parameter and a tick cycle of 50 μs, then the resulting PWM signal will have a frequency of 200 Hz and a resolution of 1%.

A new duty cycle can be set with the `set_duty()` member function. It includes a range check and an atomic manipulation of the software shadow register. The new duty cycle is latched in from the shadow register at the end of each full period of the counter. This avoids incomplete PWM periods when setting the duty cycle in a process that is asynchronous to the call of the `service()` routine.

The example below creates a PWM signal generator on `portb.0` with the default initial duty cycle of 0%. The PWM duty cycle is subsequently set to 20%. Here, it is assumed that the PWM's `service()` routine is called with a fixed tick cycle, for instance, in an asynchronous timer interrupt service routine.

```
// Make a type definition for a PWM signal on portb.0.
typedef pwm_type<std::uint8_t,
                 std::uint8_t,
                 mcal::reg::portb,
                 UINT8_C(0)> pwm_b0_type;

// Create pwm0 on portb.0.
pwm_b0_type pwm0;

void do_something()
{
  // Set the duty cycle to 20 percent.
  pwm0.set_duty(UINT8_C(20));
}
```

9.5 A Serial SPI™ Driver Class

SPI™ is a synchronous full-duplex serial communication interface commonly used for microcontroller communication with other devices. SPI™ is a four-wire serial bus. A single bus master device initiates data frame transfer with one or more slave devices using three communication lines and one device-select line per slave device.

An example of an SPI™ bus with the master device connected to one slave device is sketched in Fig. 9.3. Data are clocked out from the bus master to the slave device on the *Master-Out-Slave-In* line (MOSI) and clocked from the slave device into the master on the *Master-In-Slave-Out* line (MISO). The flanks of the serial clock line (SCLK) provide the timebase for bit transfer, which can be quite fast reaching speeds of several mega-bits per second. Depending on the SPI™ dialect, either rising or falling edge can be used for latching the data bits, and the clock can optionally idle to high or low,

In the following paragraphs, we will develop an all-software SPI™ driver class. Instead of using a dedicated peripheral device, the all-software SPI™ driver class directly uses port toggle and port pin read functions to manually send and receive individual data bits.

The synopsis of a potential all-software SPI™ communication class is shown in the code below. The class is called `spi_software_port_driver`. This class is designed for a microcontroller bus master having 8-bit data tranceive with serial clock idle to low. This SPI™ template class is derived from a class called `communication_buffer_depth_one_byte`. This base class uses an internal data buffer having a depth of one byte and is, itself, derived from a communication base class similar to the one first introduced in Sect. 4.9.

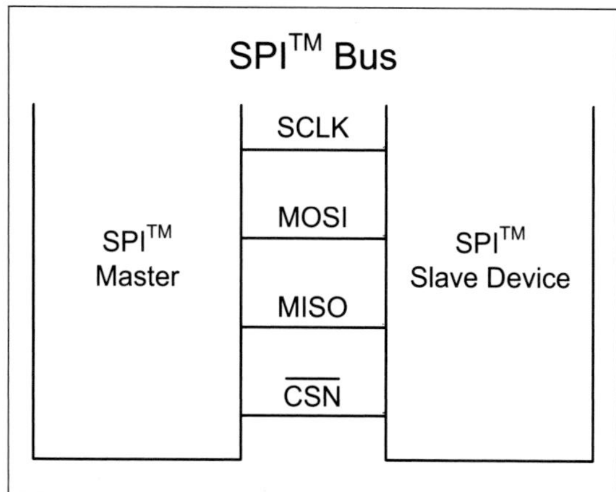

Fig. 9.3 SPI™ communication with the master device connected to a single slave device is shown

```
template<typename port_pin_sck__type,
         typename port_pin_mosi_type,
         typename port_pin_csn__type,
         typename port_pin_miso_type,
         const std::uint8_t nop_count,
         const bool has_disable_enable_interrupts>
class spi_software_port_driver
  : public util::communication_buffer_depth_one_byte
{
public:
  spi_software_port_driver();
  {
    port_pin_csn__type::set_pin_high();
    port_pin_sck__type::set_pin_low();
    port_pin_mosi_type::set_pin_low();

    port_pin_csn__type::set_direction_output();
    port_pin_sck__type::set_direction_output();
    port_pin_mosi_type::set_direction_output();
    port_pin_miso_type::set_direction_input();
  }

  virtual ~spi_software_port_driver() = default;

  virtual bool send(
    const std::uint8_t byte_to_send);

  virtual void   select()
  {
    port_pin_csn__type::set_pin_low();
  }

  virtual void deselect()
  {
    port_pin_csn__type::set_pin_high();
  }
};
```

The `spi_software_port_driver` class includes members that are intended for sending and receiving one or more data bytes. For sending one data byte, the `spi_software_port_driver` class supplies the public member function `send()`. The receive function is implemented within the base class hierarchy. The base class implements a function called `send_n()` which is designed for sending multiple-byte stream bursts.

The interface of the `spi_software_port_driver` class is intended to be completely independent of the underlying microcontroller registers. Hardware details are hidden in the implementations of the class methods. In this way, the user interface of the `spi_software_port_driver` class is completely portable.

The work of the `spi_software_port_driver` class is predominantly implemented in the send and receive algorithms. The send routine is shown below.

```
bool spi_software_port_driver::send(
  const std::uint8_t byte_to_send)
{
  base_class_type::recv_buffer = 0U;

  for(std::uint_fast8_t bit_mask = UINT8_C(0x80);
              bit_mask != UINT8_C(0);
                          bit_mask >>= 1U)
  {
    ((std::uint_fast8_t(byte_to_send & bit_mask)
      != UINT8_C(0))
        ? port_pin_mosi_type::set_pin_high()
        : port_pin_mosi_type::set_pin_low());

    detail::disable_all_interrupts
      <has_disable_enable_interrupts>();

    port_pin_sck__type::set_pin_high();
    detail::spi_nop_maker
      <nop_count>::execute_n();

    port_pin_sck__type::set_pin_low ();
    detail::spi_nop_maker
      <nop_count>::execute_n();

    if(port_pin_miso_type::read_input_value())
    {
      base_class_type::recv_buffer |= bit_mask;
    }

    detail::enable_all_interrupts
      <has_disable_enable_interrupts>();
  }

  return true;
}
```

Aside from helper functions for global interrupt enable and disable and the *nop* operation (Sects. 6.7 and 9.2), the `send()` function uses a standard "bit-banging" mechanism for data transceive. When sending a data byte, the function manually clocks in each bit-to-send and shortly thereafter reads in each bit-to-receive. Port pin manipulation is uses the `port_pin` template class from Sect. 9.1.

The time-critical sequences of this class rely on static polymorphism for utmost speed efficiency. The class itself is, however, architecturally nested at the top of a skinny class hierarchy. Instances of `spi_software_port_driver` can, therefore, be used with dynamic polymorphism through a base class pointer or reference, as discussed in Sects. 4.4 and 5.7. In fact, the `spi_software_port_driver` class is accessed through dynamic polymorphism in various practical situations in the companion code including examples `chapter04_04`, `chapter04_04a`, `chapter10_08` and `chapter10_08a`.

The SPI™ bus driver presented here is relatively simple, yet rather robust. The implementation of the `spi_software_port_driver` class in its entirety (also within its class hierarchy) can be found in the companion code. The `spi_software_port_driver` class also has a portable user interface, allowing for straightforward adaption to other target systems.

9.6 CPU-Load Monitors

Robustness and quality can be key goals of embedded microcontroller software development. Due to potential cost-sensitive constraints prevalent in the industry, however, efficiency in size and space can also be important. There can, in fact, sometimes be a tradeoff between size and space while still attempting to retain reliability.[2]

It can, therefore, be good practice to monitor the runtime of all tasks and interrupts in the project during the phases of the development cycle. Adherence to runtime limits can be tested with runtime monitoring mechanisms such as real-time measurements via port pins, software timers or in-circuit emulators.

One of the most rudimentary yet effective means for measuring the runtime of a code sequence is to toggle a digital I/O port to high directly before the sequence begins and to toggle it to low just after the sequence completes. Using this technique, we can observe timing results and statistical variances in timing with a digital oscilloscope.

Extraneous interrupt load can be eliminated from short timing measurements by disabling all interrupts for the duration of the measurement and enabling them

[2]Tradeoffs involving code size, code space and software quality are recurring themes in this book and have also been discussed in Sects. 6.1 and 6.2.

immediately thereafter.[3] Disabling and enabling all interrupts is a CPU-specific operation that can be accomplished by setting and clearing the global interrupt flag or manipulating the CPU priority or other microcontroller-specific means. Most of the real-time measurements in this book have been performed with this kind of technique.

The code that has been used to measure the runtime of the CRC32 checksum algorithm in Sects. 6.1 and 6.2, for example, is shown below.

```
#include <array>
#include <cstdint>
#include <math/checksums/crc/crc32.h>
#include <mcal_benchmark.h>
#include <mcal_cpu.h>
#include <mcal_irq.h>

std::uint32_t app_benchmark_crc;

void app::benchmark::task_func()
{
  // Define the test data '0' ... '9'.
  constexpr std::array<std::uint8_t, 9U> data =
  {{
    UINT8_C(0x31), UINT8_C(0x32), UINT8_C(0x33),
    UINT8_C(0x34), UINT8_C(0x35), UINT8_C(0x36),
    UINT8_C(0x37), UINT8_C(0x38), UINT8_C(0x39)
  }};

  // Convenient typedef of the benchmark port pin type.
  typedef
  mcal::benchmark::benchmark_port_type
  port_type;

  mcal::irq::disable_all();
  port_type::set_pin_high();

  // Calculate the CRC-32/MPEG-2 checksum.
  app_benchmark_crc =
    math::checksums::crc32_mpeg2(data.cbegin(),
                                 data.cend());
```

[3]Note, however, that disabling the interrupts for too long or forgetting to re-enable them in a timely fashion may lead to a system crash with unpredictable results.

```
  port_type::set_pin_low();
  mcal::irq::enable_all();

  if(app_benchmark_crc == UINT32_C(0x0376E6E7))
  {
    // The benchmark is OK.
    // ...
  }
}
```

This code simply uses a regular I/O port pin such as `portb.4` configured as an output pin to generate a time pulse that can be measured with a digital oscilloscope. The port pin used for the timing measurement is abstracted with a template class called `benchmark_port_type` which is **`typedef`**-ed from `port_pin` (Sect. 9.1) in `<mcal_benchmark.h>`. The port pin is toggled high before the CRC32 checksum calculation begins and low after the computation completes. The interrupts are disabled for the duration of the measurement. This measurement technique is trivially simple, yet nonetheless highly effective.

The timing result of a real-time performance benchmark is shown in Fig. 9.4. This benchmark has been carried out with a modern digital oscilloscope. The oscilloscope has been used to capture the real-time measurement within the range of its adjustable cursors. The timing result has been acquired over numerous cycles in order to obtain a stable average.

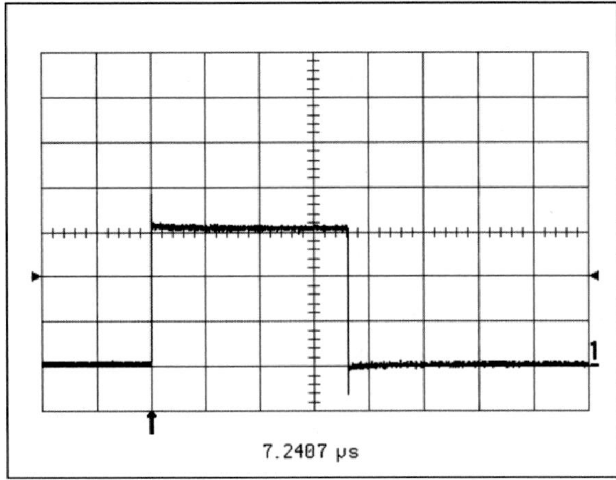

Fig. 9.4 The timing result of a real-time performance benchmark is shown. The digital oscilloscope captures the toggling of the port pin in the microsecond regime

9.7 Controlling a Seven-Segment Display

This section presents a complete example of controlling a seven-segment display[4] using our target system with the 8-bit microcontroller. The complete source code for this example can be found in the `chapter09_07` sample project in the companion code.

This is a non-trivial project that uses state-of-the-art programming technology to control a classic electronic device. In particular, this project makes combined use of various advanced programming methods including object-orientated design (Chap. 4), templates and static polymorphism (Chap. 5), low-level hardware drivers such as the `port_pin` template class (Sect. 9.1), a multitasking scheduler (Chap. 11), and the utility classes `noncopyable` and `timer` (Sects. 15.2 and 15.3). These are used to build up a layered architecture (Sect. B.2) that abstracts low-level pin-driven LED segments to images of hexadecimal digits represented on the seven-segment display with animation.

A standard seven-segment display with one digit and a decimal point is used. It has a red color with a character height of $1/2\,in$ ($\approx$ 1.27 cm). The display has a 10-pin package with two common anode pins. The display segments are low-active and light up when connected over a resistor to ground. Here, we use 750 Ω resistors resulting in a current of approximately 4.4 mA through each LED segment.[5]

The display is capable of representing recognizable images of the hexadecimal digits `0123456789AbCdEF`, where `b` and `d` are lowercase. A decimal point to the lower right of the digit can be controlled independently from the digit segments.

In this example, our target system with the 8-bit microcontroller is connected to the seven-segment display as shown in Fig. 9.5. Electrical connections between the microcontroller ports and the seven-segment display have been made with a custom break-out board and traditional wire-wrapping techniques using AWG-30 wire [12].

When working with skinny wire such as AWG-30, it can be convenient (or even necessary for proper circuit dimensioning) to understand the resistance of wire. The resistance of straight cylindrical wire is given by [11]

$$R = \frac{\rho\,L}{A}\,, \tag{9.1}$$

---

[4]See also Sect. 12.5.3.A "*LED Displays*" in [5] for additional information on seven-segment displays and other LED displays.

[5]The forward voltage of the LED in a given display segment is specified with a typical value of approximately 1.7 V such that

$$I_{seg} \approx \frac{(5.0\,-\,1.7)\,\text{V}}{750\,\Omega} \approx 4.4\,\text{mA}\,,$$

where I_{seg} is the current in one switched-on LED segment. On the microcontroller ports, the current of approximately 4.4 mA per port pin is well below the specified maximum value of 40 mA (see Table 29.1 *Absolute Maximum Ratings* in [1]).

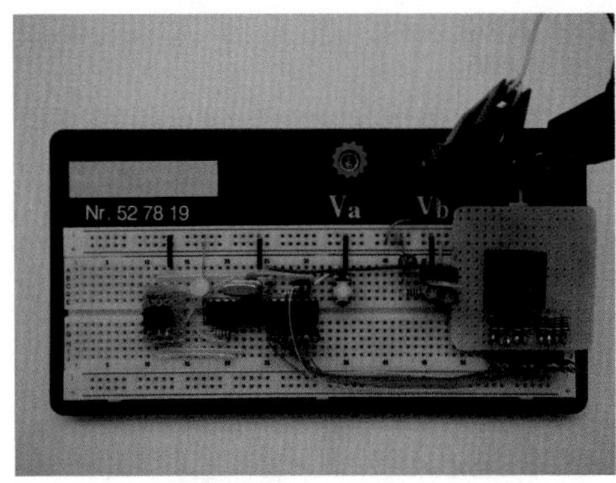

Fig. 9.5 Our target system with the 8-bit microcontroller wired to the seven-segment display is shown. The display has been fitted on a custom break-out board. Electrical connections between the microcontroller ports and the display board use traditional wire-wrapping techniques

where L is the length, A is the cross-sectional area and ρ is the *resistivity* of the material of the wire. The diameter of AWG-n wire is

$$d_n = 0.127 \times 92^{(36-n)/39} \, \text{mm} \tag{9.2}$$

for ($n = 0 \ldots 36$) and the resistivity of copper is approximately

$$\rho_{\text{Cu}} \approx 1.68 \times 10^{-8} \, \Omega \cdot \text{m} \tag{9.3}$$

from the tabulated values in[11]. The resulting resistance per 1 m of AWG-n copper wire is

$$R_{\text{Cu, AWG-}n} \approx \frac{1.68}{\pi \left(0.625 \times 92^{(36-n)/39}\right)^2} \, \Omega \text{ (per 1 meter)}. \tag{9.4}$$

The approximate resistance of 1 m of AWG-30 copper wire, for instance, is

$$\begin{aligned} R_{\text{Cu, AWG-30}} &\approx \frac{1.68}{\pi \left((5/8) \times 92^{2/13}\right)^2} \, \Omega \text{ (per 1 m)} \\ &\approx 340 \, \text{m}\Omega \text{ (per 1 m)}. \end{aligned} \tag{9.5}$$

This results in negligible resistance of around $\sim$ 20 mΩ for the short $\sim$ 6 cm, low-current signal lines connecting the seven-segment display.

In order to make room for the seven-segment display, certain component placements on the board have been changed compared with those shown in Fig. 2.1.

The pin connections between the microcontroller and the seven-segment display are listed in Table 9.2. Pinning uses a combination of port pins from `portc` and `portd`, and the +5 V supply.

Table 9.2 The pin connections between the microcontroller and the seven-segment display are listed

Pin on 7-segment display	Display Pin's function	Electrical connection	Microcontroller pin
1	Segment E	`portc.5`	28
2	Segment D	`portc.0`	23
3	Common anode	+5 V	–
4	Segment C	`portc.1`	24
5	Decimal point	`portc.2`	25
6	Segment B	`portc.3`	26
7	Segment A	`portc.4`	27
8	Common anode	+5 V	–
9	Segment F	`portd.0`	2
10	Segment G	`portd.1`	3

The hierarchy of the display classes in the `chapter09_07` sample project is shown in Fig. 9.6. The two most highly derived classes in the diagram are called `display_console` and `display_board`. These two classes are intended to be instantiated as singleton instances of base class objects and subsequently used in the application layer.

The `display_console` class simulates the seven-segment display in a console. This class is intended to be used for convenient testing of the project on a PC.[6]

The `display_board` class encapsulates the real seven-segment display on the board. This class has been designed to control the display via eight port pins on the microcontroller (i.e., as wired in Fig. 9.5).

The two base classes, `display_base` and `display_seven_segment`, contain a mixture of both public interface functions as well as abstract methods

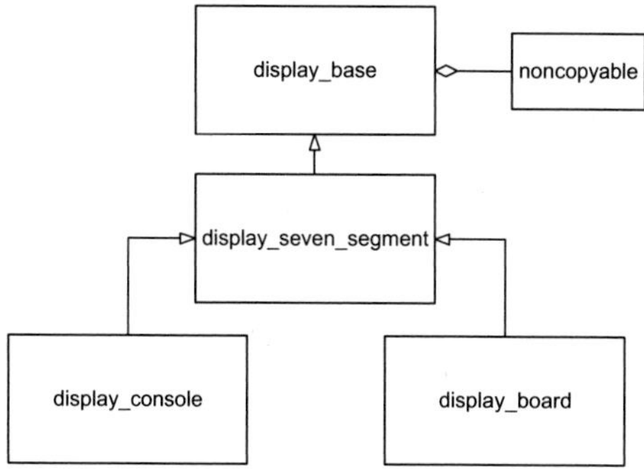

Fig. 9.6 The class hierarchy of the display classes in the `chapter09_07` project is shown

[6]Console testing is supported via cross development methods that port the entire project to a PC-based compiler. Hereby, the hardware-specific MCAL has been partially simulated in the PC environment.

(Sect. 4.6). These two classes serve the primary purpose of providing a public interface for clients of the display classes and ensuring that the necessary abstract functions are implemented.

The public interface of display_base is shown below.

```
class display_base : private util::noncopyable
{
public:
  virtual ~display_base() { }

  bool write(const std::uint8_t value_to_write)
  {
    return do_write(value_to_write);
  }

  bool read(std::uint8_t& value_to_read) const
  {
    return do_read(value_to_read);
  }

private:
  // Non-public details...
};
```

The essential functions of display_base can be used to write or read one single 8-bit character.

The display_base class inherits privately from the noncopyable utility class (Sect. 15.2). This ensures that all of the classes in the display class hierarchy can not be copied. This is desired in our design because a given display exists once and only once on a given board. An instantiation encapsulating a display is, therefore, not intended to be copied.

The display_seven_segment class adds the ability to write or read a decimal point character. In particular,

```
class display_seven_segment : public display_base
{
public:
  virtual ~display_seven_segment() { }

  bool write_dp(const bool dp_on)
  {
    return do_write_dp(dp_on);
  }
```

```
  bool read_dp(bool& dp_on) const
  {
    return do_read_dp(dp_on);
  }

private:
  // Non-public details...
};
```

As mentioned above, the actual class that embodies the seven-segment display on the real board is called `display_board` The synopsis of the `display_board` class is shown in the code below.

```
template<typename segment_a_port,
         typename segment_b_port,
         typename segment_c_port,
         typename segment_d_port,
         typename segment_e_port,
         typename segment_f_port,
         typename segment_g_port,
         typename segment_dp_port>
class display_board final :
  public display_seven_segment
{
public:
  display_board() { }

  display_board(const std::uint8_t value_to_write,
                const bool dp_on)
    : display_seven_segment(value_to_write, dp_on)
    { }

  virtual ~display_board() { }

private:
  virtual bool do_write(const std::uint8_t)

  virtual bool do_read(std::uint8_t&) const;

  virtual bool do_write_dp(const bool);

  virtual bool do_read_dp(bool&) const;
};
```

The public interface is used for construction and destruction. The private virtual methods implement write and read of a character and decimal point.

The display_board class is a template class. It accepts eight template parameters representing the eight port pins connected to the display—seven port pins for the seven segments in the digit and one port pin for the decimal point. The public interface of the display_board class provides virtual Boolean functions for reading and writing both the digit as well as the decimal point.

The port pin types corresponding to the template parameters must adhere to the public interface of the port_pin template class from Sect. 9.1. This is because the private details of the display_board class make use of some of port_pin's static public member functions such as toggle(), etc. via static polymorphism (Sect. 5.7). The display_board class and its parents in the class hierarchy can be readily ported to other microcontroller projects as long as the port_pin template class is properly supported.

A global display_board object is provided to the application layer by a subroutine that returns a singleton instance (Sect. 8.6) of the base class. This mechanism is depicted in pseudo-code below.

```
display_seven_segment& display0()
{
  // Define some board-specific types, etc.
  ...

  // Create a static display_board object...

  static display_board the_display;

  // ... and return a base class reference to it.

  return the_display;
}
```

Here, the instance is returned in the form of a non-constant reference to the base class (i.e., display_seven_segment&). This allows display0() to exhibit runtime polymorphism. In this way, the entire public abstract interface of the display class hierarchy available to the caller of display0().

The display task in the application layer uses the display0() subroutine for writing to the seven-segment display. The sixteen hexadecimal digits 01234567-89AbCdEF are sequentially represented on the display, continually cycling from 0 to F and beginning anew with the digit 0. The digit on the display is updated every second (i.e., at a rate of 1 s per digit). The decimal point is toggled once per group of sixteen hexadecimal digits to add a further detail to the display animation.

The display task also toggles the user LED on portb.5 at 1/2 Hz. This is done in the same fashion as in the chapter02_03a sample project.

Timing is derived from a simple multitasking scheduler (Chap. 11) in combination with a static instance of the `timer` utility class (Sect. 15.3). The display task is scheduled every 2 ms and the timer object provides a secondary timebase that services the display and LED every 1 *s*.

The synopsis of the display task is listed in pseudo-code below.[7]

```
void task_func()
{
  if(app_display_timer.timeout())
  {
    // Start a new 1s interval.
    app_display_timer.start_interval(
      timer_type::seconds(1U));

    // Toggle the user LED on portb.5.
    ...

    // Select the next hexadecimal digit.
    ...

    // Toggle the phase of the decimal point at
    // full cycles of sixteen hexadecimal digits.
    ...

    // Write the decimal point.
    display0().write_dp(...);

    // Write the hexadecimal digit.
    display0().write(...);
  }
}
```

As mentioned at the beginning of this section, the complete source code of the `chapter09_07` project (including various build scripts and the port to the PC-console) can be found in the companion code. The project has been tested on our target with the 8-bit microcontroller (as shown in Fig. 9.5). Program verification has been carried out using different versions of GCC ranging from 4.8.1 through 10.1.0 [2] built for the `avr-g++` target (Sect. 2.2 and Appendix C) and using C++11 or higher.[8]

[7]Here, the **namespace** resolutions have been removed from the pseudo-code for the sake of simplicity.

[8]Recall that the C++11, C++14, etc. dialects are enabled in GCC with the compiler flags `-std=c++11`, `-std=c++14`, etc.

9.8 Animating an RGB LED

In this section, we present an example that animates an RGB LED to produce a colorful light show. An RGB LED is typically composed of three discrete LEDs, in hues of red, green and blue. The light-emitting segments are housed closely within a single package. This allows for the appearance of homogeneous color mixing when the hues are turned on with varying intensity.

In addition to utilizing advanced object-oriented and template methods, this example (as in the previous exercise of `chapter09_07`) demonstrates cross-development within a PC environment. The result is an intuitive object-oriented program that runs on both our target with the 8-bit microcontroller as well as on a PC. The complete source code for this example can be found in the `chapter09_08` sample project in the companion code.

The target system is built on a solderless prototyping board, as shown in Fig. 9.7. An industry-standard off-the-shelf RGB LED is mounted on the panel. Individual color hues of red, green and blue are set with PWM signals on microcontroller ports having varying duty cycles. Instances of the PWM software template class described in Sect. 9.4 are used for this. The current through the RGB LED segments is sourced directly from the microcontroller port pins.

This RGB LED has a *common anode* connected to the 5 V supply. Because of the common anode, the PWM duty cycles are inverted. A lower value of PWM duty cycle results in a deeper color hue. The inversion of the signals takes place in a lower layer of the software prior to setting the PWM duty cycle.

The electrical characteristics of the RGB LED circuit, including PWM port connections, LED forward voltages (V_{LED}), voltages on the resistors (V_R), and resistor values (R_{LED}) are summarized in Table 9.3. This system has been designed to drive approximately 10 mA of current through each LED segment. In practice, variations among different RGB LEDs can be expected. It can, therefore, be a good

Fig. 9.7 Our target system with the 8-bit microcontroller animating the RGB LED is shown. PWM signals on `portc.3`, `portc.4` and `portc.5` control hues of red, green and blue. In this figure, a cyan-like color can be observed

Table 9.3 The electrical characteristics of the RGB LED circuit and the PWM port connections are summarized. Resistors with a tolerance of 1% are used

Hue	PWM port	V_{LED} [V]	V_R [V]	R_{LED} [Ω]
R	`portc.3`	$\sim$ 1.75	$\sim$ 3.25	$\sim$ 325
G	`portc.4`	$\sim$ 2.25	$\sim$ 2.75	$\sim$ 275
B	`portc.5`	$\sim$ 2.50	$\sim$ 2.50	$\sim$ 250

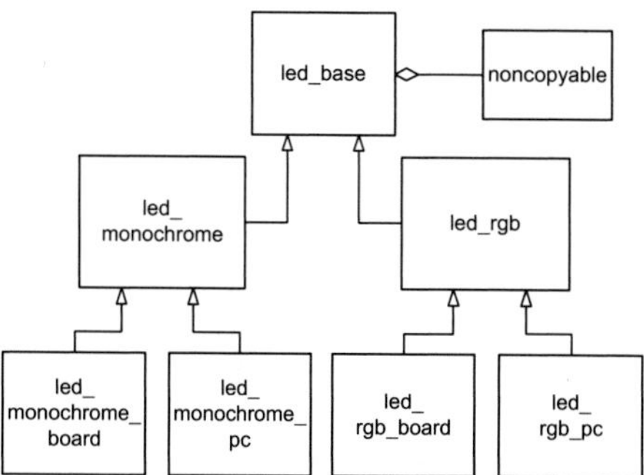

Fig. 9.8 The class hierarchy of monochrome LED objects and RGB LED objects in the `chapter09_08` project is shown

idea to measure the LED forward voltage when selecting the resistors.[9] This kind of electrical characterization can improve the results of color mixing.

The application layer computes color hues throughout the range of the color spectrum. The computed values run from 0 ... 255. The color hue values are subsequently scaled to percent 0 ... 100 when setting the PWM duty cycle. The scaled color hues are passed to the MCAL for setting the PWM signals at the hardware level. Simultaneously, the user-LED on `portb.5` is toggled at 1/2 Hz.

The style and architecture of the `chapter09_08` sample project are similar with those of the `chapter09_07` project described in Sect. 9.7. The presence of both monochrome LED objects and RGB LED objects within the class architecture, however, adds an additional level of depth to the design.

The hierarchy of the LED classes in the `chapter09_08` sample project is shown in Fig. 9.8. There is a base class called `led_base`. Successive classes are derived from this base class. The entire class hierarchy encapsulates both monochrome LED as well as RGB LED.

The most highly derived classes in this example are summarized in Table 9.4. These classes embody the actual LED objects in the software architecture. There are specific versions for both our target system with the 8-bit microcontroller as well as the PC.

The two second-most derived classes are called `led_monochrome` and `led_rgb`. The public interfaces of the base classes and of these second-most derived

[9] It might be necessary to use more than one resistor to attain the approximate desired resistance level for a given pin due to constraints imposed by the available standard resistor values.

Table 9.4 The names and purposes of the most highly derived classes used in the chapter-08_09 example are listed

Class name	Class purpose
led_monochrome_board	Control the monochrome user LED on our target with the 8-bit microcontroller
led_monochrome_pc	Control the simulated monochrome user LED on the PC
led_rgb_board	Control the RGB LED that is wired to PWM signals on portc.3, portc.4 and portc.5 on our target with the 8-bit microcontroller
led_rgb_pc	Control the simulated RGB LED on the PC

classes are intended to be used in the application layer (i.e., via singleton instance and dynamic runtime polymorphism, see also Sects. 4.4 and 8.6).

The base class in this class hierarchy is called led_base. The public interface of led_base is shown below.

```
class led_base : private util::noncopyable
{
public:
  virtual ~led_base() { }

  void on () { my_on (); is_on = true; }
  void off() { my_off(); is_on = false; }

  void toggle() { (is_on ? off() : on()); }

private:
  // Non-public details...
  // such as virtual my_on(), my_off(), etc.
};
```

In the base class, we find top-level functions such as on(), off() and toggle(). Virtual functions are added in the derived classes for carrying out the necessary class-specific operations. These include essentials such as my_on() and my_off(), which are used for turning an instance of a given LED class on or off, respectively.

The led_rgb class adds additional functions for setting and retrieving a 24-bit color value. Color can be set or retrieved in the form of a native 32-bit unsigned integer. Alternatively, three individual 8-bit hues of red, green and blue can be used.[10] In particular,

[10]Transparency is not used in the color representation of this example.

```
class led_rgb : public  led_base
{
public:
  virtual ~led_rgb();

  void set_color(const std::uint32_t color);

  void set_color(const std::uint_fast8_t hue_r,
                 const std::uint_fast8_t hue_g,
                 const std::uint_fast8_t hue_b);

  std::uint32_t get_color() const;

  std::uint_fast8_t get_hue_r() const;
  std::uint_fast8_t get_hue_g() const;
  std::uint_fast8_t get_hue_b() const;

private:
  // Non-public details...
};
```

As explained previously and listed in Table 9.4, the most highly derived classes of this example implement control of the LEDs on both the PC as well as on the board. Base class references to instances of these objects wrapped in singleton subroutines are used by the application layer. This technique was also used in the previous example `chapter09_07` of Sect. 9.7.

The animation of the LEDs is carried out in the application layer. A partial synopsis of the application task is shown below.

```
void task_func()
{
  if(app_led_monochrome_timer.timeout())
  {
    // Toggle the monochrome user LED at 1/2 \mathrm{Hz}.
    led_monochrome0().toggle();

    // Start the next timer interval
    // for the monochrome user LED.
    app_led_monochrome_timer.start_interval(
      app_led_monochrome_timer_type::seconds(1U));
  }
```

```
  if(app_led_rgb_timer.timeout())
  {
    // Animate the RGB LED with the colors
    // of the spectrum at 50 \mathrm{Hz}.

    // ...

    // Initialize the color transition state.
    static color_transition_type
      color_transition_state = red_to_yellow;

    // Make a smooth color transition and
    // increment the color transition state
    // if necessary.
    switch(color_transition_state)
    {
      // ...
    }

    // ...

    // Write the next color to the RGB LED.
    led_rgb0().set_color(
      app_led_hue_r,
      app_led_hue_g,
      app_led_hue_b);

    // Start the next timer interval
    // for the RGB LED.
    app_led_rgb_timer.start_interval(
      app_led_rgb_timer_type::milliseconds(20U));
  }
}
```

In this task, the monochrome user LED is toggled with a frequency of $1/2\,\mathrm{Hz}$. In addition, the colors of the spectrum are changed in the RGB LED with a frequency of about $50\,\mathrm{Hz}$. The color transitions run through red, yellow, green, cyan, blue, magenta, and ultimately back to red. The number of discrete colors in the complete color sequence of this example is $6 \times 256 = 1,536$. The fine granularity of changing hues makes the color metamorphosis gradual and smooth. Sequencing through a full cycle of the color spectrum in this sample takes about $1,536/\,(50\,\mathrm{Hz}) \approx 30\,\mathrm{s}$ on our target with the 8-bit microcontroller. The overall timing of the PC simulation is approximately the same.

As mentioned at the beginning of this section, the complete source code of the `chapter09_08` project can be found in the companion code. The project has been tested on our target with the 8-bit microcontroller. Program verification has been carried out with various versions of GCC `avr-g++` ranging from 4.8.1 through 10.1.0 [2] using C++11, C++14 and C++17 [8–10].[11] The code in this example has also been tested with several PC-based compilers.

References

1. ATMEL®, *8-bit ATMEL® Microcontroller with 4/8/16/32K Bytes In-System Programmable Flash (ATmega48A, ATmega48PA, ATmega88A, ATmega88PA, ATmega168A, ATmega168PA, ATmega328, ATmega328P)*, Rev. 8271D–AVR–05/11 (ATMEL®, 2011)
2. Free Software Foundation, *The GNU Compiler Collection Version 4.6.2* (2012). http://gcc.gnu.org
3. Free Software Foundation, *The GNU Compiler Collection Version 7.2.0* (2017). http://gcc.gnu.org
4. W. von Hagen, *The Definitive Guide to GCC* (Apress, Berkeley, 2006)
5. P. Horowitz, W. Hill, *The Art of Electronics, Third Edition, Twelfth Printing* (Cambridge University Press, Cambridge, 2017)
6. ISO, *ISO 11898–1:2003 : Road Vehicles – Controller Area Network (CAN) – Part 1: Data Link Layer and Physical Signaling* (International Organization for Standardization, Geneva, 2003)
7. ISO/IEC, *ISO/IEC 9899:1999 : Programming Languages – C* (International Organization for Standardization, Geneva, 1999)
8. ISO/IEC, *ISO/IEC 14882:2011 : Information Technology – Programming Languages – C++* (International Organization for Standardization, Geneva, 2011)
9. ISO/IEC, *ISO/IEC 14882:2014 : Information Technology – Programming Languages – C++* (International Organization for Standardization, Geneva, 2014)
10. ISO/IEC, *ISO/IEC 14882:2017 : Programming Languages – C++* (International Organization for Standardization, Geneva, 2017)
11. Wikipedia, *Electrical resistivity and conductivity* (2020). http://en.wikipedia.org/wiki/Electrical_resistivity_and_conductivity
12. Wikipedia, *American wire gauge* (2012). http://en.wikipedia.org/wiki/American_wire_gauge

[11]When using GCC, the language standards C++11, C++14, C++17 and C++20 can be activated with the command line switches `-std=c++11`, `-std=c++14`, `-std=c++17` and `-std=c++20`, respectively.

Chapter 10
Custom Memory Management

Effective microcontroller programming in C++ mandates dependable memory management beyond that offered by the language's default mechanisms. Some of the countless situations in microcontroller programming that require customized memory management include dynamic creation polymorphic objects, using STL containers, mapping hardware peripherals and efficiently interfacing with external memory devices. This chapter describes memory management methods that are robust and reliable enough to perform these tasks while adhering to the strict constraints of limited microcontroller memory resources. Section 10.8 toward the end of this chapter presents an advanced case study that uses external memory ICs combined with custom iterators and containers to compute up to 100,001 decimal digits of the mathematical constant π. This is detailed project is adapted further in Sect. 10.9 to use the ample RAM on a powerful 32-bit Arm®-based single-board computer.

10.1 Dynamic Memory Considerations

Dynamic memory allocation is useful in C++ programming, in particular for creating polymorphic objects. The operators **`new`** and **`delete`** can be used for dynamic memory allocation and deallocation in C++.

The **`new`** operator allocates memory for an object in a heap of dynamic memory. If sufficient memory is available and allocation succeeds, **`new`** initializes the object in the allocated memory by calling its constructor and returns a pointer to the object. If insufficient memory is available, **`new`** either returns **`nullptr`** or throws an `std::bad_alloc` exception (depending on the version of **`new`** being used). Calling **`delete`** for a memory block allocated with **`new`** destroys the object by calling its destructor and frees the memory.

C. Kormanyos, *Real-Time C++*, https://doi.org/10.1007/978-3-662-62996-3_10

The syntax of **new** and **delete** is shown below.

```
class something
{
public:
  something() { }
  ~something() { }

  void do_my_thing() { }
};

void do_something()
{
  // Allocate ps with operator new.
  something* ps = new something;

  // Do something with ps.
  ps->do_my_thing();

  // Delete ps when finished with it.
  delete ps;
}
```

As described in Sect. 6.16, the use of **new** and **delete** can be inappropriate for microcontrollers with strictly limited heaps of, say, a few tens or hundreds of bytes. Consider the example above. In a typical microcontroller situation, the subroutine `do_something()` might be called thousands of times—even millions of times. It might only take a few calls, or at most a few hundred calls of `do_something()` and/or similar subroutines to completely fragment a microcontroller's tiny heap beyond repair.

One potential solution to this problem is to overload the global operators **new** and **delete** to provide a memory allocation mechanism for individual classes. This technique can be effective for making selected dedicated class-specific allocators. For additional information on overloading the global operators **new** and **delete** for a particular class, see Eckel [12], Chap. 13, Sect. "*Overloading new & delete for a class*". Flexible memory management, however, often requires allocation methods that are generic and can be used with any kind of object. So we need to investigate other methods of memory management for microcontroller programming.

10.2 Using Placement-new

Fortunately, **new** is also available in its so-called *placement* version, known as placement-**new**. Placement-**new** allows programmers to explicitly control a dynamically created object's placement in memory (i.e., its physical address).

Placement-**new** is the essential ingredient for generic memory management in microcontroller programming. It allows one to determine *where* (in other words at which address) a given dynamic allocation should be carried out in memory. The caller of placement-**new** is responsible for finding and managing the memory chunks used in calls to placement-**new**. These can be carefully defined memory locations such as the stack in a subroutine call or a local or global static memory pool.

There are several versions of placement-**new**. The form shown below is the most useful one for the purposes of this chapter.

```
void* operator new(size_t, void*) noexcept;
```

This version of placement-**new** creates a pointer to a single object. Placement-**new** does not **throw** any exceptions. The first input parameter to placement-**new** (the one of type `size_t`) gives the size of the object in bytes. The second input parameter (the one of type **`void*`**) specifies the *place* in memory where the new object should be created.

For example, placement-**new** can be used to place an instance of `something` in a subroutine-local memory pool on the stack.

```
class something
{
  // ...
};

void do_something()
{
  std::uint8_t pool[sizeof(something)];

  something* ps = new(pool) something;

  // Do something with ps.
  ps->do_my_thing();

  // Do not delete ps when finished with it.

  // The destructor needs to be called manually.
  ~ps();
}
```

In this example, ps is created with placement-**new** rather than the global operator **new**. Instead of using memory from the heap, ps is placed in a memory pool on the stack. Every time do_something() is called, ps is created on the stack. The memory used for storing ps is recycled because the stack is cleared upon subroutine return. Since the heap is not used, there is no risk of fragmenting or overflowing the heap, as might occur when using the global operator **new**.

The code sample above presents an uncommon sight in C++ programming—an explicit call to a class destructor (i.e., the call to ~ps()). Pointers to class types created with placement-**new** require manual destructor call. They should not be deleted with the global operator **delete**. This differs from pointers created with the global operator **new**. These always need a corresponding call to **delete** which recycles the memory and also implicitly calls the destructor. Custom memory management is one of very few programming situations in C++ that requires explicit call of an object's destructor.

10.3 Allocators and STL Containers

STL containers have an additional (sometimes overlooked) template parameter that defines the so-called *allocator type* used for dynamic memory management. For example, the full template definition of std::vector has not only an elem_-type parameter for the element type but also a second alloc_type parameter for the allocator type. In particular,

```
namespace std
{
  template
    <typename elem_type,
     typename alloc_type = std::allocator<elem_type>>
  class vector
  {
    // ...
  };
}
```

The second template parameter alloc_type is the allocator type. This is the allocator that a given instantiation of std::vector uses to allocate and deallocate elements when dynamically changing its size. If otherwise left unspecified, the value of this allocator type is the STL's templated default allocator class std::allocator instantiated for the type of element in the container.

The key to using STL containers effectively in microcontrollers is to replace the default allocator with a specialized custom allocator. The default allocator uses the global operators **new** and **delete** which, as mentioned previously, can be inappropriate for microcontroller programming. Custom allocators can use memory policies that rely on placement-**new** acting on, for example, a pool of local stack memory or a chunk of re-usable static RAM, etc.

The code below uses `std::vector` with the default allocator.

```
#include <vector>

// A vector with three 32-bit uints.
std::vector<std::uint32_t> v(3U);
```

The code below is almost the same. However, it uses `std::vector` with a custom allocator.

```
#include <vector>
#include "my_allocator.h"

std::vector<std::uint32_t,
            my_allocator<std::uint32_t>> v(3U);
```

Here, `my_allocator` is assumed to have memory allocation and deallocation mechanisms suitable for the microcontroller's memory.

10.4 The Standard Allocator

In order to be used with STL containers, a custom allocator must adhere to the interface of the standard allocator, `std::allocator`. The partial synopsis of the standard library's default allocator class is shown below.

```
namespace std {

template<typename T>
class allocator
{
public:
  typedef std::size_t        size_type;
  typedef std::ptrdiff_t     difference_type;
  typedef T                  value_type;
  typedef value_type*        pointer;
  typedef const value_type* const_pointer;
  typedef value_type&        reference;
  typedef const value_type& const_reference;
```

```
  allocator() noexcept;
  allocator(const allocator&) noexcept;

  template<class U>
  allocator(const allocator<U>&) noexcept;

  ~allocator() noexcept;

  template <class U>
  struct rebind { typedef allocator<U> other; };

  size_type max_size() const noexcept;

  pointer address(reference) const;
  const_pointer address(const_reference) const;

  pointer allocate(size_type,
    typename allocator<void>::const_pointer = nullptr);

  void construct(pointer, const value_type&);

  void destroy(pointer);

  void deallocate(pointer, size_type);
};

} // namespace std
```

The complete specification of the behavior and requirements of the default allocator can be found in [14], with details in Sect. 20.1.5 (especially Table 32) and Sect. 20.6.9 therein. Consult also Sect. 19.3 of [15] for a detailed description of the data types and operations of `std::allocator`.

10.5 Writing a Specialized `ring_allocator`

In the following, we will write a custom `ring_allocator`. The ring allocator obtains its memory from a static pool that behaves like a ring buffer. Memory is consumed as needed for allocation and automatically recycled in the ring buffer.

The functions needing specialization in a custom allocator are `max_size()`, `allocate()` and `deallocate()` (Sect. 19.2 in [15]). Armed with this list, writing a custom allocator using specialized memory management instead of global **new** and **delete** is straightforward.

We will begin with a base class that predominantly handles the ring allocator's memory management. In particular,

```
class ring_allocator_base
{
public:
  typedef std::size_t size_type;

protected:
  ring_allocator_base() { }

  // The ring_allocator's buffer size.
  static constexpr size_type buffer_size = 64U;

  // The ring_allocator's memory allocation.
  static void* do_allocate(const size_type);
};
```

The ring_allocator_base class defines the buffer_size. It is 64 bytes in this example. The ring allocator base class also defines a static function called do_allocate(). The do_allocate() function is responsible for the nuts and bolts of the memory allocation in the ring buffer. In particular,

```
void*
ring_allocator_base::do_allocate(const size_type size)
{
  // Define a static buffer and memory pointer.
  static std::uint8_t  buffer[buffer_size];
  static std::uint8_t* get_ptr = buffer;

  // Get the newly allocated pointer.
  std::uint8_t* p = get_ptr;

  // Increment the pointer for the next allocation.
  get_ptr += size;

  // Does this allocation overflow the top
  // of the buffer?
  const bool is_wrap =
    (get_ptr >= (buffer + buffer_size));
```

```
  if(is_wrap)
  {
    // Here, the allocation overflows the top
    // of the buffer. Reset the allocated pointer
    // to the bottom of the buffer and increment
    // the next get-pointer accordingly.
    p       = buffer;
    get_ptr = buffer + size;
  }

  return static_cast<void*>(p);
}
```

The do_allocate() subroutine returns a non-constant **void**-pointer to the next free chunk of memory in its ring buffer. A local static buffer called buffer and a ring pointer named get_ptr are defined in the subroutine. The get_ptr variable cycles through the ring buffer, always pointing to the next block of free memory. When the top of the requested memory block exceeds the top of the buffer, get_ptr wraps around to the beginning of the buffer—in the sense of a ring buffer.

Armed with the memory allocation mechanism of the ring allocator base class, it is straightforward to write the derived ring_allocator template class. For example,

```
template<typename T>
class ring_allocator : public ring_allocator_base
{
public:
  // ...

  size_type max_size() const noexcept
  {
    // The max. size is based on the buffer size.
    return buffer_size / sizeof(value_type);
  }

  pointer allocate(size_type count,
    ring_allocator<void>::const_pointer = nullptr)
  {
    // Use the base class ring allocation mechanism.
    void* p = do_allocate(count * sizeof(value_type));

    return static_cast<pointer>(p);
  }
```

```
  void deallocate(pointer, size_type)
  {
    // Deallocation does nothing.
  }

  // ...
};
```

This code sample shows possible implementations of the three subroutines needing specialization when creating the custom ring allocator—max_size(), allocate() and deallocate(). The most significant details of these functions include:

- The max_size() member. This function evaluates the maximum available memory size based on the buffer_size.
- The allocate() function. Memory allocation uses the memory management scheme of the do_allocate() function in the base class.
- The deallocate() function, which is empty. Memory is simply recycled and re-used in the ring buffer without being cleared or otherwise modified. The deallocate() function can, therefore, be empty.

The allocate() function of the ring allocator calls do_allocate() as its sole instance for memory allocation. The ring buffer cycles through and eventually wraps around to its start. This means that previously allocated memory is overwritten without taking any particular precautions or even warning the caller about buffer overrun. Users of the ring_allocator, then, need to be acutely aware of this limitation and set the size of the internal buffer accordingly for the intended use of this allocator.

With additional software, an out-of-memory check could optionally be added to the class if needed, possibly in conjunction with a mechanism for properly handling an out-of-memory exception. See Sect. 10.7 for further details on this.

Memory alignment is not taken into consideration in the allocation mechanism of the ring_allocator. If memory alignment on, say, 4-byte or 8-byte boundaries is necessary, a simple modulus check needs to be added to the size passed to the allocation routine.

10.6 Using ring_allocator and Other Allocators

The ring_allocator has been designed to be particularly effective when used with subroutine-local STL containers. Consider, for instance, a subroutine that prepares a made-up login response.

```
// Type definition for the ring allocator of uint8_t.
typedef ring_allocator<std::uint8_t> alloc_type;

// Type definition of a vector using alloc_type.
typedef
std::vector<std::uint8_t, alloc_type> response_type;

// Create the login response in a vector.
void login_response(response_type& rsp)
{
  // Reserve memory in the vector.
  // This uses the ring allocator.
  rsp.reserve(5U);

  // Fill the login data in the response vector.
  rsp.push_back(UINT8_C(0x55)); // The login-OK key.
  rsp.push_back(UINT8_C(0x31)); // Data rsp[1] = '1'.
  rsp.push_back(UINT8_C(0x32)); // Data rsp[2] = '2'.
  rsp.push_back(UINT8_C(0x33)); // Data rsp[3] = '3'.

  // Make a byte checksum of the response payload.
  const std::uint8_t checksum =
    std::accumulate(rsp.begin(),
                    rsp.end()
                    UINT8_C(0));

  // Append the checksum to the login response.
  rsp.push_back(checksum);
}
```

The `login_response()` subroutine prepares a communication frame responsible for responding to a login request. These bytes represent a fictional login handshake frame consisting of a key byte (`0x55`), a response with three data bytes (`'1'`, `'2'`, `'3'`) and a byte-wise checksum over the previous four bytes in the frame.

The data bytes in the login response are stored in an `std::vector` that uses the custom `ring_allocator`. The significance of this for the real-time C++ programmer is that the `login_response()` subroutine can be called time and time again—thousands of times, millions of times, etc.—without causing any memory fragmentation whatsoever. Memory for the login response is merely taken from the internal pool of the ring allocator and the modest memory consumption of the login response does not overflow the capacity of the allocator's buffer.

The `ring_allocator` is an efficient, bare-bones allocator. Its allocation routine is fast, and the overhead of deallocation is entirely eliminated because its memory is simply recycled through the ring buffer. As mentioned above, though, care must be taken when using `ring_allocator` (or something similar) to ensure that the allocator's buffer is large enough to prevent buffer overrun for the use-cases at hand.

Other kinds of custom allocators can also be written for various situations that commonly arise in microcontroller programming. One may, for example, consider writing a `static_allocator` that has a one-shot, non-recyclable memory pool. This could be useful for static constant STL container objects such as version strings, lookup tables, etc. that are created once and remain unchanged for the duration of the program. Another example of a well-known custom allocator is one that holds a pointer to a buffer called an *arena*. This kind of arena pool can be used to create a stack-based allocator. In addition, it is possible to wrap a constant address in, say, a `mapped_allocator`. This can be used to overlay a memory-mapped vector onto a memory-aligned set of hardware registers such as a DMA in a microcontroller peripheral device.

Custom allocators make it possible to embed the power of STL containers and algorithms working on them in remarkably tiny microcontrollers—safely and efficiently—in environments bounded by strict memory limitations. Using custom STL allocators that are tailored to the needs of the application can potentially add a new dimension of elegance and ease to microcontroller programming.

10.7 Recognizing and Handling Memory Limitations

Because we are not using C++ exceptions in this book, the `ring_allocator` described in the previous section does not include checks for out-of-memory or for excessive block size. A standards-adherent custom allocator should, however, include checks for both an out-of-memory error as well as an excessive-length error. STL authors will, therefore, typically support C++ exceptions when requesting memory from an allocator.

An ideal allocator should throw an `std::bad_alloc` exception if the allocator is out of memory. In addition, it should throw an `std::length_error` exception if the requested block size exceeds the size returned from `max_size()`. The code below depicts a possible implementation of the `reserve()` method that includes support for `std::length_error`.

```
#include <memory>
#include <exception>

template<typename T,
         typename alloc = std::allocator<T>>
```

```
class vector
{
public:
  // ...

  void reserve(size_type count);
  {
    // Calculate the requested block-size.
    const size_type size = count * sizeof(value_type);

    // Obtain the maximum size available.
    const size_type the_max
      = allocator_type().max_size();

    // Is the maximum size exceeded?
    if(size > the_max)
    {
      // Throw a length error exception.
      throw std::length_error();
    }

    // Reserve the requested count.
    // ...
  }

  // ...
};
```

Before allocating any memory, the `reserve()` method queries the allocator's `max_size()` to find out if the requested memory size exceeds the available size. If the allocator's `max_size()` will be exceeded by the requested allocation, then there is insufficient memory and an `std::length_error` exception is thrown.

Developers can check for exceptions using a **`try-catch`** clause. We will now modify the `login_response()` subroutine from the previous section to catch a length error exception that may potentially be thrown when attempting to reserve the response vector.

```
// Type definition for the ring allocator of uint8_t.
typedef ring_allocator<std::uint8_t> alloc_type;

// Type definition of a vector using the alloc_type.
typedef
std::vector<std::uint8_t,
            alloc_type> response_type;
```

```
// Create the login response in a vector.
void login_response(response_type& rsp)
{
  // Try to reserve 5 bytes in the vector.
  try
  {
    rsp.reserve(5U);
  }
  catch(const std::length_error& e)
  {
    // Catch a length error exception.

    // Implement an error reaction.
    // ...
  }

  // ...
}
```

C++ exception handling can potentially improve the reliability of embedded real-time software. C++ exception handling may, however, increase the code size of the project by several tens of kilobytes, depending on the characteristics of the compiler implementation of exception handling. Enabling and using C++ exceptions should, therefore, only be undertaken if sufficient resources are available.

10.8 Off-Chip Memory and Computing 100,001 Digits of π

Embedded software projects often use increased memory by adding different types of off-chip or off-bus memory such as non-volatile NVM, EEPROM, card-based memory, volatile SRAM, video RAM, etc. Computationally intensive applications may very well require, in particular, more RAM than is available on-chip in the microcontroller. At the same time, RAM tends to be quite limited in today's microcontrollers because of its high requirements on silicon use and chip area.[1]

One practical, tangible way to increase the amount of available RAM can be to use external memory ICs. Examples `chapter10_08` and `chapter10_08a` focus particularly on handling read/write access to external serial and parallel SRAM chips. We will use external memory ICs to extend the available static RAM of our target with the 8-bit microcontroller to as much as ~2 M byte.

[1]Ratios of around 1/8 or 1/16 RAM-per-ROM (on-chip) seem to be typical for common microcontrollers in the industry. On our target with the 8-bit microcontroller, for instance, the standalone single-chip microcontroller has 2 k byte RAM for 32 k byte ROM.

The extended memory is used for calculations of thousands of digits of the mathematical constant π (Sect. 12.2), up to more than 100,001 decimal digits.

Within the context of examples `chapter10_08` and `chapter10_08a`, we will utilize various advanced technologies including

- complex algorithms,
- distribution of algorithmic complexity among the calls of a state machine,
- creation of specialized iterator and container templates for abstracting off-chip RAM access allowing external SRAM to be used almost like regular on-chip memory in the usual C++ way,
- building hardware prototypes requiring attention to detail and laboratory skills, especially example `chapter10_08a`, requiring two external 16-bit port expander chips, an SMT-to-DIP adaption for the breadboard and numerous carefully fitted wire connections.

To calculate π, we will use a so-called *spigot* algorithm, the algorithmic particularities of which are explained in great detail below. We begin with the calculation of 10,001 decimal digits of π. The expected truncated, non-rounded result is[2]

$$\pi_{10{,}001} = 3.14159 \ldots 5678\,. \tag{10.1}$$

A glance forward to Table 10.2 shows that ∼140 k byte RAM are required. The hardware setup used to successfully perform this memory-demanding 10,001 digit π calculation is shown in Fig. 10.1. It uses a variation of our target system with

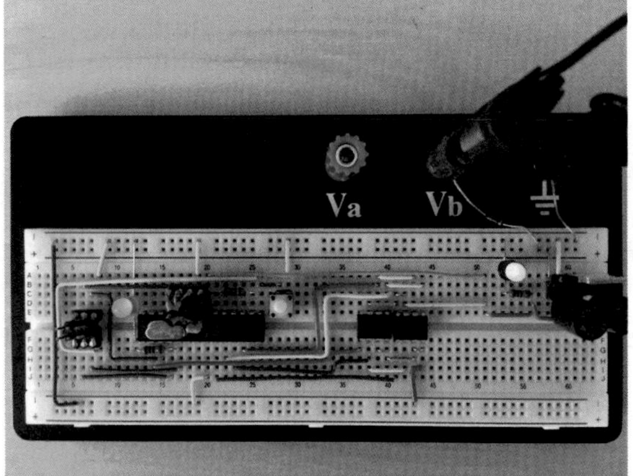

Fig. 10.1 Our target system with the 8-bit microcontroller calculating 10,001 decimal digits of π in example `chapter10_08` is shown. Two external serial SRAM memory chips connected to the all-software SPI™ communication interface of Sect. 9.5 can be observed. The calculation of 10,001 decimal digits of π with this setup requires about 3 h

[2]The expected result can be compared with, for instance, the value obtained from an AGM calculation in the `chapter10_08-001_pi_millions_with_boost.cpp` code snippet shown later in this section near the description of Eq. 10.9 and one extra digit beyond 10,001 is used.

Table 10.1 The pin connections between the microcontroller and the SRAM chips in example `chapter10_08` are listed

Pin on SRAM chip (0,1)	SRAM chip's function	Electrical connection	Microcontroller pin
1_0	$\overline{\text{CS}}_0$	`portc.4`	27
6_0	SCK_0	`portc.3`	26
2_0	SO_0	`portc.2`	25
5_0	SI_0	`portc.1`	24
1_1	$\overline{\text{CS}}_1$	`portc.5`	28
6_1	SCK_1	`portc.3`	Shared with SCK_0
2_1	SO_1	`portc.2`	Shared with SO_0
5_1	SI_1	`portc.1`	Shared with SI_0

the 8-bit microcontroller. Two off-chip SPI™ serial SRAM ICs of type Microchip® 23LC1024 [18] are employed for the RAM memory extension. The memory ICs are placed adjacent to each other and located in the center-right portion of the board in Fig. 10.1.

The pin connections between the microcontroller and the SRAM chips are listed in Table 10.1. The all-software SPI™ driver from Sect. 9.5 is used to control the two SRAM chips. The three SPI™ control lines (MOSI, MISO, SCK) use the same microcontroller pins for each SRAM chip. The individual chips are selected via setting the corresponding chip-select-not pin to low ($\overline{\text{CS}}_0$ or $\overline{\text{CS}}_1$).

We will now begin with the creation of specialized iterator and container templates for abstracting off-chip RAM access. Unlike some larger microcontrollers, our target system with the 8-bit microcontroller lacks any kind of hardware or bus interface support for SRAM extension.[3] The SRAM interface hardware and software, therefore, need to be built entirely from scratch.

We begin with the creation of a specialized software SRAM iterator. Our SRAM iterator employs a dedicated SRAM pointer specially designed for read/write access to external memory ICs. In particular, a template utility class called `mcal::memory::sram::sram_ptr` is used. This self-made pointer class is an abstraction of a pointer that provides low-level read/write access to the external serial SRAM memory chips via SPI™. The essentials of the public interface of `mcal::memory::sram::sram_ptr` are partially summarized below.

[3]Larger chips in the family such as the Microchip® ATmega2560 [19, 20] do, however, have direct bus interface support for up to 64 k byte off-chip SRAM using a 74HC series latch. In addition, the subject of example `chapter10_09` in Sect. 10.9 uses a powerful single-board computer with ample 32-bit bus addressable RAM. These kinds of RAM interfaces will, however, not be used in this particular example.

```
namespace mcal { namespace memory { namespace sram {

template<typename ValueType,
         typename AddressType,
         typename AddressDifferenceType>
class sram_ptr
{
public:
  // Types reference, difference_type, etc.

  // Constructors.
  sram_ptr();

  // ...

  // Pointer access via dereferencing.
  reference operator*();

  const reference operator*() const;

        // ...

  // Pointer increment, decrement, etc.
  sram_ptr& operator++();
  sram_ptr& operator--();

  // ...
};

} } } // namespace mcal::memory::sram
```

This pointer abstraction is equipped with functions for both incrementing and decrementing addresses as well as reading from and writing to specific memory locations. There are both constant as well as non-constant versions of the dereference operator (**operator***()). These are intended to hook up to low-level memory access driver primitives such as read and write of single bytes or multiple-byte stream bursts.

On top of the SRAM pointer, higher level abstractions including an SRAM iterator template named `mcal::memory::sram::sram_iterator` and an array-like container called `mcal::memory::sram::sram_array`, have been written. These provide convenient and familiar STL-like container read/write access to the external SRAM memory ICs. After the buildup of these levels of abstraction to SRAM access, we now have, in summary, seamless C++-style read/write pointer, iterator and array access to the external SRAM chips. These shield the high-level program layers from the low-level details that depend on the specific kind of memory being used.

The pointer, iterator and array abstractions used here for read/write SRAM access are similar to those used in the read-only case for reading ROM in example `chapter06_14` of Sect. 6.14. In addition, the read/write iterator for SRAM access described here could just as well alternatively be based on using Iterator Façade from Boost [1], as was also briefly indicated in Sect. 6.14.

We will now consider the mathematics of example `chapter10_08`. The mathematical starting point of this example is a so-called *spigot* algorithm [6, 24, 33]. Spigot algorithms can be used to produce sequences of digits of mathematical constants. The most recently generated digits are computed in these algorithms sequentially from left to right, regardless of the values of the previously calculated digits. In this way, spigot algorithms have symbolic or intuitive similarity with a household water spigot that drips or pours out water from its opening. Spigot algorithms in various numerical bases are known for certain mathematical constants such as e, $\log 10$, π and others. This list fortunately also includes π in the familiar base 10.

A simplified form of a spigot algorithm for π is provided in Eq. 6.1, Sect. 6.1, page 78 of [6]. In particular,

$$\pi = 2 + \frac{1}{3}\left(2 + \frac{2}{5}\left(2 + \frac{3}{7}\left(2 + \ldots\right)\right)\right). \tag{10.2}$$

The authors of [6] go on to implement a well-described C-language program based on code and mathematical theory from [24]. The program calculates decimal digits of π in sequential groups of 4 digits. For the particular implementation therein, a maximum of 54,932 decimal digits can be calculated before a sequence of four zeros in a row forcefully halts the recursion in the program.

In our book, a related program has been created for examples `chapter10_08` and `chapter10_08a`. This program is called the π spigot program. It uses a C++11 template design that incorporates a base class called `pi_spigot_base`. The class types used for the actual π spigot calculations are called `pi_spigot_single` and `pi_spigot_state`. These are both derived directly from the base class.

Our π spigot program is capable of using a variable number of loop digits ℓ, with a granularity ranging from $4 \leq \ell \leq 9$. This feature is supported through the template parameter `LoopDigit`, mirrored through the class-local **`constexpr`** member variable `loop_digit`.

With `loop_digit` set to 9, for instance, the recursion-stopping sequence of four zeros at digit position 54,932 that hinders the program in [6] does not terminate the calculation in the π spigot program. Because of this convenient fact, the π spigot program with, for instance, $\ell = 9$ and multiplication results stored in `std::uint64_t` can be used for π calculations with results ranging from 10 up to 1,000,000 decimal digits and beyond. As shown below, however, the required memory and calculation time increase significantly with rising digit count.

Some of the declarations of the `pi_spigot_single` class are shown in the code below. This class can be used to compute digits of π in a single blocking call with one process, thread or core entirely dedicated to the nested inner loops of the program without multitasking or thread overhead.

The digits of π themselves are computed in a template method called `calculate()`. In particular,

---

```
// The pi spigot program.
// ...

template<const std::uint32_t ResultDigit,
         const std::uint32_t LoopDigit>
class pi_spigot_base
{
public:
  static constexpr std::uint32_t loop_digit =
    LoopDigit;

  // ...
};

// ...

template<const std::uint32_t ResultDigit,
         const std::uint32_t LoopDigit>
class pi_spigot_single
  : public pi_spigot_base<ResultDigit,
                          LoopDigit>
{
public:
  pi_spigot_single() = default;

  virtual ~pi_spigot_single() = default;

  template<typename ItIn,
           typename ItOut>
  void calculate(ItIn  input_first,
                 ItOut output_first)
  {
    // Use pi_spigot::calculate() to calculate
    // result_digit decimal digits of pi.
```

```
        // The caller is responsible for providing
        // both input memory for the internal
        // calculation details as well as output
        // memory for the result digits of pi.

        // ...
    }

    // ...
};
```

Runtime and operation count values for selected runs of the π spigot program on several systems are summarized together with associated memory usage in Table 10.2. The column showing runtime on a PC reflects execution time of calculating the corresponding digits of π on one single PC core. A π spigot object of type `pi_spigot_single` has been used for the PC measurements in the table.[4]

There are two columns showing runtime on our target with the 8-bit microcontroller. These depict the execution time needed to calculate the corresponding digits of π with the state machine version of the π spigot algorithm using an object of type `pi_spigot_state`. Times for two individual hardware setups using either serial or parallel SRAM are tabulated. These calculation times also include the overhead from a running in a state machine implementation within the idle task of the multitasking scheduler, which is rather significant.

In Table 10.2, we find that memory consumption grows linearly with digit count. The computational complexity and resulting runtime of the program scale approximately quadratically with the number of digits in the result. This means

Table 10.2 Runtime and operation count of the π spigot program together with associated memory usage are summarized for various numbers of digits. Groups of 9 digits are used for the template parameter `loop_digit` (i.e., $\ell = 9$)

Digits	Operations	Runtime [s] PC	Runtime [s] 8-bit μC serial SRAM	Runtime [s] 8-bit μC parallel SRAM	RAM [k byte]
1,000,001	1.9×10^{11}	2100			13,000
500,001	4.8×10^{10}	520			6600
100,001	1.9×10^{9}	21		5.4×10^{5}	1400
50,001	4.8×10^{8}	5.3		1.4×10^{5}	630
10,001	1.9×10^{7}	0.23	9.3×10^{3}	5.5×10^{3}	140
5001	4.8×10^{6}	0.055	2.3×10^{3}	1.4×10^{3}	67
1001	1.9×10^{5}	0.002	9.4×10^{1}	5.6×10^{1}	13

[4]Potential distribution among multiple cores has not yet been investigated for this implementation, even though this seems feasible.

that run-time performance drops significantly for large digit results due to rapidly increasing operation count.

Both memory consumption as well as operation count for the π spigot program can, in fact, be calculated exactly in closed form.[5] The mathematical analysis thereof is shown in the following paragraphs.

The required memory m in $\left[\text{byte}\right]$ is given by

$$m = 4 \left\lfloor \frac{d\left(\left\lfloor \frac{10\ell}{3} \right\rfloor + 1\right)}{\ell} \right\rfloor \left[\text{byte}\right] , \tag{10.3}$$

where bottom-edged brackets such as $\lfloor x \rfloor$ designate the integral floor of x. ℓ is the value of the `loop_digit` template parameter ranging from $4 \le \ell \le 9$. d is the number of decimal digits of π requested. The numeral 4 represents four bytes per internal storage unit of type `std::uint32_t`.

With $\ell = 9$ and $d = 50{,}001$, for instance, the required memory $m\,(9\,|\,50{,}001)$ is

$$\begin{aligned} m\,(9\,|\,50{,}001) &= 4 \left\lfloor \frac{50{,}001\left(\left\lfloor \frac{10\times 9}{3} \right\rfloor + 1\right)}{9} \right\rfloor \left[\text{byte}\right] \\ &= 4 \times 172{,}225 \left[\text{byte}\right] \\ &= 688{,}900 \left[\text{byte}\right] \\ &\approx 0.7 \times 10^6 \left[\text{byte}\right] , \end{aligned} \tag{10.4}$$

which is just shy of 1 *M*byte and agrees with the corresponding entry in Table 10.2.

The operation count N can be obtained from the two nested loops in the π spigot program. These can be represented with a summation that has a closed form result. We find that the operation count for this implementation is given by

$$\begin{aligned} N &= \sum_{\substack{j=0 \\ \ell\,|\,j}}^{d} \left\lfloor \frac{(d-j)\left(\left\lfloor \frac{10\ell}{3} \right\rfloor + 1\right)}{\ell} \right\rfloor \\ &= -\frac{1}{2}\left(\left\lfloor \frac{d}{\ell} \right\rfloor + 1\right) \left\{ \left(\left\lfloor \frac{10\ell}{3} \right\rfloor + 1\right) \left\lfloor \frac{d}{\ell} \right\rfloor - 2 \left\lfloor \frac{d\left(\left\lfloor \frac{10\ell}{3} \right\rfloor + 1\right)}{\ell} \right\rfloor \right\} , \end{aligned} \tag{10.5}$$

[5] In the π spigot program here, we use a so-called *bounded* algorithm intended to compute a specific number of digits with a fixed amount of memory reserved for the computation (see also § 3 in [33]).

where the syntax of the summation notation containing the expression $\ell\,|\,j$, means that j is looped from $0 \ldots d$ in increments of granularity ℓ. As mentioned above, Eq. 10.5 verifies the expected quadratic computational complexity of the operation count N of the π spigot program. When calculating d decimal digits of π, this computational complexity scales roughly with order $O\left(\alpha\, d^2\right)$, where α is a constant with $\alpha \lesssim 1$ that depends on the `loop_digit` parameter ℓ. For example $\alpha \sim 0.2$ for $\ell = 9$.[6]

Using again a summation granularity in the `loop_digit` parameter of $\ell = 9$ for $d = 50{,}001$ decimal digits, the operation count $N\,(9\,|\,50{,}001)$ is given by

$$\begin{aligned} N\,(9\,|\,50{,}001) &= -\frac{1}{2}\,(5556)\,\{172{,}205 - 344{,}450\} \\ &= 478{,}496{,}610 \\ &\approx 4.8 \times 10^8\,, \end{aligned} \tag{10.6}$$

also in accordance with the corresponding entry in Table 10.2.

It is a fascinating and richly educational technical challenge in real-time C++ to adapt the π spigot program to our target system with the 8-bit microcontroller and run it successfully. In its original state as a PC program, however, it cannot be used without significant modification on this device having only 2 $k$byte of on-chip SRAM.

Consider for instance, the subject of example `chapter10_08`, which is the calculation of 10,001 decimal digits of π using the π spigot program with parameter $\ell = 9$. This calculation requires nearly 140 k byte of SRAM and approximately 19 million operations (Table 10.2 and Eqs. 10.4 through 10.6).

The following adaptations of hardware and software have been undertaken on our target system with the 8-bit microcontroller in order to successfully run the π spigot program with 10,001 digits.

- Use two serial SPI™ SRAM chips to easily handle the ~140 k byte of memory required. Here we use chips of type Microchip® 23LC1024 [18] having 128 k byte per chip providing a total of 256 k byte.[7]
- Employ the specialized external SRAM templates `mcal::memory::sram::sram_iterator` and `mcal::memory::sram::sram_array` to provide convenient and familiar STL-like container read/write access to the external SRAM memory ICs.
- Store a few more than 10,001 decimal digits of π in constant program memory for checking the result. The methods for accessing constant program memory presented in Sect. 6.14 are used for this.

[6]See also the discussion in Sect. 6.3 which discusses how a given algorithm's computational complexity can often be characterized by its input length.

[7]Alternatively for higher digit counts we could use, for example, one or more parallel asynchronous SRAM bricks with memories in the M byte range.

- Modify the inner loops of the π spigot calculation to use a state machine design. The state machine is intended to run efficiently in successive, numerous, brief single passes that do not clog the multitasking scheduler (Chap. 11).
- A π spigot object of type `pi_spigot_state` having **`static`** storage is used throughout the calculations. This object retains its calculation values from one successive iteration to the next.
- Service the state machine of the π spigot calculation in the idle task of the multitasking scheduler (see also Sect. 11.5).
- The calculation runs and reruns again and again successively without pause or break.
- The approximate percentage of completion of a given calculation cycle is output as a PWM duty cycle on `portb.1` generated from a peripheral timer.

Upon completion of these adaptions, the π spigot program calculating 10,001 decimal digits of π in `chapter10_08` runs successfully on both our target with the 8-bit microcontroller as well as the PC. As mentioned in the list above, numerical correctness is ascertained with a constant table in program code containing $\gtrsim$10,001 decimal digits of π, whereby the new digits produced in a given iteration of the calculation are compared on the spot with the known tabulated digits.

We will now describe example `chapter10_08a` which extends the π spigot program to higher digit counts. In this exercise, the π spigot program has been enlarged even further to use a parallel SRAM brick of type Cypress® MoBL® CY62167GN [11] having 2 *M*byte of asynchronous parallel SRAM. This hardware setup is depicted in Fig. 10.2.[8]

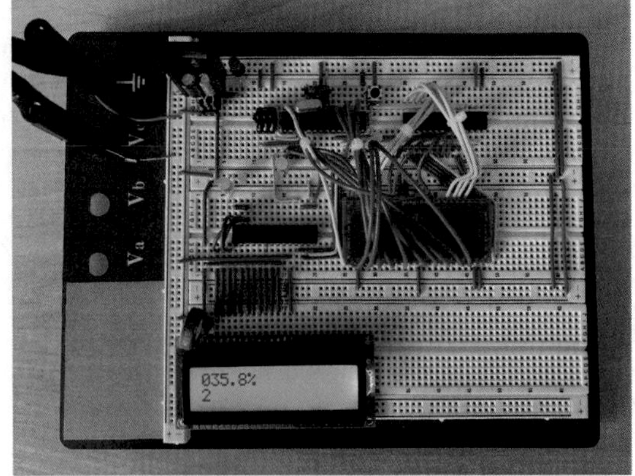

Fig. 10.2 Our target system with the 8-bit microcontroller calculating 100,001 decimal digits of π is shown. A 2 M byte parallel SRAM brick and two serial port expander chips are used. Progress in percent is reported on LCD line 1. Line 2 displays the number of successful calculations in this power-on cycle. Each 100,001 digit run requires ~6.2 days on this system

[8]A similar hardware setup utilizing an SRAM IC of type Cypress® MoBL® CY62158E [10] having 1 M byte of SRAM can also be employed for prototyping. With the 1 M byte setup, it is possible to extend the π spigot calculation to 50,001 digits. When a 2 M byte SRAM chip is used, π spigot calculations up to 100,001 decimal digits and somewhat beyond can be carried out, as listed in Table 10.2.

The wiring of this example is non-trivial and requires careful attention to detail. Fitting the SRAM chip on the breadboard uses an SMT-to-DIP adapter. The use of this adapter, itself, requires rather advanced soldering skills.[9]

Additional digital ports are obtained with two discrete serial port expander chips of type Microchip® MCP23S17 [17], the same port expander type that has been used in the setup featured in Fig. 4.2 of Sect. 4.4. Calculation progress in percent is displayed on an LCD display of type Newhaven NHD-0216K1Z-FSW-FBW-L [23]. The LCD uses typical industry standard port pin control. See also the examples and their documentation in the companion code for additional circuit details.

In example `chapter10_08a`, we calculate up to 100,001 decimal digits of π. There is literally not enough space available in the 32 k byte ROM code region to store both program code as well as such a large control value. An array containing 1012 tabulated values of each 100th digit of π is used for partial verification of up to 101,200 digits. In particular,

```
// Taken from pi_digits_100th_pi_digits.h

namespace math { namespace constants {

// ...

template<>
struct pi_digits_100th_pi_digits<1012U>
{
  using array_type =
   mcal::memory::progmem::array<
    std::uint8_t,
    mcal_progmem_uintptr_t(UINT32_C(1012))>;

  using const_pointer =
    typename array_type::const_pointer;

  static const_pointer pi_digits_control() noexcept
  {
    static const array_type value MY_PROGMEM =
    {{
      3, // : 0

      9, // : 100
      6, // : 200
      3, // : 300
```

[9]For additional information on electronic circuit construction, soldering and safety when doing hobby electronics, see [21, 28].

```
        4, // : 400
        2, // : 500
        2, // : 600
        5, // : 700

        // ...
      }};
    }
  }

} }
```

In addition to checking each 100th digit of π, a standard 160-bit checksum algorithm is used. Each and every character digit retrieved from the π spigot calculation is processed on-the-fly in the checksum. Final checksum comparison is performed at the completion of the π calculation.

Consider, for instance, the truncated, non-rounded value of 100,001 digits of π

$$\pi_{100,001} = 3.14159 \ldots 4646 . \tag{10.7}$$

The 160-bit checksum h_{160} of these 100,001 decimal digits, where each digit is represented as a single character, is similar to

$$h_{160}\,(\texttt{"314159"}\ \ldots\ \texttt{"4646"}) = \texttt{D9D5}\ldots_{16} . \tag{10.8}$$

One of the essential real-time C++ technologies used in example chapter-10_08a is the implementation of read/write operations from/to the many-pinned SRAM IC carried out by the processor in our target system with the 8-bit microcontroller. For controlling the SRAM brick, this example uses a template class called memory_sram_parallel_cypress_cy62167gn. Its public interface is sketched below.

```
template
  <typename sram_parallel_port_pin_addr20_type,
   typename sram_parallel_port_addr04_to_19_type,
   typename sram_parallel_port_pin_addr03_type,
   typename sram_parallel_port_pin_addr02_type,
   typename sram_parallel_port_pin_addr01_type,
   typename sram_parallel_port_pin_addr00_type,
   typename sram_parallel_port_pin_ce1not_type,
   typename sram_parallel_port_pin_ce2____type,
   typename sram_parallel_port_pin_oe_not_type,
```

```
      typename sram_parallel_port_pin_we_not_type,
      typename sram_parallel_port_data08_type,
      const std::uint8_t nop_count,
      const bool has_disable_enable_interrupts>
class memory_sram_parallel_cypress_cy62167gn final
  : private util::noncopyable
{
public:
  void write(
    const std::uint32_t address_to_write,
    const std::uint8_t source_byte_to_write);

  void write_n(
    const std::uint32_t address_to_write,
    const std::size_t   count,
    const std::uint8_t* source_input_to_write);

  std::uint8_t read(
    const std::uint32_t address_to_read);

  void read_n(
    const std::uint32_t address_to_read,
    const std::size_t   count,
    std::uint8_t* dest_to_store_read_data);

  // ...
};
```

This is a highly speed-optimized template class that provides functions for writing and reading single bytes or multiple-byte stream bursts. The selection of template parameters allows for a compromise between runtime efficiency and the number of available ports on the microcontroller. The comparatively slowly-changing upper sixteen address bits, for instance, are intended to be placed on a cohesive 16-bit port that reads and writes all bits at once for the sake of efficiency. In this example, a port expander is needed for the upper sixteen address bits. More quickly changing pins including the lower address nibble bits and the SRAM chip control lines such as write-enable, etc. can be placed on fast microcontroller port pins. The eight I/O data bits can be placed on an 8-bit microcontroller port for fast data read and write (in this example `portd.0–7`).

The π spigot program used in examples `chapter10_08` and `chapter10_08a` is terse and relatively easy to understand. It is effective for low digit counts and offers rich exemplary utility. This π spigot program and other spigot-based π programs in general are, however, rather slow for large digit counts. Consider once again the increasing operation counts and corresponding runtime values listed in

Table 10.2. In this table we do, in fact, observe that the calculation time of the π spigot program grows quadratically with increasing digit count, as predicted by Eq. 10.5. These runtime characteristics make ultra high-digit calculations with spigot algorithms impractical, especially on our target with the 8-bit microcontroller.

For many fans of π calculations, however, it just has to be millions of decimal digits of π or even more. Readers seeking much larger digit counts, for instance, in a higher performance environment might consider investigating π programs that use a quadratically convergent AGM iteration (i.e., arithmetic geometric mean [6, 7]) or Chudnovsky-type rapid series expansion [31]. These, when combined with an efficient big number package, can be used for very fast ultra high-precision calculations of π (or selected other values).

Consider, for instance, the Schönhage variation of the Gauss AGM iteration for π. It is based on Algorithm 16.149 in Chap. 16 on page 236 of [6], which can be originally found in [29].

$$
\begin{aligned}
&\text{Initialize :}\\
&\quad a_0 := 1\\
&\quad A_0 := 1\\
&\quad B_0 := 0.5\\
&\quad s_0 := 0.5\\
&\text{Iterate :}\\
&\quad T := (A_k + B_k) / 4\\
&\quad b_k := \sqrt{B_k}\\
&\quad a_{k+1} := (a_k + b_k) / 2\\
&\quad A_{k+1} := a_{k+1}^2\\
&\quad B_{k+1} := 2\,(A_{k+1} - T)\\
&\quad s_{k+1} := s_k + 2^{k+1}\,(B_{k+1} - A_{k+1})\\
&\text{Then :}\\
&\quad p_n = \frac{A_n + B_n}{s_n} \xrightarrow{2} \pi
\end{aligned}
\tag{10.9}
$$

The pseudo-code below sketches the template subroutine `pi()`. It uses the Gauss AGM iteration for π from Eq. 10.9 and is intended to perform PC-based calculations of millions of digits of π.

```
// chapter10_08-001_pi_millions_with_boost.cpp

// Compute pi using a quadratically convergent
// Gauss AGM, in the Schoenhage variant.

// ...

template<typename float_type>
const float_type& pi(...)
{
  // ...
}

// ...
```

Calculating, for instance, one million digits of π with the subroutine `pi()` shown above in combination with `Boost.Multiprecision` [16] and its `gmp_float` backend based on GMP [13] or MPIR [22] takes $\lesssim 2$ s. This is about 1000 times faster than the calculation of one million digits of π obtained from the spigot program described above executed on the same PC host system (Table 10.2).

For the sake of completeness, the verbose timing information produced by the subroutine `pi()` in the program `chapter10_08-001_pi_millions_with_boost.cpp` running on a PC host system is shown in Fig. 10.3. The source code of the entire ultra high-precision π AGM program is available in the code

```
Base-10 digits of iteration  1:        2
Base-10 digits of iteration  2:        4
Base-10 digits of iteration  3:        9
Base-10 digits of iteration  4:       20
Base-10 digits of iteration  5:       42
Base-10 digits of iteration  6:       85
Base-10 digits of iteration  7:      172
Base-10 digits of iteration  8:      346
Base-10 digits of iteration  9:      695
Base-10 digits of iteration 10:     1394
Base-10 digits of iteration 11:     2790
Base-10 digits of iteration 12:     5584
Base-10 digits of iteration 13:    11172
Base-10 digits of iteration 14:    22349
Base-10 digits of iteration 15:    44703
Base-10 digits of iteration 16:    89410
Base-10 digits of iteration 17:   178826
Base-10 digits of iteration 18:   357657
Base-10 digits of iteration 19:   715320
Iteration loop done, compute inverse
The pi calculation is done.
================================================
Computed 1000001 digits of pi.
Total computation time : 1.87 seconds
================================================
Writing the output file.
```

Fig. 10.3 The calculation of one million digits of π in 19 AGM iterations on a PC host system is shown. This run required $\lesssim 2$ s. Observe the quadratic convergence of the algorithm which approximately doubles the number of precise digits in each successive iteration

snippets. In our implementation, slight algebraic simplifications of the initialization and optimizations of the iteration loop have been undertaken.

10.9 Using Ample RAM on Arm®-Based Single-Board Computer

Sometimes regardless of how many optimizations are performed certain applications simply *require* significant amounts of RAM. The bounded π spigot program from the previous section calculating 100,001 decimal digits of π, for instance, needs approximately 1.4 M byte RAM, as listed in Table 10.2. A single-board computer [32] having ample on-board RAM can potentially be a good choice for such applications.

This section describes example `chapter10_09`. In this example, we adapt the π spigot program from example `chapter10_08a` to run on a commercially available single-board computer.

We use the well-known 32-bit Arm®-based Raspberry Pi®Zero WH single-board computer [25].[10] This single-board computer is equipped with a modern and powerful 32-bit ARM1176JZF-S™ processor [2] clocked at 1 GHz. The processor is interfaced to 512 M byte of synchronous dynamic RAM (SDRAM) and several additional high-performance peripherals. The Arm11™ is integrated in the Broadcom® BCM2835 system-on-chip [8, 9].

The 32-bit Arm®-based Raspberry Pi®Zero WH single-board computer system in example `chapter10_09` calculating 100,001 decimal digits of π on a solderless prototyping breadboard is shown in Fig. 10.4. The 100,001 digit π calculation

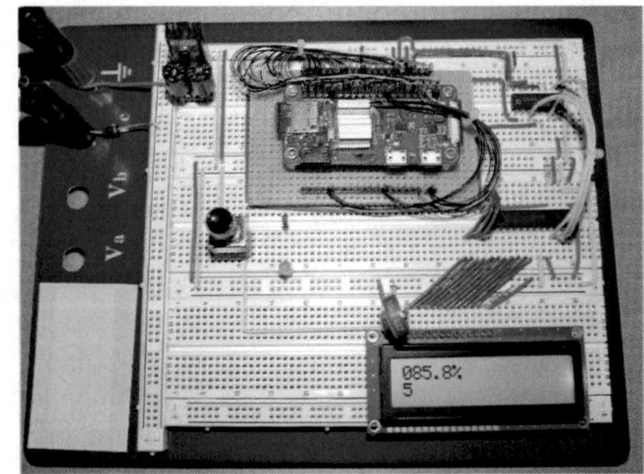

Fig. 10.4 The 32-bit Arm®-based Raspberry Pi®Zero WH single-board computer system in example `chapter10_09` calculating 100,001 decimal digits of π is shown. In this power-on cycle, the system has completed five full π calculations and is about 90% finished with its sixth

[10] In the name Raspberry Pi®Zero WH, the abbreviation *WH* stands for *Wireless* with *Header*. This single-board computer system has wireless connectivity capabilities and an optional double-row of 2.54 mm pins is soldered to the 40-pin header in the factory. This example, however, also works with the Raspberry Pi® Zero as well (without the *WH* option).

requires ~2500 s (about 42 min) and uses 1.4 M byte of this system's abundant quantity of 512 M byte of easy-to-access on-board SDRAM.

With more than enough on-board SDRAM available for the π calculation, circuit design is relatively straightforward. Just a few external components are needed to represent the computation's progress on an industry standard character-based LCD of type Newhaven NHD-0216K1Z-FSW-FBW-L [23]. Pin connections are summarized in Tables 10.3 and 10.4.

Table 10.3 The GPIO pins, their associated pins on the Raspberry Pi®Zero WH's 40-pin header, their functions and their connections in example `chapter10_09` are listed

GPIO/40-pin header	Function	AND-Gate	Port expander
GPIO12/H32	Debug and benchmark timing	in 12/13, out 11	
GPIO16/H36	$\overline{\text{CS}}$ (of all-software SPI™ driver)	in 9/10, out 8	11
GPIO18/H12	SCK (of all-software SPI™ driver)	in 1/2, out 3	12
GPIO19/H35	MOSI (of all-software SPI™ driver)	in 4/5, out 6	13

Table 10.4 The pin connections of the port expander chip in example `chapter10_09` are listed

Port expander	Function	Connection
1	GPB0	LCD DB0
2	GPB1	LCD DB1
3	GPB2	LCD DB2
4	GPB3	LCD DB3
5	GPB4	LCD DB4
6	GPB5	LCD DB5
7	GPB6	LCD DB6
8	GPB7	LCD DB7
9	V_{DD}	+5 V
10	V_{SS}	GND
11	$\overline{\text{CS}}$	GPIO16/H36 (via AND-gate in 10/9, out 8)
12	SCK	GPIO18/H12 (via AND-gate in 1/2, out 3)
13	SI	GPIO19/H35 (via AND-gate in 4/5, out 6)
15	A0	GND
16	A1	+5 V
17	A2	GND
18	$\overline{\text{RESET}}$	Switch closed (non-pressed): +5 V Switch open (pressed): 16 kΩ pulldown to GND
19–20	INTA/B	Not connected
21–24	GPA0–3	Not connected
25	GPA4	750 Ω to LED1
26	GPA5	LCD RS
27	GPA6	LCD R/W
28	GPA7	LCD E

In this example, the Raspberry Pi®Zero WH is used directly out of the box with non-modified factory settings. Traditional wire-wrapping with AWG-30 wire [30] twisted with a hand-held tool has been used to connect the needed pins on the Raspberry Pi®Zero WH's 40-pin header with a homemade breakout board that is, itself, fitted on the breadboard.

The electrical conversion from the Broadcom® BCM2835's 3.3 V CMOS logic level to the 5 V TTL needed by other components on the board (such as the LCD) uses a classic 7408 quad AND-gate. Although a quad AND-gate simply happened to be in the drawer at the time of fitting the breadboard and can be seen in Fig. 10.4, using a hex-buffer could slightly reduce the circuitry even further as there would be no need to tie the individual AND-gate inputs together.

The +5 V supply pins and ground pins in this setup have double and quadruple strands of AWG-30 wire. Multiple strands of wire reduce resistance, voltage drop and parasitic power dissipation in supply lines to minimal levels. See also the discussion on the resistance of wire in Sect. 9.7 spanning from Eqs. 9.1 through 9.5. It makes sense to consider voltage drop and power dissipation on the +5 V supply line when using skinny wire (such as AWG-30 wire) because this system draws a maximum current up to $\lesssim$200 mA.

The 5 V supply pins, for instance, have 4 strands of AWG-30 copper wire with lengths of perhaps 6 cm $\sim$ (1/ 17) m. From Eq. 9.5, the resulting resistance on the +5 V supply line R_{5V} is

$$R_{5V} \approx \left(\frac{1}{4}\right)\left(\frac{1}{17}\,\text{m}\right) 340\,\frac{\text{m}\Omega}{\text{m}} \approx 5\,\text{m}\Omega\,. \qquad (10.10)$$

For a maximum of $\lesssim$200 mA current, the voltage drop on the +5 V supply line dV_{5V} is

$$dV_{5V} \lesssim \frac{1}{5}\,\text{A} \times 5\,\text{m}\Omega \approx 1\,\text{mV}\,, \qquad (10.11)$$

and the power dissipation in the +5 V supply line dP_{5V} is

$$dP_{5V} \lesssim \left(\frac{1}{5}\,\text{A}\right)^2 \times 5\,\text{m}\Omega \approx \frac{1}{5}\,\text{mW}\,, \qquad (10.12)$$

both of which can be confidently neglected for this setup.

A little custom-sawed heat sink has been fashioned from a piece of corrugated, flat-bottomed, semi-hollow aluminum bar found in the recycle bin. It has been pasted with heat-conducting double-sided tape to the top of the Broadcom® BCM2835 chip for cooling.

A port expander chip of type Microchip® MCP23S17 [17] controls the LCD port pins and a second user LED called LED1. This port expander chip is of the same variety as the one that has been used in examples `chapter04_04`, `chapter04_04a`, `chapter10_08` and `chapter10_08a`.

A reset button is located in the center-left portion of the board in Fig. 10.4. Having reversed polarity, this switch button is in the closed state when non-pressed and in the open state when pressed. In particular when the reset button is pressed, the Raspberry Pi®Zero WH +5 V supply line is switched to open-circuit and both the port expander chip $\overline{\text{RESET}}$ pin as well as the LCD supply are pulled to ground over 16 kΩ. Letting go of the reset button to its non-pressed state creates semi-synchronized reboot conditions for the Raspberry Pi®Zero WH and the LCD display and resets the port expander chip. So these components basically restart nearly in unison when the reset button is briefly pressed and shortly thereafter released to its non-pressed state.

A minimalistic do-it-yourself MCAL has been written for this target in order to provide a few peripheral drivers including a lightweight GPIO port driver.

The all-software SPI™ driver of Sect. 9.5 has been adapted via adjusting it's port timing for the faster CPU. It communicates with the external port expander chip.

Two 32-bit up-counting timer registers `clo` and `chi` are used to provide a consistent 64-bit system tick with a frequency of approximately 1 MHz (see also Sect. 9.3). For a description of the registers `clo` and `chi`, see Chap. 12 "*System Timer*", especially Table 12.1 in [8].

Some portions of the relevant system tick code are summarized below. Note how this implementation also subtracts any potential already-elapsed ticks (i.e., `initial_count`) accrued from the execution of the bootloader.

```
// Taken from mcal_gpt.cpp

struct mcal_gpt_system_tick final
{
public:
  // ...

  static std::uint64_t get_tick()
  {
    const std::uint64_t elapsed =
        get_consistent_microsecond_tick()
      - initial_count;

    return elapsed;
  }

private:
  static std::uint64_t initial_count;

  // ...
```

```
  static std::uint64_t
    get_consistent_microsecond_tick();

  // ...
};

mcal::gpt::value_type
  mcal::gpt::secure::get_time_elapsed()
{
  const std::uint64_t elapsed =
    (gpt_is_initialized()
      ? mcal_gpt_system_tick::get_tick()
      : UINT64_C(0));

  return value_type(elapsed);
}
```

The time-slicing multitasking scheduler (Chap. 11) used on the Raspberry Pi®Zero WH in this example is the same one that has been used throughout the other examples in this book on our target with the 8-bit microcontroller. The time base of the multitasking scheduler uses the consistent 64-bit software system tick described above.

As was the case in example `chapter10_08a`, the π spigot calculation in example `chapter10_09` is also implemented as a state machine. In fact the identical header-only code is used to implement the `pi_spigot_state` class. The state machine is serviced in the idle task of the multitasking scheduler.

Numerical verification of the π result in example `chapter10_09` uses both a table of the 100th digits of π as well as a standard 160-bit checksum calculated over the digits of π represented as characters. This approach is the same as the one taken to check the numerical results in example `chapter10_08a` described near Eqs. 10.7 and 10.8.

The Raspberry Pi®Zero WH in example `chapter10_09` is used in so-called *bare metal* mode without any operating system. It is somewhat uncommon to run single-board computers of the Raspberry Pi® product line in an OS-less fashion. Furthermore, in the domain of this particular rudimentary example, we are not taking advantage of the powerful graphics, camera or connectivity features of this mighty single-board computer system.[11] Running the Raspberry Pi®Zero WH OS-less, however, does provide complete control over the microcontroller code and run-time characteristics of the Arm1176JZF-S™ processor, potentially making this example enriching for those interested in the art of pure bare metal programming.

[11] See, for instance, [26, 27] for additional suggestions regarding literature about making more complete use of the full features of Raspberry Pi®.

The Raspberry Pi®Zero WH's large chunk of 512 M byte of SDRAM, although separate from the microcontroller die, is directly addressable by the processor's bus system. This is depicted in the illustration "*BCM2835 ARM Peripherals*" on page 5 of [8, 9]. Therefore the software, once booted, loaded from micro SD card and started, has seamless bus interface support for the entire SDRAM with flat 32-bit addressing. This is done with direct hardware bus access to the SDRAM address space without needing special, manually-written RAM iterators or pointer abstractions such as those that were required in examples `chapter10_08` and `chapter10_08a` in the previous section for our target with the 8-bit microcontroller.

The well-established Raspberry Pi® boot mechanism is utilized. For this, the boot files `bootcode.bin` and `start.elf`, the optional `config.txt`, and the application file `kernel.img` (in binary form) are stored on a raw formatted micro SD card. A CPU clock of 1 GHz (the default setting of `arm_freq`) and SDRAM frequency of 450 MHz (the default setting of `sdram_freq`) have been configured. These are set to default by simply omitting their associated entries in `config-.txt`.

The very simple version of `config.txt` used in example `chapter10_09` is shown below. The two entries included are for setting the minimum allowed requirements for the GPU (graphics processing unit). All other entries retain their default settings.

```
gpu_freq=600
gpu_mem=32
```

`kernel.img` is the actual application software. It is extracted in the later stages of the build process from the absolute object `ELF`-file using the program `objcopy`. Note that `objcopy` is a GCC-specific tool usually available in GCC's binary utilities (binutils). Other targets and other tool chains such as `avr-g++`, include similar binary extraction programs (see also Sect. 2.2). These could possibly have different names and parameters but the same general functionality.

Upon power-up, `kernel.img` is loaded by the Raspberry Pi® bootloader from micro SD card into SDRAM at address `0x00008000`. The bootloader then transfers control to (i.e., jumps to) address `0x00008000`. Standard Arm® startup procedure is used. In accordance with this, the interrupt vector table has been linked to address `0x00008000`. The interrupt vector table can be found in the dedicated assembly file `int_vect.s`.

The population of the interrupt vector table is sketched below. User interrupts are not used in this particular example, even though there are various entries reserved for them. Only the entry of the startup subroutine `__my_startup()` is actually needed.

```
// Taken from bcm2835_raspi_b/startup/int_vect.s

.section .isr_vector, "ax"

b __my_startup
b __int_vect_undef_instr_handler
b __int_vect_sw_interrupt_handler
b __int_vect_prefetch_abort_handler
b __int_vect_data_abort_handler
b __int_vect_unused_05_handler
b __int_vect_irq_handler
b __int_vect_fiq_handler
```

The entries in the interrupt table are written in the form of assembly branch instructions to a particular subroutine address. The application entry point, for instance, is provided as a branch instruction to the address of `__my_startup()` in the first entry of the interrupt vector table. So when the bootloader jumps to the start of the interrupt vector table at address `0x00008000`, the controller simply subsequently branches (i.e., jumps) again to `__my_startup()` and immediate program execution begins there. More details on `__my_startup()` are provided below.

As mentioned above, both `kernel.img` as well as its associated program data will be read/written/executed directly from/to/out of SDRAM, all via 32-bit bus interface unit of the Arm®-core. This makes accessing all of the 512 M byte of SDRAM quite convenient. The application's various memory ranges can simply be defined in the linker definition file (Sect. 8.4) and both program code as well as data subsequently use these memory regions directly.

The topology of the memory regions in the linker definition file in example `chapter10_09` is shown below.

```
/* Taken from bcm2835_raspi_b.ld */

/* Set up stacks with total size of 16K. */
/* ... */

/* Set up memory regions. */
MEMORY
{
  ROM    (rwx) : ORIGIN = 0x00008000,
                 LENGTH = 0x00008000
  RAM    (rwx) : ORIGIN = 0x00010000,
                 LENGTH = 0x00004000
```

```
  STACKS(rwx)  : ORIGIN = 0x00014000,
                 LENGTH =   _sys_stack_size
                          + _svc_stack_size
                          + _abt_stack_size
                          + _und_stack_size
                          + _irq_stack_size
                          + _fiq_stack_size
  POOL   (rwx) : ORIGIN = 0x00100000,
                 LENGTH = 512M - 1M
}

/* ... */
```

The application code is linked to start at address `0x00008000` in the `ROM` region. The program's `RAM` region including the sections `.bss` and `.data` follows at address `0x00010000`. There are several kinds of stacks in this system. These are placed in the self-made 16 k byte `STACKS` region having base address `0x00014000`.

A custom-created memory region called `POOL` has been placed at a significantly higher address of `0x00100000`. A section named `.dram_noinit_pool` has been put in the `POOL` region. This section contains the empty, non-initialized array data for the bulk of the program's memory used for the π calculation and its result.

As briefly indicated above, a lightweight, custom startup code called `__my_startup()` has been written. In particular,

```
// Taken from bcm2835_raspi_b/startup/crt0.cpp

extern "C" void __my_startup() { /* ... */ }
```

`__my_startup()` sets the stack pointers, performs static RAM initialization, calls static constructors and completes the partial initialization of the processor (those initialization parts that the bootloader left out) before jumping to and never returning from `main()`. Low-level configuration of Arm® processors is an advanced operating system topic that goes slightly beyond the scope of this book. For additional details on this topic, see also [3], in particular Subsects. [4] and [5]. For more information on startup code and the jump to `main()`, see also Chap. 8, especially Sects. 8.1, 8.2, 8.3 and 8.7.

CPU initialization is implemented in the `mcal_cpu` module. A partial synopsis of some relevant parts of its details in namespace `mcal::cpu::detail` is provided below.

```
// Taken from mcal_cpu_detail_secure.h
namespace mcal { namespace cpu { namespace detail {

class secure final
{
  friend inline void mcal::cpu::detail::init()
  {
    initialize_vfp_unit();
    clear_branch_prediction_array();
    fill_tlb_entries();
    enable_mmu();
    enable_branch_prediction();
    enable_caches();
  }

  // ...
};

} } } // namespace mcal::cpu::detail
```

We will now consider some of the performance-enhancing memory management aspects that are used in example `chapter10_09`. In addition to setting up the stacks, initializing the floating-point unit (FPU), enabling branch prediction and the like, the startup code also configures the Arm® TLB, starts the Arm® MMU and activates instruction and data caching in the target processor's 16 k byte L1 cache (see also [3–5, 8]).[12]

Optimization of memory management is expected to be particularly effective in this example. This is because the application's running code and its data together (with the exception of the large input and output data arrays for the π calculation itself) potentially fit entirely within the 16 k byte L1 cache. This can be seen in a snippet from the example's size report `bin/chapter10_09_size.txt` shown in the following listing.

[12]At the time of writing the fourth edition of this book, it is hoped that the lightweight, self-written startup code correctly initializes the Arm1176JZF-S™ processor to reach its full performance. This has, however, not been entirely verified. The Arm® MMU and Arm® TLB, for instance, have been setup in a rather basic way. Potential refinements thereof could possibly enhance performance further.

```
bin/chapter10_09.elf   :
section              size         addr
.isr_vector            32        32768
.startup              336        32800
.text               10016        33136
.ARM.exidx              8        43152
.data                  12        65536
.bss                  316        65552
```

This size report shows, for instance, that the `.text` section which contains most of the program code takes up ~ 10 k byte. The RAM sections `.data` and `.bss` occupy together $\lesssim$400 byte. Essentially all code sequences and variables in these sections are, therefore, excellent candidates for being entirely cached in the processor's 16 k byte L1 cache. The compilation leading to this size report used GCC `arm-none-eabi-g++` version 9.3.1 with optimization `-O2` plus the options `-finline-functions` and `-finline-limit=32`, and language standard `-std=c++11`.

Using memory management and chaching does, in fact, profoundly improve the overall performance of this application in this example. Temporarily deactivating these features reveals a performance difference of slightly more than a factor of 4. This can be confirmed by commenting out `fill_tlb_entries()` and `enable_mmu()` in `mcal::cpu::detail::init()` shown above.

We will now investigate the overall performance of example `chapter10_09`. The π spigot program compiles builds, runs predictably, and also retains its numerical correctness in a wide variety of environments including:

- our target with the 8-bit microcontroller (with external SRAM),
- the powerful 32-bit Arm®-based Raspberry Pi®Zero WH single-board computer (with 512 M byte on-board SDRAM),
- any suitable PC or similar host system.

Table 10.5 lists runtime data for the π spigot program calculating 100,001 digits of π within these three vastly different environments. The values in the column *Relative* are calculated with respect to the runtime using one single core on a PC host. This relative value is set to 1 for this particular PC host. The runtimes of the calculations on the Raspberry Pi®Zero WH (example `chapter10_09` here) and on the 8-bit μC with a 2 M byte external asynchronous parallel SRAM brick (example `chapter10_08a` in Sect. 10.8) are approximately 25 and 5400 times larger, respectively.

These timing data reflect the overhead of the algorithm having been implemented as a state machine serviced within the idle task of the multitasking scheduler. We also note that the spigot algorithm is known to be a rather inefficient $O\left(N^2\right)$ algorithm for calculating π, as noted in Eq. 10.5 and the description thereof in Sect. 10.8.

Table 10.5 Runtime data for the π spigot program calculating 100,001 digits of π within three vastly different environments are listed

Environment	Runtime [s]	Relative	Comments
PC Host	1.0×10^2	1	3.4 GHz 64-bit CPU with 32 G byte main memory @ 1.333 GHz. Used `x86_64-w64-mingw32-g++` 8.2.0 with `-O2 -std=c++11`.
Raspberry Pi®Zero WH	2.5×10^3	25	1 GHz 32-bit CPU with 512 M byte on-board SDRAM @ 450 MHz. See also footnote 12, Page 274. Used `arm-none-eabi-g++` 9.3.1 with `-O2 -std=c++11`.
8-bit μC	5.4×10^5	5400	16 MHz 8-bit CPU with 2 *M*byte external asynchronous parallel SRAM brick. Used `avr-g++` 9.2.0 with `-O3 -std=c++11`.

The π spigot program exhibits a very high level of portability. The application layer and algorithm implementations are essentially identical with those used in example `chapter10_08a`. Their advanced design lends insight into the usefulness of cross development and exemplifies how to develop complex real-time software that runs properly and uniformly on multiple systems.

References

1. D. Abrahams, J. Siek, T. Witt, *Iterator Façade* (2020). http://www.boost.org/doc/libs/1_73_0/libs/iterator/doc/iterator_facade.html
2. Arm® Limited, *Arm1176JZF-S™ Technical Reference Manual, Rev. H* (2020). http://developer.arm.com/documentation/ddi0301/h
3. Arm® Limited: *Arm1176JZF-S™ Technical Reference Manual, Rev. H, Chap. 6: Memory Management Unit* (2020). http://developer.arm.com/documentation/ddi0301/h/memory-management-unit
4. Arm® Limited: *Arm1176JZF-S™ Technical Reference Manual, Rev. H, Chap. 6: Memory Management Unit, Subsection: About the MMU, Sub-subsection: Memory region attributes, Sub-sub-subsection: C and B bit, and type extension field encodings* (2020). http://developer.arm.com/documentation/ddi0301/h/memory-management-unit/memory-region-attributes/c-and-b-bit--and-type-extension-field-encodings
5. Arm® Limited: *Arm1176JZF-S™ Technical Reference Manual, Rev. H, Chap. 6: Memory Management Unit, Subsection: About the MMU, Sub-subsection: TLB organization* (2020). http://developer.arm.com/documentation/ddi0301/h/memory-management-unit/tlb-organization
6. J. Arndt, C. Haenel, *π Unleashed* (Springer, Heidelberg, 2001)
7. J.M. Borwein, P.B. Borwein, *Pi and the AGM: A Study in Number Theory and Computational Complexity* (Wiley, New York, 1987)

8. Broadcom® Corporation, *BCM2835 ARM Peripherals* (Broadcom® Europe Ltd., Cambridge, 2012)
9. Broadcom® Corporation, *BCM2835 ARM Peripherals* (Internet link) www.raspberrypi.org/app/uploads/2012/02/BCM2835-ARM-Peripherals.pdf (2020)
10. Cypress Semiconductor Corporation, *Document Number: 38-05684 Rev. *L: CY62158E MoBL® 8-Mbit (1M × 8) Static RAM*, San Jose, CA, Revised 20 July 2015
11. Cypress Semiconductor Corporation, *Document Number: 001-93628 Rev. *D: CY62167GN MoBL® 16-Mbit (1M × 16/2M × 8) Static RAM*, San Jose, CA, Revised 23 June 2017
12. B. Eckel, *Thinking in C++ Volume 1: Introduction to Standard C++*, 2nd edn. (Pearson Prentice Hall, Upper Saddle River, 2000)
13. GMP, *GNU Multiple Precision Arithmetic Library* (2020). http://gmplib.org
14. ISO/IEC, *ISO/IEC 14882:2011 : Information Technology – Programming Languages – C++* (International Organization for Standardization, Geneva, 2011)
15. N.M. Josuttis: *The C++ Standard Library: A Tutorial and Reference*, 2nd edn. (Addison-Wesley, Boston, 2012)
16. J. Maddock, C. Kormanyos, *Boost Multiprecision* (2020). www.boost.org/doc/libs/1_73_0/libs/multiprecision/doc/html/index.html
17. Microchip, *MCP23S17 16-Bit SPI I/O Expander with Serial Interface* (2020). www.microchip.com/wwwproducts/en/MCP23S17
18. Microchip, *23LC1024 2.5–5.5V 1Mb SPI Serial SRAM* (2020). www.microchip.com/wwwproducts/en/23LC1024
19. Microchip, *ATmega2560* (2020). www.microchip.com/wwwproducts/en/ATmega2560
20. Microchip, *ATmega640/V-1280/V-1281/V-2560/V-2561/V Datasheet-DS40002211A*, (Microchip®, 2020)
21. S. Monk, *Make Your Own PCBs with EAGLE®* (McGraw Hill Education, New York, 2017)
22. MPIR (from wbhart), *Multiple Precision Integers and Rationals* (2020). http://github.com/wbhart/mpir
23. Newhaven Display International, *NHD-0216K1Z-FSW-FBW-L Character Liquid Crystal Display Module* (2020). www.newhavendisplay.com/specs/NHD-0216K1Z-FSW-FBW-L.pdf
24. S. Rabinowitz, S. Wagon, A spigot algorithm for the digits of Pi. Am. Math. Mon. **102**, 195–203 (1995)
25. Raspberry Pi Foundation, *Raspberry Pi Zero* (2020). www.raspberrypi.org/products/raspberry-pi-zero
26. raspberrypi.org, *The MagPi Magazine: The official Raspberry Pi Magazine* (2020). http://magpi.raspberrypi.org
27. raspberrypi.org, *The MagPi Magazine: The official Raspberry Pi magazine (Sect. Books)* (2020). http://magpi.raspberrypi.org/books
28. P. Scherz, S. Monk, *Practical Electronics for Inventors*, 4th edn. (McGraw Hill Education, New York, 2016)
29. A. Schönhage, A.F.W. Grotefeld, E. Vetter, *Fast Algorithhms, A Multitape Turing Machine Implementation* (BI Wissenschaftsverlag, Zürich, 1994)
30. Wikipedia, *American Wire Gauge* (2020). http://en.wikipedia.org/wiki/American_wire_gauge
31. Wikipedia, *Chudnovsky Algorithm* (2020). http://en.wikipedia.org/wiki/Chudnovsky_algorithm
32. Wikipedia, *Single-Board Computer* (2020). http://en.wikipedia.org/wiki/Single-board_computer
33. Wikipedia, *Spigot Algorithm* (2020). http://en.wikipedia.org/wiki/Spigot_algorithm

Chapter 11
C++ Multitasking

A multitasking scheduler is an indispensable tool for providing temporal and functional software distribution. In this chapter, we design a cooperative C++ multitasking scheduler that performs a top-down call of its tasks using time slices and a basic priority mechanism. This multitasking scheduler is compact and portable and can be used for a wide variety of projects ranging from small to large. Toward the end of this chapter, we will discuss additional multitasking features such as extended scheduling with yield and sleep functions, a sample exemplifying preemptive multitasking scheduling, and the C++ thread support library.

11.1 Multitasking Schedulers

The basic operation of a multitasking scheduler is depicted in Fig. 11.1. In general, a multitasking scheduler runs, possibly indefinitely, in a loop and uses a *scheduling algorithm* to identify and call *ready* tasks. Here, ready is the state of needing to be called. The scheduler's ready-check usually involves timing and possibly event or alarm conditions. In this way, a multitasking scheduler distributes software functionality among various modules and time slices.

Consider the multitasking scheduler shown below. This basic multitasking scheduler is designed to schedule three tasks, `task_a()`, `task_b()` and `task_c()`.

```
#include <array>
#include <algorithm>

void task_a() { /* ... */ }
void task_b() { /* ... */ }
void task_c() { /* ... */ }
```


C. Kormanyos, *Real-Time C++*, https://doi.org/10.1007/978-3-662-62996-3_11

```
typedef void(*function_type)();
typedef std::array<function_type, 3U> task_list_type;

const task_list_type task_list
{
  { task_a, task_b, task_c };
}

void scheduler()
{
  for(;;)
  {
    std::for_each(task_list.begin(),
                  task_list.end(),
                  [](const function_type& func)
                  {
                    func();
                  });
  }
}
```

Every multitasking scheduler uses some form of scheduling algorithm to search for ready tasks. In the case of the `scheduler()` above, for example, the searching algorithm is trivially simple. It uses neither timing nor priority nor any other kinds of events or alarms. Since each task is ready to be called at any given time, the ready condition for a given task is simply unconditional-**`true`**. Accordingly, each task is called via lambda expression in the `std::for_each()` algorithm of the multitasking scheduler as soon as its corresponding iterator in the `task_list` is reached. The outer **`for`**`(;;)`-loop causes the multitasking scheduler to run indefinitely.

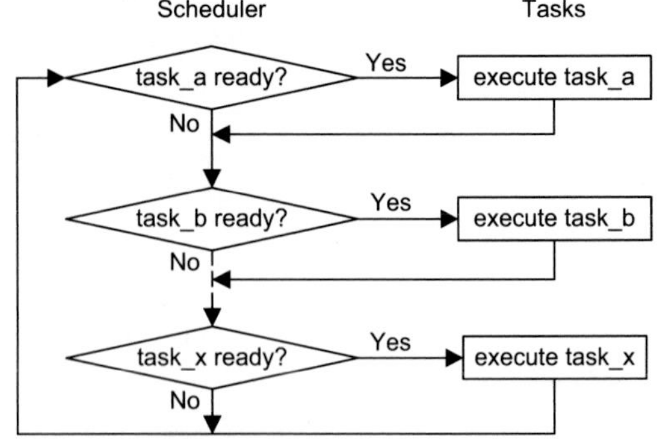

Fig. 11.1 A multitasking scheduler and its tasks, `task_a`, `task_b`, ... `task_x`, are sketched

This multitasking scheduler is extraordinarily simple, requiring only a few tens of bytes of program code and no RAM whatsoever. It sequentially calls the tasks in its `task_list`, indefinitely without pause, break or return.

Even though the rudimentary temporal distribution of this multitasking scheduler may be inadequate for most practical situations, this example does, nonetheless, clearly exhibit the general concept of a multitasking scheduler. In the upcoming sections, we will add timing and a more sophisticated scheduling mechanism to this multitasking scheduler.

11.2 Task Timing

We will now discuss timing aspects for our multitasking scheduler. Imagine that the multitasking scheduler should call `task_a()`, `task_b()` and `task_c()` at even multiples of 2, 8 and 16 ms, respectively.

With this call scheduling, there are time points at which two or more tasks need to be called back-to-back. For example, at even multiples of 8 ms, both `task_a()` as well as `task_b()` need to be called. At even multiples of 16 ms, all three tasks need to be called. This could lead to a timing crunch.

Table 11.1 The call schedules for `task_a()`, `task_b()` and `task_c()` with call cycles of (2, 8, 16 ms) and call offsets of (0, 7, 13 ms) are shown

System tick [ms]	`task_a()`	`task_b()`	`task_c()`
0	•		
1		•	
2	•		
3			•
4	•		
5			
6	•		
7			
8	•		
9		•	
10	•		
11			
12	•		
13			
14	•		
15			
16	•		
17		•	
18	•		
19			•

In order to avoid timing bottlenecks or at least lessen their impact, call offsets can be added to the call cycle timing of the scheduler. Small-valued prime numbers are well-suited for schedule offsets. For example, we will select for `task_b()` an offset of 7 ms and for `task_c()`, an offset of 13 ms, while `task_a()` retains its 0 ms offset.

The first few scheduled task call times using these offsets are shown in Table 11.1. The bottleneck situation has been effectively removed. As can be seen in the table, `task_a()` is always called at system tick values which are multiples of two—and these are always even-numbered. Both `task_b()` as well as `task_c()`, however, are always called at odd-numbered values of the system tick. Therefore, the call of `task_a()` is never scheduled simultaneously with the calls of either `task_b()` or `task_c()`. Furthermore, simultaneous scheduling of `task_b()` and `task_c()` has been eliminated because the call cycles of these two tasks no longer intersect.

11.3 The Task Control Block

A class which encapsulates the scheduling characteristics of a task is often called a *task control block*, sometimes also known as a TCB. Typical things in a task control block may include:

- The task to be scheduled
- The timing characteristics of the task's scheduling
- A scheduling function that checks for task-ready
- A task execution mechanism
- Optional event or alarm information

The scheduling characteristics of `task_a()`, `task_b()` and `task_c()`, for example, can be represented with the task control block shown below.

```
class task_control_block
{
public:
  typedef void (*function_type)();

  typedef timer<mcal::gpt::value_type> timer_type;
  typedef timer_type::tick_type tick_type;

  task_control_block(const function_type f,
                     const tick_type c,
                     const tick_type o = 0U)
    : function(f),
      cycle(c),
      time(o) { }
```

```
  bool execute();

private:
  const function_type function;
  const tick_type cycle;
  timer_type time;
};
```

The `task_control_block` class has three member variables, `function`, `cycle` and `time`. The variable `function` is a constant pointer to a **`void`** function with static linkage. This is the function that is encapsulated in the task control block, in other words it is the task that is to be called by the scheduler. The variables `cycle` and `time` contain the task cycle in milliseconds and its interval timer. The interval timer uses the `timer` utility described later in Sect. 15.3.

The `time` member of the task control block is initialized with the offset of the task. The type of the `time` member is `timer_type`, a class-local type that is scaled to the width of the system tick, Sect. 9.3. A less wide timer type could optionally be used to optimize the RAM storage requirements of the task control block. This, however, assumes that the necessary intervals can still be represented by this type.

The member function `execute()` checks if a task is ready and, if so, calls it. In particular,

```
bool task_control_block::execute()
{
  // Check if the task is ready via timeout.
  if(time.timeout())
  {
    // Increment the task's interval timer
    // with the task cycle.
    time.start_interval(cycle);

    // Call the task.
    function();

    return true;
  }
  else
  {
    return false;
  }
}
```

After a ready task is called, its interval timer is incremented with the task `cycle` and the `execute()` function returns **`true`**. Otherwise, `execute()` leaves the state of the task unchanged and returns **`false`**. Since `execute()` returns a Boolean result, it can be used with a predicate-based searching algorithm, as will be shown below.

11.4 The Task List

The `task_list` is a list of `task_control_block` objects that define the task and timing characteristics of the application. For our system with `task_a()`, `task_b()` and `task_c()` and the timing characteristics shown in Table 11.1, a potential initialization of the `task_list` is shown below.

```
#include <array>

typedef
std::array<task_control_block, 3U> task_list_type;

void task_a() { /* ... */ }
void task_b() { /* ... */ }
void task_c() { /* ... */ }

task_list_type task_list
{{
  task_control_block
  {
    task_a,
    task_control_block::timer_type::milliseconds(2),
    task_control_block::timer_type::milliseconds(0)
  },
  task_control_block
  {
    task_b,
    task_control_block::timer_type::milliseconds(8),
    task_control_block::timer_type::milliseconds(7)
  },
  task_control_block
  {
    task_c,
    task_control_block::timer_type::milliseconds(16),
    task_control_block::timer_type::milliseconds(13)
  }
}};
```

The task_list is stored in an std::array containing three objects of type task_control_block. These represent the task control blocks of task_a(), task_b() and task_c(), and they are to be scheduled with cycles of 2, 8, 16 ms and offsets of 0, 7, 13 ms, respectively.

11.5 The Scheduler

Armed with our task_control_block and the task_list, we will now write a multitasking scheduler(). In particular,

```
#include <algorithm>

void scheduler()
{
  for(;;)
  {
    // Find the next ready task using std::find_if.
    std::find_if(task_list.begin(),
                 task_list.end(),
                 [](task_control_block& tcb) -> bool
                 {
                   // Call the ready task.
                   return tcb.execute();
                 });
  }
}
```

In this multitasking scheduler(), the outer **for**(;;)-loop continuously polls the task_list and never pauses, breaks or returns. The std::find_-if() algorithm sequentially loops through the task_list. If a ready task is found, it is called via lambda function in combination with the execute() method of the task_control_block.

A ready task that is called thereby breaks the loop in std::find_if(). If no ready task is found, the outer **for**-loop continues polling the task_list waiting for the next ready task. During times when no task is ready, the so-called *idle* task is executed. Several background activities can typically be carried out in the idle task, a popular one being to trigger the watchdog timer.

The STL's std::find_if() algorithm implements a simple task priority mechanism. Recall that std::find_if() locates the iterator of the first occurrence of an element in a range that satisfies the given find condition. In other words, it finds the iterator to the reference of a task_control_block in the task_list whose execute() function returns **true**. If, however, no task is ready, the iterator at the end of the task_list is found. All of this means that `std::find_if()` performs a priority-based search. The order of the tasks in the `task_list` defines the priority of the tasks.

The multitasking scheduler implemented with the `scheduler()` function is designed to be called one time only, for example, in `main()`. For instance, the multitasking scheduler might be called after initializing the MCAL. This has been discussed previously in Sect. 8.8. In particular,

```
namespace mcal
{
  void init();
}

void scheduler();

int main()
{
  // Initialize the microcontroller layer.
  mcal::init();

  // Call the multitasking scheduler
  // and never return.
  scheduler();
}
```

Our multitasking scheduler can be used with a wide variety of projects ranging from small to large. It is efficient. In fact, the entire size of the multitasking scheduler including the implementation of the `task_control_block` and the `task_list` including three tasks only requires a few hundred bytes of code.

Our multitasking scheduler also has a high degree of portability. The only things needed to port to another microcontroller are the system tick and the `timer`'s conversion to milliseconds.

11.6 Extended Multitasking

The example of the multitasking scheduler shown in the previous sections has called its tasks in a *top-down* fashion. This means that tasks have been implemented as run-capable entities that are called by the scheduler via top-down subroutine call. Each task always runs to completion before returning control to the scheduler.

At times, such basic tasks are insufficient for certain multitasking design needs. For example, it is often desired to wait in a task for an indefinite time within a deeply nested, polling loop. Perhaps the task needs to wait for a critical communication response or a reaction from a hardware device. This is shown in the code sample below.

```
// External functions in the application.
bool initialize_state();
bool response_ready();
void handle_response();

// An example of an extended task.
void extended_task()
{
  // The task initialization.
  const bool state_is_valid = initialize_state();

  // The task worker loop.
  for(;;)
  {
    if(state_is_valid)
    {
      // Wait indefinitely for a response.
      while(!response_ready())
      {
        // Yield control to the scheduler.
        os::yield();
      }

      // Handle the communication response.
      handle_response();
    }
  }
}
```

In this sample, the extended task initializes its state and then enters a loop that waits indefinitely for a communication response. When waiting for the response, `extended_task()` calls `os::yield()` in order to yield control to the scheduler.

The extended task's yield gives the scheduler the opportunity to check if any other tasks with higher priority are pending and execute them if so. In this way, a running task can hand over control to the scheduler, allowing other potentially ready tasks to run. The scheduler returns control to the task at the same place at which control was yielded and also ensures that the task has the same state as before. This form of multitasking is known as cooperative multitasking with extended tasks.

When switching from one task to another, the scheduler is responsible for saving and restoring the task's *context*, in other words its state. This is called context switching. Context switching can be understood in very simple terms. The scheduler needs to remember *where the task was* and also *what the task was doing* at the time of the yield in order to properly save and restore a context. In the listing above, *where the task was* is in the **`while`**–loop that calls `response_ready()`. *What the task was doing* is waiting for a communication response. From the perspective of the CPU, however, the *where* is represented by the value of instruction pointer (or an equivalent CPU register). The *what* is described in terms of the values of the CPU registers and, possibly, a task stack.

Be aware that context switching is written in target-specific assembly language. Context switching also requires additional resources. This includes runtime for the context save and restore, and, in particular, RAM for context storage and individual task stacks. These efficiency factors should be taken into account when considering the use of an extended multitasking scheduler.

11.7 Preemptive Multitasking

Certain applications may need preemptive multitasking and synchronization objects such as a mutex. When deciding whether or not to employ preemptive multitasking, however, it is essential to carefully consider the expected benefits compared with the costs. This is because preemptive scheduling and the use of synchronization mechanisms may lead to significantly increased resource consumption and design complexity.

In particular, preemptive multitasking might result in a more obscure relation between the written code and its runtime characteristics. Preemptive multitasking requires added resources because each preemptive task requires its own individual stack and context storage. Furthermore, widespread use of synchronization mechanisms might introduce additional potential sources of error related to re-entrance and concurrency.

Many experienced embedded systems programmers decide to use preemptive multitasking, but use it sparingly. It can often possible to reduce the use of preemption to just a few tasks or to only one preemptive task such as a single idle task, while other tasks use cooperative scheduling. Typical operations in the idle task might include lengthy background calculations that have non-critical timing such as running a checksum on program code, collecting runtime or other statistics, etc. Keep a watchful eye on runtime characteristics when using preemptive multitasking and ensure that object encapsulations and interrelations remain clear and efficient. If the project, nonetheless, really needs preemptive multitasking, then by all means use it.

For preemptive multitasking, one may consider using a third-party operating system. There is a wide variety of popular and robust real-time operating systems [3] available with various styles of licensing. These RTOS-es are often written using a sensible combination of C and assembly, whereby short assembly sequences are typically needed for save/restore of task contexts.

Most of these RTOS-es are stable, well-tested and have been ported to a variety of architectures. Some of these RTOS-es can optionally be used with preemptive scheduling and synchronization objects.

Example `chapter11_07` presents a simple use of preemptive multitasking scheduling. In this example, we use two tasks, a background task called `app_led_task_background()` and an application task named `app_led_task_toggle_led0()`. These are sketched in the code synopsis below.

```
namespace
{
  using app_led_timer_type =
    util::timer<std::uint32_t>;

  app_led_timer_type app_led_timer_background;
  app_led_timer_type app_led_timer_toggle_led0;
}

extern "C"
void app_led_task_background(void*)
{
  // This background task runs perpetually
  // without pause, break or yield.

  for(;;)
  {
    while((!app_led_timer_background.timeout()))
    {
      ;
    }

    app_led_timer_background.start_interval(
      app_led_timer_type::milliseconds(50U));

    mcal::led::led1().toggle();
  }
}

extern "C"
void app_led_task_toggle_led0(void*)
{
  // This application task is designed
  // to yield every 70ms. It has higher
  // priority than the background task
  // and will, in fact, preemptively interrupt
  // the background task.
```

```
  for(;;)
  {
    mcal::wdg::secure::trigger();

    if(app_led_timer_toggle_led0.timeout())
    {
      app_led_timer_toggle_led0.start_interval(
        app_led_timer_type::seconds(1U));

      mcal::led::led0().toggle();
    }

    OS_TASK_WAIT_YIELD(OS_TASK_MSEC(70U));
  }
}
```

The app_led_task_background() task runs perpetually in the background without pause, break or yield. The background task also toggles a second LED with a frequency of $\sim 10\,\text{Hz}$. This should simulate any kind of algorithmic or control activity that might potentially be taking place in the idle times of the system.

The app_led_task_toggle_led0() is intended to carry out scheduled cyclic duties of the application. This task yields control to the multitasking scheduler every 70 ms. The toggling of the LED at $\sim 1/2\,\text{Hz}$, also commonly exhibited by other examples in this book, is carried out in the application task. The application task has higher priority than the background task and will, in fact, preemptively interrupt the background task.

As mentioned above, the app_led_task_toggle_led0() task yields control to the multitasking scheduler every every 70 ms. This action is carried out with the use of two macros. In particular,

```
OS_TASK_WAIT_YIELD(OS_TASK_MSEC(70U));
```

These macros have generic names. As such, they are designed to abstract a typical scheduling call and its delay time (in ms) in a fashion that is independent of the underlying scheduler being used. This philosophy facilitates seamless portability of tasks to other RTOS-es without the necessity of changing their code.

The use of preemptive multitasking gives the appearance that more than one task is being carried out simultaneously by the single controller. This is, however, not actually the case since there is but one single core in our target with the 8-bit microcontroller.

The context switch of the scheduler is the key to multitasking. This example provides intuitive insight into the temporal distribution of preemptive multitasking with a very small memory and resource footprint.

11.8 The C++ Thread Support Library

C++ offers support for multithreading in its thread support library. Although implementation of the C++ thread support library might be difficult to find among microcontroller compilers.

Thread support is predominantly implemented in the `<thread>` library which, itself, makes secondary use of additional headers including `<condition_variable>`, `<chrono>` and `<ratio>`. The specification of the `<thread>` library can be found in Chap. 30 of [2]. The `<atomic>` and `<mutex>` libraries can be used for synchronizing access to shared data if a preemptive threading environment is used.

The code sample below uses C++ threads.

```
#include <chrono>
#include <thread>

void thread_1()
{
  for(;;)
  {
    // Do something in thread_1.
    // ...

    // Yield control to the scheduler for 2ms.
    std::this_thread::sleep_for(2ms);
  }
}

void thread_2()
{
  for(;;)
  {
    // Do something in thread_2.
    // ...

    // Yield control to the scheduler for 7ms.
    std::this_thread::sleep_for(7ms);
  }
}
```

```
void do_something()
{
  // Create two threads, thread_1 and thread_2.
  std::thread t1(thread_1);
  std::thread t2(thread_2);

  // Wait for thread_1 and thread_2 to finish.

  // In this example, the join() functions will wait
  // indefinitely because neither thread returns.

  t1.join();
  t2.join();
}
```

This example creates two `std::thread` objects, `t1` and `t2`. The first thread carries out its internal work and subsequently yields control to the scheduler for 2 ms, whereas the second thread has a cycle time of 7 ms. The cooperative multitasking yield is accomplished with the standard library's `sleep_for()` subroutine. Notice how the convenient timing mechanisms from the `<chrono>` library can be used compatibly with the thread support library. The durations of the sleep times in milliseconds are eloquently expressed using the standard library suffix `ms` (see Sect. 3.17 on user-defined literals).

After creating the two threads, the `do_something()` subroutine waits for both threads to complete before returning. This is accomplished with the `join()` method. In this example, however, the program will wait indefinitely because both threads are programmed to run without return.

The syntax and design of the C++ thread support library were strongly influenced by the POSIX standard [1]. In addition, C++ threads had been long implemented in Boost's `Boost.Thread` library prior to becoming part of the C++ language in C++11. So anyone familiar with POSIX *pthreads* from `<pthread.h>` or who has worked with `Boost.Thread`, should be able to understand and use C++11 threads with no trouble at all.

References

1. ISO/IEC, *ISO/IEC 9945:2003 : Information Technology – Portable Operating System Interface (POSIX)* (International Organization for Standardization, Geneva, 2003)
2. ISO/IEC, *ISO/IEC 14882:2011 : Information Technology – Programming Languages – C++* (International Organization for Standardization, Geneva, 2011)
3. Wikipedia, *Comparison of Real-Time Operating Systems* (2020). http://en.wikipedia.org/wiki/Comparison_of_real-time_operating_systems

Part III
Mathematics and Utilities for Real-Time C++

Chapter 12
Floating-Point Mathematics

This chapter describes floating-point mathematics for real-time C++ using built-in floating-point types such as **float double** and **long double**. The first sections of this chapter introduce floating-point arithmetic, mathematical constants, elementary transcendental functions and higher transcendental functions. The last sections of this chapter cover more advanced topics including complex-numbered mathematics, compile-time evaluation of floating-point functions and generic numeric programming.

12.1 Floating-Point Arithmetic

Floating-point arithmetic can be used effectively in real-time C++. For example, the simple function below computes the floating-point area of a circle of radius r, where the area a is given by

$$a = \pi r^2 . \tag{12.1}$$

```
float area_of_a_circle(float r)
{
  constexpr float pi = 3.14159265358979323846F;

  return (pi * r) * r;
}
```


C. Kormanyos, *Real-Time C++*, https://doi.org/10.1007/978-3-662-62996-3_12

The C++ standard specifies three built-in floating-point types, **float**, **double** and **long double**.[1] The standard, however, does not specify any details about the internal representations of these types.

Basically, the standard merely states that **double** needs to provide at least as much precision as **float**, and that **long double** must provide at least as much precision as **double**. The way that the compiler internally stores and treats floating-point types remains implementation-defined. See Sect. 3.9.1, § 8 in [11] for additional details.

Most suppliers of high-quality compilers strive to provide conformance with the floating-point standard IEEE-754:2008 [7]. This standard specifies (among other things) the following.

- Single-precision is usually implemented as **float**, which is required to be four bytes in width and to provide 24 binary digits of precision ($\sim$ 7 decimal digits).
- Double-precision is often implemented as **double**, which is required to be eight bytes in width and to provide 53 binary digits of precision ($\sim$ 15 decimal digits). When using our target with the 8-bit microcontroller, `avr-g++` (starting with version 10 and higher) supports double-precision floating-point with the command line option `-mdouble=64`.
- Quadruple-precision[2] is occasionally implemented as **long double**, which is required to be sixteen bytes in width and to provide 113 binary digits of precision ($\sim$ 33 decimal digits).

The IEEE-754 floating-point standard covers an enormous amount of information on single-precision, double-precision and quadruple-precision floating-point representations including rounding characteristics, subnormal numbers such as infinity (∞) and *not-a-number* (NaN), conversion to and from integer, etc. We will not discuss all of these details here due to space considerations. A comprehensive treatment of floating-point arithmetic can be found in the definitive reference work on the topic by Muller et al. [16].

Some microcontrollers have hardware support for floating-point arithmetic using a *floating-point unit* (FPU). An FPU can make floating-point arithmetic as efficient as integer calculations—or even more so. Many small-to-medium microcontrollers, however, do not have an FPU, and floating-point calculations are performed with a software floating-point emulation library. Floating-point emulation can be slow and may introduce large amounts of library code in the executable program. The real-time C++ programmer should attempt to be aware of the potentially high resource consumption of floating-point arithmetic.

C++ supports many floating-point functions including elementary transcendental functions, floating-point classification functions, rounding functions, absolute value functions, etc. These functions are predominantly included in the `<cmath>` and `<cstdlib>` libraries (Sect. 12.3). In addition, care was taken during the

[1] We primarily use **float** and **double** in this book.

[2] Quadruple-precision is not commonly implemented for microcontroller compilers.

specifications of C++11 and C99 to improve consistency in floating-point functions between C and C++ [8, 11].

As mentioned above, floating-point arithmetic in C++ supports the concept of infinity and other non-representable subnormal floating-point values. Consider finite, positive x with $x \in \mathbb{R}$ and x representable in the compiler's floating-point implementation of IEEE-754:2008. In this floating-point system, for example, the result of $x/0$ is ∞ and the result of $\sqrt{-x}$ is NaN. Subnormal representations and floating-point limits are supported in the C++ language with the `std::numeric_limits` template, as described in Sect. A.5.

Some developers use the symbol $\mathbb{F}$ to denote the set of numbers representable in a floating-point system. In this book, however, we simply use $\mathbb{R}$ for the sake of convenience.

We will now perform some additional floating-point math using the built-in **float** type. Consider the sinc function that often arises in fields such as optics, scattering and radiation theory,

$$\operatorname{sinc} x = \frac{\sin x}{x} . \tag{12.2}$$

We will use the following approximation scheme to calculate the sinc function.

$$\operatorname{sinc} x = \begin{cases} 1 , & \text{for } |x| < \epsilon , \\ 1 - \dfrac{x^2}{6} + \dfrac{x^4}{120} - \dfrac{x^6}{540} , & \text{for } |x| < 0.03 , \\ \dfrac{\sin x}{x} , & \text{otherwise} , \end{cases} \tag{12.3}$$

where $x \in \mathbb{R}$ and x is of type **float**. Here, ϵ represents the smallest number distinguishable from 1 that can be represented by **float** (in other words ϵ = `std::numeric_limits<float>::epsilon()`, as described in Sects. 13.5 and A.5).

The corresponding code for the sinc function is shown below.

```
#include <cmath>
#include <limits>

float sinc(const float& x)
{
  if(std::fabs(x) <
      std::numeric_limits<float>::epsilon())
  {
    return 1.0F;
  }
```

```
  else if(std::fabs(x) < 0.03F)
  {
    const float x2 = x * x;

    const float sum = ((       - 1.984126984E-04F
                         * x2 + 8.333333333E-03F)
                         * x2 - 1.666666667E-01F)
                         * x2;

    return 1.0F + sum;
  }
  else
  {
    return std::sin(x) / x;
  }
}
```

As shown in Eq. 12.3, the sinc function is symmetric about the origin which allows us to use the absolute value function `std::fabs()` from `<cmath>` in key locations. See also Sect. 12.3 for further information on `<cmath>`. Very small arguments with $|x| < \epsilon$ return 1. Small arguments with $|x| < 0.03$ use a Taylor series of order 6. Larger arguments with $|x| \geq 0.03$ use the library function `std::sin()` combined with division (in other words, $\sin(x)/x$). The polynomial expansion in the Taylor series uses the method of Horner, as described in [13], Vol. 2, Sect. 4.6.4 in the paragraph named "*Horner's Rule*".

12.2 Mathematical Constants

Some mathematical constants [4] such as $\sqrt{2}$, π, $\log 2$, e, γ and others appear time and time again in mathematical formulas. It makes sense, then, to implement these numbers in a dedicated fashion. In C++, it is straightforward to implement mathematical constants as variable templates (Sect. 5.12) representing compile-time constant values.

Here, we use approximately 40 decimal digits after the decimal point. This slightly exceeds the precision of quadruple-precision floating-point with 113 binary digits, or $\sim$ 33 decimal digits. Even if the application does not need this many digits, the precision is available for any extended-use situation that may arise. Since the values are compile-time constant, the extra digits do not add any overhead.

The variable template `pi` below, for example, provides a scalable compile-time constant floating-point approximation of π.

```
template<typename T>
constexpr T pi =
  T(3.1415926535'8979323846'2643383279'5028841972L);
```

Using template constants in code is simple. For example, this new version of `area_of_a_circle()` uses the `pi` variable template to compute the **`float`** area of a circle of radius r.

```
float area_of_a_circle(const float& r)
{
  return (pi<float> * r) * r;
}
```

A selection of useful mathematical constants is implemented in the variable templates below, including Pythagoras' constant ($\sqrt{2} \approx 1.41421 \ldots$),

```
template<typename T>
constexpr T sqrt2 =
  T(1.4142135623'7309504880'1688724209'6980785697L);
```

Archimedes' constant ($\pi \approx 3.14159 \ldots$),

```
template<typename T>
constexpr T pi =
  T(3.1415926535'8979323846'2643383279'5028841972L);
```

the natural logarithm of two ($\log 2 \approx 0.69314 \ldots$),

```
template<typename T>
constexpr T ln2 =
  T(0.6931471805'5994530941'7232121458'1765680755L);
```

the natural logarithmic base ($e \approx 2.71828 \ldots$),

```
template<typename T>
constexpr T e =
  T(2.7182818284'5904523536'0287471352'6624977572L);
```

the Euler-Mascheroni constant ($\gamma \approx 0.57721\ldots$),

```
template<typename T>
constexpr T euler_gamma =
  T(0.5772156649'0153286060'6512090082'4024310422L);
```

and Apéry's constant ($\zeta(3) \approx 1.20205\ldots$).

```
template<typename T>
constexpr T zeta_three =
  T(1.2020569031'5959428539'9738161511'4499907650L);
```

Boost [2] provides a wide selection of scalable mathematical constants in its `Boost.Math.Constants` library. The syntax of Boost's mathematical constants library is similar to the syntax in the examples above.[3]

C++20 added a collection of common mathematical constants such as $\sqrt{2}$, π, $\log 2$, e, etc. in the `<numbers>` header. As has been done previously in this section, the standardized mathematical constants are also implemented as variable templates that can be instantiated for **`float`**, **`double`** and **`long double`**.

In order to reduce conflicts with same-named symbols in existing previous code, the mathematical constants have been injected into the nested namespace `std::-numbers`. For example,

```
#include <numbers>

constexpr float  pi_f = std::numbers::pi_v<float>;
constexpr double pi_d = std::numbers::pi_v<double>;
```

12.3 Elementary Functions

As mentioned previously, C++ supports many floating-point mathematical functions and elementary transcendental functions in its C-compatibility headers `<cmath>` and `<cstdlib>`. Basically, `<cmath>` and `<cstdlib>` include everything in the C99 library headers `<math.h>` and `<stdlib.h>` and also add overloaded versions of the functions for **`float`** and **`long double`** (in addition to the original versions for **`double`**).

[3]Boost uses template functions in its interface to mathematical constants whereas variable templates (Sect. 5.12) are used here.

The <cmath> and <cstdlib> libraries have a host of functions related to the floating-point number system including, among others, trigonometric, exponential, logarithmic, power, hyperbolic, rounding, absolute value functions, etc. Again, see Sect. 26.8 in [11] for details on the specifications of <cmath> and <cstdlib>.

The code below, for example, computes sin(1.23) for **float**.

```
#include <cmath>

const float s = std::sin(1.23F);
```

Floating-point functions can require significant resources. The results of floating-point benchmarks on our target with the 8-bit microcontroller are shown in Table 12.1. Multiplication, division and square root are the fastest functions. More complicated functions such as hyperbolic arc-cosine and Gamma (Sect. 12.4) require significantly more resources.

An interesting perspective on the runtime characteristics of floating-point functions can be obtained by comparing the floating-point benchmark results in Table 12.1 with those of the CRC32 calculation in Sects. 6.1 and 6.2. For our target with the 8-bit microcontroller, the CRC32 is a non-trivial, computationally intensive task that needs about 300 bytes of code and a bit more than 300 μs. The floating-point hyperbolic arc-cosine computation has a similar runtime but requires significantly more code—possibly due to the inclusion of significant parts of the software floating-point library.

The performance of floating-point elementary function calculations may vary considerably from one microcontroller to another. In particular, floating-point elementary function calculations might be greatly accelerated if an FPU is used. In addition, there can even be strong variations in size and performance when switching from one compiler to another or when using different implementations of the underlying floating-point library. In order to understanding floating-point

Table 12.1 Resource consumptions for single-precision floating-point functions on our target with the 8-bit microcontroller are shown

Function	Result (**float**)	Result (known)	Runtime [μs]	Code size [byte]
1.23×3.45	4.2435	Exact	10	420
$1.23/3.45$	0.3565217	0.3565217391...	30	430
$\sqrt{1.23}$	1.109054	1.1090536506...	30	290
$\sqrt{1.23^2 + 3.45^2}$	3.662704	3.6627039192...	60	1,080
sin(1.23)	0.9424888	0.9424888019...	110	890
log(3.45)	1.238374	1.2383742310...	140	1,050
exp(1.23)	3.421230	3.4212295363...	170	1,270
acosh(3.45)	1.909823	1.9098229687...	240	1,670
$\Gamma(3.45)$	3.146312	3.1463120534...	280	2,550

efficiency in the project, some simple benchmarking in hard real-time such as the kind summarized in Table 12.1 above can be performed.

12.4 Special Functions

Some special functions of pure and applied mathematics such as Bessel functions, orthogonal polynomials, elliptic integrals, the Riemann zeta function, etc. are specified in both TR1 [9] as well as in the *optional* special functions part of the C++ standard library [10] (since C++11). As of C++17, however, these mathematical special functions have been incorporated into the standard [12]. Here, the general term *special functions* means higher transcendental functions as described in depth in Erdélyi's three-volume treatise on the subject [3] and also in [1, 17].

Since implementations of special functions are, in fact, relatively new in the C++ standard and because they can be quite difficult to calculate accurately and efficiently, compiler support for them may be very limited among embedded targets. For these reasons, it may be necessary at some point in time to either write certain special functions oneself or arrange for dedicated compiler support for them in cooperation with the compiler supplier.

In general, the complexity of computing special functions increases the *higher* a function gets. In particular, the Gamma function for modest digit counts $\Gamma(x)$ is often considered a relatively straightforward special function to compute.[4] Orthogonal polynomials are thought to be more difficult to compute than the Gamma function. Bessel functions such as $J_\nu(x)$, which require the Gamma function, are frequently judged to be yet more difficult to compute, etc.

Writing a library of special functions that is accurate, efficient and supports correct range checking and handling of subnormal values is a task beyond the scope of this book. To get better acquainted with the ways of programming special functions in real-time C++, though, we will write an implementation of the Gamma function $\Gamma(x)$ for $x \in \mathbb{R}$ for single-precision **`float`**.

The Gamma function $\Gamma(x)$ is the extension of the integer factorial function to both real as well as complex numbers x with $x \in \mathbb{C}$. The relation between the Gamma function and the factorial is $\Gamma(n + 1) = n!$, where $n \in \mathbb{Z}^+$ is a positive integer or zero. The behavior of the Gamma function is shown in Fig. 12.1 for $x \in \mathbb{R}$ with $0 \lesssim x \leq 4$. The Gamma function has a complex-valued singularity at the origin and grows rapidly for increasing argument (i.e., like the factorial). Notice at the right-hand side of the graph the expected value of $\Gamma(4) = 3! = 6$.

---

[4]Even though some compilers do not include Gamma functions, both $\Gamma(x)$ as well as $\log \Gamma(x)$ are intended to be available in the optional special functions of C++11 and also in the mandatory `<cmath>` library of C++17 for $x \in \mathbb{R}$ for **`float`**, **`double`** and **`long double`**.

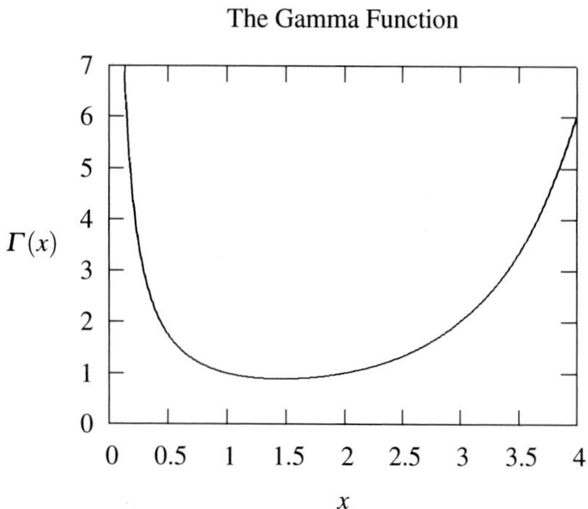

Fig. 12.1 The Gamma function $\Gamma(x)$ for $x \in \mathbb{R}$ with $0 \lesssim x \leq 4$ is shown. The Gamma function $\Gamma(x)$ has a singularity at the origin and grows rapidly for increasing x

Our computational scheme for computing $\Gamma(x)$ is primarily based on polynomial expansion. In particular, we use

$$\Gamma(x) = \begin{cases} \text{reflection of } \Gamma(x) \text{ for } x < 0, \\ \text{NaN for } x = 0, \\ \text{inverse of the Taylor series of } 1/\Gamma(x) \text{ for } 0 < x < 0.1, \\ \text{polynomial expansion of } \Gamma(x+1) \text{ for } 0.1 \leq x < 1, \\ 1 \text{ for } x = 1 \text{ and } x = 2, \\ \text{upward recursion of } \Gamma(x) \text{ for } x > 1, x \neq 2, \\ \text{and } +\infty \text{ for overflow when } x \text{ is large or near } 0. \end{cases} \tag{12.4}$$

We have chosen to use polynomial expansion and recursion in this book because the resulting code is compact and easy to understand. Many numerical specialists prefer to use a Lanczos-type approximation for small-to-medium values combined with an asymptotic Stirling-type expansion for large arguments to compute $\log \Gamma(x)$ and subsequently take the exponent of it for $\Gamma(x)$. This is, for example, done in GCC for targets that support the Gamma function.

The small-argument Taylor series for $\dfrac{1}{\Gamma(x)}$ is given by

$$\begin{aligned} \frac{1}{\Gamma(x)} &= x + \gamma x^2 - 0.6558780715\, x^3 - 0.0420026350\, x^4 \\ &\quad + 0.1665386114\, x^5 - 0.0421977346\, x^6 + \ldots , \end{aligned} \tag{12.5}$$

where $\gamma = 0.5772156649\ldots$ is the Euler-Mascheroni constant.

An effective polynomial expansion for $\Gamma(x+1)$ is given by

$$\Gamma(x+1) = \left(\sum_{n=0}^{9} a_n x^n\right) + \epsilon(x), \tag{12.6}$$

where the relative error $|\epsilon(x)| \lesssim 3 \times 10^{-8}$ and the coefficients a_n are given by[5]

$$\begin{aligned}
a_0 &= 0.9999999703 \\
a_1 &= -0.5772069549 \\
a_2 &= 0.9887589417 \\
a_3 &= -0.9035083713 \\
a_4 &= 0.9539074630 \\
a_5 &= -0.8649108124 \\
a_6 &= 0.6721315341 \\
a_7 &= -0.3860871683 \\
a_8 &= 0.1405004023 \\
a_9 &= -0.0235850272\,.
\end{aligned} \tag{12.7}$$

These coefficients have been computed with a computer algebra system. A least-squares curve-fit of a table of $\Gamma(x+1)$ with 81 equidistant points in the range $0 \le x \le 1$ has been used. The polynomial fit has been performed with 50 decimal digits of precision.

For our calculation, we also need both reflection of the Gamma function

$$\Gamma(-x) = -\frac{\pi}{x\,\Gamma(x)\,\sin \pi x}, \tag{12.8}$$

as well as upward recursion of the Gamma function

$$\Gamma(x+1) = x\,\Gamma(x)\,. \tag{12.9}$$

[5]A similar polynomial expansion for $\Gamma(x+1)$ is given in Sect. 6.1.36 of [1], originating from the work of C. Hastings in [6]. In the polynomial expansion in Eq. 12.6 here, however, the number of coefficients has been increased from Hastings' original 8 up to 10. With 10 coefficients, this approximation reaches a precision slightly better than the approximate 7 decimal digits of single-precision `float`.

Armed with all these mathematical equations, we are finally ready to implement the core part of our Gamma function calculation. We will call it `gamma1()`. It computes the **`float`** value of $\Gamma(x)$ for $0 < x < 1$. In particular,

```
#include <cmath>

float gamma1(const float& x)
{
  // Compute Gamma(x) for 0 < x < 1 (float).
  if(x < 0.1F)
  {
    // Small-argument Taylor series for 1/gamma.
    const float sum = (((((((     + 0.0072189432F
                             * x - 0.0096219715F)
                             * x - 0.0421977346F)
                             * x + 0.1665386114F)
                             * x - 0.0420026350F)
                             * x - 0.6558780715F)
                             * x + 0.5772156649F)
                             * x + 1)
                             * x;

    return 1.0F / sum;
  }
  else
  {
    // Do the order-9 polynomial fit.
    const float g = ((((((((    - 0.0235850272F
                           * x + 0.1405004023F)
                           * x - 0.3860871683F)
                           * x + 0.6721315341F)
                           * x - 0.8649108124F)
                           * x + 0.9539074630F)
                           * x - 0.9035083713F)
                           * x + 0.9887589417F)
                           * x - 0.5772069549F)
                           * x + 0.9999999703F;

    // Note: We use one downward recursion here.
    return g / x;
  }
}
```

To make the complete implementation of tgamma(), we need to include range checks, handling of subnormals, possible upward recursion of the result and reflection for negative arguments. For example,

```
namespace math
{
  float tgamma(float x);
}

template<typename T>
constexpr T pi =
  T(3.1415926535'8979323846'2643383279L);

float math::tgamma(float x)
{
  // Is the argument a subnormal?
  if(!std::isfinite(x))
  {
    return x;
  }

  // Check for pure zero argument.
  if(x == 0.0F)
  {
    return std::numeric_limits<float>::quiet_NaN();
  }

  // Check for overflow and underflow.
  if(     (x > 35.0F)
      || ((x > -1.0E-4F) && (x < 1.0E-4F))
    )
  {
    return std::numeric_limits<float>::infinity();
  }

  // Is the argument 1 or 2?
  if((x == 1.0F) || (x == 2.0F))
  {
    return 1.0F;
  }
```

```
  // Use a positive argument for the Gamma calculation.
  const bool b_neg = (x < 0.0F);

  x = std::fabs(x);

  // Get any integer recursion and scale the argument.
  const std::uint_fast8_t nx =
    static_cast<std::uint_fast8_t>(std::floor(x));

  x -= static_cast<float>(nx);

  // Calculate gamma of the scaled argument.
  float g = gamma1(x);

  // Do the recursion if necessary.
  for(std::uint_fast8_t i = UINT8_C(0); i < nx; ++i)
  {
    g *= x;

    ++x;
  }

  // Return (and possibly reflect) the result.
  if(b_neg == false)
  {
    return g;
  }
  else
  {
    const float sin_pi_x = std::sin(pi<float> * x);

    return -pi<float> / ((x * g) * sin_pi_x);
  }
}
```

This implementation of the `tgamma()` function is relatively complete. In practice, though, it should throw an `std::out_of_range` exception for arguments that are too large or so close to zero or negative integers that the results will be subnormal. In addition, it may be preferable to switch from recursion to Stirling's approximation for arguments above, say, $x \geq 10$ since many upward recursions can be costly. Even with its limitations, though, this version of `tgamma()` is a compact efficient Gamma function for **`float`** that may be adequate if the compiler does not include one. A variation of this implementation of `tgamma()` is included in the reference project of the companion code.

Table 12.2 Calculations of `tgamma(x)` are compared with known values of $\Gamma(x)$

x	`tgamma(x)`	$\Gamma(x)$
0.5	1.77245 38	1.7724538509 ...
8.76	24203.830	24203.81462 ...
0.02	49.442211	49.4422101631 ...
−3.45	0.29302 791	0.2930279565 ...

The numerical results of our `tgamma()` function are compared with known control values in Table 12.2. The relative deviations of the calculated values lie in the range $|\epsilon(x)| \lesssim 10^{-7}$—accurate to within the approximate 7 decimal digits of single-precision **`float`**.

Another example of a special function often needed in real-time C++ is the cylindrical Bessel function $J_\nu(x)$. The Taylor series for $J_\nu(z)$ is

$$J_\nu(z) = \left(\frac{1}{2}z\right)^\nu \sum_{k=0}^{\infty} \frac{\left(-\frac{1}{4}z^2\right)^k}{k!\,\Gamma(\nu + k + 1)}, \qquad (12.10)$$

where $z, \nu \in \mathbb{C}$, see Eq. 9.1.10 in [1] and Eq. 10.2.2 in [18].

Eq. 12.10 is a simple enough series. Accurately calculating Bessel functions over a wide range of arguments and orders is, however, relatively complicated. Numerical methods for computing the Bessel function $J_\nu(x)$ and other special functions are described in detail in [5] (in a language-neutral form) and in [23] (in traditional Fortran 77).

In addition, Boost's `Boost.Math` library [2] includes portable and well-tested C++ implementations of numerous higher transcendental functions for both built-in floating-point types as well as user-defined types. `Boost.Math` includes many utilities, tools and all of the mathematical special functions specified in TR1 [9] and C++17. The `Boost.Math` library is also designed to interact with its user-defined extended multiple-precision library `Boost.Multiprecision` [14].

As mentioned in the beginning of this section, a lot of mathematical special functions have been incorporated in the specification of C++17. These can be found in the `<cmath>` library. This allows for straightforward use of special functions such as Gamma-type functions, Bessel functions, elliptic integrals, zeta functions, etc., assuming the compiler implements them.[6]

The code sample below, for instance, shows how to conveniently retrieve the approximate value of the cylindrical Bessel function $J_{12/10}(34/10)$ for built-in **`float`**.

[6]At the time of C++17, the newly-specified mathematical special functions are limited to real-valued implementations only.

```
#include <cmath>

const float jv = std::cyl_bessel_j(1.2F, 3.4F);

// 0.275794
```

Elliptic integrals are also available in <cmath>. Consider, for example, the incomplete elliptic integral of the first kind given by [22],

$$F(\varphi, k) = \int_0^{\varphi} \frac{d\theta}{\sqrt{1 - k^2 \sin^2 \theta}} . \tag{12.11}$$

The following code snippet computes the **float** value of $F(1/2, \pi/2)$.

```
#include <cmath>

constexpr float pi_half = pi<float> / 2.0F;

const float e1 = std::ellint_1(0.5F, pi_half);

// 1.68575
```

A more detailed investigation of another mathematical special function from <cmath> can be motivated by a well-known series involving the Riemann zeta function $\zeta(x)$ and the Euler-Mascheroni constant γ. In particular, we find from [21] that

$$\gamma = 1 - \sum_{n=2}^{\infty} \frac{\zeta(n) - 1}{n} . \tag{12.12}$$

Based on this series we can use the `std::riemann_zeta()` function from <cmath>, to compute an approximation of γ. This is shown in the following code.

```
#include <algorithm>
#include <array>
#include <cmath>
#include <cstdint>
#include <numeric>

float euler_gamma_approx()
{
  std::array<float, 14U> arg_list;

  float f = 1.0F;
```

```
  // Generate a list of floating-point
  // arguments ranging from 2.0 to 15.0.
  std::generate_n(arg_list.begin(),
                  arg_list.size(),
                  [&f]() -> float
                  {
                    return f += 1.0F;
                  });

  // Calculate the gamma approximation.
  const float sum =
    std::accumulate(
      arg_list.cbegin(),
      arg_list.cend(),
      0.0F,
      [](const float prev, const float& n) -> float
      {
        return     prev
               + ((std::riemann_zeta(n) - 1.0F) / n);
      });

  // Result: 0.577218, compare with 0.5772156649....
  const float euler_gamma = 1.0F - sum;

  return euler_gamma;
}
```

This series calculation uses 14 individual calls of the Riemann zeta function to produce the Euler-Mascheroni constant γ with about 5 decimal digits of precision. Even though this is not a particularly efficient calculation of γ, this example does, nonetheless, provide a strong test of the compiler's implementation of `std::riemann_zeta()` for positive integral arguments.

A benchmark of mathematical special functions can be found in the `chapter12_04` example. Highly detailed calculations of certain function values are carried out in this sample, providing an effective stress-test for the compiler's floating-point implementation.[7] Not all of these functions are included in the C++ standard, so they are implemented (only for small parameter ranges) in the example.

[7]The floating-point implementation could use either a hardware FPU or a software floating-point emulation library.

The code sizes and runtimes are measured for calculations of a cylindrical Bessel function[8]

$$J_{11/9}(\gamma) \approx 0.1890533652, \tag{12.13}$$

a generalized hypergeometric series[9]

$${}_4F_5\left(\left\{\frac{3}{7}, \frac{3}{8}, \frac{3}{9}, \frac{3}{10}\right\}; \left\{\frac{7}{13}, \frac{7}{14}, \frac{7}{15}, \frac{7}{16}, \frac{7}{17}\right\}; \log 2\right) \approx 1.5835963139, \tag{12.14}$$

and a generalized Legendre function of the first kind on the real axis within the unit circle[10]

$$P_{1/11}^{14/19}\left(\frac{2}{7}\right) \approx 0.2937838815. \tag{12.15}$$

The runtimes and code sizes of the mathematical special functions calculations of the `chapter12_04` example are provided in Table 12.3. Our target with the 8-bit microcontroller has been used with GCC 7.2.0 and optimization level `-O2` for this benchmark. The temporal measurement method using a digital port and an oscilloscope described in Sect. 9.6 has been employed to determine the runtime.

---

[8]This calculation uses a Taylor series (see Eq. 9.1.10 in [1])

$$J_\nu(x) = \left(\frac{1}{2}x\right)^\nu \sum_{k=0}^{\infty} \frac{\left(-\frac{1}{4}x^2\right)^k}{k!\,\Gamma(\nu + k + 1)},$$

also shown in Eq. 12.10.

[9]This calculation uses a Taylor series in combination with products of the coefficients (see Eq. 16.2.1 in [19])

$${}_pF_q\left(\{a_p\}; \{b_q\}; x\right) = \sum_{k=0}^{\infty} \frac{(a_1)_k \ldots (a_p)_k}{(b_1)_k \ldots (b_q)_k} \frac{x^k}{k!}.$$

[10]This calculation uses a hypergeometric representation (see Eq. 8.1.2 in [1])

$$P_\nu^\mu(x) = \frac{1}{\Gamma(1-\mu)} \left(\frac{1+x}{1-x}\right)^{\mu/2} {}_2F_1\left(-\nu,\ \nu+1;\ 1-\mu;\ \frac{1-x}{2}\right),$$

which ultimately uses a Taylor series as well.

Table 12.3 The resource consumptions in the benchmark of mathematical special functions in the `chapter12_04` example are provided

Function	Runtime [μs]	Code size [byte]
$J_{\nu}(x)$	800	400
${}_pF_q\left(\{a_p\};\{b_q\};x\right)$	1,600	2,600
$P_{\nu}^{\mu}(x)$	2,000	600

12.5 Complex-Valued Mathematics

The C++ standard library supports complex-valued mathematics with its template data type `std::complex`. The `std::complex` data type is defined in `<complex>` and specified for (and *only* for) the built-in types **`float`**, **`double`** and **`long double`**.

The public interface of the `std::complex` class supports basic arithmetic operators, elementary transcendental functions, the norm, polar coordinates, etc. See Sects. 26.4.1–26.4.9 in [11] for a complete synopsis of the `<complex>` library.

Consider x and y of type `std::complex<float>` given by

$$x = 1.23 + 3.45i$$

$$y = 0.77 + 0.22i\,. \tag{12.16}$$

The following code computes the complex values

$$z_1 = x/\,y$$

$$z_2 = \sin(x)\,, \tag{12.17}$$

where z_1 and z_2 are of type `std::complex<float>`.

```
std::complex<float> x(1.23F, 3.45F); // (1.23 + 3.45 I)
std::complex<float> y(0.77F, 0.22F); // (0.77 + 0.22 I)

std::complex<float> z1;
std::complex<float> z2;

z1 = x / y;          // (2.6603774 + 3.7204117 I)
z2 = std::sin(x); // (14.859343 + 5.2590045 I)
```

The `<complex>` library also supports, among others, common complex operations such as norm and absolute value. For the same complex values x and y, consider the norm and absolute value given by

$$
\begin{aligned}
n_x &= \|x\| = (\Re x)^2 + (\Im x)^2 \\
a_y &= |y| = \sqrt{(\Re y)^2 + (\Im y)^2}\,.
\end{aligned} \tag{12.18}
$$

The following code computes the **`float`** values of n_x and a_y.

```
std::complex<float> x(1.23F, 3.45F); // (1.23 + 3.45 I)
std::complex<float> y(0.77F, 0.22F); // (0.77 + 0.22 I)

float nx = std::norm(x); // 13.4154
float ay = std::abs(y);  // 0.800812
```

Setting and retrieving the real and imaginary parts of a complex number is done with the member functions `real()` and `imag()`. For instance,

```
std::complex<float> z(0); // (0 + 0 I)

z.real(1.23F); // Set the real part.
z.imag(3.45F); // Set the imag part.

float zr = z.real(); // Get the real part, 1.23.
float zi = z.imag(); // Get the imag part, 3.45.
```

It is straightforward to create non-trivial complex-valued computations that can also use complex-valued elementary functions. We will now convert the computation of the real-valued sinc function from Sect 12.1 to a complex-valued calculation. The code sample below computes the complex-valued sinc function for `std::complex<float>`.

```
#include <complex>
#include <limits>

namespace
{
  using local_complex_type = std::complex<float>;
}

local_complex_type sinc(const local_complex_type& z)
{
  if(std::abs(z) <
      std::numeric_limits<float>::epsilon())
```

```
  {
    return 1.0F;
  }
  else if(std::abs(z) < 0.03F)
  {
    const local_complex_type z2 = z * z;

    const local_complex_type sum
      = ((      - 1.984126984E-04F
          * z2 + 8.333333333E-03F)
          * z2 - 1.666666667E-01F)
          * z2;

    return 1.0F + sum;
  }
  else
  {
    return std::sin(z) / z;
  }
}
```

Performing a quick test of the computation yields

$$\operatorname{sinc}(1.2 + 3.4i) \approx (2.70868 - 3.15559\, i) \; . \tag{12.19}$$

The calculated result for 32-bit built-in **float** compares well with the control value of $(2.70868\,1783\ldots - 3.15558\,5490\ldots\, i)$.

In general, complex-valued floating-point calculations are at least four times slower than corresponding real-valued computations. The rule of thumb here is that mathematical software does the majority of its work with multiplication—an $O\left(N^2\right)$ operation. Since complex numbers have two components, real and imaginary, the computational effort of complex-valued math can be expected to be at least four times that of real-valued math (i.e., $O(N^2) \rightarrow 2^2 \sim 4$).

For two cases in point, consider the work of multiplying two complex numbers

$$(a + ib) \times (c + id) = (ac - bd) + i\,(ad + bc) \; , \tag{12.20}$$

and that of evaluating the sine of a complex number

$$\sin(x + iy) = \sin x \, \cosh y + i \, \cos x \, \sinh y \, . \tag{12.21}$$

Table 12.4 Timing and code size of complex-valued floating-point calculations

Function	Runtime [µs]	Code size [byte]
$(1.23 + 3.45i) \times (0.77 + 0.22i)$	60	900
$\sqrt{1.23 + 3.45i}$	190	1,600
$\sin(1.23 + 3.45i)$	590	1,700
$\log(1.23 + 3.45i)$	400	1,900
$\exp(1.23 + 3.45i)$	400	1,600
$\operatorname{acosh}(1.23 + 3.45i)$	830	3,200

The multiplication algorithm in Eq. 12.20 requires four real-valued multiplications and two additions.[11] The computation of the trigonometric sine function in Eq. 12.21 requires the evaluation of four real-valued elementary transcendental functions.[12]

It can be interesting to measure the efficiency of complex-valued calculations. Table 12.4 shows the runtime and code size for various complex-valued functions performed with `std::complex<float>` on our target with the 8-bit microcontroller.[13]

Comparisons of runtime and size characteristics between complex-valued and real-valued calculations confirm the expectation that complex-valued math is more

[11]There is also a well-known alternate scheme for multiplication of complex numbers that requires only *three* real-valued multiplications, but five additions. In particular,

$$(a + ib) \times (c + id) = (\alpha - \beta) + i(\alpha + \gamma),$$

where

$$\begin{aligned}\alpha &= a(c + d)\\ \beta &= d(a + b)\\ \gamma &= c(b - a).\end{aligned}$$

This alternate scheme for multiplication of complex numbers may or may not be faster than the original $O(N^2)$ scheme on a given CPU architecture.

[12]Note here, however, that the sometimes supported function `sincos()` may boost efficiency because both $\sin x$ as well as $\cos x$ are required. In addition, only one exponential calculation of e^y (and its inverse) is needed because

$$\cosh y = \frac{e^y + e^{-y}}{2},$$

$$\sinh y = \frac{e^y - e^{-y}}{2}.$$

[13]This particular implementation of `std::complex` is provided in the self-written subset of the C++ standard library and STL for our target with the 8-bit microcontroller. It can be found in the companion code of this book. In addition, this interpretation of `std::complex` is nearly identical with the self-written `extended_complex` class presented in Sect. 16.6.

resource-intensive than real-valued math. Consider, for example, some of the computations of the sine function that we have described previously. On our target with the 8-bit microcontroller, the real-valued calculation requires 110 μs and 890 bytes of code (Table 12.1 row 5), whereas the complex-valued calculation takes 590 μs and 1, 700 bytes of program space (Table 12.4 row 3).

Aside from potential resource consumption issues that need to be kept in mind, there are no other significant technical reasons to avoid using complex-valued floating-point math in real-time C++. So if a project can benefit from complex-valued math and the performance constraints can be satisfied, then the `<complex>` library can safely be used.

12.6 Compile-Time Evaluation of Functions with **constexpr**

Compile-time evaluation of floating-point functions uses the **constexpr** keyword. For example, we can re-factor the `area_of_a_circle()` function from Sects. 12.1 and 12.2 for compile-time evaluation via **constexpr**.

```
template<typename T>
constexpr T area_of_a_circle(T r)
{
  return (pi<T> * r) * r;
}
```

This function returns the floating-point value representing the approximate area of a circle with radius r as a compile-time constant. For example, to compute the area of a circle with approximate **float** radius 1.23 ($a \sim 4.752916$), we simply use

```
constexpr float a = area_of_a_circle(1.23F);
```

Using **constexpr** floating-point values in this way allows for portable and legible compile-time evaluation of even non-trivial floating-point functions such as trigonometric functions.

Consider, for instance, an order 19 polynomial approximation of the sine function,

$$\sin x = \sin\left(\frac{\pi}{2}\chi\right) = \left(\sum_{n=1,n\ \text{odd}}^{n=19} a_n \chi^n\right) + O\left(10^{-20}\right), \tag{12.22}$$

using the scaled argument

$$\chi = x \left(\frac{2}{\pi}\right) \tag{12.23}$$

in the range $-1 \leq \chi \leq 1$, where the coefficients a_n are given by

$$\begin{aligned}
a_1 &= 1.5707963267948966192276341 \\
a_3 &= -6.4596409750624625337325359 \times 10^{-1} \\
a_5 &= 7.9692626246167038770053004 \times 10^{-2} \\
a_7 &= -4.6817541353186228516958362 \times 10^{-3} \\
a_9 &= 1.6044118478699232812460184 \times 10^{-4} \\
a_{11} &= -3.5988432339708525153771884 \times 10^{-6} \\
a_{13} &= 5.6921726597221657560994942 \times 10^{-8} \\
a_{15} &= -6.6880017863298194595553955 \times 10^{-10} \\
a_{17} &= 6.0640855645940930588123490 \times 10^{-12} \\
a_{19} &= -4.2468171354841523379493663 \times 10^{-14} .
\end{aligned} \tag{12.24}$$

These coefficients have also been computed with a computer algebra system using a least-squares fitting technique.

It takes a bit of typing, cleverly crafted **#define**s, and careful considerations about argument reduction, reflection and the like. It is, however, relatively straightforward to write a compile-time sine function for floating-point arguments based on Eqs. 12.22–12.24. In particular, the subroutine below performs a compile-time computation of $\sin x$ for floating-point argument x with better than 20 decimal digits of precision.[14]

```
// Scale the argument.
#define CHI_S T(T(x * 2) / pi<T>)

// Take the absolute value of CHI.
#define IS_NEG bool(CHI_S < T(0))
#define CHI_A  T(IS_NEG ? -CHI_S : CHI_S)
```

[14]This implementation uses solely range reduction, reflection and the polynomial approximation. To obtain the highest possible precision-conserving characteristics, however, it may be better to use Taylor series approximations near the turning points at $x = 0$ and $x = \pi/2$ after the range reduction. See [15] for further details on techniques for range reduction.

```
// Do the argument reduction.
#define NPI2 std::uint32_t(CHI_A / 2)
#define NPI  std::uint32_t(                        \
               (CHI_A - (NPI2 * 2) > T(1))         \
                 ? NPI2 + 1                        \
                 : NPI2)

#define CHI  T(CHI_A - T(NPI * 2))
#define CHI2 T(CHI * CHI)

// Do the order-19 polynomial expansion.
#define SUM                                           \
  (((((((((- T(4.2468171354841523379493663E-14L)    \
    * CHI2 + T(6.0640855645940930588123490E-12L)) \
    * CHI2 - T(6.6880001786329819459555395E-10L)) \
    * CHI2 + T(5.6921726597221657560994942E-08L)) \
    * CHI2 - T(3.5988432339708525153771884E-06L)) \
    * CHI2 + T(1.6044118478699232812460184E-04L)) \
    * CHI2 - T(4.6817541353186228516958362E-03L)) \
    * CHI2 + T(7.9692626246167038770053004E-02L)) \
    * CHI2 - T(6.4596409750624625337325359E-01L)) \
    * CHI2 + T(1.5707963267948966192276341E+00L)) \
    * CHI

// Reflect the result if necessary.
#define NEEDS_REFLECT bool((NPI % 2) != 0)

namespace math { namespace const_functions {

template<typename T>
constexpr T sin(T x)
{
  return ((NEEDS_REFLECT == IS_NEG) ? SUM : -SUM);
}

} } // namespace math::const_functions
```

Here, the **constexpr** version of the `sin()` function has been implemented within **namespace** `math::const_functions`. Thereby, it can be differentiated from global `::sin()` and the standard library's `std::sin()` in `<cmath>` which are often used without namespace resolution.

Using `math::const_functions::sin()` for compile-time calculations of the sine function in code is simple. In the example below, for instance, the compiler computes the approximate double-precision representation of sin (1/ 2).

```
constexpr double y = math::const_functions::sin(0.5);
```

If `y` is subsequently used in a subroutine, the compiler should be able to compute the value of the sine function at compile time. Investigations of the compiler-generated assembly code reveal that the compiler directly replaced the variable `y` with the 8-byte hexadecimal representation of

$$\sin(1/2) \approx 0.47942553860420301 = \texttt{0x3FDE'AEE8'744B'05F0}. \tag{12.25}$$

This is an extremely efficient form of constant folding.[15] In fact, using the **constexpr** subroutine `math::const_functions::sin()` reduces the runtime effort of computing $\sin x$ for compile-time constant x to essentially zero, that of merely loading a constant value computed by the compiler into CPU registers.[16]

With a bit of additional effort, compile-time constant versions of cosine and tangent can also be written. In particular,

```
namespace math { namespace const_functions {

template<typename T>
constexpr T cos(T x)
{
  return -sin<T>(x - T(pi<T> / 2));
}

template<typename T>
constexpr T tan(T x)
{
  return sin<T>(x) / cos<T>(x);
}

} } // namespace math::const_functions
```

[15] This benchmark was investigated with GCC version 4.8.1 for `avr-unknown-elf` and GCC version 4.8.3 for a well-known 32-bit microcontroller.

[16] In this example, the floating-point representation of **double** is 8 bytes wide and conforms with double-precision floating-point representation in IEEE-754.

It is possible to use compile-time evaluation of functions to compute essentially any function, bounded only by the compiler's internal limits. It is possible to extend the number of coefficients in polynomial expansions and the like to obtain even higher precision. In addition, template metaprogramming can be employed for more complicated range reduction if needed. Compile-time evaluation of floating-point functions may potentially be a new research topic in the area of high-performance numerical computing made possible by the abilities of **constexpr** in C++11.

12.7 Generic Numeric Programming

Some forms of generic numeric programming employ C++ templates to use the same code for different data types and function objects.[17] We have already encountered generic numeric programming previously in this chapter. In particular, recall the templated function `area_of_a_circle()` from Sect. 12.6.

```
template<typename T>
constexpr T area_of_a_circle(T r)
{
  return (pi<T> * r) * r;
}
```

This subroutine has strong generic character because it can be used with various floating-point types to provide results with differing precisions. For example, if **float** and **double** correspond to IEEE-754 single-precision and double-precision, respectively, on a given system, then the following results are obtained for the area of a circle with radius 1.23.

```
constexpr float f = area_of_a_circle(1.23F);
// 4.75292

constexpr double d = area_of_a_circle(1.23);
// 4.752915525616
```

We will now add even more power to generic numeric programming using not only different floating-point types but also function objects as template parameters. Consider some well-known central difference rules for numerically computing the

[17]See also [20] for a description of a fundamental relationship between mathematics and generic programming.

first derivative of a function $f'(x)$ with $x \in \mathbb{R}$. In particular,

$$f'(x) \approx m_1 + O(dx^2)$$

$$f'(x) \approx \frac{4}{3}m_1 - \frac{1}{3}m_2 + O(dx^4)$$

$$f'(x) \approx \frac{3}{2}m_1 - \frac{3}{5}m_2 + \frac{1}{10}m_3 + O(dx^6), \tag{12.26}$$

where the difference terms m_n are given by

$$m_1 = \frac{f(x+dx) - f(x-dx)}{2\,dx}$$

$$m_2 = \frac{f(x+2dx) - f(x-2dx)}{4\,dx}$$

$$m_3 = \frac{f(x+3dx) - f(x-3dx)}{6\,dx}, \tag{12.27}$$

and δx is the step-size of the derivative.

The third expression in Eq. 12.26 is a three-point central difference rule. It calculates the first derivative of $f(x)$ with respect to x to $O(dx^6)$, where δx is the given step-size. If the step-size is 0.01, for example, this derivative calculation is expected to provide results having about 6 decimal digits of precision—just about right for the 7 decimal digits of single-precision **float**.

We will now make a generic template subroutine using this three-point central difference rule. In particular,[18]

```
template<typename value_type,
         typename function_type>
value_type derivative(const value_type x,
                      const value_type dx,
                      function_type function)
{
  // Compute the derivative using a three point
  // central difference rule of O(dx^6).
```

[18]Here, we rearrange the terms in the third expression of Eq. 12.26 such that

$$f'(x) \approx \frac{(15m_1 - 6m_2 + m_3)\,dx}{10\,dx},$$

where δx is the step-size.

```
  const value_type dx1 = dx;
  const value_type dx2 = dx1 * 2;
  const value_type dx3 = dx1 * 3;

  const value_type m1 =
    (function(x + dx1) - function(x - dx1)) / 2;

  const value_type m2 =
    (function(x + dx2) - function(x - dx2)) / 4;

  const value_type m3 =
    (function(x + dx3) - function(x - dx3)) / 6;

  const value_type fifteen_m1 = 15 * m1;
  const value_type six_m2     =  6 * m2;
  const value_type ten_dx1    = 10 * dx1;

  return ((fifteen_m1 - six_m2) + m3) / ten_dx1;
}
```

The `derivative()` template function can be used to compute the first derivative of any continuous function to $O(dx^6)$. Consider, for example, the first derivative of $\sin x$ evaluated at $x = \pi/3$, in other words

$$\frac{d}{dx}\sin x\bigg|_{x=\frac{\pi}{3}} = \cos\left(\frac{\pi}{3}\right) = \frac{1}{2}\,. \tag{12.28}$$

The code below computes this derivative with about 6 decimal digits of precision using the `derivative()` function.

```
const float x = pi<float> / 3.0F;

// Should be very near 0.5.
const float y =
  derivative(x,
             0.01F,
             [](const float& x) -> float
             {
               return std::sin(x);
             });
```

The expected value is $1/2 = 0.5$. The compiler that was used to test this code sequence obtained 0.50000286. This result is within the expected tolerance of $O\left(dx^6\right)$ with $dx = 1/100 = 0.01$.[19] This code also makes use of the `pi` variable template from Sect. 12.2 and a lambda expression—both of which are C++ language elements with strong generic character as well.

The `derivative()` template function can also be used with function objects. Consider the quadratic equation,

$$ax^2 + bx + c = 0 . \tag{12.29}$$

The code below implements a template function object that encapsulates the left-hand side of the quadratic equation.

```
template<typename T>
class quadratic
{
public:
  const T a;
  const T b;
  const T c;

  quadratic(const T& a_,
            const T& b_,
            const T& c_) : a(a_),
                           b(b_),
                           c(c_) { }

  T operator()(const T& x) const
  {
    return ((a * x + b) * x) + c;
  }
};
```

The first derivative of the quadratic equation can be computed in closed form. In other words,

$$\frac{d}{dx}\left(ax^2 + bx + c\right) = 2ax + b . \tag{12.30}$$

[19]When using binary floating-point representations, however, best results are typically obtained from derivative central difference rules with a step-size of the form $(1/2)^n$. Using a somewhat *larger* step size of $1/64 = 0.015625$, for example, produces a result of 0.50000173, which is even slightly better than the result of 0.50000286 obtained with the *smaller* step-size of $1/100 = 0.01$.

The `derivative()` template function can handily compute the first derivative of the `quadratic` function object. In particular, the code below computes

$$\frac{d}{dx}\left(\frac{12}{10}x^2 + \frac{34}{10}x + \frac{56}{10}\right)\Bigg|_{x=\frac{1}{2}} = \frac{12}{10} + \frac{34}{10} = 4.6\,. \tag{12.31}$$

```
const float x = 0.5F;

// Should be very near 4.6.
const float y =
  derivative(x,
             0.01F,
             quadratic<float>(1.2F, 3.4F, 5.6F));
```

The expected value is 4.6. The compiler that was used to test this code sequence obtained 4.60000086, which is well within the expected tolerance of $O\left(dx^6\right)$.

The versatile `derivative()` template function exemplifies generic numeric programming because both the floating-point type (`value_type`) as well as the function-type (`function_type`) are template parameters. This means that the `derivative()` template function can be used equally well with both built-in floating-point types (**`float`**, **`double`**, **`long double`**) as well as user-defined types such as extended precision floating-point types (i.e., as in [14]), fixed-point types (Chap. 13), etc. Furthermore, the `derivative()` template function accepts all valid function types in its third input parameter including functions having static linkage, lambda expressions, and function objects alike.

A similar generic template method can be used for computing the numerical definite integral of a function. Recall the definite integral of a real-valued function $f(x)$ from a to b, in other words

$$\int_a^b f(x)\,dx\,. \tag{12.32}$$

The `integral()` template function shown below uses a recursive trapezoid rule to perform this kind of numerical integration.[20] In particular,

```
template<typename real_value_type,
         typename real_function_type>
real_value_type integral(
  const real_value_type& a,
  const real_value_type& b,
  const real_value_type& tol,
  real_function_type real_function)
```

[20] See also Sect. 5.2.2 in [5] for additional information on this recursive trapezoid rule.

```
{
  std::uint_fast32_t n2(1);

  real_value_type step = ((b - a) / 2U);

  real_value_type result =
    (real_function(a) + real_function(b)) * step;

  const std::uint_fast8_t k_max = UINT8_C(32);

  for(std::uint_fast8_t k(0U); k < k_max; ++k)
  {
    real_value_type sum(0);

    for(std::uint_fast32_t j(0U); j < n2; ++j)
    {
      const std::uint_fast32_t two_j_plus_one =
        (j * UINT32_C(2)) + UINT32_C(1);

      sum +=
        real_function(a + (step * two_j_plus_one));
    }

    const real_value_type tmp = result;

    result = (result / 2U) + (step * sum);

    const real_value_type ratio =
      std::abs(tmp / result);

    const real_value_type delta = std::abs(ratio - 1U);

    if((k > UINT8_C(1)) && (delta < tol))
    {
      break;
    }

    n2 *= 2U;

    step /= 2U;
  }

  return result;
}
```

We will now use the `integral()` template function to compute the value of a cylindrical Bessel function. Consider the well-known integral representation of the cylindrical Bessel function of integer order on the real axis. In particular,[21]

$$J_n(x) = \frac{1}{\pi} \int_0^{\pi} \cos\left(x \sin\theta - n\theta\right) d\theta\,, \quad \text{for } x \in \mathbb{R},\, n \in \mathbb{Z}. \tag{12.33}$$

The template code below implements `cyl_bessel_j()` based on the integral representation in Eq. 12.33.[22]

```
template<typename float_type>
float_type cyl_bessel_j(const std::uint_fast8_t n,
                        const float_type& x)
{
  const float_type epsilon =
    std::numeric_limits<float_type>::epsilon();

  const float_type tol = std::sqrt(epsilon);

  const float_type jn =
    integral(float_type(0),
             pi<float_type>,
             tol,
             [&x,&n](const float_type& t) -> float_type
             {
               return
                 std::cos(x * std::sin(t) - (n * t));
             })
    / pi<float_type>;

  return jn;
}
```

Here, we use standard mathematical functions combined with generic template methods. A lambda function is used for passing the integral representation of the Bessel function to the recursive trapezoid mechanism in `integral()`.

[21] See, for example, Eq. 10.9.1 in [18].

[22] This implementation of `cyl_bessel_j()`, however, only converges well for limited parameter ranges such as small x, $n \lesssim 5$.

We will now use the `cyl_bessel_j()` template to compute the approximate value of $J_2(1.23)$ for single-precision **`float`**. In other words,

```
const float j2 = cyl_bessel_j(UINT8_C(2), 1.23F);

// Computed result: 0.1663694
// Known value:     0.1663693837...
```

The result of the computation of `j2` is 0.1663694. This computed result agrees with the known value of $J_2(1.23) \approx 0.1663693837\ldots$ to within the approximate seven decimal digits of precision had by single-precision **`float`**.

As of C++17, the value of this cylindrical Bessel function can also be verified with `std::cyl_bessel_j()`, from the mathematical special functions found in the `<cmath>` library. In particular,

```
#include <cmath>

const float j2 = std::cyl_bessel_j(2, 1.23F);

// 0.166369
```

Generic numeric programming can be quite useful in real-time C++ because it is flexible and scalable. Since generic numeric programming utilizes template methods, the results can be highly optimized by the compiler. This can result in exceptionally efficient algorithms.

References

1. M. Abramowitz, I.A. Stegun, *Handbook of Mathematical Functions,* 9th *Printing* (Dover, New York, 1972)
2. B. Dawes, D. Abrahams, *Boost C++ Libraries* (2017). http://www.boost.org
3. A. Erdélyi, W. Magnus, F. Oberhettinger, F.G. Tricomi, *Higher Transcendental Functions*, vol. 1–3 (Krieger, New York, 1981)
4. S.R. Finch, *Mathematical Constants* (Cambridge University Press, Cambridge, 2003)
5. A. Gil, J. Segura, N.M. Temme, *Numerical Methods for Special Functions* (Society for Industrial and Applied Mathematics, Philadelphia, 2007)
6. C. Hastings, *Approximations for Digital Computers* (Princeton University Press, Princeton, 1955)
7. IEEE Computer Society, *IEEE Std 1003.1 – 2008*. IEEE Standard 754–2008 (2008). http://ieeexplore.ieee.org/servlet/opac?punumber=4610933
8. ISO/IEC, *ISO/IEC 9899:1999 : Programming Languages – C* (International Organization for Standardization, Geneva, 1999)

9. ISO/IEC, *ISO/IEC TR 19768:2007 : Information Technology – Programming Languages – Technical Report on C++ Library Extensions* (International Organization for Standardization, Geneva, 2007)
10. ISO/IEC, *ISO/IEC 29124:2010 : Information Technology – Programming Languages, Their Environments and System Software Interfaces – Extensions to the C++ Library to Support Mathematical Special Functions* (International Organization for Standardization, Geneva, 2010)
11. ISO/IEC, *ISO/IEC 14882:2011 : Information Technology – Programming Languages – C++* (International Organization for Standardization, Geneva, 2011)
12. ISO/IEC, *ISO/IEC 14882:2017 : Programming Languages – C++* (International Organization for Standardization, Geneva, 2017)
13. D.E. Knuth, *The Art of Computer Programming Volumes 1–3, Third Edition* (Addison-Wesley, Boston, 1998)
14. J. Maddock, C. Kormanyos, *Boost Multiprecision* (2019). http://www.boost.org/doc/libs/1_70_0/libs/multiprecision/doc/html/index.html
15. J.M. Muller, *Elementary Functions: Algorithms and Implementation, Third Edition* (Springer (Birkhäuser), New York, 2016)
16. J.M. Muller, N. Brisebarre, F. de Dinechin, C.M. Jeannerod, V. Lefèvre, G. Melquiond, N. Revol, D. Stehlé, T. Torres, *Handbook of Floating-Point Arithmetic* (Birkhäuser, Boston, 2010)
17. F.W.J. Olver, D.W. Lozier, R.F. Boisvert, C.W. Clark (eds.), *NIST Handbook of Mathematical Functions* (Cambridge University Press, Cambridge, 2010)
18. F.W.J. Olver, D.W. Lozier, R.F. Boisvert, C.W. Clark (eds.), F.W.J. Olver, L.C. Maximon, *NIST Handbook of Mathematical Functions, Chap. 10, Bessel Functions* (Cambridge University Press, Cambridge, 2010)
19. F.W.J. Olver, D.W. Lozier, R.F. Boisvert, C.W. Clark (eds.), R.A. Askey, A.B. Olde Daalhuis, *NIST Handbook of Mathematical Functions, Chap. 16, Generalized Hypergeometric Functions and Meijer G–Function* (Cambridge University Press, Cambridge, 2010)
20. A.A. Stepanov, D.E. Rose, *From Mathematics to Generic Programming* (Addison-Wesley, Boston, 2014)
21. Wikipedia, *Riemann zeta function* (2017). http://en.wikipedia.org/wiki/Riemann_zeta_function
22. Wikipedia, *Elliptic integral* (2017). http://en.wikipedia.org/wiki/Elliptic_integral
23. S. Zhang, J. Jin, *Computation of Special Functions* (Wiley, New York, 1996)

Chapter 13
Fixed-Point Mathematics

Many embedded systems applications need to perform floating-point calculations. As mentioned in the previous chapter, however, small-scale microcontrollers may not have hardware support for floating-point calculations with a floating-point unit (FPU). To avoid potentially slow floating-point emulation libraries manipulating 32-bit single-precision **`float`** or even 64-bit double-precision **`double`**, many developers elect to use integer-based fixed-point arithmetic. The first part of this chapter describes fixed-point data types and presents a scalable template class representation for fixed-point. In the second part of this chapter, we will use our fixed-point class to compute some elementary transcendental functions, discuss fixed-point efficiency and develop a specialization of `std::numeric_limits`.

13.1 Fixed-Point Data Types

A fixed-point number is an integer-based data type representing a fractional number, optionally signed, having a fixed number of integer digits to the left of the decimal point and another fixed number of fractional digits to the right of the decimal point.[1] A fixed-point data type is usually used to hold a real value. Two fixed-point values, however, could also be used as the real and imaginary components of a complex class, such as an extended complex numbers class similar to the one used in Sect. 16.6. Fixed-point data types are commonly implemented in base-2 or base-10. Fixed-point calculations can be highly efficient in microcontroller programming because they use a near-integer representation of the data type.

[1] See Chap. 9 in [5] and also [7] for more information on fixed-point numbers.

C. Kormanyos, *Real-Time C++*, https://doi.org/10.1007/978-3-662-62996-3_13

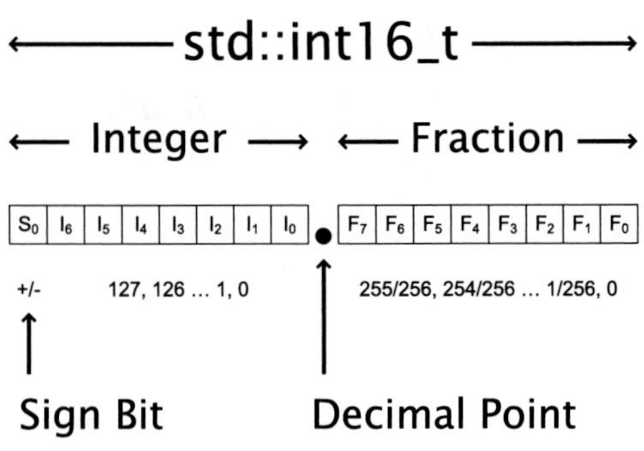

Fig. 13.1 A representation of the Q7.8 fixed-point type is shown

Consider a base-2 fixed-point system consisting of an integer representation with four binary digits, having two integer digits to the left of the decimal point and two fractional digits to the right of the decimal point. In this system, the fractional number 1.5 could be represented as an integer with binary value `0b0110` (i.e. decimal value 6). Here, the fractional value has been left-shifted by 2 (multiplied by 4) in order to fit within the integer representation. The decimal point in this fixed-point system lies between bits $\{0 \ldots 1\}$ and bits $\{2 \ldots 3\}$.

High-performance implementations of fixed-point numbers for modern microcontrollers commonly use base-2. In Fig. 13.1, for example, a common base-2, signed, 16-bit fixed-point representation is depicted. It has one sign bit, 7 binary integer digits to the left of the decimal point, and 8 binary fractional digits to the right of the decimal point.

This is known as a Q7.8 fixed-point type using the *Q-notation*. In the unambiguous Q-notation, the entire fixed-point number is represented as a single two's-complement signed integer with an implicit sign bit. For example, Q15.16 describes a fixed-point type with one sign bit, 15 integer bits and 16 fractional bits. The Q15.16 representation can be stored in a 32-bit signed integer.

Fixed-point numbers generally do not have an exponent field, lending them a near-integer representation. Therefore, manipulations of fixed-point numbers such as addition, subtraction, multiplication and division can use integer algorithms which can be simpler and potentially more efficient than those of conventional floating-point representations.

The Q7.8 representation can hold real numbers ranging from

$$\pm \left\{ \texttt{0x00.01} \ldots \texttt{0x7F.FF} \right\}, \tag{13.1}$$

in other words from

$$\pm \left\{ \frac{1}{2^8} \cdots \left(2^7 - \frac{1}{2^8} \right) \right\}, \tag{13.2}$$

which is approximately equal to

$$\pm \left\{ 0.004 \ldots 127.996 \right\}. \tag{13.3}$$

The decimal point has been symbolically included in the hexadecimal representation of Eq. 13.1 in an intuitive fashion. The Q7.8 fixed-point representation has slightly more than 2 decimal digits of precision both to the left of the decimal point as well as to the right of the decimal point. Note that the fractional part of the Q7.8 representation has one binary digit more of precision than the integer part due to the sign bit in the integer part.

Since the decimal point has a fixed position in the underlying integer data type, smaller numbers have decreased precision. In fact, the minimum value of the Q7.8 representation is $\left(1/2^8\right) \approx 0.004$, with merely *one* binary digit of precision. In addition, fixed-point representations lacking an exponent usually have smaller range than floating-point types. In particular, the maximum value of the Q7.8 representation is approximately $+127.996$.

Fixed-point types generally have less range and reduced precision compared with floating-point representations. The underlying reason for this is the near-integer representation of fixed-point types. This is, however, exactly what lends them their improved performance. Fixed-point trades reduced range and decreased precision in favor of potentially improved efficiency using simpler integer algorithms.

It is possible to vary the fundamental integer size and/or the decimal split characteristics when defining fixed-point types. This can be done in order to obtain different performances or other numerical ranges. For example, a signed, 32-bit Q15.16 representation could be used for a fixed-point type with optimized performance on a 32-bit architecture. If storage size or performance on an 8-bit platform are considerations, then an unsigned, 8-bit Q0.8 representation could be used. The Q0.8 representation is able to store fixed-point numbers with positive values less than one with about two decimal digits of precision. The Q0.8 representation could be useful, for example, if the application only needs to implement a couple of trigonometric calculations, such as sine and cosine functions with just a few digits of precision. Whatever the fixed-point representation, one must be aware of its range. In addition, utmost care must be taken to remain within the numerical limitations at all times when performing fixed-point calculations.

It is also possible to dynamically vary the characteristics of a fixed-point type's decimal split during runtime. This may be desired for optimizing the results of numerical calculations within specific ranges. For example, calculations of the exponential function of, say, $e^2 \ldots e^3$ have results that range from about $7 \ldots 20$. Comparing these values with the results of calculations of the sine or cosine functions, for instance, shows that the exponential function benefits from more digits to the left of the decimal point and fewer to the right. So preferentially shifting the decimal point of the fixed-point type a few places to the right in order to make room for more digits in the integer part will generally improve fixed-point calculations of the exponential function.

In this book, however, dynamic modification of the decimal split is not done because it can lead to additional sources of error and a more complicated implementation. In my opinion, it may be best to consider the kinds of calculations planned for a particular application up front and, based on the analysis, limit the required range to some reasonable values, such as $0.001 \ldots 1,000$. Once the fixed-point range has been defined, a dedicated fixed-point type adequate for the given range can be selected up front.

13.2 A Scalable Fixed-Point Template Class

A class representation of a specialized numeric type in C++ should behave like a built-in type as closely as possible. In other words, it should be possible to perform operations on the specialized type such as assignment, binary arithmetic, comparison, etc. In order to accomplish this, the author of a specialized numeric class usually needs to implement some or all of the following features.

- Make a copy constructor from the self-type and additional constructors from other built-in types.
- Implement assignment operators from the self-type and other built-in types.
- Write overloads for the assignment operator and also for arithmetic compound assignment operators such as **operator**+=, **operator**-=, **operator***=, **operator**/=, etc.
- Make the global unary operators **operator**+ and **operator**- as well as the operators for the pre-forms and post-forms of increment and decrement **operator**++ and **operator**--.
- Implement standard global operators for binary arithmetic operations including **operator**+, **operator**-, **operator***, **operator**/, etc.
- Write global comparison operators for the specialized type as well as other built-in types such as **operator**<, **operator**<=, **operator**==, **operator**!=, **operator**>=, **operator**>, etc.
- Optionally implement a template specialization of `std::numeric_limits` for the numeric type.

These steps have been carried out in the reference project of the companion code to make a specialized `fixed_point` class. The `fixed_point` class implements a relatively complete representation of fixed-point arithmetic in C++. This class is based on a scalable template that supports varying decimal digits of precision depending on the width of the underlying template parameter.

A partial synopsis of the fixed_point template class is shown in the listing below. Complete implementation details can be found in the source code of the reference project.

```
// The scalable fixed_point template class.
template<typename integer_type>
class fixed_point
{
public:
  // Signed representation of the fixed_point type.
  typedef integer_type signed_value_type;

  // Default constructor.
  fixed_point();

  // Constructors from POD.
  fixed_point(const char);
  fixed_point(const signed char);
  fixed_point(const unsigned char);
  fixed_point(const signed short);
  fixed_point(const unsigned short);
  fixed_point(const signed int);
  fixed_point(const unsigned int);
  fixed_point(const signed long);
  fixed_point(const unsigned long);
  fixed_point(const float&);
  fixed_point(const double&);

  // Copy constructor.
  fixed_point(const fixed_point&);

  // Copy construction from another fixed-point type.
  template<typename other_type>
  fixed_point(const fixed_point<other>&);

  // Copy assignment operators from POD.
  fixed_point& operator=(const char);
  fixed_point& operator=(const signed char);
  fixed_point& operator=(const unsigned char);
  fixed_point& operator=(const signed short);
  fixed_point& operator=(const unsigned short);
  fixed_point& operator=(const signed int);
```

```
  fixed_point& operator=(const unsigned int);
  fixed_point& operator=(const signed long);
  fixed_point& operator=(const unsigned long);
  fixed_point& operator=(const float&);
  fixed_point& operator=(const double&);

  // Copy assignment operator.
  fixed_point& operator=(const fixed_point&);

  // Copy assignment from another fixed-point type.
  template<typename other>
  fixed_point& operator=(const fixed_point<other>&);

  // Negation.
  void negate();

  // Pre-increment and pre-decrement.
  fixed_point& operator++();
  fixed_point& operator--();

  // Compound assignment operations.
  fixed_point& operator+=(const fixed_point&);
  fixed_point& operator-=(const fixed_point&);
  fixed_point& operator*=(const fixed_point&);
  fixed_point& operator/=(const fixed_point&);

  // Conversion operations.
  float             to_float() const;
  double            to_double() const;
  signed_value_type to_int() const;
  std::int8_t       to_int8() const;
  std::int16_t      to_int16() const;
  std::int32_t      to_int32() const;

private:
  // Internal data representation.
  signed_value_type data;

  // Internal structure for special constructor.
  typedef nothing internal;

  // Special constructor from data representation.
  fixed_point(const internal&,
              const signed_value_type&);
```

```
  // Comparison functions.
  // ...

  // Other private implementation details.
  // ...
};

// Global post-increment and post-decrement.
// Global binary mathematical operations.
// Global binary comparison operations.
// Global math functions and transcendental functions.

// ...
```

In the `fixed_point` class, the decimal split is always in the middle of the underlying integer representation of the type. The size of the template parameter `integer_type` sets the scale of the `fixed_point` class. Here, the `integer_type` parameter is assumed to be one of the signed fixed-size integer types such as `std::int16_t`, `std::int32_t`, etc. If `integer_type` is `std::int16_t`, for example, then the `fixed_point` class represents Q7.8 fixed-point numbers. With a larger `integer_type` such as `std::int32_t`, the `fixed_point` class represents Q15.16 fixed-point numbers.

Dedicated types have been defined for the fixed-point representations that can be made from the `fixed_point` class. In particular,

```
// Define four scalable fixed_point types.
typedef fixed_point<std::int8_t>  fixed_point_3pt4;
typedef fixed_point<std::int16_t> fixed_point_7pt8;
typedef fixed_point<std::int32_t> fixed_point_15pt16;
typedef fixed_point<std::int64_t> fixed_point_31pt32;
```

For our target with the 8-bit microcontroller, the first three can be used effectively. On this 8-bit platform, though, the manipulation of signed 64-bit integers required for the Q31.32 representation is excessively costly and this fixed-point type should be avoided. On our target with the 32-bit microcontroller, however, the Q31.32 representation can be quite efficient. When selecting the right fixed-point types for a system, it may be beneficial to analyze runtimes and assembly listings in order to find the right trade-off between performance, range and precision.

13.3 Using the `fixed_point` Class

Using the `fixed_point` class is straightforward. For example, we will set the value of a Q7.8 fixed-point variable `r` to approximately 1.23.

```
// r is approximately 1.23.
const fixed_point_7pt8 r(1.23F);
```

Here, the fixed-point variable `r` is constructed from the **`float`** representation of 1.23. It can, however, be more efficient to construct fixed-point values using pure integers instead of, say, **`float`** or **`double`**. In particular, we will create the variable `r` again—this time using an integer constructor.

```
// r is approximately 1.23.
const fixed_point_7pt8 r(fixed_point_7pt8(123) / 100);
```

In this case, `r` uses an intermediate fixed-point object created from the integer 123 which is subsequently divided by the integer 100. In general, this kind of fixed-point construction should offer the best performance, even with subsequent integer division. In fact, depending on the compiler's capabilities and the characteristics of the underlying fixed-point type, the compiler may be able to directly initialize this kind of expression using constant-folding. One does need to carefully benchmark the results in order to verify that this is, in fact, the case for a particular fixed-point type on a given architecture.

It is also essential to be aware of the range limitations of fixed-point types. For example, when setting the intermediate value in the constructor shown above to 123, we are not far away from the maximum value of 127 that can fit in the integer part of the Q7.8 representation. An initial value of, say, 234 would overflow the integer part of the Q7.8 representation.

It is easy to write functions using the `fixed_point` class. Consider the template function below that computes the fixed-point area of a circle.

```
template<typename fixed_point_type>
fixed_point_type
area_of_a_circle(const fixed_point_type& r)
{
  return (fixed_point_type::value_pi() * r) * r;
}
```

In particular, we will use this template with the Q7.8 fixed-point type to compute the approximate area of a circle with radius 1.23.

```
// r is approximately 1.23.
const fixed_point_7pt8 r(fixed_point_7pt8(123) / 100);

// a is approximately 4.723.
const fixed_point_7pt8 a = area_of_a_circle(r);
```

The result for the area a is $\sim$ 4.723, which differs from the actual value of 4.75291 ... by merely 0.6%.

The fixed_point class can be seamlessly mixed with other built-in integral and floating-point types in mathematical expressions. For example, a simple template subroutine that implements the left-hand side of a cubic equation with signed integer polynomial coefficients could be implemented like this.

```
template<typename fixed_point_type,
         const int_fast8_t c0,
         const int_fast8_t c1,
         const int_fast8_t c2,
         const int_fast8_t c3>
fixed_point_type cubic(const fixed_point_type& x)
{
  return (((c3 * x + c2) * x + c1) * x) + c0;
}
```

As mentioned above, the fixed_point class can also be used with built-in **float**. In particular, consider an order 5 polynomial approximation of the trigonometric sine function

$$\sin x = 1.5704128\,\chi - 0.6425639\,\chi^3 + 0.0722739\,\chi^5 + \epsilon(x)\,, \qquad (13.4)$$

where

$$\chi = x\left(\frac{2}{\pi}\right). \qquad (13.5)$$

This polynomial approximates $\sin x$ in the range $-\pi/2 \leq x \leq \pi/2$ (in other words $-1 \leq \chi \leq 1$) with relative error $|\epsilon(x)| \lesssim 0.0002$.

The polynomial approximation in Eq. 13.4 can be implemented with a template subroutine using the fixed_point class as follows.[2]

[2]This is, though, a somewhat naive and incomplete fixed-point implementation of the sine function. It loses performance via use of **float** and is missing range reduction and reflection. A more efficient and complete fixed-point implementation of the sine function will be shown in the following section.

```
template<typename fixed_point_type>
fixed_point_type sin(const fixed_point_type& x)
{
  // Scale x to chi (+-pi/2 to +-1).
  fixed_point_type chi(x * 0.6366198F);

  // Calculate chi^2 for the polynomial expansion.
  fixed_point_type chi2 = chi * chi;

  // Do the order-5 polynomial expansion.
  return ((          0.0722739F
          * chi2 - 0.6425639F)
          * chi2 + 1.5704128F)
          * chi;
}
```

We will now use the Q15.16 fixed-point representation to compute the approximate value of sin $(1/2)$.

```
// 0.47937
fixed_point_15pt16 y = sin(fixed_point_15pt16(1) / 2);
```

The result for y is 0.47937, which differs from the actual value of approximately $0.47942\ldots$ by less than 1 part in $10,000$.

13.4 Fixed-Point Elementary Transcendental Functions

Fixed-point math can be used to create elementary transcendental functions such as trigonometric functions, exponential functions or logarithmic functions. Such functions can be quite efficient and might significantly outperform corresponding functions using built-in floating-point types such as **`float`** or **`double`**. For further information on efficient algorithms for elementary transcendental functions, the interested reader can consult [2, 3, 6].

Consider, for example, the naive fixed-point implementation of the trigonometric sine function based on Eq. 13.4 in the previous section. We will now re-design this naive implementation using more efficient *integer* construction of the polynomial coefficients (instead of construction from **`float`**) and also to include range reduction and reflection.

The algorithm for computing the fixed-point sine function uses the following scheme:

- argument transformation from x to χ according to Eq. 13.5,
- argument reduction via removing multiples of π,
- reflection for negative arguments and odd integral multiples of π,
- and polynomial expansion according to Eq. 13.4.

A possible implementation of the fixed-point sine function according to this scheme is shown below.

```
friend inline fixed_point sin(const fixed_point& x)
{
  // This function uses fixed_point's internals
  // and is, therefore, a friend of fixed_point.

  // Transform x to chi (+-pi/2 to +-1).
  fixed_point
    chi(x * fixed_point::value_two_over_pi());

  // Take the absolute value for argument reduction.
  const bool is_neg = (chi < 0);

  if(is_neg)
  {
    chi.negate();
  }

  // Do the argument reduction.
  std::uint_fast8_t npi = UINT8_C(0);

  // Remove multiples of pi (1 in the units of chi).
  if(chi.data > fixed_point::decimal_split_value)
  {
    const std::uint_fast8_t npi1 =
      (chi.data >> 1) >> fixed_point::decimal_split;

    npi = ((chi - (npi1 * 2U) > 1U) ? npi1 + 1U
                                    : npi1);

    chi -= fixed_point(npi * 2U);
  }

  const fixed_point chi2 = chi * chi;
```

```
  // Do the polynomial expansion in terms of chi.
  const fixed_point sum =
  ((
    fixed_point(internal(), // near 0.072273923
      UINT64_C(0x0'1280'8B37) >> (32 - decimal_split))
    * chi2 -
    fixed_point(internal(), // near 0.642563935
      UINT64_C(0x0'A47F'11EE) >> (32 - decimal_split)))
    * chi2 +
    fixed_point(internal(), // near 1.570412766
      UINT64_C(0x1'9206'922F) >> (32 - decimal_split)))
    * chi;

  // Reflect the result if necessary.
  const bool needs_reflect = ((npi % 2U) != 0U);

  return ((is_neg == needs_reflect) ? sum : -sum);
}
```

The `sin()` function has been implemented as a **`friend`** of the `fixed_point` class because it makes use of the private decimal split value and a private constructor from `fixed_point`. These are optimizations specifically intended to improve the performance of this implementation of the sine function. In general, one should try to find and incorporate these and similar kinds of optimizations when devising fixed-point functions because they can drastically improve the efficiency of fixed-point functions.

Using the fixed-point sine function in code is straightforward. For example, the code sequence below computes the approximate fixed-point values of $\sin(1/2)$ for several different fixed-point representations.

```
// 0.438: relative error 960/10,000
fixed_point_3pt4 y0 = sin(fixed_point_3pt4(1) / 2);

// 0.4766: relative error 60/10,000
fixed_point_7pt8 y1 = sin(fixed_point_7pt8(1) / 2);

// 0.47937: relative error 1/10,000
fixed_point_15pt16 y2 = sin(fixed_point_15pt16(1) / 2);

// actual value:
// 0.4794255386...
```

Table 13.1 The performance and efficiency of the computation of sin (1.23) for various fixed-point types and `float` on our target with the 8-bit microcontroller are shown. The runtime values exclude the time needed for `float` construction from 1.23

fp Type	sin (1.23)	Error	Runtime [μs]	Relative time $\left(\frac{\texttt{fixed\_point}}{\texttt{float}}\right)$	Code size [byte]
Q3.4	0.438	10^{-1}	8	0.1	300
Q7.8	0.4766	10^{-3}	17	0.2	520
Q15.16	0.47937	10^{-4}	50	0.5	1,170
`float`	0.4794255	10^{-8}	105	–	890
Known value	0.4794255386 ...	–			

This implementation of the fixed-point sine function includes range reduction and reflection and can, therefore, be used in a robust computational environment. There are, however, potential improvements including proper handling of excessively large arguments and subnormal numbers such as infinity and NaN. These features can be optionally included in the sine function if the underlying fixed-point class supports subnormals.

The computational complexity of fixed-point transcendental functions increases with increasing precision and width of the underlying fixed-point type used in the computations. Table 13.1 compares the performance and efficiency characteristics of the computation of sin (1.23) for various fixed-point types and `float` on our target with the 8-bit microcontroller. On this architecture, the fixed-point calculations are significantly faster and generally smaller than the corresponding `float` implementation in the C++ standard library.[3]

Another common elementary transcendental function that can be readily implemented in fixed-point is the exponential function e^x for $x \in \mathbb{R}$. The exponential function has a very wide range of results that are of interest. One of the most effective methods for reaching a large part of the range of e^x is based on argument scaling via removing integral multiples of log 2 from x.

In particular, we start with

$$e^x = e^{\alpha - n \log 2}, \tag{13.6}$$

where we select

$$n = \frac{x}{\log 2}, \tag{13.7}$$

such that $-\log 2 \le \alpha \le \log 2$. The final result of the exponential function is obtained from

$$e^x = e^{\alpha}\, 2^n. \tag{13.8}$$

[3]As mentioned previously, though, our fixed-point sine function does not properly treat subnormals, whereas the `float` version in the C++ standard library does include this formal correctness.

After approximating e^{α}, the final multiplication by 2^n requires only a shift operation. This is very efficient in binary fixed-point arithmetic.

For our calculation, we will approximate e^{α} for $-\log 2 \leq \alpha \leq \log 2$ using the polynomial

$$e^{\alpha} = 1 + c_1 \alpha + c_2 \alpha^2 + c_3 \alpha^3 + c_4 \alpha^4 + \epsilon(\alpha), \tag{13.9}$$

where the relative error $|\epsilon(\alpha)| \lesssim 2 \times 10^{-4}$.

The coefficients c_n are given by

$$\begin{aligned} c_1 &= 0.9978546 \\ c_2 &= 0.4994721 \\ c_3 &= 0.1763723 \\ c_4 &= 0.0435108 . \end{aligned} \tag{13.10}$$

The code corresponding to Eqs. 13.6 through 13.10 for the fixed-point exponential function can be implemented as shown below.

```
friend fixed_point exp(const fixed_point& x)
{
  // Scale the argument by removing multiples of ln2.
  fixed_point x_over_ln2(x);
  x_over_ln2 *= fixed_point::value_one_over_ln2();

  const std::int_fast8_t n = x_over_ln2.to_int8();

  fixed_point alpha(x);
  alpha -= (fixed_point::value_ln2() * n);

  // Do the polynomial expansion in terms of alpha.
  fixed_point sum =
  (((
    fixed_point(internal(), // near 4.3510841353E-2
      UINT64_C(0x0'0B23'8740) >> (32 - decimal_split))
    * alpha +
    fixed_point(internal(), // near 1.7637226246E-1
      UINT64_C(0x0'2D26'BC00) >> (32 - decimal_split)))
    * alpha +
    fixed_point(internal(), // near 4.9947209750E-1
      UINT64_C(0x0'7FDD'6C80) >> (32 - decimal_split)))
    * alpha +
    fixed_point(internal(), // near 9.9785463267E-1
      UINT64_C(0x0'FF73'5F00) >> (32 - decimal_split)))
    * alpha;
```

```
  sum.data += decimal_split_value;

  // Scale the result by 2^n if necessary.
  if(n > 0)
  {
    sum.data <<= n;
  }
  else if(n < 0)
  {
    sum.data >>= (-n);
  }

  return sum;
}
```

Using the fixed-point exponential function is easy. The code sample below, for instance, computes the approximate fixed-point values of $\exp(3.7)$ for both the Q7.8 as well as the Q15.16 fixed-point representations. The result of $\exp(3.7)$, however, overflows the Q3.4 representation, so Q3.4 cannot be used for this calculation.

```
fixed_point_7pt8 y1
  = exp(fixed_point_7pt8(37) / 10);
// 40.625: relative error 44/10,000

fixed_point_15pt16 y2
  = exp(fixed_point_15pt16(37) / 10);
// 40.4341: relative error 3/10,000

// Actual value:
// 40.4473043601...
```

To complement the exponential function, we will compute the logarithm function $\log x$ for $x \in \mathbb{R}$ and $x > 0$. In our approximation, we will first compute the base-2 logarithm $\log_2(x+1)$ in the range $0 \leq x \leq 1$. Argument scaling is done by removing integer powers of 2 from x. After scaling, the result of the natural logarithm is obtained from the well-known relation

$$\log x = \log 2 \times \log_2 x \,. \tag{13.11}$$

The logarithm function calculates $\log_2(x + 1)$ using the polynomial approximation

$$\log_2 (x + 1) = d_1 x + d_2 x^2 + d_3 x^3 + d_4 x^4 + \epsilon (x) , \tag{13.12}$$

where the coefficients d_n are given by

$$\begin{aligned} d_1 &= 1.4384189 \\ d_2 &= -0.6771900 \\ d_3 &= 0.3218538 \\ d_4 &= -0.0832229 , \end{aligned} \tag{13.13}$$

and the relative error $|\epsilon(x)| \lesssim 1 \times 10^{-4}$.

Arguments ranging from $0 < x < 1$ use the negated result from one recursive call of the logarithm function with the argument inverted. In other words,

$$\log (x) = -\log \left(\frac{1}{x} \right) . \tag{13.14}$$

A `fixed_point` implementation of the logarithm function based on Eqs. 13.12–13.14 is shown below.

```
friend inline fixed_point log(const fixed_point& x)
{
  // Check for negative arguments.
  if(x.data < 0)
  {
    return fixed_point(0);
  }

  unsigned_value_type x2_data(x.data);

  if(x2_data == decimal_split_value)
  {
    // The argument is identically equal to one.
    return fixed_point(0);
  }
  else if(x2_data < decimal_split_value)
  {
    // Invert and negate for 0 < x < 1.
    return -log(1 / x);
  }
```

```
  std::uint_fast8_t n2 = 0U;

  // Remove even powers of two from the argument.
  while(x2_data > (decimal_split_value * 2))
  {
    ++n2;
    x2_data >>= 1;
  }

  const fixed_point my_x2 =
    fixed_point(internal(),
                x2_data - decimal_split_value);

  // Do the order-4 polynomial expansion.
  const fixed_point sum =
  (((
  - fixed_point(internal(),      // near 8.3222941295E-2
      UINT64_C(0x0'154E'1943) >> (32 - decimal_split))
    * my_x2 +
    fixed_point(internal(),      // near 3.2185380545E-1
      UINT64_C(0x0'5265'02D0) >> (32 - decimal_split)))
    * my_x2 -
    fixed_point(internal(),      // near 6.7718997268E-1
      UINT64_C(0x0'AD5C'5271) >> (32 - decimal_split)))
    * my_x2 +
    fixed_point(internal(),      // near 1.4384189488
      UINT64_C(0x1'703C'3967) >> (32 - decimal_split)))
    * my_x2;

  // Account for 2^n, scale the result and return.
  return (sum + n2) * value_ln2();
}
```

We now have fixed-point implementations for the sine, exponential and logarithm functions. We can use these basic functions to compute other associated functions such as the remaining trigonometric functions and the hyperbolic trigonometric functions.

For example, it is straightforward to derive the fixed-point cosine and tangent functions from the sine function. In particular,

```
friend inline fixed_point cos(const fixed_point& x)
{
  return -sin(x - half_pi());
}
```

```
friend inline fixed_point tan(const fixed_point& x)
{
  const fixed_point s(sin(x));
  const fixed_point c(cos(x));

  if(s.data >= decimal_split_value || c.data == 0)
  {
    return fixed_point(0);
  }
  else
  {
    return
      fixed_point( internal(),
                   (s.data << decimal_split) / c.data);
  }
}
```

The hyperbolic trigonometric functions can be derived from the exponential function using the well-known algebraic relations

$$\sinh x = \frac{e^x - e^{-x}}{2} \tag{13.15}$$

$$\cosh x = \frac{e^x + e^{-x}}{2} \tag{13.16}$$

$$\tanh x = \frac{\sinh x}{\cosh x} = \frac{e^x - e^{-x}}{e^x + e^{-x}} . \tag{13.17}$$

When computing hyperbolic trigonometric functions, the computation of e^{-x} can be replaced with more efficient division using the reflection relation

$$e^{-x} = \frac{1}{e^x} . \tag{13.18}$$

The corresponding code for the fixed-point hyperbolic trigonometric functions is shown below.

```
friend inline fixed_point sinh(const fixed_point& x)
{
  // Compute exp(x) and exp(-x)
  const fixed_point ep = exp(x);
  const fixed_point em = 1 / ep;
```

```
  // Subtract exp(-x) from exp(x) and divide by two.
  fixed_point result(ep - em);
  result.data >>= 1;

  return result;
}

friend inline fixed_point cosh(const fixed_point& x)
{
  // Compute exp(x) and exp(-x)
  const fixed_point ep = exp(x);
  const fixed_point em = 1 / ep;

  // Add exp(x) and exp(-x) and divide by two.
  fixed_point result(ep + em);
  result.data >>= 1;

  return result;
}

friend inline fixed_point tanh(const fixed_point& x)
{
  // Compute exp(x) and exp(-x)
  const fixed_point ep = exp(x);
  const fixed_point em = 1 / ep;

  // Do the division and return the result.
  return (ep - em) / (ep + em);
}
```

Inverse trigonometric functions can be computed from polynomial approximations as well. For instance, the reference project in the companion code uses[4]

$$\sin^{-1} x = \frac{\pi}{2} - (1 - x)^{\frac{1}{2}} \left(a_0 + a_1 x + a_2 x^2 + a_3 x^3 \right) + \epsilon(x) , \qquad (13.19)$$

for $0 \leq x \leq 1$. The coefficients a_n are given by

$$\begin{aligned} a_0 &= 1.5707288 \\ a_1 &= -0.2121144 \\ a_2 &= 0.0742610 \\ a_3 &= -0.0187293 , \end{aligned} \qquad (13.20)$$

[4]This polynomial has been taken from Abramowitz and Stegun [1], § 4.4.45. It originates with the work of C. Hastings [4].

and the relative error is $|\epsilon(x)| \lesssim 5 \times 10^{-5}$. Negative arguments use odd reflection with $\sin^{-1} x = -\sin^{-1} |x|$ for $-1 \leq x < 0$.

The inverse cosine function is derived from the inverse sine function using

$$\cos^{-1} x = \frac{\pi}{2} - \sin^{-1} x . \tag{13.21}$$

The inverse tangent function uses

$$\frac{\tan^{-1} x}{x} = 1 - 0.3282530\, x^2 + 0.1617571\, x^4 - 0.0484948\, x^6 + \epsilon(x) , \tag{13.22}$$

for $0 \leq x \leq 1$. The coefficients have been derived with computer algebra and the relative error $|\epsilon(x)| \lesssim 1 \times 10^{-4}$. Arguments greater than 1 use

$$\tan^{-1} x = \frac{\pi}{2} - \tan^{-1}\left(\frac{1}{x}\right) . \tag{13.23}$$

Negative arguments use odd reflection with $\tan^{-1} x = -\tan^{-1} |x|$ for $x < 0$.

The inverse hyperbolic trigonometric functions can be computed with well-known relations involving logarithmic functions. In particular,[5]

$$\sinh^{-1} x = \log\left(x + \sqrt{x^2 + 1}\right) \tag{13.24}$$

$$\cosh^{-1} x = \log\left(x + \sqrt{x^2 - 1}\right) \tag{13.25}$$

$$\tanh^{-1} x = \frac{1}{2} \log\left(\frac{1 + x}{1 - x}\right) . \tag{13.26}$$

In this section, we have used polynomial approximations combined with argument reduction and reflection to compute real-valued fixed-point elementary transcendental functions. Excellent results for calculating transcendental function in fixed-point can be obtained from numerous other techniques including table-lookup methods, Taylor series, Newton iteration, Padé approximations, Chebyshev polynomial expansions, CORDIC (COordinate Rotation DIgital Computer) algorithms, etc.

CORDIC algorithms provide efficient shift-and-add methods for computing hyperbolic and trigonometric functions. CORDIC methods are commonly used when the cost of multiplication is significantly higher than addition, subtraction, shift and table lookup. Fast CORDIC algorithms have the potential disadvantage of

[5] Here we use $x \in \mathbb{R}$ for all three inverse hyperbolic trigonometric functions. For $\cosh^{-1} x$, we limit the range of the argument to $x \geq 1$. For $\tanh^{-1} x$, we limit the range of the argument to $|x| < 1$ combined with odd reflection with $\tanh^{-1} x = -\tanh^{-1} |x|$ for $-1 < x < 0$.

requiring large tables, making scalability difficult and resulting in potentially large code size.

13.5 A Specialization of std::numeric_limits

Numeric limits are only provided for built-in types including floating-point types, integer types and **bool**. The author of a specialized numeric type such as the fixed_point class is, therefore, responsible for providing a template specialization of std::numeric_limits.

Consider, for example, the Q15.16 fixed-point representation. It has 15 binary digits to the left of the decimal point and 16 binary digits to the right of the decimal point. A possible implementation of the std::numeric_limits template class the Q15.16 fixed-point representation is listed below.

```
namespace std
{
  template<>
  class numeric_limits<fixed_point_15pt16>
  {
  public:
    static constexpr bool is_specialized = true;

    static constexpr fixed_point_15pt16 min()
    { return
        fixed_point_15pt16(nothing(), 1); }

    static constexpr fixed_point_15pt16 max()
    { return
        fixed_point_15pt16(nothing(),
                           INT32_C(0x7FFFFFFF)); }

    static constexpr fixed_point_15pt16 lowest()
    { return min(); }

    static constexpr int digits        = 16;
    static constexpr int digits10      =  4;
    static constexpr int max_digits10  =  5;
    static constexpr bool is_signed    = true;
    static constexpr bool is_integer   = false;
    static constexpr bool is_exact     = false;
    static constexpr int radix         = 2;
    static constexpr T epsilon()
```

```
    { return
        fixed_point_15pt16(nothing(), 7); }

    static constexpr T round_error()
    { return
        fixed_point_15pt16(nothing(),
                           INT32_C(0x8000)); }

    static constexpr int min_exponent   = -15;
    static constexpr int min_exponent10 = -4;
    static constexpr int max_exponent   = 14;
    static constexpr int max_exponent10 = 4;

    static constexpr bool has_infinity      = false;
    static constexpr bool has_quiet_NaN     = false;
    static constexpr bool has_signaling_NaN = false;
    static constexpr float_denorm_style has_denorm =
      denorm_absent;
    static constexpr bool has_denorm_loss = false;
    static constexpr T infinity()
    { return fixed_point_15pt16(); }
    static constexpr T quiet_NaN()
    { return fixed_point_15pt16(); }
    static constexpr T signaling_NaN()
    { return fixed_point_15pt16(); }
    static constexpr T denorm_min()
    { return fixed_point_15pt16(); }

    static constexpr bool is_iec559   = false;
    static constexpr bool is_bounded = false;
    static constexpr bool is_modulo   = false;
    static constexpr bool traps       = false;
    static constexpr bool tinyness_before = false;
    static constexpr float_round_style round_style =
      round_toward_zero;
  };
}
```

Certain members of `numeric_limits<fixed_point_15pt16>`, such as the value of **`true`** for `is_specialized`, are self-explanatory. Understanding the values of other class members can be more subtle. The `digits` member, for example, contains only the binary digits to the right of the decimal point. This is fair because any non-trivial fixed-point calculations will lose about half their digits due to truncation or argument reduction.

The `digits10` member is derived from `digits`. The maximum and minimum values are given by the internal representations of `0x7FFFFFFF` and `1`, respectively. The `nothing` structure, as described in Sect. 15.1, is used in the fixed-point constructor to set these values without left-shifting them.

The `epsilon()` member represents the smallest number that, when subtracted from 1, results in a value that differs from 1. Since this fixed-point type has four decimal digits of precision to the right of the decimal point, `epsilon()` for this type is equal to 0.0001. In other words, `epsilon()` should return

$$\frac{\texttt{0xFFFF}}{10,000} \approx \texttt{7.} \tag{13.27}$$

Specializations of `std::numeric_limits` for the `fixed_point` types in the reference project of the companion code are implemented as a generic template. Details can be found in the source code.

References

1. M. Abramowitz, I.A. Stegun, *Handbook of Mathematical Functions,* 9th *Printing* (Dover, New York, 1972)
2. W.J. Cody, W. Waite, *Software Manual for the Elementary Functions* (Prentice Hall, Upper Saddle River, 1980)
3. J.W. Crenshaw, *Math Toolkit for Real-Time Programming, First Edition* (CMP Books, Lawrence, 2000)
4. C. Hastings, *Approximations for Digital Computers* (Princeton University Press, Princeton, 1955)
5. J. LaBrosse, *Embedded Systems Building Blocks: Complete and Ready-to-Use Modules in C* (CMP Books, Lawrence, 1999)
6. J.M. Muller, *Elementary Functions: Algorithms and Implementation, Third Edition* (Springer (Birkhäuser), New York, 2016)
7. Wikipedia, *Fixed-point arithmetic* (2012). http://en.wikipedia.org/wiki/Fixed-point_arithmetic

Chapter 14
High-Performance Digital Filters

There may be no other signal-processing tool more widely used in embedded software than the digital filter because even the simplest applications usually read some kinds of input signals that need filtering. In this chapter, we will implement several types of finite impulse response (FIR) filters. The first section of this chapter presents a simple order 1 floating-point FIR filter. In order to obtain high performance for filters on microcontrollers without a floating-point unit or digital signal processor (DSP), however, the filters in the rest of this chapter use pure-integer mathematics combined with template design.

14.1 A Floating-Point Order-1 Filter

Consider the floating-point filter

$$y_1 = (1 - \beta)\, x_0 + \beta x_1\,, \tag{14.1}$$

where the weight β ranges from $0 \ldots 1$. The index convention here uses the highest index for the newest sample in the delay line. Successively lower indexes are used for older samples, reaching index 0 for the oldest sample.

Equation 14.1 is a floating-point order 1 low-pass FIR filter. The frequency response of this filter is given by

$$H\left(e^{i\omega}\right) = \frac{1}{\beta} + \frac{e^{-i\omega}}{1-\beta}\,, \tag{14.2}$$

where ω is the frequency in radians per sample.

C. Kormanyos, *Real-Time C++*, https://doi.org/10.1007/978-3-662-62996-3_14

At this point, we could investigate a host of theoretical characteristics of this filter, such as the Z-transform of the impulse response, the absolute value of the frequency response or the phase response. The rich theory of digital filters and digital signal processing are, however, beyond the scope of this book. So we will just concentrate on how to program digital filters. Readers can find additional information on digital filters in Refs. [1–3].

The order 1 FIR low-pass filter from Eq. 14.1 can be implemented with a template class. For example,

```
template<typename T>
class fir_01_fp
{
public:
  typedef T result_type;
  typedef T value_type;

  fir_01_fp(const value_type val = 0) : result(val)
  {
    std::fill(values.begin(), values.end(), val);
  }

  void new_sample(const std::array<value_type, 2U>& b,
                  const value_type& val)
  {
    // Shift the delay line.
    values[0U] = values[1U];

    // Put the new sample in the delay line.
    values[1U] = val;

    // Calculate the FIR algorithm.
    result =    (b[0U] * values[0U])
              + (b[1U] * values[1U]);
  }

  const result_type& get_result() const
  {
    return result;
  }

private:
  result_type result;
  std::array<value_type, 2U> values;
};
```

The class fir_01_fp is a template filter class. As indicated by the trailing "fp" in its name, fir_01_fp is designed for floating-point types. For instance, fir_01_fp can be effectively used with floating-point types such as **float**, **double**, **long double**, the fixed_point class from the previous chapter, etc.

The fir_01_fp class has member variables for both the delay line (values) as well as the filter result (result). Notice how the delay line in values is stored as an array. The public interface of fir_01_fp has two functions, one called new_sample() and another called get_result().

Using fir_01_fp in code is straightforward. For example,

```
fir_01_fp<float> f(4.0F);

constexpr std::array<float, 2U> b
{
  { 0.875F, 0.125F }
};

void do_something()
{
  // The result of the first call is 16.0.
  f.new_sample(b, 100.0F);
}
```

The filter coefficients β and $(1 - \beta)$ from Eq. 14.1 are $\frac{1}{8}$ and $\frac{7}{8}$, respectively. They are stored in the array as the floating-point values 0.125 and 0.875. The filter f is initialized with 4.0. Thereby, both values of the delay line are initialized to 4.0.

In the first call to the new_sample() function, f's member variable result is set to

$$\texttt{result} = (0.875 \times 4.0) + (0.125 \times 100.0) = 16.0\,. \qquad (14.3)$$

The new_sample() function executes the filter algorithm and sets the new value of the filter result each time it is called. Users of fir_01_fp are expected to call the new_sample() method in a periodic cycle, thereby providing the value of the new sample and the desired filter coefficients as input parameters. The sum of the filter coefficients should always be equal to 1.0.

The template coefficients stored in b are passed to the new_sample() function as a constant reference to std::array. In this case, using a pass-by-reference (instead of pass-by-value) is essential for maintaining the performance of the filter function.

The filter's `get_result()` member function can be used for accessing the filtered result at any time. For example,

```
const float my_filter_result = f.get_result();
```

The `fir_01_fp` template filter class could potentially be used on microcontroller platforms that support fast floating-point math. Many small microcontrollers, however, lack a hardware floating-point unit (FPU) and floating-point math is emulated with software. This can be very inefficient. Double-precision math is excruciatingly slow on embedded microcontrollers without a hardware FPU. Even single-precision and fixed-point math are often unduly inefficient for many practical microcontroller applications.

For this reason, a floating-point filter such as `fir_01_fp` may be too slow for microcontrollers. In order to reach the desired high performance for embedded systems, we need to design filters that use integer math.

14.2 An Order-1 Integer Filter

When implementing integer filters instead of floating-point filters, one of the first design steps encountered is to express the floating-point sample values and coefficients in terms of normalized integer values. This can be accomplished by rewriting the order 1 FIR filter expression from Eq. 14.1 in integer form,

$$y_1 = \frac{\beta_0 x_0 + \beta_1 x_1 + \frac{1}{2}\left(\beta_0 + \beta_1\right)}{\beta_0 + \beta_1}, \tag{14.4}$$

where y_1, x_0, x_1, β_0 and β_1 are unsigned integer values and the extra term in the numerator, $\frac{1}{2}\left(\beta_0 + \beta_1\right)$, handles unsigned integer rounding.

Equation 14.4 can be implemented in a scalable, optimized fashion using the template class shown below.

```
template<const std::size_t resol = 4U,
         typename sample_t       = std::uint16_t,
         typename value_t        = sample_t,
         typename result_t       = sample_t>
class fir_01
{

public:
  typedef sample_t           sample_type;
  typedef value_t            value_type;
```

```
  typedef result_t           result_type;
  typedef std::int_fast16_t weight_type;

  fir_01(const sample_type& val = 0U)
    : result(val * resol)
  {
    std::fill(values.begin(),
              values.end(),
              result);
  }

  template<const weight_type B0,
           const weight_type B1>
  void new_sample(const sample_type& val)
  {
    values[0U] = values[1U];

    values[1U]
      = val * static_cast<value_type>(resol);

    value_type new_val =   (B0 * values[0U])
                         + (B1 * values[1U]);

    result = (new_val + ((B0 + B1) / 2)) / (B0 + B1);
  }

  result_type get_result() const
  {
    return (result + (resol / 2U)) / resol;
  }

private:
  result_type result;
  std::array<value_type, 2U> values;
};
```

The class `fir_01` is a scalable template filter class. The last three template parameters, `sample_t`, `value_t` and `result_t`, are scaling parameters that can be used to define the dimension of the filter. They can be set to 8-bit, 16-bit, 32-bit or even 64-bit. These three template parameters provide for scalability with several degrees of freedom because the sizes of the variables representing the filter sample, the delay line and the filter result can be set independently.

The first template parameter, `resol`, provides a resolution scale by multiplying each new sample with a constant integer. Closer approximation to the analog filter regime is obtained for higher values of the `resol` parameter. The resolution scale is removed from the filter result in the `get_result()` function.

Care should be taken to ensure that `resol` is a multiple of two. Only then will the rounding correction (given by `resol/2`) be exact. Furthermore, the best performance can be achieved if `resol` is a power of 2^n, where n is a small positive integer value. This is because the compiler can replace the division with a fast, efficient shift operation. See Sect. 6.11.

The class `fir_01` is a template, and its `new_sample()` function is a template function within a template class. The template parameters of `new_sample()` are the filter coefficients, `B0` and `B1`. These are constant signed integers of type `std::int_fast16_t`. Since the filter coefficients are compile-time constants, the filter algorithm can be optimized to a high degree, see Sect. 6.12. Just as described above for the `resol` parameter, the sum of $\left(|\mathrm{B0}| + |B1|\right)$ should also be a small integer power of two such that the rounding correction is exact and such that the compiler can replace division by $\left(|\mathrm{B0}| + |B1|\right)$ with an efficient shift operation.

Care must be taken to select the proper dimension of a filter such that the entire range of sample values can be filtered without numerical overflow. At the same time, the filter operations need to be matched to the CPU architecture.

For example, we will dimension a filter running on a 16-bit machine. Imagine a filter that should be designed to sample 10-bit ADC values ranging from $0 \ldots 1023$. Furthermore, say that this filter will be sampled with a high frequency, such as in an interrupt service routine. For this 16-bit microcontroller, the high performance of 16-bit math is mandatory, as opposed to costly 32-bit operations. In this case, all three template parameters (`sample_t`, `value_t` and `result_t`) should be set to `std::uint16_t`. The samples need 10 bits. Therefore, there are 6 bits remaining to be split among the coefficients and the resolution. The resolution could be set to 4, requiring two bits. This leaves four bits for the filter coefficients. Thus, the filter coefficients, `B0` and `B1` can range from $1 \ldots 15$, whereby the sum of $\left(|\mathrm{B0}| + |B1|\right)$ should always be equal to 16.

A filter with larger sample values or higher valued coefficients may need to be dimensioned with wider data types for one or more of the template parameters. For example, the following template parameters could be selected for a high-frequency filter running, for example, on a 32-bit machine.

$$
\begin{aligned}
\texttt{sample\_t} &= \texttt{std::uint16\_t} \\
\texttt{value\_t} &= \texttt{std::uint32\_t} \\
\texttt{result\_t} &= \texttt{std::uint16\_t}\,. \qquad (14.5)
\end{aligned}
$$

A filter with these dimensions can be used to filter samples within the entire range of `std::uint16_t` (0 ... 65535) because the type of `value_t` is `std::uint32_t`. This is large enough to hold the internal values of the filter algorithm without overflow. Examples showing how significantly a filter's dimension impacts its runtime performance will be shown in Sect. 14.4.

Using an `fir_01` object in code is straightforward. For example,

```
typedef fir_01<> filter_type;
filter_type f(4U);

void do_something()
{
  // The result of the first call is 16.
  f.new_sample<7, 1>(100U);
}
```

This sample code creates an `fir_01` object called `f`. The type of its first template parameter, `sample_t`, is `std::uint16_t`, which is the default template parameter. By way of default, the other two template parameters, `value_t` and `result_t` are also set to the type of `sample_t` (i.e., `std::uint16_t`).

This example has numerical values similar to the example of the floating-point filter in the previous section. The filter is initialized with an initial value of 4. The sample function of the filter is called in `do_something()` with a sample value of 100. The filter coefficients (`B0` and `B1`) are 7 and 1, respectively. The `new_sample()` function places the new sample value of 100 at the top of the delay line. It is weighted with the coefficient 1. The old value in the delay line is the initialization value of 4. It is weighted with the coefficient 7. The result of calling the filter's template subroutine `new_sample<7, 1>(100)` is

$$\frac{(7 \times 4) + (1 \times 100) + (8/2)}{8} = 16\,, \tag{14.6}$$

where 16 is a rounded pure integer result.

It is interesting to study the disassembled source code listing which the compiler produces when compiling the code of this example. The constructor code is efficient because the compiler can unroll the loop in `std::fill()`. Thereby, the values of `result` and those in the delay line can be directly initialized with 16, evaluated via constant folding from ($|$`resol`$|$ $\times$ 4) $=$ 16.

Similarly, the filter algorithm of the `new_sample()` subroutine can be highly optimized. The compiler can replace all of the multiplication operations in the inner product of the filter algorithm with fast shift-and-add operations. This, combined with constant folding, makes the filter code extremely efficient. This is a very significant result which is essential for obtaining high performance with integer template filters. A further optimization is the normalization with the coefficient sum. The division by $\left(|\mathrm{B0}| + |B1|\right) = 8$ can be replaced with a right shift of 3.

In this example, every part of the filter sampling function can been inlined and optimized by the compiler. There is no function call to `new_sample()` and there are no parameters passed to the subroutine. The disassembled source of `new_sample()` is near to, or possibly even is, as optimally efficient as compiled code can be—approaching the efficiency of assembly programming itself.

The sampling subroutine can be used with equal efficiently in both interrupt service routines as well as normal task levels. This is a very satisfying result which exemplifies how the power of C++ templates can be utilized to obtain the highest possible filter performance.

14.3 Order-*N* Integer FIR Filters

We will now extend the techniques used for the order 1 FIR filter in the previous section to order N FIR filters. The order N FIR filter is defined by the difference equation

$$y_n = b_0\,x[n] + b_1\,x[n-1] + \ldots + b_N\,x[n-N]\,, \tag{14.7}$$

where $x[n]$ are the delay line values, y_n is the filter result, b_i are the coefficients and N is the filter order. An order N FIR filter has $N + 1$ terms on the right hand side. These are the filter samples weighted with their coefficients. They are commonly referred to as *taps*. Equation 14.7 can also be expressed as

$$y_n = \sum_{i=0}^{N} b_i\,x[n-i]\,. \tag{14.8}$$

The order 1 filter template class from the previous section can be extended to order N using Eqs. 14.7 and 14.8. A synopsis of a template class that can be used to implement these filter algorithms is shown below.

```
template<const std::size_t order,
         const std::size_t resol = 4U,
         typename sample_t = std::uint16_t,
         typename value_t  = sample_t,
         typename result_t = sample_t>
class fir_order_n
{
public:
  static_assert((order > 0U) && (order < 48U),
        "error: filter order must be from 1 to 48");

  fir_order_n() { }
```

```
  explicit fir_order_n(const sample_t&) { }

  template<typename... dummy_parameters>
  void new_sample(const sample_t&) { }

  result_t get_result() const { return result_t(0); }
};
```

The template class `fir_order_n` has the same template parameters as the template class `fir_01`, plus one additional template parameter `order` that represents the order of the filter. As can be deduced from the class synopsis, this class is meant to serve only as a template for further specializations of the `order`. Each individual class implementation of the *N*th filter `order` must be explicitly programmed as separate template specialization.

An example of the template class specialization of `fir_order_n` for order 5 is shown below.

```
template<const std::size_t resol,
         typename sample_t,
         typename value_t,
         typename result_t>
class fir_order_n<5U,
                  resol,
                  sample_t,
                  value_t,
                  result_t>
{
public:
  typedef sample_t sample_type;
  typedef value_t  value_type;
  typedef result_t result_type;

  fir_order_n() : result(0)
  {
    std::fill(data.begin(), data.end(), result);
  }

  explicit fir_order_n(const sample_type& x)
    : result(value_type(x) * resol)
  {
    std::fill(data.begin(), data.end(), result);
  }
```

```
  template<const std::int_fast16_t B0,
           const std::int_fast16_t B1,
           const std::int_fast16_t B2,
           const std::int_fast16_t B3,
           const std::int_fast16_t B4,
           const std::int_fast16_t B5>
  void new_sample(const sample_type& x)
  {
    // Shift the delay line.
    std::copy(data.begin() + 1U,
              data.end(),
              data.begin());

    // Store the new sample at top of delay line.
    *(data.end() - 1U) = value_type(x) * resol;

    // Calculate the FIR algorithm.
    const value_type new_val
      =   value_type(data[0U] * B0)
        + value_type(data[1U] * B1)
        + value_type(data[2U] * B2)
        + value_type(data[3U] * B3)
        + value_type(data[4U] * B4)
        + value_type(data[5U] * B5);

    constexpr std::int_fast16_t weight
      = B0 + B1 + B2 + B3 + B4 + B5;

    result = (new_val + (weight / 2)) / weight;
  }

  result_type get_result() const
  {
    return (result + (resol / 2U)) / resol;
  }

private:
  result_type result;
  std::array<value_type, 6U> data;
};
```

Aside from the constructor and some convenient type definitions, the template class specialization of `fir_order_n` has only one function with significant algorithmic complexity, `new_sample()`. It is in the `new_sample()` method that the FIR algorithm in Eq. 14.7 is implemented. Notice how the delay line is shifted and the new sample, weighted with the resolution, is put at the top of the delay line.

The `new_sample()` function in `fir_order_n` is a template function with six integral template parameters. This explains why each individual order N filter needs to be implemented as a template class specialization. It is because every different value of the template parameter `N` needs to have its own specific template variation of the `new_sample()` subroutine with $\text{N}+1$ template parameters for the filter coefficients.

This design choice may be considered somewhat inconvenient. There are, however, not very many ways to accomplish this without making individual specializations containing template implementations of the `new_sample()` function. A variadic template (Sect. 5.9) that accepts a variable number of template parameters *could* be considered. This would, however, allow template users to supply non-integer template parameter types for the filter coefficients, potentially resulting in undefined behavior. In light of these conditions, each individual order N `fir_order_n` class has been explicitly specialized providing a place in code at which the specific template variations of `new_sample()` can be defined.

A collection of template specializations of `fir_order_n` filters including filter order ranging from 1 ... 48 is available in the reference project of the companion code. In order to avoid tedious typing work and to ensure that the implementations are error free, these template specializations have been created with a simple, automatic code generator which has been specifically written for this purpose.

Using `fir_order_n` objects in code is simple and intuitive. The following sample code, uses an order 5 low-pass filter that is dimensioned for 16-bit unsigned math with a coefficient sum of 32 and a resolution scale of 4. The coefficient sum uses 5 bits and the resolution scale uses 2 bits. Together, they use a total of 7 bits from the 16 bits available, leaving 9 bits remaining for the range of the sample values. This filter can filter 9-bit unsigned integer values ranging from 0 ... 511.

```
typedef fir_order_n<5U> filter_type;

filter_type f(4U);

void do_something()
{
  f.new_sample<5, 5, 6, 6, 5, 5>(100U);
}
```

The result of the filter operation is

$$\frac{(5 \times 4) + (5 \times 4) + (6 \times 4) + (6 \times 4) + (5 \times 4) + (5 \times 100) + 16}{32} = 19\,, \tag{14.9}$$

where 19 is the rounded pure integer result.

As is the case for the order 1 filter in the previous section, the examination of the disassembled source code listing for this filter operation reveals highly optimized code. The generation and investigation of this listing are left as exercises for the reader. In the benchmark carried out, all parts of the `new_sample()` function were successfully inlined by the compiler. Furthermore, because the filter coefficients are available at compile time and since the coefficient sum is a power of 2, the compiler replaced slow multiply and divide operations with fast shift-and-add operations in the FIR algorithm.

A filter with larger dimensions and a greater number of filter parameters is shown in the code sample below.

```
typedef fir_order_n<17U,
                    64U,
                    std::uint16_t,
                    std::uint32_t> filter_type;

filter_type f(4U);

void do_something()
{
  f.new_sample<-2, -2, -2, -1, 3, 9, 15, 20, 24,
               24, 20, 15, 9, 3, -1, -2, -2, -2>(100U);
}
```

This is an order 17 low-pass FIR filter. It is also known as an 18-tap filter because it has 18 filter coefficients. The sum of the filter coefficients is 128 and the resolution scale is 64. The symmetry of the coefficients has been exploited to write all 18 template parameters of the `new_sample()` function in a legible fashion. This filter uses `std::uint32_t` to represent the internal algorithm values because they do not always fit within `std::uint16_t`. This filter can filter input values within the entire range of `std::uint16_t`.

The order 17 filter in this example requires significantly more code and runtime than the order 5 filter from the previous example. This is not only because the filter has more coefficients, but also because the delay line values are 32 bits wide instead of 16. With the numerous 32-bit operations of its `new_sample()` function, this order 17 filter is *definitely* over-dimensioned for 8-bit or 16-bit targets. It would be more appropriate for 32-bit targets. However, it is possible to get the same filter quality with much less code and runtime expense using two or more cascaded filters of lower order. This technique will be discussed in Sect. 14.4. This order 17 filter can be comfortably used with 32-bit targets and examination of its disassembled source code listing shows the same kind of high-performance optimizations that were observed for the order 5 filter above—inlining, unrolling, shift-and-add, etc.

The filter coefficients for the order 17 filter operation have been obtained with a *filter design tool*. Scaling and rationalization of the coefficients has done with the filter design tool to obtain pure integer coefficients. Thereby care has been taken to ensure that the coefficient sum of 128 is an unsigned integer power of two.

14.4 Some Worked-Out Filter Examples

This section presents some worked out filter examples. The results have been prepared for visualization within a PC environment and also tested in real-time on two different microcontrollers.

Consider the unfiltered raw signal S shown with connected open circles ($\circ$) in Fig. 14.1. This signal could, for example, result from a voltage measurement fed to a 10-bit ADC input. The main component of the signal is a sine wave with a frequency of 60 Hz, an amplitude of 150 and an offset of 250. Added to this underlying sine wave is a strong, asynchronous noise component. The noise has 10 times the signal's frequency ($10 \times 60 = 600\,\text{Hz}$), $\frac{1}{5}$ of its amplitude ($150/5 = 30$) and an offset of 0.317 ms.

The mathematical representation of the signal S is given by

$$S = 250 + 150 \times \left[\sin(0.12\pi t) + \frac{1}{5} \sin(0.317 + 1.2\pi t) \right], \tag{14.10}$$

where t is the time in *ms*.

We will now filter this signal with an order N, low-pass FIR filter such that the noise component with a frequency of 600 Hz is strongly suppressed and the main

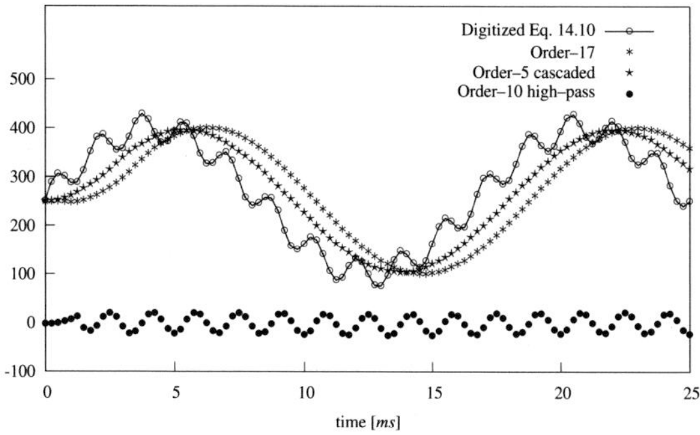

Fig. 14.1 Test results for various filters are shown. The connected open circles (*opencircle*) show the digitized test data. The asterisks (*asterisk*) show the results of an order 17 low-pass filter. The stars (*star*) show the results of two cascaded order 5 low-pass filters. The solid circles (*filledcircle*) show the results of an order 11 high-pass filter

component at 60 Hz passes through the filter with as little attenuation as possible. This is a typical filter design problem. The first step in designing the filter is to consider the sampling frequency. Imagine that about 3–4 samples should be taken per half-wave of noise. As mentioned above, the noise has a frequency of 600 Hz. So, if there should be, say, $3\frac{1}{2}$ samples per half-wave of noise, then the resulting sampling frequency T_s is given by

$$T_s = 3\frac{1}{2} \; (2 \times 600\,\text{Hz}) = 4,200\,\text{Hz} \approx 4,000\,\text{Hz}, \tag{14.11}$$

where T_s has been rounded down to 4 kHz. The corresponding sampling period is 250 μs.

To design this filter, we will select a pass-band upper frequency of 200 Hz and a stop-band lower frequency of 600 Hz, with a stop-band attenuation of 40 dB. A ripple of 1 dB is allowed within the pass-band. The pass-band upper frequency of 200 Hz is high enough to expect good signal passing at 60 Hz, and the stop-band lower frequency of 600 Hz with 40 dB attenuation should effectively suppress the noise.

Supplying these filter parameters to the filter design tool and instructing the tool to compute the unbound optimum number of taps produces 18 double-precision coefficients for an 18-tap, order 17 filter. These double-precision coefficients correspond to the scaled integer coefficients in the order 17 filter of Sect. 14.3. In fact, these filter parameters have been used to generate them.

For the purpose of testing this order 17 filter, a PC-based simulation has been written. A separate program has been used to generate 101 digitized points from Eq. 14.10 using the desired sampling frequency of 4 kHz. These are the test data. They are shown in Fig. 14.1. The test data span $1\frac{1}{2}$ full periods of the 60 Hz signal and about 15 full periods of the signal's noise. The code below shows the test data, stored in a static constant STL array with 101 elements.

```
#include <cstdint>
#include <array>

const std::array<std::uint16_t, 101U> data =
{
  {
    250U, 288U, 306U, 301U, 287U, 288U, 312U, 351U,
    381U, 386U, 371U, 354U, 357U, 381U, 412U, 428U,
    417U, 390U, 370U, 372U, 392U, 411U, 409U, 383U,
    347U, 326U, 328U, 343U, 350U, 333U, 296U, 258U,
    241U, 246U, 258U, 256U, 231U, 190U, 158U, 150U,
    162U, 176U, 170U, 141U, 106U,  87U,  93U, 116U,
    132U, 125U, 100U,  77U,  75U,  97U, 129U, 147U,
    141U, 123U, 113U, 127U, 162U, 198U, 215U, 209U,
    195U, 197U, 224U, 264U, 297U, 306U, 296U, 285U,
```

```
    293U, 325U, 363U, 386U, 383U, 364U, 352U, 363U,
    392U, 420U, 427U, 409U, 381U, 368U, 377U, 400U,
    414U, 403U, 371U, 338U, 324U, 332U, 348U, 348U,
    322U, 282U, 250U, 240U, 250U
  }
};
```

The code below uses the order 17 filter that we have just designed to filter these test data.

```
#include <iostream>
#include <math/filters/fir_order_n.h>

typedef fir_order_n<17U,
                    64U,
                    std::uint16_t,
                    std::uint32_t> filter_type;

void do_something()
{
  filter_type f(data[0U]);

  std::cout << f.get_result() << "\n";

  std::for_each(
    data.begin() + 1U,
    data.end(),
    [&f](const std::uint16_t& s)
    {
      f.new_sample
      <-2, -2, -2, -1, 3, 9, 15, 20, 24,
       24, 20, 15, 9, 3, -1, -2, -2, -2>(s);

      std::cout << f.get_result() << "\n";
    });
}
```

The order 17 filter, `f`, sequentially filters the test data in `do_something()` using STL's `for_each()` algorithm in combination with a lambda expression. The filter results are printed to the standard output.

The results of this filter simulation are shown in Fig. 14.1. As can be seen in the figure, the filter quality is excellent. The main component of the signal at 60 Hz passes through the filter essentially unattenuated. The noise at 600 Hz has, for all practical purposes, been eliminated. The filtered signal has a phase shift corresponding to the delay line of the 18-tap filter.

The `new_sample()` function of the order 17 filter runs quickly on 32-bit targets, requiring just a few microseconds. For example, it requires approximately 9.6 μs on our target with the 32-bit microcontroller. Since the sample rate is 4 kHz and the corresponding sample period is 250 μs, the filter operation requires approximately $9.6/250 \approx 3.8\%$ of the total CPU power. This filter can, therefore, be comfortably used with this target. The sample rate could even be doubled or fourfolded if higher frequencies need to be filtered.

However, this order 17 filter has many 32-bit operations. In fact, it needs at least nineteen 32-bit move operations alone for shifting the delay line. In addition, roughly twice again as many operations are required for the filter algorithm itself, and most of these are also 32-bit operations. So this filter is actually over dimensioned for most applications using 16-bit or 8-bit architectures. In comparison with the runtime of 9.6 μs on the 32-bit target, the `new_sample()` function requires approximately 56 μs on our 8-bit target, and this corresponds to $56/250 \approx 22\%$ of the total CPU power with a 4 kHz sampling rate. This is too much CPU load for the filter function on this target.

Similar filter quality can be obtained using 16-bit operations that are more appropriate for smaller architectures such as our target with the 8-bit microcontroller. One way to accomplish this is by using two or more cascaded filters with much lower order. For example, we will use two cascaded, 16-bit order 5 filters instead of the order 17 filter. When using these, it should be possible to significantly reduce the CPU load on the 8-bit target.

To design an order 5 filter for this purpose, the filter parameters previously used to design the order 17 filter can be used. This time, however, the number of taps is limited to 6. The resulting integer coefficients are (5, 5, 6, 6, 5, 5). The code sample below shows how to use two cascaded 16-bit, order 5 filters with these coefficients.

```
#include <iostream>

typedef fir_order_n<5U> filter_type;

void do_something()
{
  filter_type f1(data[0U]);
  filter_type f2(f1.get_result());

  std::cout << f2.get_result() << std::endl;

  std::for_each(
    data.begin() + 1U,
    data.end(),
    [&f1, &f2](const std::uint16_t& s)
    {
```

```
        f1.new_sample<5, 5, 6, 6, 5, 5>(s);

        filter_type::result_type r = f1.get_result();

        f2.new_sample<5, 5, 6, 6, 5, 5>(r);

        std::cout << f2.get_result() << std::endl;
    });
}
```

This code uses two filters, `f1` and `f2`. The filter result of `f1` is supplied to the `new_sample()` function of `f2`. In this way, the filters are cascaded.

The results of this filter operation on the test data are also shown in Fig. 14.1. The filter quality is just as good as that of the order 17 filter. However, the required CPU power has been significantly reduced. This cascaded filter operation is acceptable for 16-bit architectures with a sampling frequency of 4 kHz. The runtime of the `new_sample()` function on the 8-bit target has been reduced from 56 μs for the order 17 filter to 22 μs for two cascaded order 5 filters. In other words, with a sampling period of 250 μs, the fraction of the total CPU power invested in filter sampling has been reduced from the unacceptably high level of approximately 22 % to the tolerable amount of $22/250 \approx 9\,\%$.

As a final example, we will filter the test data with a high-pass filter. This time, the filter design tool needs parameters for a high-pass filter. We use a stop-band upper frequency of 80 Hz with an attenuation of 40 dB and a pass-band lower frequency of 600 Hz with a pass-band ripple of 1 dB. The result is an order 10, eleven tap high-pass filter with the integer coefficients (1, 2, 4, 6, 8, −40, 8, 6, 4, 2, 1).

The results of this filter are signed. Therefore, precautions for signed arithmetic and rounding need to be included in the filter algorithms. This has been done in the companion code, but not explicitly listed here.

Programming the PC simulation with the signed high-pass filter is left as an exercise for the reader. The results that have been obtained when researching for this book are shown in Fig. 14.1. A few samples are needed before the high-pass filter attenuates the 60 Hz part of the signal, leaving only the ripple at 600 Hz part—as per design goal for this high-pass filter.

References

1. R.G. Lyons, *Understanding Digital Signal Processing* (Prentice Hall, Upper Saddle River, 2004)
2. A.V. Oppenheim, R.W. Schafer, *Digital Signal Processing* (Prentice Hall, Upper Saddle River, 1975)
3. L. Thede, *Analog and Digital Filter Design Using C* (Prentice Hall, Upper Saddle River, 1996)

Chapter 15
C++ Utilities

This chapter presents a selection of C++ utilities that are useful for solving recurring problems in microcontroller programming.

15.1 The `nothing` Structure

Consider the implementation of the `nothing` structure below.

```
struct nothing { };
```

The `nothing` structure contains no members and encapsulates no functionality whatsoever. Although the `nothing` structure does not actually do anything itself, it can be quite useful as a place holder for other function and template parameters.

Recall the `fixed_point` class from Sect. 13.2. Consider the constructors of the `fixed_point` class that accept integral types as input parameters. These constructors perform a left-shift of their input parameter before using it to initialize the internal representation of the fixed-point number. This accounts for the fixed position of the decimal point. For a simplified version of the Q7.8 fixed-point representation, for example, we have something like the following.

```
// A simplified Q7.8 fixed-point representation.
class fixed_point
{
public:
  fixed_point(std::uint16_t u) : value(u << 8) { }
```


C. Kormanyos, *Real-Time C++*, https://doi.org/10.1007/978-3-662-62996-3_15

```
private:
  std::uint16_t value;
};
```

At the same time, the values of special fixed-point numbers such as mathematical constants have a known integral representation in this fixed-point system. The integral representation of the numerical constant π in this fixed-point system, for example, is `0x0324`. To accommodate construction from a known integral value that is not supposed to be left-shifted, the `fixed_point` class has an additional private constructor that takes an integral type parameter and a `nothing`-type structure. In other words,

```
// A simplified Q7.8 fixed-point representation.
class fixed_point
{
public:
  // Construct from integer with left-shift.
  fixed_point(std::uint16_t u) : value(u << 8) { }

  // Create pi with the special constructor.
  static fixed_point value_pi()
  {
    return fixed_point(nothing(), 0x0324U);
  }

private:
  std::uint16_t value;

  // Constructor from integer without left-shift.
  fixed_point(const nothing&,
              std::uint16_t u) : value(u) { }
};
```

Here, the `nothing` structure provides for unambiguous differentiation between the normal constructor from `std::uint16_t` with left-shift and the private constructor from `std::uint16_t` without left-shift. If the `nothing` structure were not used, the two constructors would be ambiguous. The special private constructor from an integer without left-shift is used to efficiently return the value of π in the `value_pi()` method.

We will now use the `nothing` structure to create a template class that represents a collection of three things. We will call this class a `triple`. The `triple` class can be made by using three template parameters and supplying defaults for them. For instance,

```
struct nothing {};

template <typename first_type  = nothing,
          typename second_type = nothing,
          typename third_type  = nothing>
class triple
{
public:
  // Constructor with default values.
  triple(const first_type&  t1_  = first_type(),
         const second_type& t2_  = second_type(),
         const third_type&  t3_  = third_type())
    : t1(t1_),
      t2(t2_),
      t3(t3_)
  {
  }

  // Element access.
  first_type&  first()  { return t1; }
  second_type& second() { return t2; }
  third_type&  third()  { return t3; }

private:
  first_type  t1;
  second_type t2;
  third_type  t3;
};
```

The `triple` class is similar to the `std::pair` class in the standard library's `<utility>` header. The `triple` class, however, has three elements, whereas `std::pair` has two.

Using the `triple` class is straightforward. The code below, for example, uses a `triple` containing a **`char`**, an **`int`** and an instance of a structure.

```
struct something
{
  something() { }
};

triple<char, int, something>
```

```
  things('a', 123, something());

void do_something()
{
  if(things.first() == 'a')
  {
  }
}
```

Techniques using a nothing-like class type are often employed to implement std::tuple for compilers that lack C++11 support for variadic templates.

15.2 The noncopyable Class

In Sect. 4.8, we first discussed non-copyable classes. Frequently, we would like to prohibit intentional and unintentional copying of a class object. A potential implementation of a non-copyable mechanism for classes is shown in below. This implementation is based on the noncopyable class in Boost.

```
class noncopyable
{
protected:
  noncopyable() {}
  ~noncopyable() {}

private:
  // Emphasize: The following members are private.
  noncopyable(const noncopyable&) = delete;

  const noncopyable& operator=(const noncopyable&)
    = delete;
};
```

Here, the copy constructor and copy assignment operator have been declared private and explicitly qualified with **delete**. This causes all classes that are privately derived from noncopyable to be non-copyable because derived classes inherit the private non-copyable members.

It is common in microcontroller programming to purposely prohibit class copying. Consider, once again, an LED mapped to a port pin. We will use an led class similar to the one in Sect. 1.1.

```
class led
{
public:
  // The led class constructor.
  led(const port_type p,
      const bval_type b) : port(p),
                           bval(b)
  {
    // ...
  }

  void toggle() const
  {
    // ...
  }

private:
  // Private member variables of the class.
  port_type port;
  bval_type bval;
};
```

As in Sect. 1.1, we can create an instance of the `led` class on microcontroller port bin `portb.5`. In particular,

```
// Create led_b5 on portb.5.
led led_b5
{
  mcal::reg::portb,
  mcal::reg::bval5
};
```

Here, `led_b5` is directly associated with `portb.5` and with no other pin. In the present form, however, it is possible to copy `led_b5`. The copy operation below, for instance, can successfully be compiled.

```
// Create led_b5 on portb.5.
led led_b5
{
  mcal::reg::portb,
  mcal::reg::bval5
};
```

```
// Copy led_b5 to another led instance.
led led_other = led_b5;
```

Probably, though, we would prefer to prohibit copying the `led` class in this fashion. This policy will help ensure that only one class instance uses the hardware pin at one time. The modified version of the `led` class shown below inherits privately from the `noncopyable` class.

```
class noncopyable { /* ... */ };

// Make the led class noncopyable.
class led : private noncopyable
{
  // ...
};
```

Here, the `led` class has been made non-copyable by simply inheriting privately from `noncopyable`.

The `noncopyable` utility simplifies typing and reduces the burden of code upkeep because the non-copyable attribute can simply be inherited via private derivation. This eliminates the need to manually implement a private copy constructor and copy assignment operator for each non-copyable class, as was shown in Sect. 4.8.

15.3 A Template `timer` Class

A timer class can be used for diverse timing applications in real-time C++. For example, the visible LED toggling in Sect. 2.3 has used a 1 *s* blocking delay to create a toggle frequency of 1 / 2 Hz. In addition, the multitasking scheduler in Sect. 11.2 has included interval timing for task scheduling.

We will now present a template `timer` class. The synopsis of the public interface of our `timer` class is shown below.

```
template<typename unsigned_tick>
class timer
{
public:
  // A class-specific tick type.
  typedef unsigned_tick tick_type;
```

```
  // Utility functions for creating timespans.
  template<typename other>
  static tick_type microseconds(const other&);

  template<typename other>
  static tick_type milliseconds(const other&);

  template<typename other>
  static tick_type seconds(const other&);

  template<typename other>
  static tick_type minutes(const other&);

  template<typename other>
  static tick_type hours(const other&);

  // Constructors.
  timer();
  explicit timer(const tick_type&);
  timer(const timer&);

  // Copy assignment operator.
  timer& operator=(const timer&);

  // Interval and relative timeout functions.
  void start_interval(const tick_type&);
  void start_relative(const tick_type&);

  // The timeout, now, and delay functions.
  bool timeout() const;
  static tick_type now();
  static void blocking_delay(const tick_type&);
};
```

This `timer` class provides the following operations in its public interface.

- Query the current time point with `now()`.
- Set relative timeouts with `start_relative()`.
- Set interval timeouts with `start_interval()`.
- Wait in a blocking delay with `blocking_delay()`.

This implementation of the `timer` class requires a timebase in hard real-time. This may, for example, originate from an underlying microcontroller peripheral timer. Here, we use the procedural `get_time_elapsed()` function from the

MCAL, as described in Sect. 9.3. In particular, the `timer`'s `now()` function simply returns the elapsed time from `get_time_elapsed()`. In other words,

```
template<typename unsigned_tick>
class timer
{
public:
  typedef unsigned_tick tick_type;

  // ...

  static tick_type now()
  {
    // Return the elapsed time in microseconds.
    return mcal::gpt::get_time_elapsed();
  }
};
```

In our example, the resolution of the underlying timebase is microseconds. The overlying `timer` class obtains the same microsecond resolution.

Since the `timer` class is a template, it can be scaled to various widths such as 16-bit or 32-bit. For example, we can set a relative timeout for a time point that lies 250 μs in the future using a 16-bit timer. In particular,

```
// Use a convenient type definition.
typedef timer<std::uint16_t> timer_type;

// Set a time point 250us in the future.
timer_type time(timer_type::microseconds(250U));
```

A polling task can query if the `timer` object has timed out by calling the `timeout()` member function. For instance,

```
void do_something()
{
  if(time.timeout())
  {
    // Do something at this time.
  }
}
```

The `timer` class, or a class similar to it, can also be used as a building block together with callbacks to encapsulate the functionality of event and alarm objects.

To do this, a `timer` object might be included as a member of a larger alarm or event object. These composite objects may be stored in a container and manipulated with a scheduling mechanism to fully implement events and alarms.

15.4 Linear Interpolation

Linear interpolation is a method of curve fitting on data points using linear polynomials. The need to perform linear interpolation on an ordered set of data points arises frequently in real-time microcontroller programming. Operations like sensor calibration and analysis of position data can often be carried out quickly and with sufficient accuracy using linear interpolation. The data points shown in Fig. 15.1, for example, are suitable for linear interpolation.

An example of linear interpolation using Eq. 15.2 is shown in Fig. 15.1. Linear interpolation with a straight line between the two (x, y) points (10, 44) and (20, 53) gives $y = 48$ at $x = 15$. Here, we are using integer calculations.

We will consider linear interpolation using a straight line between two points (x_0, y_0) and (x_1, y_1). The equation for the straight line between these two points is

$$\frac{y - y_0}{x - x_0} = \frac{y_1 - y_0}{x_1 - x_0}. \tag{15.1}$$

Solving Eq. 15.1 for an unknown value y at a known value x results in

$$y = y_0 + (x - x_0)\,\frac{y_1 - y_0}{x_1 - x_0}. \tag{15.2}$$

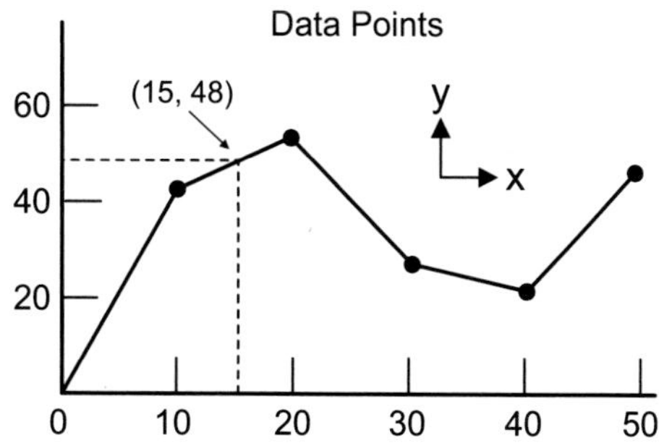

Fig. 15.1 A set of data points suitable for linear interpolation is shown

A template subroutine for straight-line linear interpolation based on Eq. 15.2 is shown in the code below.

```
template<typename point_iterator,
         typename x_type,
         typename y_type = x_type>
y_type linear_interpolate(point_iterator pts_begin,
                          point_iterator pts_end,
                          const x_type& x,
                          const y_type& offset)
{
  if(pts_begin == pts_end)
  {
    // There are no data points to interpolate.
    return y_type();
  }
  else if(    (x <= pts_begin->x)
          || (pts_begin + 1U == pts_end))
  {
    // We are beneath the lower x-range or there
    // is only one data point to interpolate.
    return pts_begin->y;
  }
  else if(x >= (pts_end - 1U)->x)
  {
    // We are above the upper x-range.
    return (pts_end - 1U)->y;
  }
  else
  {
    // Find interpolation pair with binary search.
    point_iterator it
      = std::lower_bound(pts_begin,
                         pts_end,
                         point<x_type>(x));

    // Do the linear interpolation.
    const x_type xn       = (it - 1U)->x;
    const x_type delta_xn = it->x - xn;
    const x_type delta_x  = x - xn;
    const y_type yn       = (it - 1U)->y;
    const y_type delta_yn = it->y - yn;
```

```
    const y_type delta_y
      = (delta_x * delta_yn) / delta_xn;

    return (yn + delta_y) + offset;
  }
}
```

Following some elementary bounds checking, the core of this linear interpolation function uses the `std::lower_bound()` algorithm to find the pair of interpolation points. The `linear_interpolate()` subroutine thereby profits from the high efficiency of `std::lower_bound()` which uses a binary search for sequences having random access iterators.

The fourth input parameter to `linear_interpolate()` called `offset` has a dual role. It allows an optional non-zero offset to be applied to the result of the linear interpolation. In addition, the `offset` parameter provides the compiler with enough information to automatically deduce all of the template parameters.

The `linear_interpolate()` subroutine is designed to work particularly well with a template point class type such as the one shown in Sect. 5.4. The lower-bound algorithm tests for inequality using **operator**<. In order to be used with `linear_interpolate()`, then, the `point` class needs to have an implementation of **operator**<. Here, the sense of *less-than* is based on the x-value of a point. In other words, the point $(x_i,\ y_i)$ is less than the point $\left(x_j,\ y_j\right)$ if $x_i\ <\ x_j$.

A modified implementation of the `point` class that supports **operator**< is shown below.

```
template<typename x_type,
         typename y_type = x_type>
class point
{
public:
  x_type x;
  y_type y;

  point(const x_type& x_ = x_type(),
        const y_type& y_ = y_type()) : x(x_),
                                       y(y_) { }

  bool operator<(const point& other) const
  {
    return (x < other.x);
  }
};
```

Using `linear_interpolate()` with a collection of points is straightforward. The sample below, for instance, performs the linear interpolation that is depicted in Fig. 15.1.

```
// The data points.
const std::array<point<std::uint16_t>, 6U> points
{
  {
    point<std::uint16_t> {  0U,  0U },
    point<std::uint16_t> { 10U, 44U },
    point<std::uint16_t> { 20U, 53U },
    point<std::uint16_t> { 30U, 28U },
    point<std::uint16_t> { 40U, 22U },
    point<std::uint16_t> { 50U, 47U }
  }
};

const std::uint16_t y
  = linear_interpolate(points.begin(),
                       points.end(),
                       std::uint16_t(15U),
                       std::uint16_t( 0U));

// The value of y is 48.
```

The `linear_interpolate()` subroutine can be used with built-in integral and floating-point types. It can also be used with user-defined types such as the `fixed_point` class in Sect. 13.2. If used exclusively for integral types, it may be beneficial to include a simple rounding correction in the division of the linear interpolation equation.

15.5 A `circular_buffer` Template Class

A circular buffer can be an efficient storage queue that is useful for communication interfaces and other input-output operations. The SPI™ driver class in Sect. 9.5, for example, uses circular buffers for its transmit and receive queues.

A possible implementation of a template circular buffer class is shown below.

```
template<typename T,
         const std::size_t N>
class circular_buffer
{
```

```
public:
  typedef T                   value_type;
  typedef       value_type* pointer;
  typedef const value_type* const_pointer;
  typedef       std::size_t size_type;
  typedef       value_type& reference;
  typedef const value_type& const_reference;

  circular_buffer(
      const T& value        = value_type(),
      const size_type count = size_type(0U))
    : in_ptr (buffer),
      out_ptr(buffer)
  {
    const size_type the_count =
      (std::min)(N, count);

    std::fill(in_ptr,
              in_ptr + the_count,
              value);

    in_ptr += the_count;
  }

  circular_buffer(const circular_buffer& other)
    : in_ptr (other.in_ptr),
      out_ptr(other.out_ptr)
  {
    std::copy(other.buffer,
              other.buffer + N,
              buffer);
  }

  circular_buffer& operator=(
      const circular_buffer& other)
  {
    if(this != &other)
    {
      in_ptr   (other.in_ptr);
      out_ptr  (other.out_ptr);
      std::copy(other.buffer,
                other.buffer + N,
                buffer);
    }
```

```
    return *this;
  }

  size_type capacity() const { return N; }

  bool empty() const
  {
    return (in_ptr == out_ptr);
  }

  size_type size() const
  {
    const bool is_wrap = (in_ptr < out_ptr);

    return size_type((is_wrap == false)
      ? size_type(in_ptr - out_ptr)
      : N - size_type(out_ptr - in_ptr));
  }

  void clear()
  {
    in_ptr  = buffer;
    out_ptr = buffer;
  }

  void in(const value_type value)
  {
    if(in_ptr >= (buffer + N))
    {
      in_ptr = buffer;
    }

    *in_ptr = value;

    ++in_ptr;
  }

  value_type out()
  {
    if(out_ptr >= (buffer + N))
    {
      out_ptr = buffer;
    }
```

```
    const value_type value = *out_ptr;

    ++out_ptr;

    return value;
  }

  reference front()
  {
    return ((out_ptr >= (buffer + N))
              ? buffer[N - 1U]
              : *out_ptr);
  }

  const_reference front() const
  {
    return ((out_ptr >= (buffer + N))
              ? buffer[N - 1U]
              : *out_ptr);
  }

  reference back()
  {
    return ((in_ptr  >= (buffer + N))
              ? buffer[N - 1U]
              : *in_ptr);
  }

  const_reference back() const
  {
    return ((in_ptr  >= (buffer + N))
              ? buffer[N - 1U]
              : *in_ptr);
  }

private:
  value_type buffer[N];
  pointer    in_ptr;
  pointer    out_ptr;
};
```

The `circular_buffer` class supports input and output queuing of elements. There are some STL-like members such as `size()` and `empty()`. Full support for STL iterators, however, has not been included in this implementation. A more refined circular buffer class with iterator support and STL compliance is included in Boost [1].

Using the `circular_buffer` class is simple. For instance,

```
typedef
circular_buffer<std::uint8_t, 4U>
buffer_type;

void do_something()
{
  buffer_type buffer;

  // Put three bytes into the buffer.
  buffer.in(1U);
  buffer.in(2U);
  buffer.in(3U);

  // The size of the buffer is 3.
  const buffer_type::size_type count = buffer.size();

  // The buffer is not empty.
  const bool is_empty = buffer.empty();

  // Extract the first element.
  const buffer_type::value_type value = buffer.out();

  // The size of the buffer is now 2.
  count = buffer.size();
}
```

15.6 The Boost Library

The Boost library is a large collection of generic utilities aimed at a wide range of C++ users and application domains. The Boost libraries extend the functionality of C++ beyond the language specification. Boost contains many individual libraries, including libraries for generic utilities, numeric and lexical operations, mathematics and numbers, threading and concurrency, image processing, networking, task scheduling, regular expressions, etc. The Boost libraries are known for their high quality, partly because a candidate library is subjected to peer reviews before being accepted to Boost.

Some of the concepts in this chapter originate from Boost. For example, the concept of the `noncopyable` class in Sect. 15.2 has been taken from the utilities part of Boost. The `circular_buffer` class in Sect. 15.5 is similar to Boost's `circular_buffer`.

The Boost website indicates that Boost aims to provide reference implementations potentially suitable for standardization [1]. This makes Boost a great place to follow the development of the C++ language. In fact, some of Boost's active members are on the C++ standards committee, and a variety of Boost libraries have been included in the C++11 standard [2], see also [3].

References

1. B. Dawes, D. Abrahams, *Boost C++ Libraries* (2012). http://www.boost.org
2. ISO/IEC, *ISO/IEC 14882:2011 : Information technology – Programming languages – C++* (International Organization for Standardization, Geneva, 2011)
3. B. Karlsson, *Beyond the C++ Standard Library: An Introduction to Boost* (Addison Wesley, Boston, 2005)

Chapter 16
Extending the C++ Standard Library and the STL

The C++ standard library and the STL provide a wide selection of functions, classes and generic containers that can be used in common programming situations. There are, however, times when just the right container or function for a particular programming task is missing from the standard library and the STL. In the first part of this chapter, we will extend the C++ standard library and the STL by developing a custom `dynamic_array` container that has a functionality that lies between those of `std::array` and `std::vector`. Furthermore, one often encounters a good C++ compiler that lacks large parts of the C++ standard library such as the STL, C99 compatibility, the time utilities in `<chrono>` or the thread support library. The middle part of this chapter shows how to emulate partial standard library support with certain self-written parts of the C++ standard library and the STL, including a potential extension of the `<complex>` library. The final part of this chapter includes a wide integer support, potential extensions of `<random>` and example `chapter16_08` which finds 128-bit prime numbers. This chapter concludes with a discussion of the freestanding implementation potentially well-suited for real-time C++.

16.1 Defining the Custom `dynamic_array` Container

The `std::array` container can be used when the number of elements is known at compile time. For instance,

```
// Fixed-size array of four counters init. to 1.
std::array<unsigned, 4U> counters
{
  { 1U, 1U, 1U, 1U }
};
```


C. Kormanyos, *Real-Time C++*, https://doi.org/10.1007/978-3-662-62996-3_16

```
void do_something()
{
  // Increment the counters.
  std::for_each(std::begin(counters),
                std::end  (counters),
                [](unsigned& u)
                {
                  ++u;
                });

  // It is not possible to resize the array.
}
```

On the other hand, the `std::vector` container is designed for dynamic allocation. Using vector's constructors or member functions such as `push_back()`, `resize()`, `insert()`, `erase()`, etc., the number of elements in a vector can be changed from zero to the maximum capacity during the entire lifetime of the object. For example,

```
// Dynamic vector of four counters init. to 1.
std::vector<unsigned> counters(4U, 1U);

void do_something()
{
  // Increment the counters.
  std::for_each(std::begin(counters),
                std::end(counters),
                [](unsigned& u)
                {
                  ++u;
                });

  // We can resize the vector.
  counters.push_back(counters.front());
}
```

Basically, std::array is efficient but has the limitation of constant compile-time size. While std::vector does offer flexible resizing during runtime, it also has slight performance and storage disadvantages caused by its dynamic allocation mechanisms.

At times it may be convenient to use a container with characteristics that lie *between* those of std::array and std::vector. For example, consider a container that can be dynamically allocated one time in the constructor and retains its size for the lifetime of the object. This container offers the flexibility of dynamic sizing at creation time without the added overhead needed for reallocation. We will call this container dynamic_array. For example,

```
// A dynamic array of four counters initialized with 1.
dynamic_array<unsigned> counters(4U, 1U);

void do_something()
{
  // Increment the counters.
  std::for_each(std::begin(counters),
                std::end(counters),
                [](unsigned& u)
                {
                  ++u;
                });

  // It is not possible to resize the dynamic_array.
}
```

Here, we have created a dynamic_array of counters and initialized them with 1. Although it is possible to dynamically set the number of elements in this container during construction, the size can not be modified thereafter. In this way, dynamic_array is a kind of hybrid container that combines the efficiency of an array with the dynamic sizing (albeit via one-shot allocation) of std::vector.

As will be described below, the custom dynamic_array container will be designed to fulfill the general requirements for sequential STL containers.[1] In this way, the dynamic_array container is predominantly consistent with the STL and also fills a functional niche between the fixed-size std::array and that

[1] The general requirements for STL containers are specified in 23.2.1 of [9] and listed in Tables 96 and 97 therein.

of the dynamic `std::vector`. This can be considered a kind of user-defined *extension* of the STL that, even though not formally standardized in ISO/IEC [9], can potentially be useful in generic programming.

16.2 Implementing and Using `dynamic_array`

We will now present an implementation of `dynamic_array`. The class definition of `dynamic_array` is similar to that of `std::array` but also has features in its constructors closely resembling those of the constructors of `std::vector`.[2] The class synopsis of a possible implementation of `dynamic_array` is shown in the code sample below.

```
#include <algorithm>
#include <initializer_list>
#include <iterator>
#include <memory>

template<typename T,
         typename alloc = std::allocator<T>>
class dynamic_array
{
public:
  // Type definitions.
  typedef       alloc             allocator_type;
  typedef       T                 value_type;
  typedef       T&                reference;
  typedef const T&                const_reference;
  typedef       T*                iterator;
  typedef const T*                const_iterator;
  typedef       T*                pointer;
  typedef const T*                const_pointer;
  typedef       std::size_t     size_type;
  typedef       std::ptrdiff_t difference_type;
  typedef       std::reverse_iterator<iterator>
                  reverse_iterator;
  typedef       std::reverse_iterator<const_iterator>
                  const_reverse_iterator;

  // Constructors.
```

[2]Consult Sect. 23.3.2 in [9] for an overview of `std::array` and Sect. 23.3.6 for a summary of `std::vector`.

```
dynamic_array();
dynamic_array(size_type);
dynamic_array(
  size_type,
  const value_type&,
  const allocator_type& = allocator_type());

dynamic_array(const dynamic_array&);

template<typename input_iterator>
dynamic_array(
  input_iterator,
  input_iterator,
  const allocator_type& = allocator_type());

dynamic_array(
  std::initializer_list<T> lst,
  const allocator_type& = allocator_type());

// Destructor.
~dynamic_array();

// Iterator members:
iterator               begin  ();
iterator               end    ();
const_iterator         begin  () const;
const_iterator         end    () const;
const_iterator         cbegin () const;
const_iterator         cend   () const;
reverse_iterator       rbegin ();
reverse_iterator       rend   ();
const_reverse_iterator rbegin () const;
const_reverse_iterator rend   () const;
const_reverse_iterator crbegin() const;
const_reverse_iterator crend  () const;

// Size and capacity.
size_type size    () const;
size_type max_size() const;
bool      empty   () const;

// Element access members.
reference       operator[](const size_type);
const_reference operator[](const size_type);
```

```
  reference       front();
  const_reference front() const;
  reference       back ();
  const_reference back () const;

  reference       at(const size_type);
  const_reference at(const size_type) const;

  // Element manipulation members.
  void fill(const value_type&);

  void swap(dynamic_array&);

private:
  const size_type N;
  pointer         elems;

  // Note: dynamic_array can not be copied
  // with operator=().
  dynamic_array& operator=(const dynamic_array&);
};
```

The dynamic_array class has the standard type definitions and iterator support required for a sequential STL container such as value_type, iterator, size_type, etc. In addition, the dynamic_array class has several constructors responsible for allocation and initialization of the elements. Consider, for example, the third of dynamic_array's constructors shown in the class synopsis. This constructor could be implemented as follows.

```
dynamic_array(size_type count,
              const value_type& v,
              const allocator_type& a) : N(count)
{
  const size_type the_size =
    std::max(size_type(1U), N);

  elems = allocator_type(a).allocate(the_size);

  if(N > size_type(0U))
  {
    std::fill_n(begin(), N, v);
  }
  else
```

```
  {
    elems[0U] = value_type();
  }
}
```

Here, the elements of the dynamic array are allocated and initialized with the value stored in the second parameter of the constructor. None of the functions in dynamic_array other than the constructors modify the number of elements in the container, meaning that once a dynamic_array is created, it keeps its size for its entire lifetime. The remaining implementation details of the dynamic_array class can be found in the companion code.

The dynamic_array container fulfills most of the general requirements for sequential STL containers. It can, therefore, be used with the standard algorithms of the STL. The code sample below, for instance, initializes a dynamic_array with three data bytes from an std::initializer_list and calculates the byte checksum thereof.

```
util::dynamic_array<int> values ( { 1, 2, 3 } );

int sum = std::accumulate(values.begin(),
                          values.end(),
                          0);
```

The dynamic_array container can also be used with other functions and class types. Consider, for example, a potential interface to a communication class.

```
class communication
{
public:
  communication() { }
  ~communication() { }

  bool send(const dynamic_array<std::uint8_t>& cmd);
  bool recv(dynamic_array<std::uint8_t>& rsp);
};
```

Here, the communication class has member functions send() and recv() responsible for sending and receiving communication frames, respectively. Data transfer in transmission and reception is carried out using dynamic_array containers holding 8-bit data bytes.

16.3 Writing Parts of the C++ Library if None Is Available

Some C++ compilers, even very good ones, do not provide implementations of the C++ library and the STL. At times, even if the C++ library and the STL are available, the implementations provided by the compiler may be incomplete or outdated and could lack some new and potentially useful C++ language features.

If certain components of the C++ library and the STL are missing, it may be possible to manually write them. This assumes, however, that the development and testing of these components can be carried out with the reliability mandated by real-time C++.

Throughout this book, for example, the code samples have used many parts of the C++ library and the STL. For the most part, these samples have been successfully tested and executed on several 8-bit and 32-bit microcontrollers. Some of the GCC ports used for these tests, however, include only an incomplete C++ standard library and lack the STL entirely. In order to resolve this problem, parts of the C++ library and STL components were explicitly written for this book. The implementations of these can be found in the reference project of the companion code.

Writing a complete implementation of the C++ library and the STL that closely adheres to the standard and provides optimal efficiency is a large-scale programming endeavor. In fact, this is generally considered to be a task for the most experienced C++ specialists because it requires the utmost in programming skill, deep understanding of compiler optimization techniques, meticulous attention to detail and an extensive testing effort.

Writing a complete standards-adherent C++ library might be a task that lies beyond the capabilities of most of us. It can, nonetheless, be feasible and practical to write a small subset of the C++ standard library and the STL. In the following section, we will consider a strategy for writing a subset of the C++ library.

16.4 Implementation Notes for Parts of the C++ Library and STL

It may make sense to select a single location for storage of library headers and any necessary source files when writing a subset of the C++ library and the STL. This can, for example, be a single root directory combined with additional sub-directories for the platform-specific library parts. For instance, the directory structure for the self-written subset of the C++ library for the GCC port for our target with the 8-bit microcontroller is shown in Fig. 16.1. Selecting a single location for self-written library headers simplifies the process of adding the path information to the compiler's default search paths, as described in Sect. 1.6.

The selection of which C++ library components to write may be primarily based on usefulness and ease of implementation. Consider the subset of the C++ library and the STL listed below.

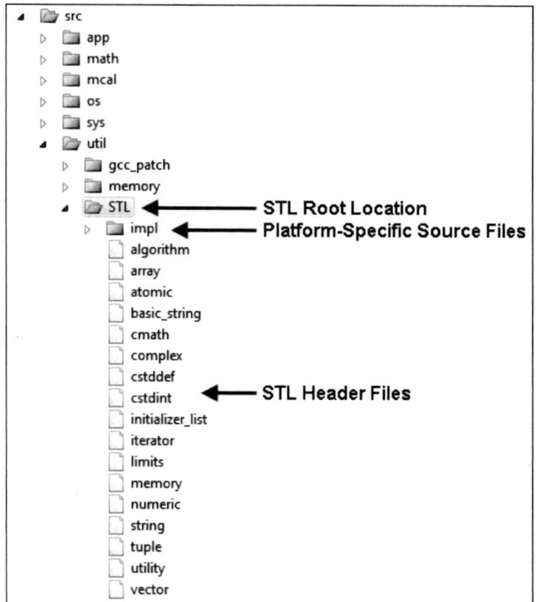

Fig. 16.1 The directory structure for the self-written subset of the C++ library and the STL written for this book is shown

- The fixed-size integer types including those with an exact number of bits, those with at least a specific number of bits and the fastest types with at least a certain number of bits.
- Partial support for `std::array`, optionally not including reverse iterators.
- Commonly used yet simple-to-write functions from the `<algorithm>` library such as the min/max functions, `std::min()`, and `std::max()`, and others operating on sequential iterators such as `std::for_each()`, `std::fill()`, `std::copy()`, `std::find_if()`, and others.
- Selected parts of `<type_traits>`, in particular `std::enable_if` and a variety of templates used for checking types such as `std::is_integral`.
- Common mathematical functions from `<cmath>` if floating-point calculations with elementary functions are anticipated in the project.

Fixed-size integer types are defined in `<cstdint>`. If the C++ compiler has C99 compatibility and supports the C99 fixed-size integer types, then it is a simple matter to inject these types into the namespace `std`. For example,

```
// A partial implementation of <cstdint>

// Include the C99 fixed-size integers.
#include <stdint.h>

namespace std
```

```
{
  // Types with an exact number of bits.
  using ::uint8_t;
  using ::uint16_t;
  using ::uint32_t;
  using ::uint64_t;

  // Types with at least a certain number of bits.
  using ::uint_least8_t;
  using ::uint_least16_t;
  using ::uint_least32_t;
  using ::uint_least64_t;

  // Fastest types with at least a certain
  // number of bits.
  using ::uint_fast8_t;
  using ::uint_fast16_t;
  using ::uint_fast32_t;
  using ::uint_fast64_t;
}
```

If the C++ compiler does not have C99 compatibility, then the fixed-size integer types must be defined. This can be readily accomplished using simple **typedef**s of platform-dependent built-in types such as **char**, **short**, **int**, **long** and possibly **long long**. This does, however, result in slight portability issues because the widths of the built-in types are compiler-dependent. These portability issues are easily managed because the fixed-size integer types need be set up only once for a given platform. Once this is done, it is relatively straightforward to separate processor-specific versions of header files such as `<cstdint>` in different directories or to use preprocessor definitions to achieve separation within larger header files.

A partial implementation of `std::array` is shown in the listing below. This implementation does not include support for reverse iterators.

```
// A partial implementation of <array>

#include <algorithm>
#include <cstddef>

namespace std
{
  template <typename T, size_t N>
  struct array
```

```
{
  // Type definitions:
  typedef T&         reference;
  typedef const T&   const_reference;
  typedef T*         iterator;
  typedef const T*   const_iterator;
  typedef size_t     size_type;
  typedef ptrdiff_t  difference_type;
  typedef T          value_type;
  typedef T*         pointer;
  typedef const T*   const_pointer;

  // Data elements:
  T elems[N];

  // iterators:
  iterator begin() { return elems; }
  iterator end()   { return elems + N; }
  const_iterator begin() const
  { return elems; }
  const_iterator end() const
  { return elems + N; }
  const_iterator cbegin() const
  { return elems; }
  const_iterator cend() const
  { return elems + N; }

  // Size-related members:
  constexpr size_type size() { return N; }
  constexpr size_type max_size() { return N; }
  constexpr bool empty() { return false; }

  // Element access members:
  reference operator[](size_type n)
  { return elems[n]; }
  const_reference operator[](size_type n) const
  { return elems[n]; }
  const_reference at(size_type n) const
  { return elems[n]; }
  reference       at(size_type n)
  { return elems[n]; }
  reference front()
  { return elems[0U]; }
```

```
    const_reference front() const
    { return elems[0U]; }
    reference back()
    { return elems[N - 1U]; }
    const_reference back() const
    { return elems[N - 1U]; }

    T* data() { return elems; }
    const T* data() const { return elems; }

    // Element manipulation members:
    void fill(const T& u) { fill_n(begin(), N, u); }
    void swap(const array<T, N>& other)
    { swap_ranges(begin(), end(), other.begin()); }
  };
}
```

This implementation of `std::array` makes use of other parts of the C++ standard library including the highly useful types `std::size_t` and `std::ptrdiff_t` as well as the algorithms `std::fill_n()` and `std::swap_ranges()`. So these parts of the library must also be available for this implementation of `std::array`.

The min/max algorithms `std::min()` and `std::max()` can be implemented as shown below.

```
// Implement part of <algorithm>

namespace std
{
  // Sample implementation of std::min.
  template<typename T>
  const T& min(const T& a, const T& b)
  {
    return (a < b ? a : b);
  }

  // Sample implementation of std::max.
  template<typename T>
  const T& max(const T& a, const T& b)
  {
    return (a > b ? a : b);
  }
}
```

Some examples of sequential STL algorithms that navigate through iterators include `std::fill()`, `std::for_each()` and `std::find_if()`. These algorithms have linear complexity and are relatively easy to implement. The following code samples show possible implementations of these algorithms.

A potential implementation of `std::fill()` is presented in the code below.

```
// Implement part of <algorithm>

namespace std
{
  // Sample implementation of std::fill.
  template<typename forward_iterator,
           typename value_type>
  void std::fill(forward_iterator first,
                 forward_iterator last,
                 const value_type& value)
  {
    // Fill each element in [first, last) with value.
    while(first != last)
    {
      *first = value;

      ++first;
    }
  }
}
```

A sample implementation of `std::for_each()` follows below. This particular version of `std::for_each()` was previously described in Sect. 5.8.

```
// Implement part of <algorithm>

namespace std
{
  // Sample implementation of std::for_each.
  template<typename iterator_type,
           typename function_type>
  function_type std::for_each(iterator_type first,
                              iterator_type last,
                              function_type function)
  {
    // Apply function to each element in [first, last).
    while(first != last)
    {
      function(*first);
```

```
      ++first;
    }

    return function;
  }
}
```

A possible realization of `std::find_if()` is shown in the following code sequence.

```
// Implement part of <algorithm>

namespace std
{
  // Sample implementation of std::find_if.
  template<typename iterator_type,
           typename predicate_type>
  iterator_type std::find_if(iterator_type first,
                             iterator_type last,
                             predicate_type predicate)
  {
    // Find the first element satisfying predicate.
    while(   (first != last)
          && (false == predicate(*first)))
    {
      ++first;
    }

    return first;
  }
}
```

Some very useful parts of the `<type_traits>` library include templates that query the type of an object at compile time, such as `std::is_integral`. Writing such templates begins with the declaration of `std::integral_constant`.

A potential (but incomplete) implementation appears below.

```
// Implement part of <type_traits>

namespace std
{
  template<typename integral_value_type,
           integral_value_type integral_value>
```

```
  struct integral_constant
  {
    typedef integral_value_type value_type;

    static constexpr value_type my_value =
      integral_value;

    typedef
      integral_constant<value_type, my_value> type;

    operator value_type() const
    {
      return my_value;
    }
  };

  typedef integral_constant<bool, true>  true_type;
  typedef integral_constant<bool, false> false_type;
}
```

When equipped with `std::integral_constant`, it is straightforward to write numerous compile-time templates such as `std::is_integral`, and the like. In particular, inheriting from `std::true_type` can provide for compile-time type queries. See the self-written partial implementation of the STL in the companion code for further hints on this.

We will now investigate possible implementations of parts of the `<cmath>` library. Common elementary transcendental functions such as $\sqrt{x}$, $\sin x$, e^x, etc. are overwritten in `<cmath>`. In fact, overwrites are provided for all three built-in floating-point types **`float`**, **`double`** and **`long double`**. These mathematical functions are related to similar C99 functions in the global namespace. For C++, they are basically wrapped and injected into namespace `std`. A partial sample implementation is shown below.

```
// Implement part of <cmath>

#include <math.h>

namespace std
{
  // Overwrites of the square root function.
  inline float sqrt(float x)
  {
    return ::sqrtf(x);
  }
```

```
  inline double sqrt(double x)
  {
    return ::sqrt(x);
  }

  inline long double sqrt(long double x)
  {
    return ::sqrtl(x);
  }

  // Overwrites of the sine function.
  inline float sin(float x)
  {
    return ::sinf(x);
  }

  inline double sin(double x)
  {
    return ::sin(x);
  }

  inline long double sqrt(long double x)
  {
    return ::sinl(x);
  }

  // Overwrites of the exponent function.
  inline float exp(float x)
  {
    return ::expf(x);
  }

  inline double exp(double x)
  {
    return ::exp(x);
  }

  inline long double exp(long double x)
  {
    return ::expl(x);
  }

// ...and numerous other elementary functions.
}
```

16.5 Providing now() for <chrono>'s High-Resolution Clock

The C++ standard library supports chronological timing functions in its <chrono> library. Part of the <chrono> library includes support for various *clocks* such as a system clock and a high-resolution clock. See Sect. 20.11.7 in [9] for details on the specification of <chrono>. The standard library's high-resolution clock is called std::chrono::high_resolution_clock. It can be well-suited for providing the timebase in a real-time C++ project.

A potential synopsis of std::chrono::high_resolution_clock in <chrono> is shown below.

```
namespace std { namespace chrono {

class high_resolution_clock
{
public:
  // The resolution of the clock is microseconds.
  typedef chrono::microseconds duration;

  // Types for representation, period and time point.
  typedef duration::rep rep;

  typedef duration::period period;

  typedef chrono::time_point<high_resolution_clock,
                             duration> time_point;

  // The counter is steady. This means that
  // a call to now() always returns a later
  // timer than a previous call.

  static constexpr bool is_steady = true;

  // The platform-specific implementation of now().
  // It is declared, but not implemented.

  static time_point now() noexcept;
};

} } // namespace std::chrono
```

Here, the timebase of the high-resolution clock is a static member function called now(). An up-to-date C++ compiler with standard library support for <chrono>

should have a definition of the std::high_resolution_clock class. The subroutine now(), however, could merely be declared in the class, but not implemented. In other words, it might lack a function body. This makes perfect sense because it may be impossible for the C++ standard library authors to know which timer or counter peripheral is used for the timebase in now() or what frequency it has.

For this reason, it might be necessary to manually write a user-provided implementation of the subroutine now() for the compiler's implementation of the std::chrono::high_resolution_clock class.[3] When done properly, this is expected to make it possible to use the high-resolution chronological functions in the <chrono> library. A potential implementation of now() is shown below.

```
// Implement std::chrono::high_resolution_clock::now()
// for the standard library's high-resolution clock.

std::chrono::high_resolution_clock::time_point
  high_resolution_clock::now()
{
  // The high-resolution clock source is microseconds.
  typedef
  std::chrono::time_point<high_resolution_clock,
                          microseconds> from_type;

  // Get the consistent tick in microseconds.
  // This function should be in the mcal.
  auto microsecond_tick
    = consistent_microsecond_tick();

  // Now obtain a time point in microseconds.
  auto from_micro
    = from_type(microseconds(microsecond_tick));

  // Return the duration in microseconds.
  return time_point_cast<duration>(from_micro);
}
```

Here, the timebase of the high-resolution clock is microseconds. Based on the necessities of the project, the microcontroller performance and the capabilities of its peripherals, a different timebase can be selected. Other common choices include milliseconds and nanoseconds.

[3]Some compilers require the manual creation of an implementation-specific, non-standard user-provided function (other than now()) on which the high-resolution clock relies. Check the detailed compiler documentation when investigating this.

In the example above, `consistent_microsecond_tick()` is assumed to be a project-specific function that returns the underlying hardware system-tick in microseconds. This subroutine can, for example, be derived from a free-running timer or a timer interrupt service routine with a fixed period (see also Sect. 9.3).

16.6 Extended-Complex Number Templates

This section introduces a collection of *extended-complex* number templates. It includes both classes representing complex numbers as well as procedural functions intended for complex-valued arithmetic and elementary transcendental functions.

The extended-complex classes represent complex numbers having real and imaginary parts that can be composed of either built-in types or user-defined types (i.e., not strictly limited to built-in types). The behavior of the `<complex>` library is only specified for the built-in data types **`float`**, **`double`** and **`long double`** (Sect. 26.4, § 2 of [9] and also Sect. 12.5 of this book). In this way, extended-complex can be roughly characterized as an extension of `<complex>` to support operation with user-defined numeric types. Typical user-defined types suitable for complex number representation might include, for example, a fixed-point data type such as the one in Sect. 13.2 or a multiple-precision data type potentially from `Boost.Multiprecision` [16]. To successfully interoperate with extended-complex, however, the user-defined type should behave like a built-in types as closely as possible.

The extended-complex templates are summarized below. There are some similarities between the synopsis of extended-complex and the synopsis of `<complex>` specified in Sect. 26.4.1 of [9].

```
// Header extended_complex.h.

namespace extended_complex
{
  template<typename T>
  class complex
  {
    // Extended-complex template (user-defined type).
    ...
  }

  template<>
  class complex<float>
  {
    // Extended-complex template (float).
    ...
  }
```

```
  template<>
  class complex<double>
  {
    // Extended-complex template (double).
    ...
  }

  template<>
  class complex<long double>
  {
    // Extended-complex template (long double).
    ...
  }

  // Unary and binary arithmetic operators.
  ...

  // Comparison operators.
  ...

  // Complex and elementary transcendental functions.
  ...
} // namespace extended_complex
```

Extended-complex includes generic template implementations for user-defined types. There are also template specializations for the built-in types **`float`**, **`double`** and **`long double`**. Support is included for unary and binary arithmetic functions, comparison operations, complex functions (such as `abs()`, `norm()`, `real()`, `imag()`, `polar()`, etc.) and elementary transcendental functions (like `cos()`, `exp()`, `log()`, `pow()`, etc.). The extended-complex templates have been isolated in the namespace `extended_complex`. This resolves potential ambiguity with `std::complex` from `<complex>`.

We will now present an instructive use-case for the extended-complex library. Consider, for example, the complex-valued sinc function,[4]

$$\operatorname{sinc} z = \frac{\sin z}{z}, \quad \text{where } z \in \mathbb{C}. \tag{16.1}$$

The following code sample implements a template subroutine that is designed to return the complex-valued sinc function using extended-complex. In particular,

[4]See also Eq. 12.2 in Sect. 12.1, in which the real-valued sinc function is calculated for built-in **`float`**.

```
#include <complex>
#include <cstdint>
#include <limits>

#include <math/extended_complex/extended_complex.h>

using extended_complex::complex;
using std::complex;

template<typename float_type>
complex<float_type> sinc(const complex<float_type>& z)
{
  using std::abs;

  const float_type my_epsilon =
    std::numeric_limits<float_type>::epsilon();

  if(abs(z) < my_epsilon)
  {
    return complex<float_type>(float_type(1));
  }
  else
  {
    return sin(z) / z;
  }
}
```

Using the `sinc()` template function to obtain complex-valued results for different kinds of input data types is straightforward. For instance,

```
#include <boost/multiprecision/cpp_dec_float.hpp>
#include <math/fixed_point/fixed_point.h>

using fp_type =
  fixed_point<std::int32_t>;

using mp_type =
  boost::multiprecision::cpp_dec_float_50;

// (2.708682 - 3.155585 i)
complex f = sinc(complex(1.2F, 3.4F));
```

```
// (2.708681782584397 - 3.15558549026962 i)
complex d = sinc(complex(1.2,  3.4));

// (2.708681782584397 - 3.15558549026962 i)
complex l = sinc(complex(1.2L, 3.4L));

// (2.709 - 3.156 i)
complex fp =
  sinc(complex(fp_type(fp_type(12) / fp_type(10)),
               fp_type(fp_type(34) / fp_type(10))));

// (  2.708681782584397058298884814264410728687226\
       098006
//   - 3.155585490269623960931511396486590036803379\
//       532893 i)
complex mp =
  sinc(complex(mp_type(mp_type(12) / mp_type(10)),
               mp_type(mp_type(34) / mp_type(10))));
```

In this example, the `sinc()` template function is used with a wide variety of complex-valued data types. These include complex values comprised of both built-in floating-point types as well as complex values made from user-defined types such as the `fixed_point` class from Sect. 13.2 and the multiple-precision type `cpp_-dec_float_50` from `Boost.Multiprecision` [16].

16.7 An Embeddable Big Integer Class

In this section, we introduce a self-written, user-defined extended width big integer template class called `uintwide_t`. `uintwide_t` is available in both the reference application of the companion code as well as in its own dedicated repository [14]. This big integer template class has been specifically designed and optimized for real-time embedded microcontroller applications.

Many areas in mathematics, statistics, science and engineering use big integer types such as `uint128_t`, `uint256_t`, `uint512_t` and beyond. Big integer types generally have more bits than standard available built-in types such as unsigned versions of **`short`**, **`int`**, **`long long`** and the like, which are commonly aliased to `std::uint16_t`, `std::uint32_t`, `std::uint64_t`, etc.[5]

[5]The use of extended precision user-defined numeric types is well-established in C++. In fact, we have encountered extended precision *floating-point* types several times previously in this book when discussing mathematical topics and the `Boost.Multiprecision` library [16]. Similarly, wide *integral* types can be found in `Boost.Multiprecision`. At the time of writing the

The declaration of the `uintwide_t` template class is shown below.

```
namespace wide_integer::generic_template
{

template<const std::size_t Digits2,
         typename LimbType = std::uint32_t>
class uintwide_t
{
  // ...
};

} // namespace wide_integer::generic_template
```

`uintwide_t` resides within the namespace `wide_integer::generic_-template` and has two template parameters. The `Digits2` parameter specifies the base-2 number of binary digits (i.e., bits) in the unsigned big integer. The `LimbType` parameter determines the type of the so-called *limbs*. Limbs are stored as an array of built-in unsigned integers and provide the internal representation of the synthesized unsigned big integer type.

The `uintwide_t` template class behaves like a drop-in replacement for built-in unsigned integral types. It provides much wider numerical range than built-in types and is, in this way, acts as an extension of the C++ Standard Library.

Consider, for instance,

```
#include "generic_template_uintwide_t.h"

using uint256_t =
  wide_integer::generic_template::uintwide_t
    <256U, std::uint16_t>;
```

Here, `uint256_t` is aliased as a 256-bit unsigned wide integer type. The internal representation of `uint256_t` is stored in an array composed of sixteen limbs having type `std::uint16_t`. Each individual `uint256_t` defined in this way requires a minimum of 32 bytes of memory storage in total.

---

fourth edition of this book, there also exists an independent proposal to add big integer support to C++ using a template class called `wide_int` [10]. A working reference implementation for the proposed `wide_int` template class is available in the public domain [11]. See also [1, 4, 5, 12, 15] for comprehensive information on many kinds of computational number systems (including big integers and big floats).

`uintwide_t` includes implementations of common elementary mathematical operations such as addition, subtraction, multiplication, division, modulus, etc. In addition, various number-theoretical functions are available including, among others, square root, kth root, power-modulus, greatest common divisor, pseudo-random number generation and rudimentary primality testing.

We will now use `uintwide_t` to perform a variety of 256-bit unsigned integral calculations. Consider, for example, two 256-bit unsigned integers a and b randomly selected, with

$$a = \texttt{F4DF741DE58BCB2F37F18372026EF9CB}$$
$$\texttt{CFC456CB80AF54D53BDEED78410065DE}_{16}$$
$$b = \texttt{166D63E0202B3D90ECCEAA046341AB50}$$
$$\texttt{4658F55B974A7FD63733ECF89DD0DF75}_{16}\,. \tag{16.2}$$

Using the `uint256_t` class, it is straightforward to compute the 256-bit integer product $a \times b$ and the 256-bit integer quotient $a\,/\,b$. In particular,

```
#include "generic_template_uintwide_t.h"

const uint256_t a =
  "0xF4DF741DE58BCB2F37F18372026EF9CB"
    "CFC456CB80AF54D53BDEED78410065DE";

const uint256_t b =
  "0x166D63E0202B3D90ECCEAA046341AB50"
    "4658F55B974A7FD63733ECF89DD0DF75";

const bool result_of_mul_is_ok =
  ((a * b) == "0xE491A360C57EB4306C61F9A04F7F7D99"
                "BE3676AAD2D71C5592D5AE70F84AF076");

const bool result_of_div_is_ok =
  ((a / b) == 10U);
```

In the following example, we will compute the integer 7th root r of x, where x is a randomly selected 256-bit unsigned integer. The particular integer 7th root calculation we will perform here is

$$r = \sqrt[7]{x}\,, \tag{16.3}$$

with

$$x = \texttt{95E0E51079E1D11737D3FD01429AA745} \\ \texttt{582FEB4381D61FA56948C1A949E43C32}_{16}\,, \tag{16.4}$$

resulting in

$$r = \texttt{16067D1894}_{16}\,. \tag{16.5}$$

The corresponding code for this integer 7th root calculation is listed below.

```
#include "generic_template_uintwide_t.h"

const uint256_t x =
  "0x95E0E51079E1D11737D3FD01429AA745"
    "582FEB4381D61FA56948C1A949E43C32";

const uint256_t r = rootk(x, 7U);

const bool result_of_root_is_ok =
  (r == UINT64_C(0x16067D1894));
```

The next code sample computes the greatest common divisor (gcd) of two randomly chosen 256-bit unsigned integers. Consider the two randomly selected 256-bit unsigned integers u and v,

$$u = \texttt{D2690CD26CD57A3C443993851A70D3B6} \\ \texttt{2F841573668DF7B229508371A0AEDE7F}_{16}$$

$$v = \texttt{FE719235CD0B1A314D4CA6940AEDC38B} \\ \texttt{DF8E9484E68CE814EDAA17D87B0B4CC8}_{16}\,. \tag{16.6}$$

The greatest common divisor w of these two integers is

$$w = \gcd(u, v) = 12170749\,. \tag{16.7}$$

The corresponding code for the greatest common divisor calculation is listed below.

```
#include "generic_template_uintwide_t.h"

const uint256_t u =
  "0xD2690CD26CD57A3C443993851A70D3B6"
    "2F841573668DF7B229508371A0AEDE7F";
```

```
const uint256_t v =
  "0xFE719235CD0B1A314D4CA6940AEDC38B"
    "DF8E9484E68CE814EDAA17D87B0B4CC8";

const uint256_t w = gcd(u, v);

const bool result_is_ok =
  (std::uint32_t(c) == UINT32_C(12170749));
```

Compiler optimization settings (Sect. 6.1) and the selected width of the limb type can strongly influence the efficiency of wide-integer code (both space as well as speed). It can, therefore, be a good idea to investigate and optionally tune these characteristics when embedding this or any other big-integer library.

16.8 Customizing `<random>`

In Sect. 3.22, we briefly introduced random numbers and the `<random>` library. When using `<random>`, it is common to use a random device or a random engine combined with random sequence generator for obtaining random numbers. In this section, we will create a simple hardware-based custom random device.

At the end of this section, we present example `chapter16_08`, which uses this custom random device to generate (and represent on an LCD character display) 128-bit random prime integers checked for primality according to Miller-Rabin testing [19].

C++'s default random device is called `std::random_device`. The C++ specification does not specify the exact way *how* random values should be generated from the standard random device (see, for instance, Sect. 26.5.6, § 6 in [9]) and leaves this open to the internal details of the compiler.

Random sequencing generally tends to work best if the both the seed as well as the subsequent generation are truly random. This might be the case if a non-deterministic hardware device or another non-biased or minimally biased process is available.

In a real-time embedded environment, some possible choices for generating a random seed include reading the value of a free-running timer register or extracting the lower bits of successive analog-digital conversions on a floating channel, etc. These sources can, however, be problematic because of loss of randomness due to electrical bias leading to a non-negligible degree of predictability.

There are various other alternatives. Some developers identify a sizable chunk of uninitialized RAM having at least several kilobytes and run a CRC or hash or a similar checksum over this memory region. This can be done in the startup code before calling `main()` in order to generate a seed (see also Sect. 8.1). Again, this method is not perfect, especially if the microcontroller is not completely powered down or if it is only switched off for a short time prior to the next power cycle.

Modern high-performance microcontrollers often have a dedicated hardware unit that implements a so-called true random number generator (TRNG). In practice, the TRNG could be used to generate a seed for a secondary software component or hardware peripheral device that subsequently uses a PRNG such as Mersenne twister (Sect. 3.22) for making a more lengthy random sequence.

Another option is collecting random bits in the form of electrical digital logic signals that result from an actual physical source such as a quantum mechanical process. A common, real-world example of this involves digitizing amplified random electrical noise in a transistor junction. This is described, for instance, in Sect. 13.14.7 of [8] based on the schematic of Fig. 13.121 therein. A much simplified circuit with a similar purpose is described later in this section.

Once a semi-random source has been built or in some other way identified, bytes can be collected from it with a software random engine. Consider the code snippet below. It shows the class synopsis of `mcal::random::random_engine`. This made-up random engine is similar to, although not identical with, `std::default_random_engine`.

```
// chapter16_08-001_random_engine.cpp

namespace mcal { namespace random {

class random_engine
{
public:
  using result_type = std::uint32_t;

  random_engine() = default;

  ~random_engine() = default;

  random_engine& operator=
    (const random_engine&) = delete;

  // Differs from the standard which
        // would ordinarily return double.
  std::uint_fast8_t entropy() const;

  // Implementation dependent.
  result_type operator()() noexcept;
};

} } // namespace mcal::random
```

In this class, extraction of random values is realized by the overloaded function call operator (i.e., **operator**() ()). For instance,

```
// chapter16_08-001_random_engine.cpp

using random_engine_type =
  mcal::random::random_engine;

random_engine_type eng;

const random_engine_type::result_type r = eng();
```

The `random_engine` class is intended to be a highly specialized, implementation dependent source of random or pseudo-random values. A simple, practical implementation of a random device in the domain of hobby-quality microcontroller applications could, for instance, stream in digitized pseudo-random bits from a do-it-yourself target-specific hardware source, as follows.

An elementary circuit designed to generate semi-random electrical noise output as a bit stream is shown in Fig. 16.2. For background information on this kind of circuit, see, for instance, [25] in particular Sect. "*Zenner diode*" therein. In the circuit in this book, a reverse-biased bipolar NPN transistor such as a 2N2222A, is hooked up to exhibit breakdown similar to that of a Zenner diode in order to create a pseudo-randomly oscillating noise signal. The noisy signal rides atop a DC offset roughly equal to the breakdown voltage of the transistor's base-emitter diode, $\sim$ 8 V in this case.

A second order passive RC low-pass filter isolates the DC component of the random noise signal. The random noise signal and its DC component are fed into the inputs of a voltage comparator of type LM2903 which performs a coarse digitization of the noise. A CMOS logic inverter such as a 7404 hex NOT-gate sharpens the edges to produce a relatively clean random bit stream at its output pin. The phase and polarity of the digitized noise are predominantly irrelevant for the planned use

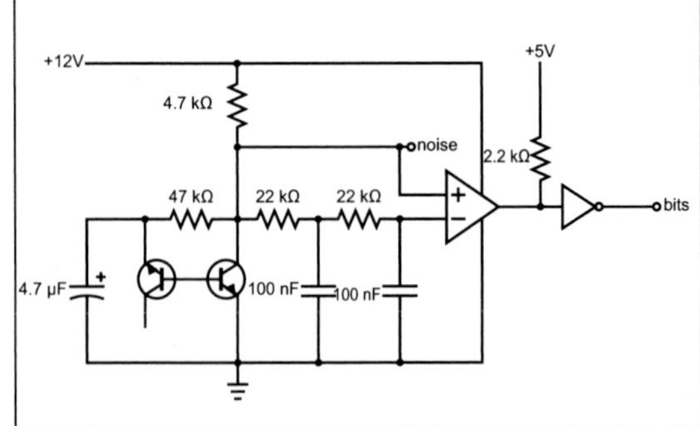

Fig. 16.2 A relatively simple do-it-yourself circuit designed for creating electrical *noise* as a stream of *bits* is shown. This circuit uses a reverse-biased transistor as a physical source of semi-random electrical noise

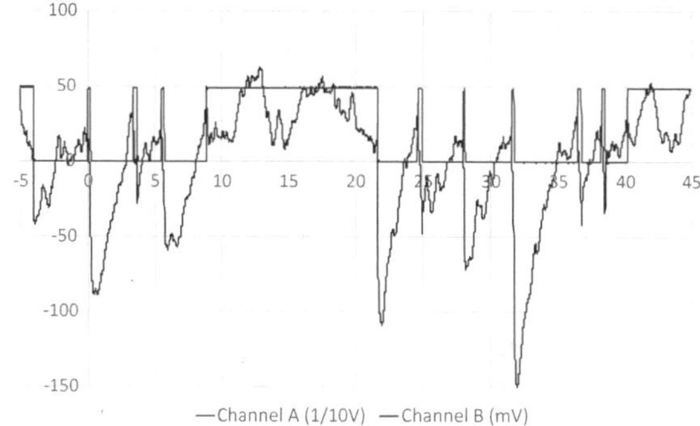

Fig. 16.3 An oscilloscope measurement showing the AC-coupled random noise signal (channel *B*, red) and its digitized output bit stream (channel *A*, blue) from a reverse-biased transistor circuit are shown. The horizontal time axis has 5 μs per division

of this bit stream. Alternatively, therefore, other different logic components could be used to refine the digital bit stream such as a 7407 non-inverting hex buffer, a 7408 quad AND-gate with inputs tied, or a 7402 quad NOR-gate with inputs tied, etc.

This circuit produces a perpetual stream of pseudo-random bits intended to be read by a microcontroller digital input port pin. The average duty cycle of the bit stream is expected to be approximately 50% with slight variances due to tolerances of the electronic components such as the comparator offset, etc.

An oscilloscope measurement showing the AC-coupled random noise signal and the digitized output bit stream resulting from a reverse-biased transistor circuit are shown in Fig. 16.3. The AC-coupled random noise has a jagged oscillating form. It is a strong, easily detectable and recognizable semi-random noise signal with an amplitude of roughly $\pm (\sim 1/4)$ V. The overall form, shape, strength and frequency of the noise signal varies depending on the exact kind of transistor or Zenner diode used and other circuit parameters. These can be empirically tuned.

The resulting digitized signal is a relatively clean bit stream having TTL logic level and a frequency near 100 kHz. The digitized random noise is intended to be sampled with a similar acquisition frequency on the input pin of a microcontroller on a per-bit basis. Bits in the stream are concatenated into pseudo-random bytes or other wider integral types via software, thereby creating random numbers that can be subsequently used in programs.

A slight variation of the `mcal::random::random_engine` class designed to use the reverse-biased transistor circuit of Fig. 16.2 as a bit stream source has been created specifically for this book. This class is called `random_engine_reverse_z_diode_raw`, as partially sketched in the following snippet.

```
// Taken from mcal/avr/mcal_random.h

namespace mcal { namespace random {
namespace detail {

template<typename SpiType,
         typename UnsignedIntegralType>
```

```
class random_engine_reverse_z_diode_raw
{
public:
  using result_type = UnsignedIntegralType;

  random_engine_reverse_z_diode_raw(
    const result_type = result_type());

  result_type operator()();
  {
    // Get a new random value
                // of type result_type.

    // ...
  }

  // ...
};

} } }
```

This random engine is used in example `chapter16_08` below in order to read random bit sequences. The all-software SPI™ driver from Sect. 9.5 (template parameter `SpiType`) reads the random bit stream and combines successive bits into bytes that are subsequently concatenated into 128-bit integers for the purpose of generating 128-bit random prime numbers.

We will now briefly describe example `chapter16_08` from the companion code. This example links the fascinating and deep prime number theorem known from mathematical number theory in an intuitive and easy-to-understand way with efficient template and object-oriented C++ running on our target with the 8-bit microcontroller.

Example `chapter16_08` uses the wide-integer library described in Sect. 16.7 to compute random 128-bit prime numbers. Primality testing is based on a Miller-Rabin algorithm [19, 21]. Miller-Rabin primality testing checks if a number is *probably* prime within the limits shown below.

Computational work is distributed among the time slices of a state machine. The state machine is serviced in the idle task of the multitasking scheduler. This is similar to the time slicing scheme utilized in examples `chapter10_08` and `chapter10_08a`. Candidate 128-bit numbers are generated with an efficient hardware random engine based on a wide-integer extension of the `mcal::random::random_engine`. In particular, this extension is performed by adapting the `random_device_reverse_z_diode` class previously mentioned above in this section.

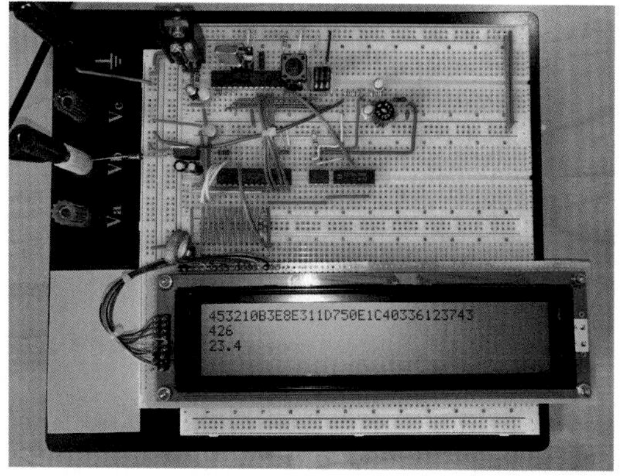

Fig. 16.4 The target hardware used in example `chapter16_08` is shown. The most recently calculated 128-bit prime is on line 1. In this power-on cycle, this system has generated a few hundred 128-bit primes (line 2). The probability that a random candidate is prime is $\sim 1/23$ (line 3). This provides deep insight into the prime number theorem, as described in the text

The target hardware used in example `chapter16_08` is shown in Fig. 16.4. The reverse-biased transistor circuit presented above in this section and drawn in Fig. 16.2 is used to generate a digitized random bit stream input. This sub-circuit occupies roughly the center-right portion of the upper third of the board. A voltage regulator of type LM7812 powered from the external voltage supply produces the +12 V rail for the random noise generator and comparator supply.[6]

The bits in the random bit stream are collected on `portc.5`. These bits are combined sequentially with some preselection in order to synthesize 128-bit integers which are subsequently tested for primality.

Prime numbers are displayed in hexadecimal base-16 uppercase representation on line 1 of the 40×4 character LCD. Line 2 of the LCD shows the total number of 128-bit prime numbers that have been generated in the current power-on cycle. The decimal value on line 3 of the LCD represents the average number of trials required in order to obtain 1 single probable prime number. Prime number and calculation visualization uses a display of type Newhaven NHD-0440AZ-FL-YBW [20]. LCD control uses the digital ports on a discrete serial port expander chip of type MICROCHIP® MCP23S17 [18].

When running on our target with the 8-bit microcontroller, the program in example `chapter16_08` generates on average $\sim$ 240 random 128-bit primes per hour, in other words requiring $\sim$ 15 seconds per prime.

The primality testing scheme is based in part on `Boost.Multiprecision`, in particular on the template functions `miller_rabin_test<>()`. The online Boost documentation provides the following description thereof [16].

"These functions perform a Miller-Rabin test for primality, ... The algorithm used performs some trial divisions to exclude small prime factors, does one Fermat test to exclude many more composites, and then uses the Miller-Rabin algorithm

---

[6]When building this circuit or otherwise engaging in hobby electronics, consider also the comments on circuit construction, soldering and safety in Footnote 9, Page 261.

straight out of Knuth Vol 2, which recommends 25 trials for a pretty strong likelihood that n is prime" [17].[7]

The Miller-Rabin test identifies unsigned integer numbers that have a strong probability of being prime. The error bound ϵ on the probability that Miller-Rabin testing falsely identifies a composite number as prime is less than 4^{-k}, where k is the number of Miller-Rabin trials performed [24].

For numbers having b binary digits, the error bound ϵ has been refined in [3] to

$$\epsilon \lesssim \left(\frac{1}{7}\, b^{15/4}\, 2^{-b/2}\right) \times 4^{-k} . \tag{16.8}$$

This results in

$$\begin{aligned}\epsilon &\lesssim \left(\frac{1}{7}\, 128^{15/4}\, 2^{-128/2}\right) \times 4^{-25} \\ &\lesssim 10^{-27}\end{aligned} \tag{16.9}$$

for 128-bit integers having $b = 128$ and when performing the execution of $k = 25$ Miller-Rabin rounds, as is done in this example here.

Primality testing in example `chapter16_08` uses the following scheme.

- At the point of random bit generation preselect 128-bit integer prime candidates n having lowest base-10 digit equal to 1, 3, 7 or 9.
- Furthermore, selectively remove candidates n having base-10 digital root [23] equal to 3, 6 or 9. The base-b digital root of an integer n, $\mathrm{dr}_b\,(n)$, can be efficiently calculated with

  $$\mathrm{dr}_b\,(n) = 1 + (n - 1) \bmod (b - 1) ,$$

  with

  $$\mathrm{dr}_{10}\,(n) = 1 + (n - 1) \bmod (9) .$$

- Require that at least one bit in the highest nibble of each prime candidate n is set. This optional condition ensures that the most significant hexadecimal digit on line 1 of the LCD is non-zero thereby establishing pretty printing for each prime number found.
- Eliminate candidates n having easy-to-identify prime factorization by using trial division of tabulated small primes ranging from 3 ... 227.

[7]Here Knuth Vol 2 refers to the description of **Algorithm P** in Sect. 4.5.4, Volume 2 of [13].

- Perform one Fermat test using the power-modulus function at $228^{n-1} \pmod n$ to rule out many non-prime candidates.
- Run 25 Miller-Rabin trials on each prime candidate n that made it this far in order to detect *very* high probability of primality according to Miller-Rabin testing.
- The primality testing algorithm has been divided into time slices and is implemented as a state machine in the class `miller_rabin_state`.

Primality testing in example `chapter16_08` has been verified with various compilers on several target systems having 8-bit, 32-bit and 64-bit architectures. PC-based tests using several independent test systems running for days upon days have independently confirmed many millions of primes originally calculated with `chapter16_08`'s primality testing algorithm. These validations provide evidence for the numerical correctness and robustness of the implementation of primality testing.

Empirical observations (also noted in the caption of Fig. 16.4) reveal that on average $\sim\ 1/23$ candidates need to be tested in order to find a single probable prime in the 128-bit range. We will now compare this with the expected theoretical density of 128-bit prime numbers.

The prime number theorem asserts that the probability that a number is prime is proportional to the prime counting function $\pi(x)$ [6, 7, 26, 27]. From Eq. 3.2 in Sect. 3.2, the asymptotic approximation of the prime counting function is given by

$$\pi(x) \sim \mathrm{Li}(x) . \tag{16.10}$$

where $\mathrm{Li}(x)$ is known as the offset logarithmic integral function.

Consider base-10 k-digit integers in the interval $\left[10^{k-1},\ 10^{k}\right)$ and a more easy-to-calculate asymptotic form of the prime counting function

$$\pi(x) \sim \frac{\log(x)}{x} . \tag{16.11}$$

These considerations lead to

$$\begin{aligned} N_k &\approx \frac{10^k}{\log\left(10^k\right)} - \frac{10^{k-1}}{\log\left(10^{k-1}\right)} \\ &= \left(\frac{10^{k-1}}{\log(10)}\right)\left(\frac{9k - 10}{k\,(k - 1)}\right) , \end{aligned} \tag{16.12}$$

where N_k is the approximate number of primes in the interval $\left[10^{k-1},\ 10^{k}\right)$.

Divide the number of primes in the interval by the total number of k-digit integers in the interval, which is $9 \times 10^{k-1}$. The result is

$$\begin{aligned} p_k &\approx \frac{N_k}{9 \times 10^{k-1}} \\ &= \frac{\left(\dfrac{10^{k-1}}{\log(10)}\right)\left(\dfrac{9k - 10}{k\,(k - 1)}\right)}{9 \times 10^{k-1}} \\ &= \frac{9k - 10}{9k\,(k - 1)\log(10)}, \end{aligned} \tag{16.13}$$

where p_k is the probability that a randomly chosen integer with k decimal digits is prime.

In example `chapter16_08`, the approximate number of decimal digits k is given by

$$\begin{aligned} k &\approx \frac{128 \times 301}{1,000} \\ &\approx 38.5\,, \end{aligned} \tag{16.14}$$

where we use a rudimentary scaling factor of $301/\,1,000$ to convert base-2 to base-10 digits.

The value of $k = 38.5$ decimal digits can be injected into Eq. 16.13. The result is

$$\begin{aligned} p_{38.5} &\approx \frac{9 \times 38.5 - 10}{9 \times 38.5 \times 37.5 \times 2.303} \\ &\approx \frac{1}{88.9}, \end{aligned} \tag{16.15}$$

where $p_{38.5}$ is the approximate probability that a randomly selected 128-bit integer is prime.

Random integers n having lowest base-10 digit equal to one of 1, 3, 7 or 9 have been preselected via software from the random device in example `chapter16_08`. This eliminates $6/\,10$ non-prime candidates and reduces the number of prime candidates in the pool by a factor of $4/\,10$. Furthermore, prime candidates n having base-10 digital root $\mathrm{dr}_{10}\,(n)$ equal to 3, 6 or 9 have also been selectively and purposely removed because these are divisible by 3 and thus non-prime (i.e., retain only prime candidates n having $\mathrm{dr}_{10}\,(n) \neq 3, 6, 9$). Since the base-10 digital root ranges from $1 \ldots 9$, this condition additionally eliminates $1/\,3$ of the remaining random non-primes from the pool of prime candidates.

With this preselection, the resulting chance that a candidate integer is prime is, accordingly, given by

$$
\begin{aligned}
p_{38.5}^{1,3,7,9;\,\mathrm{dr}\neq 3,6,9} &\approx \left(\frac{1}{88.9}\right) \div \left(\frac{4}{10}\right) \div \left(\frac{2}{3}\right) \\
&= \frac{10 \times 10 \times 3}{889 \times 4 \times 2} \\
&= \frac{75}{1778} \\
&\approx \frac{1}{23.7}\,.
\end{aligned}
\tag{16.16}
$$

This estimate agrees rather well with the empirical observation of $\sim\ 1/\,23$ noted both above as well as in the caption and image of Fig. 16.4.

An alternate calculation uses the offset logarithmic function from Eq. 16.10 instead of the ratio $\log(x)\,/\,x$ from Eq. 16.11 in the approximation of the prime counting function. This leads to[8]

$$
\begin{aligned}
p_{38.5} &\approx \frac{\mathrm{Li}\left(10^{38.5}\right) - \mathrm{Li}\left(10^{37.5}\right)}{9 \times 10^{37.5}} \\
&\approx \frac{(3.608\ -\ 0.371) \times 10^{36}}{2.846 \times 10^{38}} \\
&\approx \frac{3.237}{2.846 \times 10^{2}} \\
&\approx \frac{1}{87.9}\,,
\end{aligned}
\tag{16.17}
$$

resulting in

$$
\begin{aligned}
p_{38.5}^{1,3,7,9;\,\mathrm{dr}\neq 3,6,9} &\approx \left(\frac{1}{87.9}\right) \div \left(\frac{4}{10}\right) \div \left(\frac{2}{3}\right) \\
&= \frac{10 \times 10 \times 3}{879 \times 4 \times 2}
\end{aligned}
$$

[8]For large argument $x\ \gg\ 1$, the offset logarithmic function $\mathrm{Li}\,(x)$ is approximately equal to the logarithmic function $\mathrm{li}\,(x)$. Numerical values of the large argument logarithmic integral function, for instance $\mathrm{li}\left(10^{38.5}\right)\ \approx\ 3.608\ldots\ \times\ 10^{36}$ with about 4 – 5 decimal digits of precision, can be obtained in this argument range from 3 terms ($k\ =\ 0\ldots 2$) in the asymptotic expansion shown in Eq. 3.4.

$$
\begin{aligned}
&= \frac{25}{586} \\
&\approx \frac{1}{23.4}\,,
\end{aligned}
\tag{16.18}
$$

which is potentially even slightly more accurate than the already pretty good estimate provided in Eq. 16.16.

The result in Eq. 16.18 also agrees well with line 3 on the LCD in Fig. 16.4. This provides beautiful empirical numerical verification of the prime number theorem through a non-trivial and advanced C++ example running on our target with the 8-bit microcontroller.

16.9 Freestanding Implementation

The C++ standard differentiates between two kinds of compiler implementations, *hosted* and *freestanding*. A hosted implementation is expected to provide full language and library support including *all* specified headers. Whereas a so-called *freestanding* implementation can support fewer library functions and headers. For further information, consult Sect. 1.3.26, § 7 and Sect. 17.6.1.3 (Table 16) in [9] and also Sect. 6.1.1 in [22].

At the time of writing the fourth edition of this book, there is an ongoing, steady effort (see [2]) intended to extend the scope of *freestanding* to include additional mandatory headers and library functions beyond those mentioned above. Throughout this book in fact, a selective set of efficient, resource-saving library functions mostly consistent with these efforts has been favored and used almost exclusively. In particular, this selective set can be found in the self-written subset of the STL described in Sect. 16.4 and available in the reference application of the companion code. For the most part, but with certain differences such as moderate use of floating-point functions, the library subset in this book is predominantly consistent with the proposed extension of *freestanding* in [2].

Some developers consider *freestanding* to be well-suited for resource-constrained domains. In particular, these might include applications that are generally intolerant of potential overhead from certain "heavy" language elements such as use of heap, runtime type information (RTTI), exception handling, threads, floating-point function support, etc. Accordingly, *freestanding* or a future similar interpretation thereof could be a great choice for bare metal real-time embedded microcontroller programming in C++. See additional motivational notes in Sects. "*Scope*" and "*Design Decisions*" in [2].

References

1. R. Brent, P. Zimmermann, *Modern Computer Arithmetic* (Cambridge University Press, Cambridge UK, 2011)
2. B. Craig, *Document number: P0829R1, Freestanding Proposal* (2017). http://www.open-std.org/jtc1/sc22/wg21/docs/papers/2018/p0829r1.html
3. I. Damgård, P. Landrock, C. Pomerance, Average case error estimates for the strong probable prime test. Math. Comput. **61**(203), 177–194 (1993)
4. L. Fousse, G. Hanrot, V. Lefèvre, P. Pélissier, P. Zimmermann, MPFR: A multiple-precision binary floating-point library with correct rounding. ACM Trans. Math. Soft. **33**(2), (June 2007). https://doi.org/10.1145/1236463.1236468
5. GMP, *GNU Multiple Precision Arithmetic Library* (2019). http://gmplib.org
6. L.J. Goldstein, A history of the prime number theorem. Am. Math Month. (80), 599–615 (1973)
7. L. Goodman, E.W. Weisstein, *Riemann Hypothesis*. From MathWorld–A Wolfram Web Resource (2020). http://mathworld.wolfram.com/RiemannHypothesis.html
8. P. Horowitz, W. Hill, *The Art of Electronics, Third Edition, Twelfth Printing* (Cambridge University Press, Cambridge, 2017)
9. ISO/IEC, *ISO/IEC 14882:2011 : Information Technology – Programming Languages – C++* (International Organization for Standardization, Geneva, 2011)
10. I. Klevanets, A. Polukhin, *Document number: P0539R0, A Proposal to Add wide_int Template Class* (2017). http://www.open-std.org/jtc1/sc22/wg21/docs/papers/2017/p0539r0.html
11. I. Klevanets, *Int* (2017). http://github.com/cerevra/int/tree/master/v2
12. R.T. Kneusel, *Numbers and Computers, Second Edition* (Springer International Publishing, Cham Switzerland, 2017)
13. D.E. Knuth, *The Art of Computer Programming Volumes 1–3, Third Edition* (Addison-Wesley, Boston, 1998)
14. C. Kormanyos, *Wide-integer* (2020). http://github.com/ckormanyos/wide-integer
15. P. Kornerup, D.W. Matula, *Finite Precision Number Systems and Arithmetic* (Cambridge University Press, Cambridge UK, 2010)
16. J. Maddock, C. Kormanyos, *Boost.Multiprecision* (2020). http://www.boost.org/doc/libs/1_73_0/libs/multiprecision/doc/html/index.html
17. J. Maddock, C. Kormanyos, *Primality Testing* (2020). http://www.boost.org/doc/libs/1_73_0/libs/multiprecision/doc/html/boost_multiprecision/tut/primetest.html
18. Microchip, *MCP23S17 16-Bit SPI I/O Expander with Serial Interface* (2020). www.microchip.com/wwwproducts/en/MCP23S17
19. G.L. Miller, Riemann's hypothesis and tests for primality. J. Comput. Syst. Sci. **13**(3), 300–317 (1976)
20. Newhaven Display International, *NHD-0440AZ-FL-YBW CharacterLiquid Crystal Display Module* (2020). http://www.newhavendisplay.com/specs/NHD-0440AZ-FL-YBW.pdf
21. M.O. Rabin, Probabilistic algorithm for testing primality. J. Number Theory **12**(1), 128–138 (1980)
22. B. Stroustrup, *The C++ Programming Language — Fourth Edition* (Addison Wesley, Upper Saddle River, NJ, 2013)
23. Wikipedia, *Digital root* (2020). http://en.wikipedia.org/wiki/Digital_root
24. Wikipedia, *Miller-Rabin primality test* (2020). http://en.wikipedia.org/wiki/Miller-Rabin_primality_test
25. Wikipedia, *Noise generator* (2020). http://en.wikipedia.org/wiki/Noise_generator
26. Wikipedia, *Prime number theorem* (2019). http://en.wikipedia.org/wiki/Prime_number_theorem
27. E.W. Weisstein, *Prime Counting Function*. From MathWorld–A Wolfram Web Resource (2020). http://mathworld.wolfram.com/PrimeCountingFunction.html

Chapter 17
Using C-Language Code in C++

This chapter shows how to access C-language code within a C++ project. The subject of the example is CRC calculations (cyclic redundancy check). There can be good reasons to mix C and C++ code. Many developers write code in C, particularly in the realm of embedded microcontroller programming. Sometimes a convenient module exists in a C-language implementation and it may be desirable to use it in C++. Consider, for instance, a C language module that exercises a practical function. Let's imagine that this C implementation is well-tested and stable. Instead of rewriting or porting an existing, stable and tested body of code from C to C++, it might be a wiser choice to simply use the C code unchanged in the C++ project.

17.1 Accessing C Language Code in C++

Consider a function written in C, such as the one shown below.

```
// This is in a C file.

void FunctionInC(void)
{
  // ...
}
```


C. Kormanyos, *Real-Time C++*, https://doi.org/10.1007/978-3-662-62996-3_17

In this example, `FunctionInC()` is implemented in the C language and stored in a C file.

In order to call `FunctionInC()` within a C++ file, the function must be declared as a subroutine with so-called C-linkage. This can be accomplished with the declaration **extern** `"C"`. For instance,

```
// This is in a C++ file.

// Tell the C++ compiler about the C function.
extern "C" void FunctionInC(void);

void do_something()
{
  // Now the C++ compiler can access the C function.
  FunctionInC();
}
```

The **extern** `"C"` declaration tells the C++ compiler to deactivate name mangling for this function (see also Sect. 6.6). This makes `FunctionInC()` accessible in both C as well as C++.

17.2 An Existing C-Language CRC Library

When working with embedded microcontroller systems, it can be commonplace to use CRC calculations [6] to verify the integrity of one or more byte streams of data. This kind of verification can be useful for checking the content of things such as communication frames, memory blocks, etc. CRC calculations are well-established. It can, therefore, be prevalent to encounter existing C-code implementations for various CRC algorithms.

The AUTOSAR 4.3 Standard [1, 2] specifies the use of at least four kinds of CRC algorithms including bit-widths of 8, 16, 32, and 64. The main characteristics of these CRCs are summarized in Table 17.1.[1] We will use these four kinds of CRCs in this section.

Consider, for example, a potential C-language interface to a well-tested and existing procedural implementation of an 8-bit CRC. The code below shows a possible declaration of the interface to `Crc08`.[2]

[1]These characteristics and other details on many kinds of CRCs can be found in [3].

[2]Even though the CRCs used in this example are present in the AUTOSAR 4.3 standard, [2] the interface shown here does not exactly follow the same design as the interface specified in AUTOSAR [1].

Table 17.1 The main characteristics of some of the CRCs from the AUTOSAR 4.3 standard are listed (see also [1–3]). These CRCs have widths of 8, 16, 32 and 64 bits, respectively

CRC name	Bits	Polynomial	CRC(0x31 ... 0x39)
CRC8/AUTOSAR	8	0x2F	0xDF
CRC16/CCITT-false	16	0x1021	0x29B1
CRC32/AUTOSAR	32	0xF4ACFB13	0x1697D06A
CRC64/XZ	64	0x42F0E1EBA9EA3693	0x995DC9BBDF1939FA

```
void Crc08_Initialize
  (Crc8_Context_Type* Crc_Context);

void Crc08_ProcessBytes
  (const uint8_t*      DataIn,
   const size_t        DataLength,
   Crc8_Context_Type* Crc_Context);

void Crc8_Finalize
  (Crc08_Context_Type* Crc_Context);
```

This C-language interface includes functions for initialization, byte processing, and finalization. These functions are useful for performing CRC calculations. The underlying implementations are assumed to be well established within the development environment and have a *tried-and-true* character.

Assume that similar reliable C-language implementations also exist for specific kinds of `Crc16`, `Crc32` and `Crc64`. The result is a C library with a collection of trusted CRC implementations.

Using this C-based CRC library is simple. For instance,

```
// This is in a C file.

#include <stdint.h>

#include <math/checksums/crc/Crc08.h>

static const uint8_t test_data[9U] =
{
  0x31U, 0x32U, 0x33U, 0x34U,
  0x35U, 0x36U, 0x37U, 0x38U,
  0x39
};
```

```
void do_something(void)
{
  // Perform the Crc08 with the traditional
  // C-language interface.

  Crc08_Context_Type CrcContext;

  Crc08_Initialize(&CrcContext);

  Crc08_ProcessBytes(&test_data[0U],
                     sizeof(test_data),
                     &CrcContext);

  Crc08_Finalize(&CrcContext);

  // The result is 0xDF.
  const uint8_t CrcResult = CrcContext.Crc_Value;

  (void) CrcResult;
}
```

Here, a CRC8 of the ASCII characters 1 to 9 is computed, see also [5]. The expected result is `0xDF`.

17.3 Wrapping the C-Based CRC Library with C++ Classes

In this section we will take the existing C-language CRC library from Sect. 17.2 above and wrap it with C++ classes. Hereby, we focus on a practical case study that imports a non-trivial C library into C++. This is done without modifying the original legacy C code. This provides a class library that enables various CRC calculations that can be used in object-oriented C++. The complete source code for this example can be found in the `chapter17_03` sample project in the companion code.

It is straightforward to wrap the traditional C-language CRC implementations from the previous section in C++ classes. We can start by studying the C-language interface. We might then try to find a way to embody the data structures and procedural subroutines in classes.

The hierarchy of the CRC classes in this example is shown in Fig. 17.1. It is convenient to begin with an abstract base class (Sect. 4.6) that mimics the existing procedural interface. A class called `cpp_crc_base` serves this purpose. The public interface of `cpp_crc_base` is shown below.

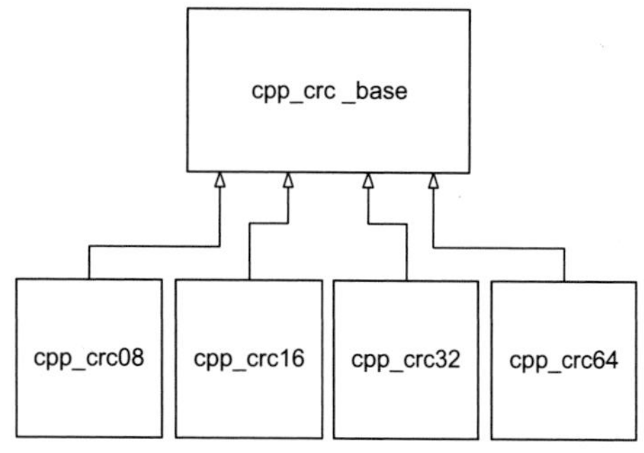

Fig. 17.1 The hierarchical architecture of C++ CRC classes in the `chapter17_03` project is shown

```
class cpp_crc_base
{
public:
  virtual ~cpp_crc_base() = default;

  void initialize();

  void process_bytes(const std::uint8_t*,
                     const std::size_t);

  void finalize();

  cpp_crc_base& operator=(const cpp_crc_base&);

  template<typename value_type>
  value_type get_result();

  template<typename value_type>
  value_type checksum(const std::uint8_t*,
                      const std::size_t);
}
```

The three centrally important functions `initialize()`, `process_bytes()` and `finalize()` are intended to be used for streaming CRC operations on byte sequences of data. The `process_bytes()` subroutine handles successive data chunks, without the need for re-initialization. Note also that `process_bytes()` does not finalize the checksum.

The template function `checksum()` provides a composite function. It will, with just one single subroutine call, perform initialization, byte processing and finalization to compute the CRC of a single data packet.

Classes corresponding to the four types of AUTOSAR CRCs are derived from `cpp_crc_base`. The public interface of the 64-bit version, for instance, is shown below.

```
class cpp_crc64 final : public cpp_crc_base
{
public:
  cpp_crc64();

  cpp_crc64(const cpp_crc64&);

  virtual ~cpp_crc64() = default;

  // ...
};
```

With this straightforward class hierarchy, it is possible to initialize and carry out CRC calculations on byte streams of data in various situations of microcontroller programming. In the application layer, a container of base class pointers is used to calculate and test four checksums in widths of 8, 16, 32 and 64 bits. The standard check of the CRC of the ASCII digits 1 through 9 (in other words `0x31...0x39`) is used.[3]

The inner loop of the application task performing the CRCs uses `std::for_each` from the STL's `<algorithm>` to carry out the checksums. The object-oriented interface of the abstract base class is called by way of the virtual function mechanism. In particular,

```
// Calculate and verify the 8-bit, 16-bit,
// 32-bit and 64-bit CRC.

std::for_each(checksums.begin(),
              checksums.end(),
              [](local_crc_base_type* my_crc)
              {
                // ...

                my_crc->initialize();

                my_crc->process_bytes(...);

                my_crc->finalize();

                // ...
              });
```

[3]See also Sect. 6.1 for a similar CRC32 measurement.

See the companion code of the chapter17_03 example for all details. This project has been verified with GCC 7.2.0 [4] using C++17.

An extension of this example called chapter17_03a is provided in the companion code. This project distributes the work of the CRC calculations over multiple time slices of a task in a multitasking environment. A straightforward state machine manages the temporal distribution of the CRC calculations.[4]

17.4 Return to Investigations of Efficiency and Optimization

We will now consider a CPU run-time measurement of the CRC calculations from the previous example. The measurement uses a microcontroller I/O port and a digital oscilloscope in accordance with the method of Sect. 9.6.

This run-time measurement has been integrated in the chapter17_03 example project. The measured runtimes (and also the code sizes) for each CRC are summarized in Table 17.2.[5] The trend is clear from the table. The code sizes and runtimes increase based on the bit width of the CRC, which is the expected tendency.

It is quite interesting to compare the efficiency characteristics of the CRC32 / -AUTOSAR calculation with those obtained for the CRC32 / MPEG-2 calculation shown previously in Sect. 6.1. These are summarized in Table 17.3. Although both

Table 17.2 The code sizes and runtimes for the AUTOSAR CRCs [1] on our target with the 8-bit microcontroller are listed. GCC 7.2.0 with optimization level -O2 has been used

CRC name	Code size CRC [byte]	Runtime CRC(0x31 ... 0x39) [µs]
CRC8/AUTOSAR	300	15
CRC16/CCITT-false	600	20
CRC32/AUTOSAR	1,200	30
CRC64/XZ	2,300	90

Table 17.3 The efficiency characteristics of CRC32/AUTOSAR (chapter17_03 example) and CRC32/MPEG-2 (Sect. 6.1) on our target with the 8-bit microcontroller are listed. GCC 7.2.0 with optimization level -O2 has been used

CRC name	Algorithm	Code size [byte]	Runtime CRC(0x31 ... 0x39) [µs]
CRC32/AUTOSAR	Table[256], 8-bit	1,200	30
CRC32/MPEG-2	Table[16], 4-bit	320	300

[4]The calculations in this example are only 9 bytes in length. The advantages of this kind of distribution using a multitasking state machine come into play when large byte streams of kilobytes or even megabytes need to be performed.

[5]For these measurements we are using our target with the 8-bit microcontroller and GCC 7.2.0.

CRCs are similar and have the same basic bit-complexity of 32 bits, the runtime values and code sizes are quite different.

This is because a larger data table featuring 256 entries and an algorithm that uses full 8-bit byte-wise data processing have been employed for the implementation of CRC32 / AUTOSAR, whereas a data table having only 16 entries and a data processing algorithm based on 4-bit nibbles have been used for CRC32 / MPEG-2.

On our target with the 8-bit microcontroller, the use of the larger data table combined with the faster byte-wise algorithm requires more storage but results in shorter runtime.[6] As described in Sect. 6.1, this is a common tradeoff (i.e., optimization of space versus speed) that arises often and recurrently in real-time embedded C++ programming.

References

1. AUTOSAR, *Automotive Open System Architecture* (2017). http://www.autosar.org
2. AUTOSAR, *AUTOSAR Classic Platform Release 4.3* (2017). http://www.autosar.org/standards/classic-platform
3. G. Cook, *CRC RevEng: Catalogue of parametrised CRC algorithms* (2017). http://reveng.sourceforge.net/crc-catalogue
4. Free Software Foundation, *The GNU Compiler Collection Version 7.2.0* (2017). http://gcc.gnu.org
5. Wikipedia, *ASCII* (2017). http://en.wikipedia.org/wiki/ASCII
6. Wikipedia, *Cyclic redundancy check* (2017). http://en.wikipedia.org/wiki/Cyclic_redundancy_check

[6]The increased storage requirement comes predominantly from the table of 256 unsigned 32-bit integers pulling 1, 024 bytes of constant data into program memory.

Chapter 18
Additional Reading

This chapter provides additional references covering background information on C, modern C++ programming, the C++ standard library and STL, C++ coding guidelines, software design, the embedded systems toolchain, and microcontroller software and hardware.

18.1 Literature List

Readers seeking additional information may find the following references helpful. Most of these references have also been mentioned in the previous chapters.

- The specification of the C language in the versions C89, C99 and C11 can be found in [2, 18, 24].
- A detailed documentation of the original C standard library is provided in [43].
- Embedded extensions to C are specified in [23].
- The formal language specifications of C++98, C++03, C++11, C++14 and C++17 are available from ISO [19, 20, 25–27]. ISO-published norms may be prohibitively expensive for hobbyists and students. Cost-free draft versions are available on the Internet and final versions can be found in any good public library.
- Comprehensive information on the C++ core language, object-oriented techniques and effective STL usage can be found in [8, 12, 13, 32, 38, 40, 41, 49].
- A detailed description of the C++ standard library extensions (TR1) can be found in [5]. The TR1 extensions were originally published in [22], and are now predominantly integrated in the C++11 standard [25].
- A well-respected, up-to-date book describing how to use C++11 and C++14 effectively is [39].

C. Kormanyos, *Real-Time C++*, https://doi.org/10.1007/978-3-662-62996-3_18

- A detailed report on C++ performance with particular focus on efficiency for embedded systems is available in [21]. This report also addresses various topics discussed in this book such as the special needs of C++ for embedded systems, space and size considerations in optimization, ROM-ability, hardware interfacing, etc. The effectiveness of C++ for embedded systems is clearly demonstrated herein.
- See [28, 36] for in-depth coverage of the containers and algorithms of the STL.
- C++ templates and template metaprogramming are described in [1, 11, 50], and [50] has been updated for C++11, C++14 and C++17 in [51].
- In [48] the authors describe a fundamental relationship between mathematics and generic programming. The code examples make extensive use generic numeric representations and C++11 and template programming.
- For comprehensive information on computational number systems, consult [6, 30, 33].
- See [35] for information on C++ I/O streams. Although not used extensively in this book, I/O streams are useful for PC-based applications. A well-rounded understanding of C++ should, therefore, include basic knowledge of I/O streams.
- The Boost libraries are intended to provide reference implementations potentially suitable for standardization [10]. This makes Boost a great place to track the future development of the C++ language. More information on the Boost libraries can be found in [29, 45].
- C++ coding guidelines can be found in [44].
- A well-respected software design book is [15].
- A comprehensive description of algorithms and computer programming with code samples written in a language-neutral form can be found in [31].[1]
- Microcontroller board design, tools, startup, processor architectures and memory topologies are discussed in [7, 42].
- Extensive and highly practical overviews of electronics with descriptions of electronic components and circuits, layout and production techniques, and much more are available in [17, 46].
- Additional details on the well-known and versatile ARDUINO® open-source microcontroller board project can be found in [3, 37, 47].
- Information on microcontroller programming in C with GNU development tools can be found in [4, 34].
- Programming microcontrollers in C from the ground up with detailed information on software design, architecture and microcontroller peripheral programming is covered in [52].
- A description of mathematical programming in real-time microcontroller environments can be found in [9]. This book includes a comprehensive collection of practical examples and numerous performance analyses.
- Detailed coverage of GNU GCC is available in [16].
- The GCC sources are available at the GNU GCC website [14].

[1]The original reference here refers to a three volume set. At the time of writing the fourth edition of this book, updated work including a fourth volume and additional fascicles is available.

References

1. D. Abrahams, A. Gurtovoy, *C++ Template Metaprogramming: Concepts, Tools and Techniques from Boost and Beyond* (Addison-Wesley, Boston, 2004)
2. ANSI, *ANSI X3.159-1989 American National Standard for Information Systems – Programming Language C* (American National Standard for Information, 1989)
3. ARDUINO®, *ARDUINO®* (2015). http://www.arduino.cc
4. M. Barr, *Programming Embedded Systems with C and GNU Development Tools, Second Edition* (O'Reilly, Sebastopol, 2006)
5. P. Becker, *The C++ Standard Library Extensions: A Tutorial and Reference* (Addison-Wesley, Boston, 2006)
6. R. Brent, P. Zimmermann, *Modern Computer Arithmetic* (Cambridge University Press, Cambridge UK, 2011)
7. J. Catsoulis, *Designing Embedded Hardware* (O'Reilly, Sebastopol, 2005)
8. J.O. Coplien, *Advanced C++ Programming Styles and Idioms* (Addison-Wesley, Boston, 1992)
9. J.W. Crenshaw, *Math Toolkit for Real-Time Programming, First Edition* (CMP Books, Lawrence, 2000)
10. B. Dawes, D. Abrahams, *Boost C++ Libraries* (2015). http://www.boost.org
11. D. Di Gennaro, *Advanced C++ Metaprogramming* (Addison-Wesley, Boston, 2011)
12. B. Eckel, *Thinking in C++ Volume 1: Introduction to Standard C++, Second Edition* (Pearson Prentice Hall, Upper Saddle River, 2000)
13. B. Eckel, *Thinking in C++ Volume 2: Practical Programming* (Pearson Prentice Hall, Upper Saddle River, 2004)
14. Free Software Foundation, *The GNU Compiler Collection Version 4.9.2* (2015). http://gcc.gnu.org
15. E. Gamma, R. Helm, R. Johnson, J. Vlissides, *Design Patterns: Elements of Reusable Object-Oriented Software* (Addison-Wesley, Boston, 1994)
16. W. von Hagen, *The Definitive Guide to GCC* (Apress, Berkeley, 2006)
17. P. Horowitz, W. Hill, *The Art of Electronics, Third Edition, Twelfth Printing* (Cambridge University Press, Cambridge, 2017)
18. ISO/IEC, *ISO/IEC 9899:1999 : Programming Languages – C* (International Organization for Standardization, Geneva, 1999)
19. ISO/IEC, *ISO/IEC 14882:1998 : Programming Languages – C++* (International Organization for Standardization, Geneva, 1998)
20. ISO/IEC, *ISO/IEC 14882:2003 : Programming Languages – C++* (International Organization for Standardization, Geneva, 2003)
21. ISO/IEC, *ISO/IEC TR 18015:2006 : Information Technology – Programming Languages, Their Environments and System Software Interfaces – Technical Report on C++ Performance* (International Organization for Standardization, Geneva, 2006)
22. ISO/IEC, *ISO/IEC TR 19768:2007 : Information Technology – Programming Languages – Technical Report on C++ Library Extensions* (International Organization for Standardization, Geneva, 2007)
23. ISO/IEC, *ISO/IEC TR 18037:2008 : Programming Languages – C – Extensions to Support Embedded Processors* (International Organization for Standardization, Geneva, 2008)
24. ISO/IEC, *ISO/IEC 9899:2011 : Programming Languages – C* (International Organization for Standardization, Geneva, 2011)
25. ISO/IEC, *ISO/IEC 14882:2011 : Information Technology – Programming Languages – C++* (International Organization for Standardization, Geneva, 2011)
26. ISO/IEC, *ISO/IEC 14882:2014 : Information Technology – Programming Languages – C++* (International Organization for Standardization, Geneva, 2014)
27. ISO/IEC, *ISO/IEC 14882:2017 : Programming Languages – C++* (International Organization for Standardization, Geneva, 2017)

28. N.M. Josuttis, *The C++ Standard Library: A Tutorial and Reference, Second Edition.* (Addison-Wesley, Boston, 2011)
29. B. Karlsson, *Beyond the C++ Standard Library: An Introduction to Boost* (Addison-Wesley, Boston, 2005)
30. R.T. Kneusel, *Numbers and Computers, Second Edition* (Springer International Publishing, Cham Switzerland, 2017)
31. D.E. Knuth, *The Art of Computer Programming Volumes 1–3, Third Edition* (Addison-Wesley, Boston, 1998)
32. A. Koenig, B.E. Moo, *Accelerated C++: Practical Programming by Example* (Addison-Wesley, Boston, 2000)
33. P. Kornerup, D.W. Matula, *Finite Precision Number Systems and Arithmetic* (Cambridge University Press, Cambridge UK, 2010)
34. J. LaBrosse, *Embedded Systems Building Blocks: Complete and Ready-to-Use Modules in C* (CMP Books, Lawrence, 1999)
35. A. Langer, K. Kreft, *Standard C++ I/O Streams and Locales: Advanced Programmer's Guide and Reference* (Addison-Wesley, Boston, 2008)
36. R. Lischner, *STL Pocket Reference* (O'Reilly, Sebastopol, 2004)
37. M. Margolis, *ARDUINO® Cookbook, Second Edition* (O'Reilly, Sebastopol, 2011)
38. S. Meyers, *Effective C++: 55 Specific Ways to Improve Your Programs and Designs, Third Edition* (Addison-Wesley, Boston, 2005)
39. S. Meyers, *Effective Modern C++: 42 Specific Ways to Improve Your Use of C++11 and C++14* (O'Reilly, Sebastopol, 2014)
40. S. Meyers, *Effective STL: 50 Specific Ways to Improve Your Use of the Standard Template Library* (Addison-Wesley, Boston, 2001)
41. S. Meyers, *More Effective C++: 35 New Ways to Improve Your Programs and Designs* (Addison-Wesley, Boston, 1996)
42. T. Noergaard, *Embedded Systems Architecture: A Comprehensive Guide for Engineers and Programmers* (Newnes Publishing, Burlington, 2005)
43. P.J. Plauger, *The Standard C Library* (Prentice Hall P T R, Englewood Cliffs, 1992)
44. Programming Research Ltd., *High Integrity C++ Coding Standard Version 4.0* (2015). http://www.codingstandard.com/HICPPCM/index.html
45. B. Schäling, *The Boost C++ Libraries* (XML Press, Laguna Hills, 2011)
46. P. Scherz, S. Monk, *Practical Electronics for Inventors, Fourth Edition* (McGraw Hill Education, New York, 2016)
47. M. Schmidt, *ARDUINO®: A Quick-Start Guide* (Pragmatic Programmers, Raleigh, 2011)
48. A.A. Stepanov, D.E. Rose, *From Mathematics to Generic Programming* (Addison-Wesley, Boston, 2014)
49. B. Stroustrup, *The C++ Programming Language — Fourth Edition* (Addison-Wesley, Upper Saddle River, NJ, 2013)
50. D. Vandevoorde, N.M. Josuttis, *C++ Templates: The Complete Guide* (Addison-Wesley, Boston, 2003)
51. D. Vandevoorde, N.M. Josuttis, D. Gregor, *C++ Templates: The Complete Guide, Second Edition* (Addison-Wesley Professional, Boston, 2017)
52. E. White, *Making Embedded Systems: Design Patterns for Great Software* (O'Reilly, Sebastopol, 2011)

Appendix A
A Tutorial for Real-Time C++

This appendix presents a short tutorial on C++. It is not intended to be a complete language tutorial, but rather a brief introduction to the most important parts of C++ for programming real-time embedded systems.

A.1 C++ Cast Operators

C++ has four template cast operators. The code below, for instance, uses the **static_cast** operator to cast from **float** to **int**.

```
// appendix0a_01-001_static_cast.cpp

float f = 3.1415926535'8979323846'264338328F;

// The value of n is 3.
int n = static_cast<int>(f);
```

The following code sequence uses the **reinterpret_cast** operator to set bit-5 in the microcontroller port register portb.

```
// appendix0a_01-002_reinterpret_cast.cpp

// The address of portb is 0x25.
constexpr std::uint8_t portb = UINT8_C(0x25);
```


C. Kormanyos, *Real-Time C++*, https://doi.org/10.1007/978-3-662-62996-3

```
// Cast std::uint8_t to std::uint8_t*.
volatile std::uint8_t* pb =
  reinterpret_cast<volatile std::uint8_t*>(portb);

// Set portb.5.
*pb |= UINT8_C(0x20);
```

The **reinterpret_cast** operator can be considered non-portable because it is capable of converting seemingly unrelated types such as the integral value of an address to an address pointer. For a detailed description of potential concerns associated with **reinterpret_cast**, see Eckel [1], Chap. 3, in the subsection on **reinterpret_cast**. When used sparingly for low-level operations such as direct memory access to registers in microcontroller programming, however, **reinterpret_cast** can be considered safe and appropriate.

This book limits its use of cast operations predominantly to the **static_cast** and **reinterpret_cast** cast operators. C++ also offers the **dynamic_cast** and **const_cast** operators. The **dynamic_cast** operator can be used to convert pointers and references, usually within the context of a class hierarchy. Dynamic casting may perform a costly but robust runtime check to ensure that the result of the cast is valid. The **const_cast** operator can change the *constant* or *volatile* qualification of an object by either setting or removing its **const** or **volatile** attribute.

A.2 Uniform Initialization Syntax

C++ has a syntax for fully uniform type initialization that works on any object. It was introduced with C++11. Uniform initialization syntax can be used alongside traditional constructor initialization with parentheses and initialization with **operator**= alike.

Uniform initialization syntax uses curly braces to hold the initial values. The code below, for instance, initializes built-in types with uniform initialization syntax.

```
// appendix0a_02-001_uniform_initialization.cpp

int n { 123 };

float f { 3.1415926535'8979323846F };
```

Aggregate types can also be initialized with uniform initialization syntax. The code below initializes a structure with two data members.

```
// appendix0a_02-002_uniform_initialization.cpp

struct my_struct
{
  int   my_n;
  float my_f;

  my_struct(const int    n = 0,
            const float& f = 0.0F) : my_n(n),
                                     my_f(f) { }
};

my_struct instance
{
  123,                         // Initial value of n.
  3.1415926535'8979323846F // Initial value of f.
};
```

In certain situations the compiler can also deduce the type of an object based on uniform initialization syntax. For example,

```
// appendix0a_02-003_uniform_initialization.cpp

struct my_struct
{
  // ...
};

my_struct function()
{
  // The compiler correctly deduces the return type.
  return
  {
    456,
    0.5772156649'0153286061F
  };
}
```

Uniform initialization syntax can be used in the constructor initialization list of a class type as well as to initialize an instance of a class type. For instance,

```
// appendix0a_02-004_uniform_initialization.cpp

struct point
{
  point(const int x = 0,
        const int y = 0) : my_x{x},
                           my_y{y} { }

  int my_x;
  int my_y;
};

point pt
{
  123,
  456
};
```

In addition, uniform initialization syntax can be used to conveniently initialize STL containers such as `std::array` and `std::vector` (Sect. A.6). Some examples are shown below.

```
// appendix0a_02-005_uniform_initialization.cpp

std::array<int, 3U> a
{
  { 1, 2, 3 }
};

std::vector<char> v
{
  { 'a', 'b', 'c' }
};
```

A.3 Overloading

Function overloading in C++ allows for the creation of several functions with the same name but different types of input and output parameters. For example,

```
// appendix0a_03-001_function_overloading.cpp

// The area of a rectangle.
float area(const float& length,
           const float& width)
{
  return length * width;
}

// The area of a circle.
float area(const float& radius)
{
  constexpr float pi = 3.1415926535'8979323846F;

  return (pi * radius) * radius;
}
```

Global functions and local functions as well as class member functions can be overloaded. It is essential, however, not to confuse class member overloading with dynamic polymorphism and the runtime virtual function mechanism, described in Sect. 4.4.

A.4 Compile-Time Assert

The **static_assert** facility checks a constant expression at compile time. The syntax of **static_assert** is

```
// appendix0a_04-001_static_assert.cpp

static_assert(expression, message);
```

Here, `expression` is a condition to be checked by the compiler and `message` contains potentially useful diagnostic text. If the result of `expression` tests **true**, then **static_assert** does nothing. Compilation continues unabatedly. If the result of `expression` tests **false**, then a compiler error ensues and the `message` text is shown like a regular compiler error.

static_assert can be used to perform compile-time diagnostics. This can be convenient for checking platform-specific requirements. For example,

```
// appendix0a_04-002_static_assert.cpp

constexpr unsigned int version = 3U;

// Print error message if version is less than 2.
static_assert(version >= 2U, "Version is too low!");
```

In this example, **static_assert** ensures that `version` is 2 or higher and issues a compiler error if not.

C++17 has made the error text in **static_assert** optional. A default text is provided if needed. This makes it possible to use **static_assert** without providing an explicit error message. For instance,

```
// appendix0a_04-003_static_assert.cpp

constexpr unsigned int version = 3U;

// Print default error message if version is not 3.
static_assert(version == 3U);
```

A.5 Numeric Limits

The C++ standard library supports numeric limits of built-in types in its `<limits>` header. The `<limits>` library provides the `std::numeric_limits` template and provides specializations for both built-in floating-point and integer types as well as **bool**. The member variable `is_specialized` is **true** for a specialization of `std::numeric_limits`.

The synopsis of the `std::numeric_limits` template class is shown below.

```
// appendix0a_05-001_numeric_limits.cpp

namespace std
{
  template<class T>
  class numeric_limits
  {
  public:
```

```
    static constexpr bool is_specialized = false;
    static constexpr T min    () { return T(); }
    static constexpr T max    () { return T(); }
    static constexpr T lowest() { return T(); }

    static constexpr int digits       = 0;
    static constexpr int digits10     = 0;
    static constexpr int max_digits10 = 0;
    static constexpr bool is_signed   = false;
    static constexpr bool is_integer  = false;
    static constexpr bool is_exact    = false;
    static constexpr int radix        = 0;
    static constexpr T epsilon()     { return T(); }
    static constexpr T round_error() { return T(); }

    static constexpr int min_exponent   = 0;
    static constexpr int min_exponent10 = 0;
    static constexpr int max_exponent   = 0;
    static constexpr int max_exponent10 = 0;

    static constexpr bool has_infinity      = false;
    static constexpr bool has_quiet_NaN     = false;
    static constexpr bool has_signaling_NaN = false;
    static constexpr float_denorm_style has_denorm
      = denorm_absent;
    static constexpr bool has_denorm_loss = false;
    static constexpr T infinity     () { return T(); }
    static constexpr T quiet_NaN    () { return T(); }
    static constexpr T signaling_NaN() { return T(); }
    static constexpr T denorm_min   () { return T(); }

    static constexpr bool is_iec559  = false;
    static constexpr bool is_bounded = false;
    static constexpr bool is_modulo  = false;
    static constexpr bool traps      = false;
    static constexpr bool tinyness_before = false;
    static constexpr float_round_style round_style
      = round_toward_zero;
  };
}
```

The specialization of `std::numeric_limits` for **int** on a platform with 32-bit **int**, for example, might be implemented as follows.

```
// appendix0a_05-001_numeric_limits.cpp

namespace std
{
  template<>
  class numeric_limits<int>
  {
  public:
    static constexpr bool is_specialized = true;

    static constexpr int min() { return 0; }
    static constexpr int max()
      { return +2147483647; }
    static constexpr int lowest()
      { return -2147483648; }

    static constexpr int digits       = 32;
    static constexpr int digits10     =  9;
    static constexpr int max_digits10 =  9;
    static constexpr bool is_signed   = false;
    static constexpr bool is_integer  = true;
    static constexpr bool is_exact    = true;
    static constexpr int radix        =  2;
    static constexpr int epsilon() { return 0; }
    static constexpr int round_error()
      { return 0; }

    static constexpr int min_exponent   = 0;
    static constexpr int min_exponent10 = 0;
    static constexpr int max_exponent   = 0;
    static constexpr int max_exponent10 = 0;

    static constexpr bool has_infinity      = false;
    static constexpr bool has_quiet_NaN     = false;
    static constexpr bool has_signaling_NaN = false;
    static constexpr float_denorm_style has_denorm
      = denorm_absent;
    static constexpr bool has_denorm_loss = false;
    static constexpr int infinity () { return 0; }
    static constexpr int quiet_NaN() { return 0; }
```

```
    static constexpr int signaling_NaN()
      { return 0; }
    static constexpr int denorm_min() { return 0; }

    static constexpr bool is_iec559        = false;
    static constexpr bool is_bounded       = false;
    static constexpr bool is_modulo        = false;
    static constexpr bool traps            = false;
    static constexpr bool tinyness_before = false;
    static constexpr float_round_style round_style
      = round_toward_zero;
  };
}
```

The `std::numeric_limits` templates allow the programmer to query information about the numeric limits of built-in types. For example,

```
// appendix0a_05-001_numeric_limits.cpp

constexpr int n_max =
  std::numeric_limits<int>::max();

constexpr int n_min =
  std::numeric_limits<int>::max();

constexpr int n_low =
  std::numeric_limits<int>::lowest();
```

Numeric limits can be conveniently used in other templates. For example,

```
// appendix0a_05-002_numeric_limits.cpp

template<typename unsigned_type>
struct hi_bit
{
  // The bit-position of the high bit.
  static constexpr int bpos
    = std::numeric_limits<unsigned_type>::digits - 1;

  // The value of the type with the high-bit set.
  static constexpr unsigned_type value
    = static_cast<unsigned_type>(1) << bpos;
};
```

Consider, for example, the scalable template structure `hi_bit` shown below. This template structure can be used to generate compile-time constant values. In particular,

```
// appendix0a_05-002_numeric_limits.cpp

constexpr std::uint8_t hi08 =
  hi_bit<std::uint8_t>::value;   // (1 <<  7)

constexpr std::uint16_t hi16 =
  hi_bit<std::uint16_t>::value; // (1 << 15)

constexpr std::uint32_t hi32 =
  hi_bit<std::uint32_t>::value; // (1 << 31)

constexpr std::uint64_t hi64 =
  hi_bit<std::uint64_t>::value; // (1 << 63)
```

Specializations of `std::numeric_limits` can also be written to provide information about the numeric limits of user-defined types.

A.6 STL Containers

The C++ standard library has a collection of *container* types in its STL. Containers store multiple elements in a single object. There are various kinds of containers in the STL. Some are optimized for fast random access, others for fast insertion and deletion, etc. The choice of which container to use depends on the programming situation at hand.

The most prevalent STL containers appearing in this book are the standard sequential containers:

- `std::array` is a fixed-length sequential array aligned in memory.
- `std::vector` is similar to `std::array`. The `std::vector` container, however, does not have fixed length. Instead, a vector has a size that can be dynamically changed at any time during its lifetime. The `std::vector` container is designed for fast random access at any index within its range.
- `std::deque` is a double-ended queue. It is designed for fast insertion and deletion at the front and back ends.
- `std::list` is a sequence that can be bidirectionally traversed, but lacks random access. The `std::list` container supports fast insertion and deletion anywhere in the sequence.
- `std::forward_list` is like `std::list`, but it can only be traversed in the forward direction.

- std::basic_string, std::string and std::wstring are used to store character-based sequences (i.e., strings). Even though strings do not fulfill all the formal requirements for sequential STL containers, many programmers think of strings as sequential containers.

The STL also includes associative containers such as std::set, std::multiset, std::map, and std::multimap. Associative containers are not sequentially ordered but rather use an internal mapping scheme such as lookup with a key-and-value mechanism.

The STL also includes a collection of standard adapters such as std::stack, std::queue and std::priority_queue. These provide different interfaces by adapting the functionality of existing standard sequential containers.

STL containers are templated, meaning they have strong generic character. Containers have various constructors, a destructor and a selection of member functions. Using STL containers is straightforward. For example,

```
// appendix0a_06-001_stl_containers.cpp

#include <vector>

void do_something()
{
  // Create v with three elements having value 0.
  std::vector<int> v(3U, 0);

  // Set the values in v to (1,2,3).
  v[0U] = 1;
  v[1U] = 2;
  v[2U] = 3;

  // The initial size is 3.
  std::vector<int>::size_type s = v.size();

  v.push_back(4);

  // The size is now 4.
  s = v.size();

  int x0 = v.at(0U); // Value of x0 is 1.
  int x3 = v.back(); // Value of x3 is 4.
```

```
  // Copy constructor from another vector.
  std::vector<int> v2(v);

  // Constructor from other input iterators.
  std::vector<int> v3(v.begin(), v.end());

  // Support for operator=().
  std::vector<int> v4 = v;
}
```

This code creates a vector of integers, an `std::vector<int>`, called `v`. The vector `v` is initially created with three elements set to zero. The three elements are subsequently set to (1,2,3) using the random-access index operator (**`operator`**`[]`). A fourth element with a value of 4 is *pushed back* onto the back end of the vector using the member function `push_back()`. The code sample also illustrates some of `std::vector`'s other convenient methods such as `size()`, `at()` and `back()`.

Containers can be copy constructed, created from another sequence of iterators and copy assigned. Additional member functions of containers include other access functions and sequence operations such as insertion, assignment, etc. See [5, 7] for complete documentation of containers and their member functions.

Template containers use member type definitions to define common member types. An example is `std::vector`'s `size_type`, shown above. Other common member types of containers include iterator types, pointer types, reference types and a value type. Again, consult [5, 7] for complete documentation of these.

STL containers are useful for embedded systems programming and are used extensively in this book and its companion code. Containers facilitate program organization and data localization. Containers of base class pointers or references allow for powerful sequential polymorphism. Containers are particularly useful in combination with STL algorithms (Sect. A.8).

A.7 STL Iterators

An *iterator* is an object designed for traversing through the elements of sequential containers and accessing their values. Iterators can be used to read and write the elements of standard STL containers. In particular, each standard STL container facilitates manipulation of its elements via iterators by providing dedicated iterator types and standardized iterator functions such as `begin()` and `end()`. For example,

```
// appendix0a_07-001_stl_iterators.cpp

#include <vector>

void do_something()
{
  // Set v to (1,2,3).
  std::vector<int> v( { 1, 2, 3 } );

  // Declare an iterator for std::vector<int>.
  std::vector<int>::iterator it;

  // Add 5 to each element in v.
  for(it = v.begin(); it != v.end(); ++it)
  {
    *it += 5;
  }

  // Now v is (6,7,8).
}
```

This code uses `std::vector`'s `iterator` type to walk through `v` in the range from `v.begin()` to the element just before `v.end()`. The code in the loop adds 5 to each individual element in `v`.

An iterator pair that delimits a range in a sequence from `First` to `Last` is denoted by

$$\left[\texttt{First, Last}\right), \tag{A.1}$$

where established convention mandates that `First` points to the first element in the sequence and `Last` points to the element that is 1 increment past the final element. The STL's *standard algorithms* (Sect. A.8) use this convention. Using this convention consistently ensures compatibility with the STL and other code. The code sample below uses a range of input iterators with the `std::copy()` function from `<algorithm>`.

```
// appendix0a_07-002_stl_iterators.cpp

#include <algorithm>
#include <array>
#include <vector>

void do_something()
```

```
{
  // Initialized src with (101, 101, 101).
  const std::vector<int> src(3U, 101);

  // Default-initialized dst.
  std::array<int, 3U> dst = {{ }};

  // Copy from vector src to array dst.
  // dst now also contains (101, 101, 101).
  std::copy(src.begin(), src.end(), dst.begin());
}
```

All iterators support incrementing (++) to advance the iterator to the next element in the sequence. Some STL iterators support decrementing (--) to lower the iterator to the previous element. In general, the *pre*-increment and *pre*-decrement forms of (++) and (--) are more efficient than the *post*-increment and *post*-decrement forms. Many programmers, therefore, preferentially use the *pre*-forms in situations for which *pre* and *post* are functionally identical. All STL iterators use the dereferencing operator (*) or the member selection operator (->) for element access.

C++ has several categories of iterators including (among others) forward iterators, bidirectional iterators and random access iterators.

There is a clear distinction between *constant* iterators and *non-constant* iterators. In particular, constant iterators are limited to read-only access. Non-constant iterators can read and write container elements.

```
// appendix0a_07-003_stl_iterators.cpp

#include <array>

void do_something()
{
  using container_type = std::array<int, 3U>;

  using const_iterator_type =
    typename container_type::const_iterator;

  using iterator_type =
    typename container_type::iterator;

  container_type cnt = {{ 1, 2, 3 }};

  iterator_type nonconst_iterator =
    cnt.begin();
```

```
  const_iterator_type const_iterator1 =
    cnt.begin();

  const_iterator_type const_iterator2 =
    cnt.cbegin();

  // Write via non-constant iterator: OK.
  *(nonconst_iterator) = 5;

  // Read via constant iterator: OK.
  const int n1 = *const_iterator1; // OK.
  const int n2 = *const_iterator2; // OK.

  // Write via constant iterator: Error.
  *(const_iterator1) = 5;

  // Write via constant iterator: Error!
  *(const_iterator2) = 5;
}
```

The "c" in `cbegin()` emphasizes that the iterator iterates over the container elements in a *constant* way, as in `const_iterator`. Some special container member iterator functions such as `begin()` and `end()` are overridden, having both constant as well as non-constant versions. Others like `cbegin()` and `cend()` are solely constant. The STL has several iterator classes that can be used standalone or as base classes for custom iterators. The standard iterator classes are defined in `<iterator>`.

A.8 STL Algorithms

The STL has an extensive collection of template algorithms specifically designed to operate on a range of iterators in a generic way. Most of the standard algorithms are defined in `<algorithm>` and some others are defined in `<numeric>` and `<memory>`.

STL algorithms are highly versatile because they can be used generically with any kind of iterator—even with regular pointers. The standard algorithms can simplify many common coding situations by transferring program complexity from the user code to the STL. More information on STL algorithms can be found in [2, 5, 7].

There are several categories of algorithms including:

- non-modifying sequence operations like `std::all_of()`, `std::count()`, `std::for_each()`, `std::search()`, etc.,
- mutating sequence operations that modify the elements in the range including algorithms such as `std::copy()`, `std::move()`, `std::fill()` and the like,
- sorting algorithms,
- binary search algorithms operating on sorted ranges,
- merge operations that act on sorted ranges,
- heap operations,
- and comparison operations including algorithms such as the min/max functions `std::min()` and `std::max()` and the generalized alphabetical compare algorithm `std::lexicographical_compare()`.

A typical function prototype of an STL algorithm is shown below.

```
// appendix0a_08-001_stl_algorithms.cpp

namespace std
{
  template<typename iterator_type,
           typename function_type>
  function_type for_each(iterator_type first,
                         iterator_type last,
                         function_type function);
}
```

This is the function prototype of `std::for_each()`, which was also shown in Sect. 5.8. The `std::for_each()` algorithm applies its function parameter (`function`) to each element in the range [`first, last`).

We will now present several examples showing how to use STL algorithms.

```
// appendix0a_08-002_stl_algorithms.cpp

#include <algorithm>
#include <vector>

void add_five(int& elem)
{
  elem += 5;
}
```

```
void do_something()
{
  // Set v to (1,2,3).
  std::vector<int> v(3U);

  v[0U] = 1;
  v[1U] = 2;
  v[2U] = 3;

  // Add 5 to each element in v, giving (6,7,8).
  std::for_each(v.begin(), v.end(), add_five);
}
```

In this example, the `add_five()` subroutine is called for each element in the range [`v.begin()`, `v.end()`). An algorithm's function parameter can be a function with static linkage that has non-subroutine-local scope.

It is also possible to use a dedicated class type for an algorithm's function parameter. This is called a *functor*, or a function object. In order to work properly, a functor must support the function call operator, **`operator`**`()`. Dedicated function objects incur overhead. It only makes sense to use one if its advantages (i.e., encapsulation, data localization and reduction of complexity) justify its costs.

An example using a *function object* in the form of a C++ **`struct`** is shown below. Also in this code sample, 5 is added to each element in `v` using `std::-for_each()`.

```
// appendix0a_08-003_stl_algorithms.cpp

#include <algorithm>
#include <vector>

struct add_five
{
  add_five() { }

  // ...

  void operator()(int& elem) const
  {
    elem += 5;
  }
};
```

```
void do_something()
{
  std::vector<int> v(3U);

  // Set v to (1,2,3).
  v[0U] = 1;
  v[1U] = 2;
  v[2U] = 3;

  std::for_each(v.begin(), v.end(), add_five());

  // Now v is (6,7,8).
}
```

Algorithms can use a so-called *lambda expression* (Sect. A.9) for the function object. For example,

```
// appendix0a_08-004_stl_algorithms.cpp

#include <algorithm>
#include <vector>

void do_something()
{
  // Set v to (1,2,3).
  std::vector<int> v(3U);

  v[0U] = 1;
  v[1U] = 2;
  v[2U] = 3;

  // Add 5 to each element in v, giving (6,7,8).
  std::for_each(v.begin(),
                v.end(),
                [](int& elem)
                {
                  elem += 5;
                });
}
```

Lambda expressions are efficient and elegant when used with algorithms because they integrate the entire functionality of the function object within the algorithm's call parameters. This also facilitates compiler optimization, see Sect. 6.18.

To complete the examples in this section, we will briefly look ahead to Sect. A.10 and initialize the vector with an `std::initializer_list`.

```
// appendix0a_08-005_stl_algorithms.cpp

#include <algorithm>
#include <initializer_list>
#include <vector>

void do_something()
{
  // Set v to (1,2,3).
  std::vector<int> v( { 1, 2, 3 } );

  // Add 5 to each element in v, giving (6,7,8).
  std::for_each(v.begin(),
                v.end(),
                [](int& elem)
                {
                  elem += 5;
                });
}
```

In this coding example, the combined use of a standard algorithm, a lambda expression and an initializer list provides for a high degree of coding efficiency and performance in C++.

There are *many* algorithms in the STL and most developers do not rigorously maintain a complete mental list of all available algorithms and in which situations to use them. The most important things to remember about the standard algorithms are that there even *are* standard algorithms in the first place and where to find help about them, for example, with help functions, additional literature, etc.

A.9 Lambda Expressions

A *lambda expression* is an anonymous function that has a body but does not have a name. Lambda expressions are stylistically eloquent and can be optimized particularly well when used with the standard algorithms of the STL.

A C++ lambda expression has the form shown below [8].

```
[capture](arguments) -> return-type { body }
```

We have already used lambda expressions with STL algorithms previously in this book. Lambda expressions can also be used as standalone function objects.

The lambda expression shown below, for example, computes the **float** value of the hypotenuse,

$$h = \sqrt{x^2 + y^2}\,. \tag{A.2}$$

```
// appendix0a_09-001_lambda_expressions.cpp

#include <cmath>

void do_something()
{
  const float x = 3.0F;
  const float y = 4.0F;

  // Capture x and y by reference.
  // The lambda expression has no input parameters.
  // The lambda expression returns the float value
  // of the hypotenuse, h.

  // The value of h is 5.
  const float h =
    [&x, &y]() -> float
    {
      return std::sqrt((x * x) + (y * y));
    }();
}
```

The local variables `x` and `y` are captured by reference. The body of the anonymous function is implemented within the scope of the curly braces. The trailing set of parentheses after the closing curly brace effects the function call.

A.10 Initializer Lists

C++11 added several useful template container classes to the STL. One of these is `std::initializer_list`. An initializer list is a sequential list of constant objects or values. Elements in an initializer list must be type-identical or type-convertible. STL containers can be conveniently initialized with an initializer list. These convenient kinds of initializations were not possible prior to the inclusion of `std::initializer_list` in the STL.

The following code sequences, for example, use `std::initializer_list` to initialize various instances of `std::vector` with compile-time constant values.

```
// appendix0a_10-001_initializer_list.cpp

#include <vector>

using container_type = std::vector<int>;

// Initialization with the assignment operator.
container_type c1 = { 1, 2, 3 };

// Initialization with the constructor.
container_type c2( { 1, 2, 3 } );

// Uniform initialization syntax.
container_type c3 { { 1, 2, 3 } };
```

Functions can accept initializer lists as parameters. In addition, initializer lists support iterators. For example,

```
// appendix0a_10-002_initializer_list.cpp

#include <initializer_list>
#include <numeric>

// Initialize 3 elements in the list.
constexpr std::initializer_list<int> lst
{
  1, 2, 3
};

// The result of the sum is 6.
const int sum = std::accumulate(lst.begin(),
                                lst.end(),
                                0);
```

Initializer lists are quite useful for embedded systems programming because, just like tuples, they provide a way to group objects while incurring low code overhead and shifting the work of the program to compile time. Because their values are potentially compile-time constant, initializer lists can potentially lend themselves very well to inline optimization and template metaprogramming.

A.11 Type Inference and Type Declaration with **auto** and **decltype**

What follows is a note for C and traditional C++ programmers. The meaning of the **auto** keyword drastically changed as C++ evolved from C++03 to C++11 and beyond. The original legacy **auto** keyword was used, in both C as well as C++03 and C++98, as a qualifier for local variables. It was a hint to the compiler to preferentially store a local variable on the stack instead of in a CPU register.

C++11, C++14 and later, however, use the **auto** keyword for automatic compile-time *type inference*. For example,

```
// appendix0a_11-001_type_inference.cpp

// The type of n is int.
auto n = 3;

// The type of u is std::uint8_t.
auto u = std::uint8_t(42U);

// The type of lst is std::initializer_list<int>.
auto lst =
{
  1, 2, 3
};
```

Type inference can reduce the complexity of code. In particular, instead of writing long iterator type names such as this:

```
// appendix0a_11-002_type_inference.cpp

const std::array<int, 3U> a = {{ 1, 2, 3 }};

// Use long type information of const_iterator.
for(std::array<int, 3U>::const_iterator i = a.cbegin();
    i != a.cend();
    ++i)
{
  // ...
}
```

automatic type inference with **auto** can be used in the following way:

```
// appendix0a_11-002_type_inference.cpp

// Use type inference of const_iterator.
for(auto i = a.cbegin(); i != a.cend(); ++i)
{
  // ...
}
```

This can be made even more generic and flexible with the STL's range access template functions `std::cbegin()` and `std::cend()`. See, for example, Sect. 24.6.5 in [4]. In particular,

```
// appendix0a_11-002_type_inference.cpp

// Use type inference of const_iterator,
// and use generic std::cbegin() and std::cend().
for(auto i = std::cbegin(a); i != std::cend(a); ++i)
{
  // ...
}
```

The related keyword `decltype` can be used to determine the underlying type of something that has been previously declared. For instance,

```
// appendix0a_11-003_decltype.cpp

// The type of a is int.
int a = 1;

// The type of b is int.
decltype(a) b = 2;
```

The keywords **auto** and `decltype` can be used effectively in numerous programming situations, in particular generic template programming.

A.12 Range-Based for(:)

C++11 added a simplified range-based **for**(:) short-hand notation for iterating over the elements of a list. This simplified range-based iteration statement allows for easy navigation through a list of elements. For example,

```
// appendix0a_12-001_range_based_for.cpp

// Set v to (1,2,3).
std::vector<char> v =
{
  char(1),
  char(2),
  char(3)
};

// Add 0x30 to each element in v,
// giving (0x31,0x32,0x33).
// Use range-based-for(:).
for(char& c : v)
{
  c += char(0x30);
}
```

This simple loop iterates over every character in `v` and adds 0x30 to each one. Even though range-based-**for**(:) is available in C++11 and beyond, both the traditional syntax of the **for**(;;)-loop as well as the `std::for_each()` algorithm still work and can be used for similar loop activities. The convenient shorthand of the range-based-**for**(:) loop can, however, potentially be more intuitive and terse.

Range-based **for**(:)-loops work for C-style arrays, initializer lists, and any type that has the normal `begin()` and `end()` functions. This includes all of the standard library containers that have `begin()` and `end()`.

A.13 Tuple

A *tuple* is the generalization of an ordered group of objects, such as a pair or a triple, a quadruple, a quin-*tuple*, a sex-*tuple*, etc. While other programming languages such as Python and Perl have had tuples for quite a while, they are relatively new in C++, available with C++11. Tuples are implemented as template classes. The template parameters of a tuple define the number of tuple objects and their types.

Consider, for example, a tuple consisting of three objects, a **float**, a **char** and an **int**. An instance of such a tuple can be created and used as shown below.

```
// appendix0a_13-001_tuple_basics.cpp

#include <tuple>

void do_something()
{
  using tuple_type = std::tuple<float, char, int>;

  // Make a tuple from float, char and int.
  tuple_type t(1.23F, char('a'), 456);

  // Get element 0 of the tuple (1.23F).
  const float f = std::get<0>(t);

  // Get element 1 of the tuple ('a').
  const char c = std::get<1>(t);

  // Get element 2 of the tuple (456).
  int n = std::get<2>(t);

  // Obtain the type of a tuple element.
  using tuple_float_type =
    std::tuple_element<0, tuple_type>::type;

  static_assert(std::is_same<float,
                tuple_float_type>::value);

  // Get the size of the tuple.
  int size = std::tuple_size<tuple_type>::value;
}
```

Tuples can be created and initialized with their constructor using appropriate arguments. The `tuple` implementation also provides a default constructor which uses the default constructors of its respective elements. The Nth element of an ordered tuple or a reference thereto can be retrieved with the template `std::get()` function. STL's `std::tuple_size` wraps the tuple element count by storing the number of elements in its member variable `value`. The `std::tuple_element` template wraps the type of a tuple element. Note in the listing that a convenient type definition has been used in order to avoid typing long and complicated tuple types.

Tuples can be copy assigned with **operator=**. They can also be copy constructed. Copy and assign use member-wise assignment. Copy and assign also require that for each element pair the destination can be converted from the source.

Tuples can be assigned using STL's `std::make_tuple()` facility. For example, the tuple in the listing above could be created with `std::make_tuple()`. In particular,

```
// appendix0a_13-002_tuple_assign.cpp

#include <tuple>

void do_something()
{
  using tuple_type = std::tuple<float, char, int>;

  tuple_type t;

  // Assign the tuple t using std::make_tuple.
  t = std::make_tuple(1.23F, char('a'), 456);
}
```

Tuples can be compared. Comparison functions use relational operators and perform pair-wise comparison. Comparison stops when the first element pair comparison yields **true**.

The code sample below depicts several straightforward copy and compare operations on a `tuple`.

```
// appendix0a_13-003_tuple_comparison.cpp

#include <string>
#include <tuple>

void do_something()
{
  using tuple_type = std::tuple<int, std::string>;

  tuple_type t1(456, "identical");
  tuple_type t2 = t1;
  tuple_type t3(t1);

  bool result;

  result = (t1 == t2);  // true
  result = (t1 == t3);  // true
```

```
  std::get<0>(t2) += 1; // 456 -> 457

  result = (t2 > t1);   // true

  // Now transform the std::string element
  // from "identical" to "xdentical".
  std::get<1>(t3).at(0U) = 'x';

  result = (t3 > t1);   // true
}
```

It is also possible to retrieve an element of a tuple based on its type. Consider the tuple presented above containing elements having type **float**, **char** and **int**.

```
// appendix0a_13-004_tuple_get_by_type.cpp

#include <tuple>

void do_something()
{
  using tuple_type = std::tuple<float, char, int>;

  // Make a tuple of a float, char and an int.
  tuple_type t(1.23F, char('a'), 456);

  // Get element of type float from tuple t.
  const float f = std::get<float>(t);

  // Get element of type char from t.
  const char c = std::get<char>(t);

  // Get element of type int from tuple t.
  const int n = std::get<int>(t);

  // ...
}
```

In this code listing, we extract the elements of the tuple `t` based on their type. This particular functionality of `<tuple>` was specified in C++14.

Tuples are immensely useful because they can group collections of objects together in a single representation. At the same time, tuples incur a minimum of code overhead because tuple elements are partly or completely available at compile-time. In particular, the template facilities `std::get()`, `std::tuple_size` and `std::tuple_element` can be optimized particularly well at compile time. Tuples lend themselves readily to template design and template metaprogramming, see Sect. 5.10.

A.14 Regular Expressions

Support for lexical parsing of regular expressions in C++ is implemented in the `<regex>` library. A complete implementation of `<regex>` involves extensive templates and a significant amount of object code. Therefore, `<regex>` is often too large scale for most microcontroller projects.

Microcontroller programming, however, usually involves other associated PC-based programs and utilities used for a variety of purposes such as manipulating files, automatic code generation, designing specialized language parsers, etc. Lexical parsing with regular expressions can drastically simplify the implementations of these programs. Therefore, the microcontroller programmer should have basic competence with `<regex>`.

Consider a regular expression designed for parsing a composite string composed of three substrings. The first substring is an alphanumeric name including underscores. The second substring is a hexadecimal number. The third substring is a base-10 unsigned integer. For example,

```
_My_Variable123     03FFB004     4
```

A regular expression for parsing this composite string is shown below:

```
// appendix0a_14-001_regex_basics.cpp

const std::regex
rx(  std::string("([_0-9a-zA-Z]+)") // Alnum name.
   + std::string("[[:space:]]+")    // 1+ spaces.
   + std::string("([0-9a-fA-F]+)")  // Hex integer.
   + std::string("[[:space:]]+")    // 1+ spaces.
   + std::string("([0-9]+)"));      // Base-10 int.
```

This regular expression (`rx`) uses POSIX syntax [3]. The `<regex>` library supports several syntaxes, POSIX being the default. The first, third and fifth strings in the definition of the regular expression are enclosed in parentheses. The parentheses indicate a *capture group* of the regular expression. A *capture group* contains an expression which should be *caught*, in other words stored, when checking for a regular expression match.

A program showing how to use this regular expression is shown in the sample code below.

```
// appendix0a_14-001_regex_basics.cpp

#include <algorithm>
#include <iostream>
#include <iterator>
#include <regex>
#include <string>

int main()
{
  const std::regex rx(  std::string("([_0-9a-zA-Z]+)")
                      + std::string("[[:space:]]+")
                      + std::string("([0-9a-fA-F]+)")
                      + std::string("[[:space:]]+")
                      + std::string("([0-9]+)"));

  const std::string str =
    "_My_Variable123    03FFB004    4";

  std::match_results<std::string::const_iterator> mr;

  if(std::regex_match(str, mr, rx))
  {
    std::copy(mr.begin(),
              mr.end(),
              std::ostream_iterator
                <std::string>(std::cout, "\n"));
  }
}
```

The `regex_match()` function is a Boolean subroutine with three input parameters. There are six different overwritten forms of `regex_match()`. The form used in the listing checks if its input string, `str`, identically matches its input regular expression, `rx`. If the regular expression matches, then `regex_match()` returns **`true`**. The match results, `mr`, contain the results of the regular expression match.

The output of the program is:

```
_My_Variable123 03FFB004 4
_My_Variable123
03FFB004
4
```

A successful match has $N + 1$ elements in the match results, where N is the number of capture groups in the regular expression. The 0th match result contains the entire string submitted to the match. In this example, there are four elements in the match results, one for the input string and three for the capture groups.

Regular expressions are templated. For example, `std::regex` is actually a type definition for `std::basic_regex<char>`. Therefore, regular expressions can be used with strings or sequences of other types. In addition, `match_results` are templated and support iterators allowing for convenient manipulation with STL standard algorithms.

Additional information on `std::regex` can be found in [6]. Even though this reference describes the `Boost.Regex` library, it is also applicable here because `std::regex` originates predominantly (with slight variations) from Boost.

A.15 The `<type_traits>` Library

The `<type_traits>` library can be used to find out or modify information about the type of an object. In particular, `<type_traits>` supports numerous useful templates such as `is_arithmetic`, `is_integral`, `is_floating_point`, `is_unsigned`, `is_signed`, `is_void`, `is_assignable`, `is_same`, and others. These utilities can be conveniently and elegantly used to find out (at compile time) useful type information about an object, which can be also helpful in generic programming with templates. The `<type_traits>` library first became available in C++11.

The code sample below, for instance, queries the underlying type of `my_int`, which type defined as `integer_type`. In particular, the sophisticated facilities of `<type_traits>` successfully determine that `integer_type` is an arithmetic signed integral type.

```
// appendix0a_15-001_type_traits.cpp

#include <type_traits>

using integral_type = int;

// Query the characteristics of integral_type.

constexpr bool type_is_arithmetic =
  std::is_arithmetic<integral_type>::value;

constexpr bool type_is_integral =
  std::is_integral<integral_type>::value;

constexpr bool type_is_signed =
  std::is_signed<integral_type>::value;
```

Additional useful templates in <type_traits> can be used to add or remove qualifiers such as **const** and **volatile**. Consider the example below which makes use of the std::remove_volatile template.

```
// appendix0a_15-002_type_traits.cpp

#include <type_traits>

void do_something()
{
// The variable pv is volatile.
volatile int* pv = nullptr;

// Remove the volatile qualifier.
auto pu = std::remove_volatile<int*>::type(pv);

// Verify that the type of pu is not volatile.
// In other words, volatile has been removed.

constexpr bool volatile_has_been_removed =
  (std::is_volatile<decltype(pu)>::value == false);
```

Additional utilities available in the <type_traits> library can be used to enable template code sequences such as declaration of class types, constructors and functions at compile time using std::enable_if. The code below shows the synopsis of an integer_wrap class that implements a trivial wrap of an integral valued member variable, the type of which is **long long**.

```
// appendix0a_15-003_type_traits.cpp

class integer_wrap
{
public:
  integer_wrap(const long long val = 0LL)
    : my_value(val) { }

  long long get_value() const
  {
    return my_value;
  }

private:
  long long my_value;
};
```

The integer_wrap class shown above features a constructor from built-in **long long**. It may, however, be convenient to enable construction of this class from all kinds of built-in integral types such as signed and unsigned versions of **char**, **short**, **int**, **long**, **long long** and the like. Writing all these constructors could be tedious, requiring a significant amount of effort for creating and maintaining the code. This overhead can be reduced by employing compile-time enable via the standard library's std::enable_if template found in <type_traits>.

We will now rework the constructor of the integer_wrap class using a template method for compile-time enable in the code snippet below.

```
// appendix0a_15-004_type_traits.cpp

#include <type_traits>

class integer_wrap
{
public:
  template
  <typename integral_type,
   typename std::enable_if
     <std::is_integral<integral_type>::value>::type* =
        nullptr>
  integer_wrap(const integral_type val = 0)
    : my_value(static_cast<long long>(val)) { }

  long long get_value() const
  {
    return my_value;
  }

private:
  long long my_value;
};
```

The second template parameter uses a somewhat complex compile-time Boolean expression involving std::enable_if and std::is_integral in combination with the default template parameter **nullptr**. This assortment of template parameters enables individual class constructors for all built-in integral types for which the Boolean expression evaluates to **true**. These include built-in integral types such as signed and unsigned versions of **char**, **short**, **int**, **long**, **long long**.

The new constructor of the integer_wrap class, in fact, embodies numerous constructors that the compiler can instantiate for all built-in integral types. This allows construction from, say, **char** to **long long** and all the signed and unsigned integral types in between. For example,

```
// appendix0a_15-004_type_traits.cpp

class integer_wrap
{
  // ...
};

integer_wrap a(char('a'));
integer_wrap u(std::uint16_t(0x5555U));
integer_wrap n(1234);
```

A.16 Using std::any and std::variant

Modern C++ includes several novel additions to the standard library. A very useful one is C++17's `std::any`, which is a template object from the `<any>` library. An instance of `std::any` can be used to store both built-in types as well as objects of *any* kind. The code sample below, for example, creates three instances of `std::any`.

```
// appendix0a_16-001_any_basics.cpp

#include <any>
#include <string>

// Create from int.
std::any ai(42);

// Create from float.
std::any af(1.23F);

// Create from std::string.
std::any as(std::string("hello"));
```

In this code snippet, three instances of `std::any` hold values of type **int**, **float** and `std::string`, respectively. The implementation of `std::any` uses templates for construction and assignment. Initializing an instance of `std::any` with the constructor or with the assignment operator uses automatic template parameter deduction based on the type of the input. So it is not necessary to explicitly provide template parameters when creating an initialized instance of std::any.

Retrieving a value from std::any can be accomplished with the std::any_cast template function. This mandates explicit use of template parameters to extract the value of the underlying type. In particular,

```
// appendix0a_16-001_any_basics.cpp

#include <any>
#include <string>

// Create from int.
std::any ai(42);

// Create from float.
std::any af(1.23F);

// Create from std::string.
std::any as(std::string("hello"));

// Retrieve int value.
int i = std::any_cast<int>(ai);

// Retrieve float value.
float f = std::any_cast<float>(af);

// Retrieve std::string value.
std::string s = std::any_cast<std::string>(as);
```

It is also possible to convert (via assignment operator) any std::any to another std::any. In fact, this even works no matter if the underlying types are the same or not. For instance,

```
// appendix0a_16-002_any_basics.cpp

#include <any>

// Create from int.
std::any ai(42);

// Create from float.
std::any af(1.23F);
```

```
void do_something()
{
  // Assign an std::any holding int
  // to an std::any holding float.
  ai = af;
}
```

It can be convenient to store multiple instances of `std::any` in an STL container. This allows us to operate on instances of `std::any` collected in a single container. The code below, for example, stores three instances of `std::any` in an `std::array` and subsequently manipulates them.

```
// appendix0a_16-003_any_and_stl_container.cpp

#include <any>
#include <algorithm>
#include <array>
#include <string>

void do_something()
{
  // Fill an array with three instances of any.
  const std::array<std::any, 3U> many
  {{
    std::any(42),                      // int
    std::any(1.23F),                   // float
    std::any(std::string("hello"))     // std::string
  }};

  // Use random access on the container elements.
  int n = std::any_cast<int>(many[0U]);

  float f = std::any_cast<float>(many[1U]);

  std::string str =
    std::any_cast<std::string>(many[2U]);

  // Query the container size.
  const std::size_t size = many.size();

  // Iterate in an algorithm
  // and use a member function.
  // 42
  // 1.23
```

```
  // hello
  // 3

  const bool has_many_values =
    std::all_of(many.cbegin(),
                many.cend(),
                [](const std::any& a) -> bool
                {
                  return a.has_value();
                });
}
```

A.17 Structured Binding Declarations

C++17 has introduced structured binding declarations. A structured binding declaration can produce an identifier that refers to an existing object or variable. For instance,

```
// appendix0a_17-001_structured_binding.cpp

// my_array is initialized to {0,1,2}.
unsigned int my_array[3U] = { 0U, 1U, 2U };

auto& [x0, x1, x2] = my_array;

// x0 is 0 and refers to my_array[0U].
// x1 is 1 and refers to my_array[1U].
// x2 is 2 and refers to my_array[2U].

void do_something()
{
  x0 += 5U;
  x1 += 5U;
  x2 += 5U;

  // x0, x1 and x2 have been incremented by 5.
  // This means that my_array is now {5,6,7}.
}
```

In this example, the identifiers `x0`, `x1` and `x2` refer to the elements of `my_array` and are used to modify the original values in the array.

Structured binding declarations can also be convenient for accessing and manipulating the elements in a tuple, see also Sects. 5.11 and A.13.

A.18 Three-Way Comparison

Three-way comparison can be quite useful. The result of three-way comparison can be either less than, equal to or greater than zero. A variety of well-established C-library functions such as `memcmp()` from `<cstring>` or `<string.h>` are based on the principle of three-way comparison.

The so-called *spaceship* operator from C++20 can be used to perform three-way comparison between two built-in types or objects. The spaceship operator is written as the concatenation of the symbols less than, equal to and greater than (**operator**<=>). For instance,

```
#include <compare>

extern std::uint_fast8_t a;
extern std::uint_fast8_t b;

auto result = a <=> b;
```

Here, `result` is a signed value that can treated as less than zero if `a < b`, zero if `a == b` and greater than zero if `a > b`. The `<compare>` header provides the abstract types required by the spaceship operator.

References

1. B. Eckel, *Thinking in C++ Volume 1: Introduction to Standard C++*, 2nd edn. (Pearson Prentice Hall, Upper Saddle River, 2000)
2. B. Eckel, *Thinking in C++ Volume 2: Practical Programming* (Pearson Prentice Hall, Upper Saddle River, 2004)
3. ISO/IEC, *ISO/IEC 9945:2003 : Information Technology – Portable Operating System Interface (POSIX)* (International Organization for Standardization, Geneva, 2003)
4. ISO/IEC, *ISO/IEC 14882:2011 : Information technology – Programming languages – C++* (International Organization for Standardization, Geneva, 2011)
5. N.M. Josuttis, *The C++ Standard Library: A Tutorial and Reference*, 2nd edn. (Addison-Wesley, Boston, 2011)
6. B. Karlsson, *Beyond the C++ Standard Library: An Introduction to Boost* (Addison-Wesley, Boston, 2005)
7. R. Lischner, *STL Pocket Reference* (O'Reilly, Sebastopol, 2004)
8. Wikipedia, *Anonymous Function* (2012). http://en.wikipedia.org/wiki/Anonymous_function

Appendix B
A Robust Real-Time C++ Environment

Real-time programming is characterized by demanding performance, size and safety constraints. This, combined with the large scope of the C++ language and a potentially complex set of development tools, can make the creation of high-quality real-time C++ software a truly challenging endeavor. In the harsh world of real-time C++, the stability of the development environment can contribute to the overall quality of the software as much or even more than the actual coding itself. This chapter discusses various aspects related to the robust real-time C++ environment.

B.1 Addressing the Challenges of Real-Time C++

Microcontroller software is usually cost sensitive, safety critical or both and demands the utmost in efficiency and robustness. The development environment and the executable program usually run on separate systems. In addition, flashing the microcontroller generally uses a connection with a hardware interface for in-system programming (ISP) with an on-chip debugger or an in-circuit emulator (ICE). This can make it particularly difficult to visualize, debug and test microcontroller software.

When addressing the challenges of real-time C++ programming, it may be best to start with a simple project and build up tools, coding competence and a collection of re-usable software components steadily and methodically. The brief checklist below describes some considerations that need to be made when doing real-time C++ programming.

✓ Select the right microcontroller for the application. Consider performance and cost aspects. Decide if the application needs a cost-sensitive 8-bit microcontroller or a more powerful, more expensive 32-bit or 64-bit microcontroller. Try to estimate how much program memory and RAM are needed and select the microcontroller accordingly. If future versions of the application are planned,

C. Kormanyos, *Real-Time C++*, https://doi.org/10.1007/978-3-662-62996-3

it may be advisable to use a scalable microcontroller family that includes pin-compatible chip derivatives accommodating potential extensions of functionality.

✓ Get a microcontroller prototype up and running. Students and hobbyists may be well served with a commercially available microcontroller starter kit including a board, a debug interface and a demo compiler. Using a starter kit can ease the learning curve by providing a functioning set of hardware, software and code examples, all in one package. If working in a production environment, try to ensure that a functioning prototype board is available early in the development cycle.

✓ Obtain a high-quality C++ compiler. Compiler availability can be an issue and successful development mandates that a good C++ compiler is available for the microcontroller. GCC [2] is cost free and known for having a high degree of language standards conformance. Professionally supplied compilers might beat the performance of GCC, particularly for low-level hardware programming requiring intimate knowledge of the microcontroller architecture. At the same time, professionally supplied compilers tend to be prohibitively expensive for students and hobbyists. Those interested in assessing compiler price and performance may want to carry out market research in combination with compiler benchmarks for the domain of the application.

✓ Depending on project necessities, make sure a microcontroller programmer, a simulator, a debugger or an ICE, or several of these are available. If other test and measurement devices such as an oscilloscope or logic analyzer are required, verify that the equipment is available. One should verify that the equipment works and that one has basic knowledge of how to use it, or knows where to find help if not.

✓ Design and use a software architecture (Sect. B.2). The architecture significantly influences the overall quality of the entire software. When doing any robust microcontroller programming in C++, it is essential to use a layered software architecture that shields the application layer from the low-level hardware-specific, non-portable register manipulation code. In this way, application software can be used and re-used, thereby improving portability and localizing the work of switching the microcontroller to the hardware layer.

✓ Establish coding competence. C++ is a rich, multifaceted language. If working alone, try to learn the C++ language as best as possible through independent study. Keep in touch with other programmers and best-practice in the community e.g., via Internet forums, additional literature, etc.

✓ Software reliability can be improved by adhering to established coding guidelines, such as [1]. Conforming to guidelines can be mandatory when working in a professional setting where proving reliability to customers may be required in an assessment or audit situation. When working on projects that demand high reliability, consider using a static syntax checker in addition to the compiler.

✓ Build up a library of re-usable code. Programming microcontrollers in C++ can be a long-term process based on years of effort. Over the course of time, a body of re-usable, portable code can be built up for programming situations that repeatedly arise. Some examples of components that I have collected in my own libraries, and partially in this book, include register manipulation mechanisms (Chap. 7), custom allocators (Chap. 10), timers (Sect. 15.3), multitasking schedulers (Chap. 11), filter functions (Chap. 14), mathematical functions (Chap. 12), convenient utilities (Chap. 15), etc.

B.2 Software Architecture

No matter how small or large a given software may be, it is essential to use a good, properly sized *software architecture*. The architecture may contribute to the overall quality of the software more strongly than any other factor. Programming skill and elegance of implementation alone can only augment software quality, not create it. The combination of solid architecture and competent coding ultimately leads to success in real-time C++.

When working in a project with a documented software architecture, one is not merely programming but engaging in software engineering and system design instead. Metaphorically speaking, software architecture comprises the foundation, floors and walls of the project; the code being the plaster, paint and furniture. In the absence of a stable and robust architecture, even good code will, in time, erode and crumble under its own weight.

Designing a software architecture can start with a simple block diagram of the major software layers and components such as the one shown in Fig. B.1. Initially, this can be a rudimentary hand-sketched diagram. Create the corresponding directories and files and fill them with preliminary namespaces, classes and functions that embody the most important interfaces. At first, classes and functions can be incomplete skeletons. Implementation details can be added later. Try to ensure that names of namespaces, classes, functions, etc. have recognizable associations with the architecture sketch.

Software architecture need not be complicated. A straightforward one with a few clearly defined layers is usually best. Consider, once again, the software architecture

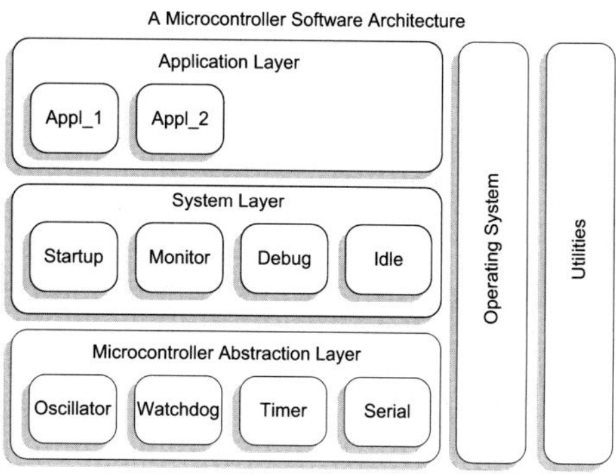

Fig. B.1 A layered microcontroller software architecture is shown

shown in Fig. B.1. This architecture consists of three layers that have successively higher levels of abstraction.

The MCAL contains microcontroller-specific peripheral drivers such as timer, watchdog or communication interfaces. Intermediate system-level software such as startup routines and monitor functions can be implemented in the System Layer. The Application Layer contains high-level application software. Modules in the application layer should be kept entirely portable. The operating system and project utilities can be used by all three layers in the architecture. Over the years, I have had good results with this kind of layered architecture in numerous projects with varying application size.

When developing a software architecture, try to achieve easy-to-understand modularity and object granularity. Avoid overly long files, classes and subroutines. It may take a few iterations until the architecture and functional granularity *feel* right. Time invested in designing software architecture is, however, time spent well because the architecture provides for long-lasting organization in a project that may potentially be worked on for years.

B.3 Establishing and Adhering to Runtime Limits

Microcontroller programming is time critical and things tend to go wrong if the software has unpredictable timing. For example, a late response from a communication attempt might be just as bad as the wrong response, regardless of its content. To address this problem, it can be helpful to establish runtime limits and adhere to them.

This can be done by identifying the priority classes of tasks and interrupts in the system and defining runtime constraints for them. Table B.1, for example, lists potential runtime limits selected for a system with three priority classes: high-priority interrupts, low-priority interrupts and the task-level priority. The runtime constraints are given in a form indicating a typical value representing the design target and a maximum limit which should never be exceeded and only sporadically neared under worst-case load conditions.

When designing an embedded microcontroller system, the most time consuming software processes should be identified up front and designed with a temporal granularity that facilitates an even distribution of the work load. In general, it is poor form to program with blocking calls that engage the CPU for long time spans such as

Table B.1 The runtime limits for a system with three priority classes are shown

Priority class	Design target [μs]	Worst-case maximum [μs]
High-priority interrupts	<10	$\lesssim 25$
Low-priority interrupts	<40	$\lesssim 100$
All tasks	<500	$\lesssim 1000$

hundreds of microseconds or even several milliseconds. It is much better to program short, fast sequences in a multitasking environment that process information or service a state machine quickly and rapidly relinquish control to other processes in the system. Interrupt service routines should be held terse and efficient. Keeping the runtime within the established limits generally leads to a more predictable software with higher quality and reliability.

References

1. Programming Research Ltd., *High Integrity C++ Coding Standard Version 4.0* (2015). http://www.codingstandard.com/HICPPCM/index.html
2. W. von Hagen, *The Definitive Guide to GCC* (Apress, Berkeley, 2006)

Appendix C
Building and Installing GNU GCC Cross Compilers

There are several reasons one might want to build GCC [4], such as to obtain the newest version of the compilers or to enable additional language features or other languages. This appendix provides step-by-step instructions for building a GNU GCC cross compiler for our target with the 8-bit microcontroller. GCC can be most easily built on ∗nix-like systems. In this example, the build is done in MinGW/-MSYS [10] using standard GNU auto-tools configure scripts and make procedures. The methods in this chapter can easily be adapted for building a cross compiler targeted to another microcontroller architecture.

C.1 The GCC Prerequisites

Building GCC has *prerequisites* [5]. This means that certain libraries must be installed and available to the build system before GCC can be built. If any prerequisites are missing, these either need to be installed or built from source before building GCC. At the time of writing this book, the prerequisites for building GCC include:

- GMP [7], the GNU multiprecision library.
- MPFR [6, 12], the GNU multiprecision floating-point library.
- MPC [11], a C library for the multiprecision arithmetic of complex numbers.
- PPL, the Parma Polyhedra Library [1], used for abstract geometrical polyhedron representation.
- Binutils [3], the binary utilities for the cross compiler such as linker, assembler, object dump, C++ name demangler, etc.

The prerequisites for building GCC evolve over time. At the time of writing the second edition of this book, the prerequisites for building GCC include:

- GMP [7], the GNU multiprecision library.
- MPFR [6, 12], the GNU multiprecision floating-point library.

C. Kormanyos, *Real-Time C++*, https://doi.org/10.1007/978-3-662-62996-3

- MPC [11], a C library for the multiprecision arithmetic of complex numbers.
- ISL [9], the integer set library used for manipulating sets of integers. GCC uses ISL for its graphite loop optimizations [5]. Building ISL requires an installed CLooG library [2], another software library used for polyhedron analysis.
- Binutils [3], the binary utilities for the cross compiler such as linker, assembler, object dump, C++ name demangler, etc.

It may seem odd that GCC has prerequisites for such exotic mathematical functions as multiprecision floating-point numbers and geometrical polyhedron representations. The multiprecision functions in GMP, MPFR and MPC are needed by GCC for compile-time calculation of floating-point mathematical expressions. The geometrical polyhedron representations in PPL (or ISL) are used for high-level optimizations including program loop analysis, parallelization and vectorization.

Perhaps the binary utilities should be considered part of the compiler rather than a prerequisite. Here, we will call the binary utilities a prerequisite simply because the build of GCC needs to use them. This, in turn, means that the binary utilities need to be built and installed prior to building GCC.

C.2 Getting Started

Building the GCC prerequisites and GCC can take several hours of manual work. At times, this work can be tedious involving intricate command lines, detailed operating system operations and careful monitoring. It may, therefore, be best to undertake building the GCC prerequisites and GCC only if ample time and peace of mind are available for this kind of endeavor. The process of building, installing and using GCC constitutes a rich topic, see [4, 8].

Sometimes building a GNU cross compiler works. At other times, it does not. There are several reasons why building GCC might fail. The prerequisites might be absent or improperly built. The binary utilities or the compiler sources might be flawed for the particular compiler version and target. Very experienced compiler builders often patch the sources of a new compiler version, thereby correcting minor flaws. The strategy thereby is to integrate the patches in a compiler bug-fix in a later subversion.

Middle-of-the-road compiler builders and users should probably avoid such advanced compiler development as patching the sources. It may, therefore, be necessary to do a bit of trial-and-error work in order to find a combination of prerequisites, binary utilities and a compiler version that harmoniously build together. The components selected in this appendix have been successfully built.

The entire build session including all the prerequisites, the binary utilities and GCC can best be organized within a single root directory. It is not a good idea to perform the build of a given component in its own source tree directory. For each component, therefore, we use two directories, one for the component's source tree and another sibling object directory next to the source tree in which the build is carried out.

We begin by creating a root directory for all the builds. Here, for example, we will use the directory /home/tmp as the root directory for performing the builds.

- Create the directory /home/tmp.

C.3 Building GMP

We will now build GMP version 5.0.5 in MinGW/MSYS.

- cd /home/tmp
- Get the GMP sources and unpack them in /home/tmp.
- Perform the command mkdir objdir-gmp-5.0.5 in order to make the GMP sibling directory.
- cd objdir-gmp-5.0.5

The source tree of GMP should be in the GMP source directory:

```
/home/tmp/gmp-5.0.5
```

We should now be in the GMP sibling object directory:

```
/home/tmp/objdir-gmp-5.0.5
```

In the objdir-gmp-5.0.5 GMP sibling object directory, configure GMP with the following command:

```
../gmp-5.0.5/configure --prefix=/usr/local \
--build=i686-pc-mingw32 --disable-shared \
--enable-static --enable-cxx CPPFLAGS="-fexceptions"
```

This configuration defines the characteristics that will be used when building GMP. It defines the prefix where the build results will be installed, specifies the build system and instructs the build to create static libraries, not dynamic link libraries.

In the objdir-gmp-5.0.5 GMP sibling object directory, make GMP with the command:

```
make --jobs=2
```

This will take a while. The optional --jobs=2 flag indicates that two processes should be used to speed up the build. It is also possible to use more processes.

In the objdir-gmp-5.0.5 GMP sibling object directory, install GMP with the command:

```
make install
```

C.4 Building MPFR

We will now build MPFR version 3.1.1 in MinGW/MSYS.

- `cd /home/tmp`
- Get the MPFR sources and unpack them in `/home/tmp`.
- Perform the command `mkdir objdir-mpfr-3.1.1` in order to make the MPFR sibling directory.
- `cd objdir-mpfr-3.1.1`

The source tree of MPFR should be in the MPFR source directory:

```
/home/tmp/mpfr-3.1.1
```

We should now be in the MPFR sibling object directory:

```
/home/tmp/objdir-mpfr-3.1.1
```

In the `objdir-mpfr-3.1.1` MPFR sibling object directory, configure MPFR with the following command:

```
../mpfr-3.1.1/configure --prefix=/usr/local \
--build=i686-pc-mingw32 --disable-shared \
--enable-static --with-gmp=/usr/local
```

This configuration defines the characteristics that will be used when building MPFR. It defines the prefix where the build results will be installed, specifies the build system and instructs the build to create static libraries, not dynamic link libraries. The configuration also tells the build of MPFR where the installation of GMP can be found.

In the `objdir-mpfr-3.1.1` MPFR sibling object directory, make MPFR with the command:

```
make --jobs=2
```

This will take a while. The optional `--jobs=2` flag indicates that two processes should be used to speed up the build. It is also possible to use more processes.

In the `objdir-mpfr-3.1.1` MPFR sibling object directory, install MPFR with the command:

```
make install
```

C.5 Building MPC

We will now build MPC version 0.9 in MinGW/MSYS.

- `cd /home/tmp`
- Get the MPC sources and unpack them in `/home/tmp`.

- Perform the command `mkdir objdir-mpc-0.9` in order to make the MPC sibling directory.
- `cd objdir-mpc-0.9`

The source tree of MPC should be in the MPC source directory:

```
/home/tmp/mpc-0.9
```

We should now be in the MPC sibling object directory:

```
/home/tmp/objdir-mpc-0.9
```

In the `objdir-mpc-0.9` MPC sibling object directory, configure MPC with the following command:

```
../mpc-0.9/configure --prefix=/usr/local \
--build=i686-pc-mingw32 --disable-shared \
--enable-static --with-gmp=/usr/local \
--with-mpfr=/usr/local
```

This configuration defines the characteristics that will be used when building MPC. It defines the prefix where the build results will be installed, specifies the build system and instructs the build to create static libraries, not dynamic link libraries. The configuration also tells the build of MPC where the installations of GMP and MPFR can be found.

In the `objdir-mpc-0.9` MPC sibling object directory, make MPC with the command:

```
make --jobs=2
```

This will take a while. The optional `--jobs=2` flag indicates that two processes should be used to speed up the build. It is also possible to use more processes.

In the `objdir-mpc-0.9` MPC sibling object directory, install MPC with the command:

```
make install
```

C.6 Building PPL

We will now build PPL version 0.12.1 in MinGW/MSYS.

- `cd /home/tmp`
- Get the PPL sources and unpack them in `/home/tmp`.
- Perform the command `mkdir objdir-ppl-0.12.1` in order to make the PPL sibling directory.
- `cd objdir-ppl-0.12.1`

The source tree of PPL should be in the PPL source directory:

```
/home/tmp/ppl-0.12.1
```

We should now be in the PPL sibling object directory:

```
/home/tmp/objdir-ppl-0.12.1
```

In the `objdir-ppl-0.12.1` PPL sibling object directory, configure PPL with the following command:

```
../ppl-0.12.1/configure --prefix=/usr/local \
--build=i686-pc-mingw32 --disable-shared \
--enable-static CPPFLAGS="-fexceptions" \
--with-gmp=/usr/local
```

This configuration defines the characteristics that will be used when building PPL. It defines the prefix where the build results will be installed, specifies the build system and instructs the build to create static libraries, not dynamic link libraries. The configuration also tells the build of PPL where the installation of GMP can be found.

In the `objdir-ppl-0.12.1` PPL sibling object directory, make PPL with the command:

```
make --jobs=2
```

This will take a while. The optional `--jobs=2` flag indicates that two processes should be used to speed up the build. It is also possible to use more processes.

In the `objdir-ppl-0.12.1` PPL sibling object directory, install PPL with the command:

```
make install
```

C.7 Building ISL

Building ISL in MinGW/MSYS (and CLooG if necessary) follow the same schema as described above for PPL. Separate up-to-date instructions for building ISL and CLooG can be found in the Internet.

C.8 Building the Binary Utilities for the Cross Compiler

We will now build the binary utilities (binutils) version 2.22 in MinGW/MSYS. The binary utilities provide tools needed by the cross compiler such as the assembler, the linker, the library archiver and assorted utilities for manipulating binary files in ELF binary format.

In this example, the binary utilities will be specifically built in preparation for building GCC version 4.6.2 for the `--target=avr-unknown-elf` cross target.

- `cd /home/tmp`
- Get the binutils sources and unpack them in `/home/tmp`.
- Perform `mkdir objdir-binutils-2.22-avr-unknown-elf` in order to make the binutils sibling directory.
- `cd objdir-binutils-2.22-avr-unknown-elf`

The source tree of the binutils should be in the binutils source directory:

```
/home/tmp/binutils-2.22
```

We should now be in the binutils sibling object directory:

```
/home/tmp/objdir-binutils-2.22-avr-unknown-elf
```

In the `objdir-binutils-2.22-avr-unknown-elf` binutils sibling object directory, configure the binutils with the following command:

```
../binutils-2.22/configure \
--prefix=/usr/local/gcc-4.6.2-avr-unknown-elf \
--target=avr-unknown-elf --build=i686-pc-mingw32 \
--disable-__cxa_atexit --disable-nls \
--disable-threads --disable-shared \
--enable-static --disable-win32-registry \
--disable-sjlj-exceptions --with-dwarf2 \
--with-gmp=/usr/local --with-mpfr=/usr/local \
--with-mpc=/usr/local --with-ppl=/usr/local
```

This configuration defines the characteristics that will be used when building the binutils. It defines the prefix where the build results will be installed, specifies the build system and instructs the build to create static libraries, not dynamic link libraries. For building the binutils, there are additional configuration flags for compiler details. The configuration also tells the build of the binutils where the installations of GMP, MPFR, MPC and PPL can be found.

In the `objdir-binutils-2.22-avr-unknown-elf` binutils sibling object directory, make the binutils with the command:

```
make --jobs=2
```

This will take a while. The optional `--jobs=2` flag indicates that two processes should be used to speed up the build. It is also possible to use more processes.

In the `objdir-binutils-2.22-avr-unknown-elf` binutils sibling object directory, install the binutils with the command:

```
make install
```

C.9 Building the Cross Compiler

We will now build GCC version 4.6.2 in MinGW/MSYS. GCC will be built for the `--target=avr-unknown-elf` cross target. GCC will be built with the newlib library [13].

- `cd /home/tmp`
- Get the GCC sources and unpack them in `/home/tmp`.
- Get the newlib sources and unpack them in `/home/tmp`.
- Perform the command `mkdir objdir-gcc-4.6.2-avr-unknown-elf` in order to make the GCC sibling directory.

The source tree of the GCC should be in the GCC source directory:

```
/home/tmp/gcc-4.6.2
```

After unpacking GCC and newlib, the newlib sources need to be copied to the GCC source tree. For newlib version 1.20.0, for example,

```
cd /home/tmp/newlib-1.20.0
cp -r newlib libgloss ../gcc-4.6.2
```

Return to the GCC sibling object directory for building GCC with:

```
cd /home/tmp/objdir-gcc-4.6.2-avr-unknown-elf
```

We should now be in the GCC sibling object directory:

```
/home/tmp/objdir-gcc-4.6.2-avr-unknown-elf
```

In the `objdir-gcc-4.6.2-avr-unknown-elf` GCC sibling object directory, configure GCC with the following command:

```
../gcc-4.6.2/configure \
--prefix=/usr/local/gcc-4.6.2-avr-unknown-elf \
--target=avr-unknown-elf --build=i686-pc-mingw32 \
--enable-languages=c,c++ --with-newlib \
--disable-__cxa_atexit --disable-nls \
--disable-threads --disable-shared --enable-static \
--disable-win32-registry --disable-sjlj-exceptions \
--with-dwarf2 --with-gmp=/usr/local \
--with-mpfr=/usr/local --with-mpc=/usr/local \
--with-ppl=/usr/local
```

This configuration defines the characteristics that will be used when building GCC. It defines the prefix where the build results will be installed, specifies the build system and instructs the build to create static libraries, not dynamic link libraries. There are additional configuration flags for compiler details including the languages to build (C and C++) and to use newlib. The configuration also tells the build of GCC where the installations of GMP, MPFR, MPC and PPL can be found.

In the `objdir-gcc-4.6.2-avr-unknown-elf` GCC sibling object directory, make GCC with the command:

```
make --jobs=2
```

This will take a while. The optional `--jobs=2` flag indicates that two processes should be used to speed up the build. It is also possible to use more processes.

In the `objdir-gcc-4.6.2-avr-unknown-elf` GCC sibling object directory, install GCC with the command:

```
make install
```

C.10 Using the Cross Compiler

We will now assume that the work of building the GCC prerequisites and GCC has been successfully completed. If this is the case, the GCC build results should be located in the installation directory:

```
/usr/local/gcc-4.6.2-avr-unknown-elf
```

Note, however, that the `/usr` directory in MinGW/MSYS could be an alias for a directory such as `/msys/1.0`.

We will now investigate the structure of the build results. In particular, two versions of the compiler should have been installed. There should be one version with tools having decorated names and a second version with tools having undecorated, plain names.

In `/usr/local/gcc-4.6.2-avr-unknown-elf`, the installation directory, there should be versions of the tools with decorated names. For example, the version of `g++` with a *decorated* name is:

```
bin/avr-unknown-elf-g++.exe
```

In `/usr/local/gcc-4.6.2-avr-unknown-elf`, the installation directory, there should also be versions of the tools with undecorated names. For example, the version of `g++` with an *undecorated* name is:

```
avr-unknown-elf/bin/g++.exe
```

Both the decorated version of the toolchain as well as the undecorated one function equivalently. It is, however, best to use only one of them at one time. Consider which version of the toolchain to use for cross development and use it consistently.

When using GCC, it can be convenient to add the path of the compiler executables to the `PATH` variable of the shell. In MinGW/MSYS, path information for the cross compiler can be added to the `PATH` variable in the file `/etc/profile`. In other ∗nix-like systems, path information for the cross compiler can added to the `PATH` variable in the file `/home/.bashrc`.

Some developers recommend not moving an installation of GCC. It is, however, possible to move a fully-built installation of GCC to another location provided the entire directory tree of the compiler is moved. In our example, for instance, this means moving all files, directories, etc. in `gcc-4.6.2-avr-unknown-elf/*` from their installed location to another place as a cohesive unit.

A GCC installation that has been built in MinGW/MSYS can also be used outside of the MinGW/MSYS environment, for example, by employing another command line interface. When doing so, it is necessary to include several dynamic link libraries from the MinGW/MSYS installation in the path of the compiler's binaries or in the build environment. This technique is used in the reference project of the companion code.

References

1. BUGSENG, *Parma Polyhedra Library (PPL)* (2012). http://www.bugseng.com/products/ppl
2. CLooG, *Chunky Loop Generator* (2015). http://www.cloog.org
3. Free Software Foundation, *GNU Binutils* (2011). http://www.gnu.org/software/binutils
4. Free Software Foundation, *GNU Compiler Collection Version 4.6.2* (2012). http://gcc.gnu.org
5. Free Software Foundation, *Prerequisites for GCC* (2015). http://gcc.gnu.org/install/prerequisites.html
6. L. Fousse, G. Hanrot, V. Lefèvre, P. Pélissier, P. Zimmermann, MPFR: a multiple-precision binary floating-point library with correct rounding. ACM Trans. Math. Soft. **33**(2), 13-es (2007)
7. GMP, *GNU Multiple Precision Arithmetic Library* (2012). http://gmplib.org
8. W. von Hagen, *The Definitive Guide to GCC* (Apress, Berkeley, 2006)
9. ISL, *Integer Set Library* (2015). http://isl.gforge.inria.fr
10. MinGW, *Home of the MinGW and MSYS Projects* (2012). http://www.mingw.org
11. MPC, *GNU MPC* (2012). http://www.multiprecision.org
12. MPFR, *GNU MPFR Library* (2013). http://www.mpfr.org
13. Red Hat, *newlib* (2013). http://sourceware.org/newlib

Appendix D
Building a Microcontroller Circuit

This appendix provides details on assembling the microcontroller circuit depicted in Fig. 2.1. Information on the circuit, the schematic and its assembly on a solderless prototyping breadboard are included.

D.1 The Circuit Schematic

Recall the microcontroller circuit on the prototyping breadboard first presented in Sect. 2.1, Fig. 2.1. The corresponding schematic for this circuit is shown in Fig. D.1 on the following page. This is a simple microcontroller circuit that can be assembled with just a handful of components. It is probably a good idea to learn about and adhere to safety when constructing electrical circuits, as described in, for instance, Sect 7.1 of [2].

Our microcontroller circuit consists of the following three main circuit groups:

1. 5 V Regulator
2. Microcontroller and Peripheries
3. JTAG Connector

The 5 V regulator group is shown in the upper right of the schematic. It is responsible for converting an input voltage ranging from about +8 V ... 24 V to the +5 V TTL voltage required by the microcontroller. The ideal input voltage range is around +9 V ... 12 V.

Moving counterclockwise, down and to the left, we encounter the second circuit group, which is the microcontroller and its peripheries. This circuit group contains the microcontroller, its crystal quartz oscillator circuit, a reset push button and the LED `D1`. Note that the LED `D1` in our circuit diagram here is the same LED that was first presented in the LED program of Chap. 1, see Fig. 1.1.

The third circuit group located to the right and above the circuit label is the JTAG connector. This is a six-pin connection that can interface to a commercially available SPI™ programmer or JTAG ICE debugger.

C. Kormanyos, *Real-Time C++*, https://doi.org/10.1007/978-3-662-62996-3

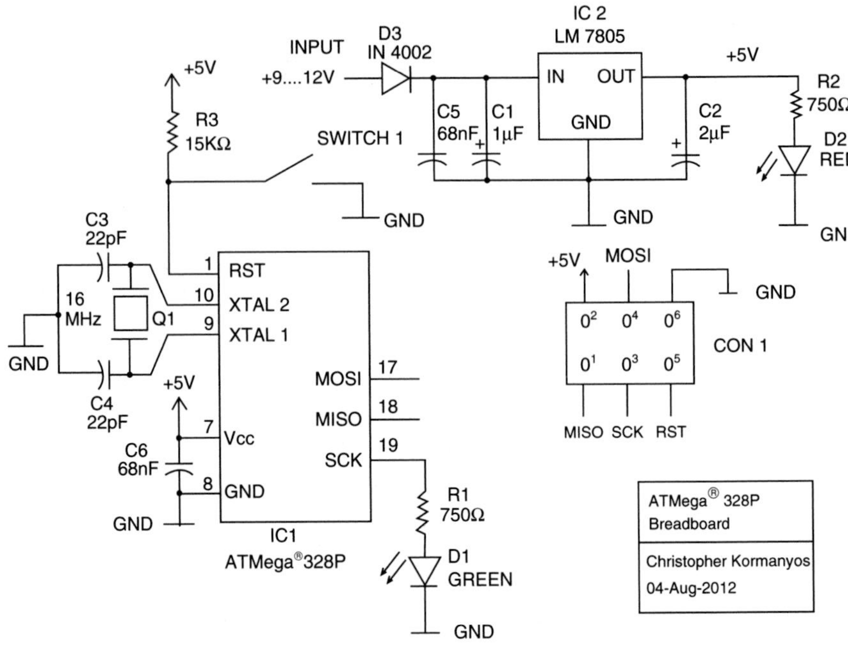

Fig. D.1 The schematic of our target system is shown

Table D.1 The discrete components in our microcontroller circuit are listed

Label	Type	Value	Function
D3	1N4002-type rectifier	100 V	Short-circuit protection
IC2	LM7805 voltage regulator	+5 V	Linear voltage regulator in TO-220 package [6]
C1	Electrolytic capacitor	~1 µF	Input stabilization
C2	Electrolytic capacitor	~2 µF	+5 V stabilization
R1, R2	1/4 Watt resistor	750 Ω	LED current limitation
D2	LED red	5–10 mA	Power indicator
C5, C6	Ceramic capacitor	68 nF	High-frequency filter
IC1	Microchip® AVR® ATmega328P [1]	–	8-bit microcontroller in DIL-28 package [5]
D1	LED green	~5–10 mA	User LED on pin 17
Q1	Quartz	16 MHz	Oscillator circuit
C3, C4	Ceramic capacitor	~10–20 pF	Oscillator circuit
R3	1/4 Watt resistor	15 kΩ	+5 V pull-up on reset
SWITCH1	mini push-button	–	Manual reset button
CON1	6-pin, 2-row 2.54 mm connector	–	SPI™ connector

A microcontroller circuit assembled on a breadboard generally does not have the robustness necessary for high-volume production. Circuit assembly on a solderless prototyping breadboard does, however, provide adequate quality for microcontroller benchmarking and compiler testing.

The part list for our microcontroller circuit is provided in Table D.1. All of the components needed for our microcontroller circuit should be available at any good electronics store.

D.2 Assembling the Circuit on a Breadboard

Our microcontroller circuit assembled with discrete components on a solderless prototyping breadboard is shown in Fig. D.2. The three main circuit groups are highlighted in rectangular boxes.

Circuit assembly uses standard breadboard methods. See, for example, Sects. 3.2–3.3 in [3] for additional information on working with a breadboard. An effort should be made to keep wire connections as short as possible and flat on the breadboard. In general, try prevent wire crossings as far as possible. Optionally, a kit containing pre-formed wires, isolated and bent for the breadboard slots, can be conveniently used for some connections.

For other connections, it may be better to make custom-length isolated wires. AWG-22 [4] conducting wire cut to length and appropriately bent for the slots is suitable for breadboard connections. AWG-22 wire has a diameter of approximately 0.6 mm. Custom breadboard wires can be isolated with commercially available skinny, round silicon tubes or small heat-shrink tubing.

Critical circuit components requiring high electromagnetic stability benefit from short, soldered connections. In our circuit on the breadboard, for example, the quartz periphery and the JTAG SPI™ connector have been fitted on secondary snap-on boards built with soldered connections.

In addition, overall stability of the board can be improved by keeping capacitors physically near the components they are meant to stabilize. For example, C1 and C2

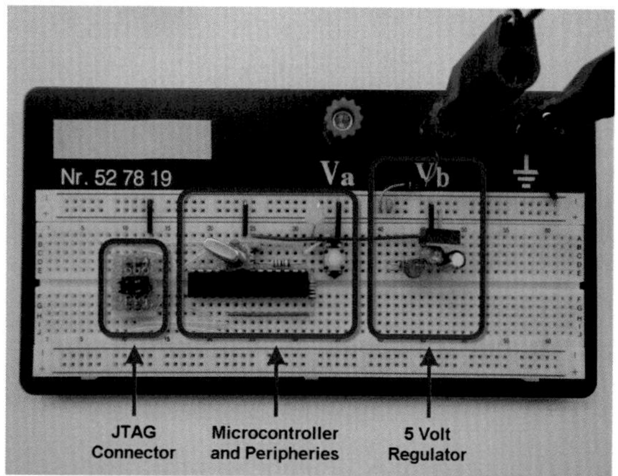

Fig. D.2 Our microcontroller circuit assembled with discrete components on a breadboard is shown

are placed near the +5 V voltage regulator, C5 is close to the input rectifier and C6 is tight on the microcontroller VCC and GND pins.

Assembling a microcontroller circuit on a breadboard requires reliable work. It is best to work methodically, properly fitting one circuit group at a time. A volt meter can be used to check the proper placement of the components and their electrical connections.

References

1. ATMEL®, *8-bit ATMEL® Microcontroller with 4/8/16/32K Bytes In-System Programmable Flash (ATmega48A, ATmega48PA, ATmega88A, ATmega88PA, ATmega168A, ATmega168PA, ATmega328, ATmega328P)*, Rev. 8271D–AVR–05/11 (ATMEL®, 2011)
2. P. Scherz, S. Monk, *Practical Electronics for Inventors*, 4th edn. (McGraw Hill, New York, 2016)
3. M. Schmidt, *ARDUINO®: A Quick-Start Guide* (Pragmatic Programmers, Raleigh, 2011)
4. Wikipedia, *American Wire Gauge* (2012). http://en.wikipedia.org/wiki/American_wire_gauge
5. Wikipedia, *Dual In-line Package* (2012). http://en.wikipedia.org/wiki/Dual_in-line_package
6. Wikipedia, *TO–220* (2012). http://en.wikipedia.org/wiki/TO-220

Glossary

Bootloader A bootloader is a small program, the job of which is to program another application via communication with another part of memory and/or another device.

Build Build is the process of building a software project including compiling the sources, linking them, extracting the executable program and optionally programming it into the microcontroller memory.

Debug Debug means finding and removing software defects caused by errors or flaws in coding, design, timing characteristics or any other mistake.

Flash, flashing Flashing is the act of programming an executable program into the FLASH program memory of the microcontroller.

Flashed Flashed is the state of the FLASH program memory of the microcontroller having undergone flash programming.

Heap The term heap commonly refers to a pool of computer memory typically used for dynamic memory allocation and deallocation.

Multitasking Multitasking is a programming technique used to distribute the work of a computer program among more than one task or process, thereby potentially improving program robustness via carefully designed temporal and functional distribution.

Stack A stack is a linear chunk of computer memory usually used for storing local variables and preserving register contents within one or more (possibly nested) subroutine or interrupt call(s).

Standard library The standard library refers to the C++ standard library (as specified in ISO/IEC 14882:2017), which is an extensive collection of types, functions, classes, generic containers and algorithms.

Startup code The startup code is the part of the program that runs before the `main()` subroutine. The startup code is responsible for initializing RAM and static constructors and subsequently calling `main()`.

C. Kormanyos, *Real-Time C++*, https://doi.org/10.1007/978-3-662-62996-3

Index

C. Kormanyos, *Real-Time C++*, https://doi.org/10.1007/978-3-662-62996-3

Printed in the United States
by Baker & Taylor Publisher Services